THE RUSSIAN TRAGEDY

By the Same Author

Paul I: A Reassessment of His Life and Reign
(editor)

Détente in the Napoleonic Era:
Bonaparte and the Russians

Tsar Paul and the Question of Madness:
An Essay in History and Psychology

Imperial Russian Foreign Policy
(editor)

The RUSSIAN TRAGEDY

The Burden of History

Hugh Ragsdale

With a foreword by Robert C. Tucker

M.E. Sharpe
Armonk, New York
London, England

Library of Congress Cataloging-in-Publication Data

Ragsdale, Hugh.
The Russian tragedy : the burden of history / by Hugh Ragsdale.
p.   cm.
Includes bibliographical references and index.
ISBN 1-56324-755-0 (cloth : alk. paper).
ISBN 1-56324-756-9 (paperback : alk. paper)
1. Russia—History. 2. Soviet Union—History. I. Title.
DK40.R34   1996
947.084—dc20   95-39310
CIP
Printed in the United States of America

The paper used in this publication meets the minimum requirements of
American National Standard for Information Sciences—
Permanence of Paper for Printed Library Materials,
ANSI Z 39.48-1984.

⊗∞

BM (c)   10   9   8   7   6   5   4   3   2   1
BM (p)   10   9   8   7   6   5   4   3   2   1

To
Martha

Contents

Foreword

Not many scholars have had the temerity to recount the thousand-year history of Russia on the modest scale of this volume. Just that has been done by Hugh Ragsdale in the pages that follow. He has, moreover, included an overview of the entire Soviet period of Russia's history, from the revolutions of 1917 to the abolition of the Soviet Union as a state formation in 1991, along with a short epilogue on Russia under Boris Yeltsin in the post-Soviet years down to 1995.

His book is notable for its pithy account of key events in Russia's history and vivid portrayals of outstanding Russian rulers such as Peter the Great and Catherine the Great in the eighteenth century as well as Tsar Alexander I in the early nineteenth and Tsar-Reformer Alexander II, under whom Russia's peasants were emancipated from serfdom by royal decree in 1861. At the same time, the narrative of events is placed within the framework of an interpretive approach that is set forth at the very outset, where we read: "The story of Russia is above all the story of the state."

In stressing the role of the state authority as the driving force of Russian history, Professor Ragsdale draws on the authority of the "political-juridical" school of Russian historiography, which developed initially in the nineteenth century. How and why it was that the state played so crucial a part in that country's history, both under the tsars and again under Soviet rulers in our century, will become plain to the reader. At the same time, the reader will note the paradoxical fact that, more than once in its history, the seemingly all-powerful Russian state structure has crumbled and collapsed. This first happened following the end of a ruling dynasty in 1598, and the ensuing fifteen years of semi-stateless chaos went down in Russian history as the "Time of Troubles." In reading the epilogue to this book, which refers to the "contemporary political chaos" in the post-Soviet Russian 1990s, the reader will understand why many Russians of our day speak of the present period as a new Time of Troubles.

While recognizing the enormous role that the state authority has played in the Russian historical process, the book takes due account of Russian culture and society as a significant part of the story. In one richly rewarding chapter the author takes us on a "literary excursion" that shows the classics of Russian literature as "the sociographers in fiction of nineteenth-century Russia" that they unwittingly but penetratingly were. Here we see Russian society mirrored in those classics: the peasant "dark people" and others in Turgenev's *Sportsman's Sketches*, Tolstoy's *Power of Darkness,* and Chekhov's "Peasants"; the gentry in Gonchararov's *Oblomov,* Turgenev's *Rudin*, and Chekhov's *Cherry Orchard*; the merchant class in a satire by Saltykov-Shchedrin and plays by Aleksandr Ostrovskii; and the Russian radical intelligentsia in Turgenev's *Fathers and Sons* and Dostoevsky's *The Possessed*. All this prepares us well for what follows on attempted reform and then revolution in the early twentieth century.

The title of this book, *The Russian Tragedy*, says something true and important about its subject matter. The Russian people's path through history has been a thorny one. We can't help but see this as we follow here such tragic episodes as the two centuries of Mongol dominion early on, the terroristic reign of Ivan the Terrible in the sixteenth century, the serfdom endured by the vast majority of Russians into the later nineteenth century, not to mention the great new tragedies in store for the nation in our own century, especially under the thirty-year-long rule of Stalin, whose villainous deeds in power stand comparison only with those of his evil German counterpart Adolf Hitler.

But still the question arises: why does Russian history, so far, merit the characterization offered it in the book's title? One possible answer, or part of the answer, that occurs to this reader is that none of the periodically undertaken attempts to reform the swollen state structure—whether Boris Godunov's or Alexander II's or Stolypin's or Gorbachev's—has successfully pointed the way to a non-tragic outcome. That is, to a less-than-authoritarian Russia in good relations with other countries, especially in the West. Always the outcome has been another breakdown, another Time of Troubles, and then another restoration of authoritarian statehood.

And this brings us to the author's concluding prognosis. He wisely abstains from predicting that post-Soviet Russian reforms will prove more successful in the end than their predecessors were. The outcome turns, as he says, on whether or not the Russians will find a way "simultaneously to a rejection of the violent absolutism of their past and yet to something more nearly their own than a perfunctory replication of liberal capitalism and its attendant values. Perhaps in the process they will learn something of use for the ills of our society as well." The story is best ended on this sensible note of uncertainty, and yet with the hope that this time, at long last, Russia will emerge into a non-tragic twenty-first century as her invariably fascinating history proceeds further.

—Robert C. Tucker
Princeton, New Jersey

Preface

The student of Russia has always had fascinating work, but the spectacle of the past few years has been extraordinary. It has been exhilarating, and it has been frustrating. Everyone will understand the exhilaration. It is the frustration that must be accounted for.

The frustration is from two sources. First, the massive commentary, analysis, and daily dissection of the Soviet apocalypse has been provided nearly exclusively by experts on contemporary affairs. These are the journalists and the social scientists. The work that they do is, of course, indispensable to our understanding, and yet it is not enough. Societies, after all, have traditions, a concept nearly forgotten in our hurried rush forward to an ever more frenetic future. And traditions have influence, a deeper and more abiding influence than we appear to realize, since we seem less and less aware of them. The journalists and the social scientists all suffer from one serious distortion of outlook— the foreshortening of perspective. There is no surer way to mesmerize our intelligence and spoil our perspective than to draw the materials for our reflection on a contemporary problem entirely from its own time and place. No one was more guilty of this mistake than Mikhail Gorbachev.

Nearly as unsatisfactory, however, has been the work of my own colleagues, the historians. C. Vann Woodward has made the point that from the time when we historians began writing principally for each other—and that seems a long time ago now—we lost the large audience that was formerly ours. Too often we both choose a subject and use a language that condemn our work to academic oblivion. And so we virtually abandoned the field of public comment on the dénouement of Soviet civilization to our colleagues of impaired vision, the journalists and social scientists.

The purpose of this book is to explain the crisis of the Soviet state and the failure of the Gorbachev reform as the natural functions of the tortured historical traditions of Russia. The Russians set out under

Gorbachev, as they had under Lenin and Peter I, to break away from their traditions. But nations do not suddenly liberate themselves from their traditions. And however burdensome their heritage, the effort to escape it—1789 in France, 1917 in Russia—may bring even greater misery.

I offer here a very personal interpretation of the awful fate of modern Russia. I emphasize the decisive perspective, the historical one. Providence has distributed her favors to the nations of this world in a strikingly unequal fashion, and several tenacious factors have been especially influential in the unhappy history of Russia.

The inauspicious environment of Russia's historical circumstances—economic and cultural lag on the one hand, strategic insecurity on the other—encouraged, perhaps demanded, the evolution of a political absolutism, a leviathan state. From one limited vantage point, this kind of government served the nation well: Russia survived and preserved its independence.

As time passed, however, the state absorbed more and more of the conventional functions of civil society. In the long run, it circumscribed the role of the people in their own fate: it deprived the nation of its voice. The nation served the state rather than the state the nation. In the process, the people grew unaccustomed—and unable—to take their fate into their own hands.

As the ever more powerful apparatus of state acquired thus a kind of political impunity, it grew increasingly insensitive and inflexible, and its inability to adjust itself to changing conditions aggravated its travail and its ultimate failure. Russia suffered in the modern world a kind of retardation rooted in the suppression of popular responsibility.

Just as the historical experience of Russians, like that of every people, is peculiar to itself, so too is their cultural outlook a unique reflection of that experience, and the attitudes of Russians have inevitably shaped their destiny as surely as have their material circumstances. If we are to appreciate impartially their own view of the world, and of themselves, without the potentially perverse skew of foreigners' accounts of them, then we must attend carefully to Russians' own self-expression. During long ages of relative illiteracy, the most characteristic form of their self-expression was their religion; and there is in Russian Orthodoxy a large element of fatalistic resignation, perhaps a natural counterpart of the overdeveloped growth of the state.

By the nineteenth century, a more important—because more articulate—mode of self-expression arose: classical Russian literature. It reflects especially well the ideas of a new social force that arose simultaneously with it: the fabled Russian revolutionary intelligentsia. It was generated initially by the eighteenth-century efforts at modernization through the imitation of European education. In the nineteenth century, the intelligentsia developed a singular self-confidence, a Manichaean conception of its own virtue and the imperial government's evil, and a titanic determination not to be denied its goals. When one camp of the intelligentsia took the government into its own hands in 1917, it began to turn its self-confident sectarian virtue into a nationwide evil.

Throughout all of this experience, Russia's trials were aggravated by its juxtaposition with that most brilliant of modern civilizations, Western Europe. The West was the modern scourge of Russia, the strategic source of a mortal security threat. At the same time, it was both the philosophical and the technological source of economic and strategic salvation. Yet if the Russian state should import not only the material and technological advances of the West but its liberal democratic politics as well, it would undermine the indispensable tradition of political authoritarianism—the hitherto unique agency of progress, strength, and security. It was an ugly dilemma, but the Soviet experiment promised delivery from the problem. In Marxism Russia presumed for a time to have found an ironic solution: to dispose of the threat of the West by destroying bourgeois civilization itself.

Paradoxically, Gorbachev's perestroika, like the revolutions that preceded it, accelerated imitation of the West in order to gain the strength to reject the Western model in the long run. Westerners themselves little appreciate the unconscious tyranny of their civilization in the world. The manifest material superiority of Western civilization aggrandizes itself at the expense of all others. The Russians are posing for us at the moment, as they have been inclined to do before, the question whether this tyranny of Western culture is just and desirable. As the euphoria of the collapse of communism dissipates, the question is worth our best consideration. (The end of history is not yet upon us—not an end that we can welcome.)

A nation in crisis turns for sustenance to the strengths of its traditions. They may bring blessings—as Charles de Gaulle demonstrated in France—or they may bring scourges—as Adolf Hitler proved in Germany. The Russians are now searching their past in an effort to recover its blessings, not its scourges.

This is a book about the truculence of tradition, the reasonableness of reform, the conflict between the two, and the consequences for what we and the Russians, in our very different conceptions, have called freedom.

Acknowledgments

Many friends and colleagues have given me the benefit of critical readings and comments on all of parts of the manuscript or have discussed various issues in it with me: David Beito, Celeste Burnum, Barbara Chotiner, David Costello, Ben Eklof, Anne R. Gibbons, Janie M. Gibbons, Grey Hodnett, Robert E. Jones, John Lukacs, Roderick E. McGrew, Michael Mendle, Kay Oliver, Norman Pereira, Carl Ragsdale, Kate Ragsdale, Blair Ruble, Paul Stephan, Eleanor Streit, Mark Teeter, and Nils Wessell. The critical comments of my two colleagues at the Russian Academy of Sciences, Valerii Nikolaevich Ponomarev and Anatolii Venediktovich Ignatiev, were especially useful; and the interest and encouragement of Robert C. Tucker of Princeton University and the editorial advice and assistance of Patricia Kolb of M.E. Sharpe have been most helpful. I am grateful to all of them, and I hope that they will find the result to justify their time and trouble.

Chronology

Kievan Rus: 859–1169

Calling of the Varangians, 859
Conversion to Christianity, 988
Destruction of Kiev by prince of Vladimir-Suzdal, 1169

Vladimir-Suzdal principality

Mongol Dominion: 1240–1480

Muscovite Russia: 1480–1689

Ivan III the Great (1462–1505)
Establishment of *pomestie* system
Liberation from Mongol yoke
Import of Western technicians
Vasilii III (1505–33)
Ivan IV the Terrible (1533–84)
Establishment of standing army
Compulsory gentry state service
Origins of serfdom
Oprichnina
Fedor I (1584–98), end of dynasty of Riurik
Time of Troubles: 1598–1613
Boris Godunov, Fedor II, False Dmitriis
Romanov dynasty established, 1613
Michael (1613–45)
Alexis (1645–76)
Zemskii sobor
Cautious Westernization
Fedor III (1676–82)
Sophia (1682–89)

Imperial Russia: 1689–1917

Peter I (1698–1725)
Establishment of Empire
Aggressive Westernization
Age of Palace Revolutions (1725–62)
Catherine II the Great (1762–96)
Conquests in Poland and Turkey
Deliberate Westernization
Cultural advancement, Age of Enlightenment
Paul (1796–1801)
Napoleonic wars
Political reaction
Alexander I (1801–25)
Cautious, tentative reform
War of 1812
Nicholas I (1825–55)
Decembrist Revolt, 1825
Reactionary politics
Crimean War, 1854–56
Alexander II (1855–81)
The Great Reforms
Emancipation of the serfs
Judicial reform
Reform of local government
Military reform
Assassination
Alexander III (1881–94)
Political reaction
Nicholas II (1894–1917)
Witte industrial program, 1892–1903
Russo-Japanese War, 1904–5
Revolution of 1905
Constitution of 1906
Stolypin agrarian reform
World War I, 1914–18
October Revolution of 1917

Soviet Russia: 1917–1991

Civil war and War Communism, 1918–20
New Economic Policy, 1921–28
Lenin's death, 1924
Stalin's emergence
First Five-Year Plan, 1928–32
Collectivization
Industrialization
Second Five-Year Plan, 1933–38
Great Purges, 1936–38
World War II, 1939–45
Reconstruction, 1945–53
Stalin's death, 1953
Khrushchev and the Thaw, 1953–64
Brezhnev and reaction, 1964–83
Interregnum
Gorbachev, 1985–91
Yeltsin, 1991-

Part I

The Historical Ingredients

❖ 1 ❖

Origins: Russia and
the Russian Political Style

*They . . . went overseas to the Varangian[s and] . . . said,
"Our land is great and rich, but there is no order in it.
Come to rule and reign over us." And . . . three brothers,
with their kinsfolk . . . migrated. The oldest, Riurik, located
himself in Novgorod.*

The Calling of the Varangians,
Primary Chronicle

*In framing a government . . . , the great difficulty is this:
you must first enable the government to control the governed; and in the next place oblige it to control itself. A
dependence on the people is, no doubt, the primary control
on the government.*

Madison, *The Federalist*, No. 51

The first fact in the evolution of Russia is one of the most sensitive:
it was founded by aliens.

The story of Russia is above all the story of the state. The Slavs who
became Russians had been where they were for generations. Their
organization was tribal. They were Drevliane (Woods People), Poliane
(Field People), Sloviane (People of the Word?), and a dozen or so
others. According to their earliest historical record, the venerable *Primary Chronicle*, there was disorder in the land, and hence, they invited
the Varangians to come and establish a government. This was around
the year 860. This compact little formula conceals a myriad of mysteries—and of controversies. The presence of disorder is hardly unknown
in the history of Russia, but issuing an invitation to foreign dominion is
hardly known anywhere in world history.

3

The Varangians were from Scandinavia. They were Vikings, Norsemen, a dynamic and far-ranging people. They made their presence felt over a large part of the European—and perhaps even North American—world. They were raiding and plundering all over the North Sea, ravaging much of France and England. As they shed their more primordial habits, they would rule Normandy, Sicily, and England—and Russia.

The Varangians came early to Novgorod and Kiev, the "mothers of Russian cities," and their influence in Russia suggests their motives in coming there. Their name in Russian—*variagi*—means traders and rowers; that is how they were perceived. They established a route, as the ancient documents have it, "from the Varangians to the Greeks," that is, to the fabled riches of what was then the crossroads of the world, the Byzantine Empire in Constantinople. The rivers of European Russia run north into the Baltic—the Lovat, the Volkhov, and the Western Dvina—and south into the Black Sea and the Caspian—the Dnieper, the Don, and the Volga. Short overland portages provide a nearly complete "river road" over the whole route. In the year 912, when Kiev dispatched envoys to draw up a treaty with the Byzantines, the Slavic influence in the list of names is hard to find: Karl, Ingjald, Farulf, Vermund, Hrollaf, Gunnar, Harold, Karni, Frithleif, Hroarr, Angantyr, Throand, Leithulf, Fast, and Steinvith.

In this fashion did a Russian state arise amidst the Slavic tribes under the auspices of the Varangians. And this fact gave birth to the "Norman theory" of the origins of the first Russian state, Kievan Rus.

Its consequences for the self-esteem of a major modern nation are easily imagined. Analogous insults would torment the Russian psyche like an ordained atavism, not excluding the present moment. One of the more poignant examples is the story of the origins of the Norman theory itself.

Peter I (d. 1725) wished to modernize his country, make it more like Western Europe. He consulted with the celebrated philosopher Gottfried Wilhelm von Leibniz to lay plans for the founding of an Academy of Sciences. The Academy was duly opened in 1725. Since Peter had died a few months previously, it was formally founded by his widow and successor, Catherine I, apparently a barely literate German peasant woman. The staff of the Academy was imported from Germany. It was two of these German scholars, Gottlieb Siegfried Bayer and August Ludwig von Schlözer, who did the first research into the history of Russia.

The Norman theory was born—nearly stillborn—on 6 September 1749. It was presented to a meeting of the Academy of Sciences by the official imperial Russian historiographer, the German scholar Gerhard Friedrich Müller, who relied on the research of his German colleague Bayer. As Müller spoke, his Russian colleague N.I. Popov interrupted to protest: "You, famous author, dishonor our nation." A tumult arose, and the meeting dispersed. The Empress Elizabeth appointed a committee to determine whether Müller's work was inimical to the interests of the nation. Müller was subsequently forbidden to continue his research, and his publications were confiscated and destroyed.[1] He was forced to turn to other subject matter, and he soon began the first serious work on the history of Siberia.

The Norman theory of the origins of Russia has always been controversial, and the significance of Norman influence has been much disputed. It appears that the cultural level of Kievan society was more advanced than that of contemporary Scandinavia. Kiev had a written literature, a written code of law, and the coining of money before these things appeared in Scandinavia. Ancient Russian borrowed words readily from neighboring cultures but few from Scandinavia. In the roughly 125 years between the coming of the Varangians (ca. 860) and the conversion of Russia to Christianity (988), there is no sound evidence of the influence of Scandinavian gods in Russian paganism. Strong evidence in support of Norman influence is clear in archaeological finds, however, and in the distinctly Scandinavian names of the early princes of Kiev and their retinues.

In any event, when Kiev was founded in the ninth century, there were no nations in Europe; there were only tribes. Europe had no East and West in the modern sense of those terms. When the Norman theory was formulated, nations were present, and East and West were recognized. The significance of these factors was undoubtedly projected anachronistically back onto the evolution of the first Russia. Modern Germans discovered ancient Teutons coming to the assistance of backward Russians—as the Teutons themselves were. If that attitude was a misinterpretation of what had happened in 860, by the year 1749 it had become a habit of thinking on both sides of the Russian cultural frontier. It remains so today, and it is one of the most enduring and painful problems of modern Russia. The persistence of the Norman theory undoubtedly owes much to the fact that both Westerners and Russians, however offensive it is to the latter, find in it a kind of familiar description of the cultural relations between them. The civilization of modern England—and of the United States—owes something to the Normans as well, but the nation on whose empire the sun never set and the self-anointed guardian of the new world order are less sensitive to questions of cultural derivation and dependence than modern Russians are.

Most of the experience of Kiev was far happier than the story of its origins. The first Russians were prosperous, as uniquely prosperous in the history of Russia as they were in the Europe of their time. Prosperity forsook modern Russia, and it was not present in the Western Europe of Kievan days. The fall of the Roman Empire and the ravages of the barbarians, the forays of the Norsemen, the expansion of Islam—all of this left travel and transport insecure in Western Europe. This was the age of manorialism, the natural economy, the great contraction of long-distance trade.

The Russians drew their prosperity from two sources. The first was trade. It was the search for trade that had brought the Varangians to Russia, and they were thus predisposed to the good civil order that favored it. The Russian "river road" gave northern and western Europeans a secure access to the eastern Mediterranean, otherwise obstructed by the Muslim–Christian conflict. The archaeological and numismatic records are clear: the trade between Scandinavia and Byzantium along the Russian rivers was active and abundant. The Russians enjoyed a trade like that of modern rather than medieval Europe.

The second source of Russian prosperity was an unusually rich agriculture. If modern Russia is notorious for the poverty of its agriculture, Kievan Russia was quite different. Kiev is the heart of Ukraine. Of the four conditions of a rich premodern agriculture—long growing season (southerly location), rich soil, open prairie (steppe), abundant moisture—Kiev had all but the last. The annual precipitation is only about twenty-four inches. Yet it was enough to make the area the "breadbasket of Europe."

As rare as prosperity in the history of Russia was the striking freedom of Kiev. The institutions of government might have been designed by a constitutional convention of Aristotle, Polybius, Montesquieu, and Burke. There are three kinds of good government, says Aristotle: monarchy, aristocracy, and polity (democracy); and each has a corresponding perversion: tyranny, plutocracy, and mob rule. In order to avoid endless conflict between the many and the few, the citizenry must comprise as large a proportion as possible of a middle class of people neither so rich as to oppress nor so poor as to be oppressed. Polybius contributed to the classical tradition of political theory by recommending a mixture of Aristotle's three good forms of government, and he illustrated the prudence of his principle in the institutions of the Roman Republic. In pursuit of the same concept, Montesquieu coined the phrases that were to characterize the American constitution: division of power, and checks and balances. Burke observed that "the nature of man is intricate; the objects of society are of the greatest possible complexity: and therefore no simple disposition or direction of power can be suitable either to man's nature, or to the quality of his affairs."[2]

Kiev did not, of course, have the benefit of this political wisdom, but its government reflected much of it nevertheless. The institutions were multiple and complex. A prince, *kniaz*, presided in monarchical fashion. The *posadnik* served as mayor in the towns. A *tysiatskii* was the urban military commander after the fashion of the Renaissance *condottiere*. Bishops exercised their influence, after the coming of Christianity, in tandem and in competition with the other institutions.

The exclusiveness of the prince's power was most effectively blocked by three institutions. A boyar *duma* constituted his aristocratic council of retainers without whose advice and consent the prince could not execute policy. A *veche* was the dominant organ of city government. Elected by plebs and merchant oligarchs, it was a semirepublican, semidemocratic town council reminiscent of the city-states of the Hanseatic League and the Italian Renaissance.

Last was a peculiar custom of legal inheritance known as the *otchina* (later *votchina*) system. The word *otchina* is from the word *otets*, father. Hence the system is also known as the patrimonial (Latin *pater*) system of land tenure. It stipulated the division of a father's property among all his sons without any conditionality of inheritance. Unlike the terms of inheritance in contemporary West European feudalism, the holder of a piece of property owed the local prince nothing for it. Therefore, if he chose to transfer his allegiance to a rival prince, even a foreign prince, the property remained irrevocably his, and his right to it and the income from it was not subject to challenge. The system obviously inhibited the centripetal aggrandizement of power.

A variation on the patrimonial system of land tenure was the *rota* system (Latin wheel, roller, alternation) of the distribution of princely power. It represents the application to royal succession of the patrimonial system of inheritance. The power and the patrimony of the grand prince of Kiev, like that of everyone else, was divided each generation among all of his surviving sons. They inherited their father's royal prerogatives and shared them collectively. The eldest son was the senior partner in this arrangement. He received a larger inheritance, and when an individual brother-prince died, those junior to him evidently moved up a step in the hierarchy of the family. The effect of the *rota* system was to give the senior prince something like undivided sovereignty of princely power in his own subprincipality and shared sovereignty of princely power in those subprincipalities of his brothers that constituted, along with his own, the Grand Principality of Kiev.

What is most important in the political institutions of Kiev is the multiple fashion in which power in the state was shared. It was roughly consonant with the conceptions of our classical political philosophers, including Montesquieu. It did not embrace, however, the axioms of the American Declaration of Independence in which men were born free and equal and endowed by their creator with unalienable rights, that is, natural rights.

Neither was Kievan freedom like that of medieval Western Europe, where individual rights derived from the legal status of the individual. Western Europe was a society of corporate orders, recognized by law and tradition, consisting, as the contemporary phrase put it, of "those who work, those who fight, and those who pray," that is, of peasant serfs, aristocratic warriors, and the Christian clergy. Each category enjoyed clear prescriptive privileges and duties. When the system matured, the aristocratic warriors would be subject to military service and be exempt from taxes. The serfs would pay taxes and be exempt from military service. The clergy would perform spiritual duties and be exempt from both taxes and military service. The natural right of equality was not there. Rather, freedom in Western Europe derived from what each estate was entitled to and exempt from.

In Kiev, there were no legally defined corporate social orders. A man was not born with a contract of rights and duties. Rather, freedom derived from the complexity of the institutions of government, from the division of its powers, from the lack of any form of political monism, and therefore from the absence of that absolutism that was to be the distinguishing feature of the future of Russia.

Toward the end of the tenth century, a prince of Kiev decided that it was time to surrender paganism and to embrace the faith of a great religion. According to the tradition, he sent missions to examine Christianity, Islam, and Judaism. Islam was rejected because, in the words of the *Chronicle,* "drink is the joy of the Russes." Christianity made a particularly favorable impression: the Russian emissaries in the magnificent Cathedral of Saint Sophia in Constantinople professed such wonder as not to know "whether they were in heaven or on earth." The prince chose Christianity in 988, and he is remembered as Saint Vladimir.

The choice was a fateful one because Vladimir selected Christianity in its Byzantine variant. At the time of the choice, there was formally only one Christian Church in the European world. The Schism of Photius, or the Great Schism, occurred in 1054, and the Russian church naturally adhered to that branch of Christendom that had inspired its own conversion. For the Roman Catholic Church of Western and Central Europe, one single language, Latin, served as the *lingua franca* of the various different national churches. The Orthodox Church in the East, however, practiced the use of local vernaculars. From virtually the beginning of their history, the Russians inadvertently chose a vehicle of communication that constituted a cultural divide between them and the heart of Europe. To view the world from the perspective of Moscow's Red Square and from Warsaw's Old Town Square is to have an instantly visible appreciation of the difference. The artistic style of the Old Town exhibits manifest influences of north German and north Italian architecture. The style of Red Square is utterly, exotically different. In this sense, the Russians quite unconsciously laid the foundation of a kind of linguistic and cultural iron curtain a thousand years ago.

The consequences were to be incalculable. It was in the future of Europe that the modern world's decisive experiences of cultural flowering and creativity were to take place, and the Russians were fated not to share most of them. They missed, for example, Thomas Aquinas's thirteenth-century reclamation of Aristotelian science and rationalism. They missed the fifteenth- and sixteenth-century Renaissance and Reformation. They missed the seventeenth-century Scientific Revolution. They participated marginally in the eighteenth-century Enlightenment.

But the Russians' experience of the Enlightenment was essentially an attempt to compress all the preceding experiences along with the Enlightenment into one grand compensatory catch-up for all that they had missed. They succeeded only well enough to recognize failure. And so in the twentieth century, they undertook a crash program of catch-up—at what horrendous cost both we and they now know only too well.

It has been suggested that the selection of a religion was one of the great tragedies of Russian history.[3] The truth of this proposition depends entirely upon the cultural values by which the question is judged. By reference to the values and standards that prevailed in Russia itself throughout most of the twentieth century, the proposition is true. The goals most sought by Russian government in the twentieth century have been material progress and power. From that perspective, the Russians would have been vastly more fortunate in 988 to have chosen the elixir of future dynamism, that is, the religion of Rome. From the perspective, however, of the Russian Orthodox believer, the rationalism and materialism of Western liberal capitalism and the rationalism and materialism of Soviet Marxist socialism are Tweedledum and Tweedledee, and one of them is as close to Antichrist as the other.

Kiev did not participate in the great West European crusades that began in 1096. It is possible that they damaged the Kievan prosperity, as they opened an alternative route for mercantile traffic to the eastern Mediterranean. As Western Europe asserted itself and entered onto a course that would lead it to the modern nation-state, Kiev slipped into decline. It is certain that the onslaughts of successive waves of bellicose nomads from the steppes of Central Asia—the Khazars, the Bulgars, the Pechenegs, the Polovtsy—inflicted devastation and strain. Perhaps even more important was the internecine division relentlessly engendered by the *rota* system. It could scarcely have been better designed to promote jealousy and conflict, especially if we consider how the claims of two generations, brother-uncles against brother-nephews, were to be weighed against each other. Royal relatives murdered each other and raised revolts that maintained the society in a state of perpetual civil war and anarchy. Kiev did not present a united front to the invaders.

The nature of Kievan civilization perhaps also adversely affected its fate. Kiev was characterized by freedom and commerce. It was evidently not conceived, and it was clearly not empowered, to nourish militarism or absolutism. It was intrinsically incompatible with such ideas. When it was challenged by nomadic militarism, Kiev was found wanting. It flourished for a time in the heart of a rich agricultural plain whose frontiers were an open invitation to movement, penetration, and invasion. Its internal structure sacrificed the demands of order to the demands of freedom. When put to the test, it produced more freedom than it could tolerate and too little order to survive. It was a lesson bitterly learned, and Moscow would remedy the mistake with a vengeance.

The experience of Kiev helps to elucidate the nature of modern Russia. It contributed to the future of Russia two important legacies: the failure of freedom and a non-European religious and cultural alignment.

In 1169, as Kiev deteriorated, a family of strong princes moved the political center of Rus north to the cities of Vladimir and Suzdal east of the forested territory of Moscow.

In 1240, the Mongols came.

The "Mongol yoke" lasted until 1480. What the Mongols achieved, positively and negatively, was astonishing. It is estimated that the population of Mongolia at the time of the death of Genghis Khan (1227—his last descendant died in Beijing in 1984) was about one million. The Mongol army is estimated to have been about 130,000 strong. The population of Russia at the time has been estimated at 10,000,000. The population of China at the time of the Mongol conquest (1260) is estimated at about 100,000,000.[4]

Being Inner Asian nomads, the Mongols centered their economy on the horse. They moved on the horse, ate horse meat, drank mare's milk, wore horse hides. The natural grasses of the steppe supported their whole economy, their whole logistics, and thus they were almost infinitely mobile. They moved rapidly, and they coordinated the movements of parallel columns by smoke signals.

One of the persistent modes of explaining the inscrutable and inexorable problem of the Russians as perceived by Europe is to identify them as Asiatic and to cite the Mongol dominion as proof. "Scratch a Russian, find a Tatar." It is not true.

The Mongols did not settle among the Russians. Rather, they established their capital Sarai far away from central Russia on the lower Volga. They did not marry among Russians on a large scale, and they were not sufficient in number to make Russia ethnically Asiatic in any event.[5] They made of Russia what was in effect a vassal state, and they left it to be administered directly by Russians themselves so long as those Russians fulfilled their obligations to their suzerain at Sarai. As in China, the Mongols brought to the conquered people, apart from military organization, a lower level of culture than their victims exemplified. Neither did the Mongols interrupt intercourse between the Russians and Europe. The Pax Mongolica established a degree of security of travel from Rome to Beijing. The experience of Marco Polo (ca. 1254–1324) and his kin is one example of it.

The non-European nature of Russia derives from other sources. It derives above all from the cultural camp defined by the Russian adherence to Orthodoxy. As we advance in Europe from the English Channel eastward, the Russians are the first major people who were never Latin and Catholic. To the ethnologist, the Russians are an Indo-European people. To the linguist, Russian is an Indo-European language. To the student of culture more generally, perhaps the anthropologist, there is something at best marginally European about Russian attitudes. No one has asked more persistently than the Russians themselves have whether they were Europeans or not. In the nineteenth century, their newly articulate identity crisis divided them passionately into Westernizers and Slavophiles. When leaving Russia to go west, the Russians of the nineteenth century habitually said, in both fact and fiction, like the Russians of our own time, that they were "going to Europe."

What impact on Russia, then, did the Mongol dominion have? The Mongols required two items of the Russians. They required an annual delivery of tribute (*dan*), and they required Russian submission to the Mongol selection and investiture of the prince of Russia, a right known as the *yarlyk*. So long as the Russians satisfied these two demands, peace prevailed—but that was not often. If the tribute fell short, or if, as more often happened, a large or small part of Russian society rebelled at the Mongol demands, then Sarai sent its characteristic instrument of enforcement, a punitive expedition.

Such an expedition would set off in the early fall. That was the time when Russia was most vulnerable, the time between the ripening of the grain and its harvesting. The Mongols would set fire to the grain fields. The population would flee in terror to the nearest fortified town. Mongol siege artillery—catapults—would bring down the walls. Then a general slaughter would begin. One man would be left alive, charged to proceed to the next town along the Mongol route of march in order to challenge it to surrender or face the fate of the last one.

Forty-eight major punitive expeditions of this sort took place during the Mongol era, approximately one every five years. The Kievan prosperity of both agriculture and commerce was wrecked. A deep depression set in. A land of cities became a land overwhelmingly rural. The consciousness of the experience is still alive in such contemporary works of art as the novels of Dmitrii Balashev, the paintings of Ilya Glazunov, and Andrei Tarkovskii's gruesome film, *Andrei Rublev*— and in the aversion of the Russians to being regarded as Asiatics.

The Mongols were not the only enemies of Russian peace in this period. Russia was also invaded from the West by the Teutonic Knights—Alexander Nevskii's famous "battle on the ice" (Lake Peipus) was fought in 1242—and the princes of Lithuania, and the land was beset by repeated feuds in the princely family itself. During the 240 years of the Mongol dominion, 223 warlike disturbances have been counted, nearly one per year.

The constitution of Kiev suffered as well. One single political prerogative was decisive in Russia, the *yarlyk*: the will of Sarai. The multiplicity of Kievan political institutions withered. Of the four principal obstacles to the consolidation of power in a single place—the *veche* (town council), the boyar *duma* (council of prince's retainers), the *votchina* (patrimonial system), and the *rota* system (sharing of princely succession)—the first two atrophied such as to lose their substance. To impose, for the sake of brevity and simplicity, a somewhat perverse perspective of hindsight on the matter, Russia was halfway home to absolutism.

Perhaps even more importantly, the cultural center and the population of Russia conceded the heartland of Kievan civilization to the brutality of the invader: Russia moved north. Ukraine was depopulated. It became for several centuries not quite a no-man's-land but a "wild field" (*dikoe pole*), a wilderness, a land of itinerant fugitives, of Cossack desperadoes, pirates on horseback. It was a kind of Wild East.

North Russia, on the other hand, acquired a new population. Its society, however, in an environment so much less hospitable to civilization than the salubrious south, was to reflect little of the character of Kiev. What emerged there was a Russia of a new kind, the kind with which the modern world is familiar. It was formed initially by the nature of the new environment and the nature of Russian relations with the Mongols. The Russian princes who were favored by the Mongols to be their faithful servants were the princes of Moscow, and it is to the Mongol scourge that the principality of Moscow was to owe its future dominion over the other Russian lands.

It was the move to the north that generated the central problem of modern Russian society and the enduring character of the modern Russian state.

The move was motivated chiefly by considerations of security. It made good sense, putting both distance and trees between the Russians and the Mongols. The trees were as important as the distance. The forests of the north did not permit the freedom of movement, the maneuverability, and the military superiority on which the Mongols' dominion of the steppes was built. Their advancing columns could not communicate so confidently in the depths of the forests. The forests did not provide the grass on which the ponies of the steppe so freely fed. Initially, then, in the move north the Russians found some relief from the pressure of their masters, even though not enough. They required some time to organize a radical readjustment to the radically new environment to which they had come. And in the long run, the power of the Mongols declined and fell as well.

Even so, the Russians paid a high price for the strategic relief that the north provided. Trade along the southern rivers, one of the two sources of Kievan prosperity, was disrupted. Worse, agricultural conditions in the north were infinitely inferior to those in the south. Of the four conditions favorable to primitive agriculture, the move north entailed deterioration in all but one. The growing season was shorter. The soil was poorer. The trees had to be cleared before the ground was cultivated. There was, however, more precipitation. The annual precipitation around Moscow is about thirty inches a year (twenty-four in Kiev). A comparison of agricultural conditions around Moscow with those around Kiev reveals one of the curses of the Russian land. Because of the vast territorial expanse and the fact that the only large sea within meteorological reach of continental Russia is the Arctic, there is an inverse relationship between the length of the growing season and the quantity of precipitation: the longer the growing season, the scanter the rainfall.

From the time when the nomads, pre-Mongol and Mongol, forced the Russian move north, a time extending over many generations, until the advent of a systematic industrial revolution in Russia, approximately the time of the First Five-Year Plan (1928), Russia was condemned to its proverbial condition of poverty, a poverty born of natural conditions that also inhibited the kind of cultural advancement that might have helped—but did not—to relieve the material problem. Modern science was to discover in the industrial resources of Soviet Russia the richest land on earth, but their advantageous exploitation awaited the hand of a progressive dictator. In the meantime, the economy languished—for centuries.

The move north, then, provided some improvement of security in exchange for a high price in prosperity. But a surprise awaited the Russians in the northwest, an ironic surprise, perhaps the unkindest, unfairest trick that fate has ever dealt them, and one perfectly impossible to have recognized at that date. Not only had they moved to economic poverty. They had also in the long run moved to greater strategic insecurity. For they had fled from a power soon to be in eclipse and settled next door to the power that was to dominate the entire world from that time hence. Already before their liberation from the Mongol yoke (1480), that Latin Catholic culture from which accident and ignorance had excluded them was generating a power complex to make that of the Mongols appear transient. Europe was giving birth to the Renaissance, and it was to be shared by all nations Latin and Catholic, their Reformation successors, and their colonial posterity. It transformed the power configuration of the world.

The critical problem that these developments posed for the Russians is best appreciated in the context of comparative history. As William McNeill has persuasively suggested, by the criterion of relations among great cultural complexes, there are three periods in world history. First is that prior to 500 B.C.E., the period of Middle Eastern cultural dominance. Second is that from 500 B.C.E. to 1500 C.E., the period that he characterizes as "Eurasian Cultural Balance." Four great civilizations maintained relative cultural parity in this period: China, India, the Middle East, and the West. The third period, 1500 to the present, is that of Western dominance.[6]

We might suggest that by McNeill's own criteria the configuration of power in the world since 1945 has shifted such as to require the recognition of a fourth period. We have grown accustomed since the

1960s, in any event, to observe a pentagonal configuration of the distribution of power in the world. Moving from west to east, there is the United States, a sometimes coherently semiunited Europe, the USSR/CIS/Russia, China, and Japan. Once upon a time there was OPEC—the Organization of Petroleum-Exporting Countries. Power has migrated far from the West, although it takes different forms in different places. Russian power is primarily military, Japanese power primarily economic, OPEC power primarily that of a quasi monopoly. Still, in the non-West the scale of power has grown sufficiently imposing to call the dominion of the West into question.

The criteria that we must use, however, in order to reach this conclusion are geographical. If we judge by cultural standards, we are still in period three. Power has migrated outward from the West in direct proportion to the exploitation—or importation—of Western civilization in non-Western cultures. The fundamentally anti-Western impulses that inspired the Russian and Chinese revolutions were given birth by Karl Marx, a German philosopher working in the British Museum. And so, for better or for worse, Western civilization remains culturally dominant.

These considerations require some qualification. Thomas Sowell has observed that cultures are not unqualifiedly superior and inferior; but, rather, they engage different challenges, perform different tricks, in ways that are superior and inferior. There is no heuristically satisfactory way to argue for comprehensive cultural superiority. China and Egypt have excelled in conscripting laboring masses to perform miracles of stone construction and irrigation. India is rich in ideas about how to put the soul to rest in a busy world. The West is master of medicine and the electronic information sciences. Different cultures, different gifts.

Western civilization undoubtedly owes it charisma and prestige, and the general impression of its superiority all over the world—a superiority recognized by most governments and many peoples—to the fact that it excels in precisely those parts of the cultural spectrum that are materially and mechanically measurable. The West produces consensually superior military power, economic prosperity, and medicine and hygiene. We can test the power of these instruments on the battlefield, in the counting house, in the laboratory. They do not, however, exhaust the spectrum of cultural quality. We cannot reasonably compare *The Tale of Genji*, *All Men Are Brothers*, and *Madame Bovary* or the Taj

Mahal, the Escorial, and the Kremlin except by reference to criteria derived from the particular culture from which one of these things comes.

Now let us consider the impact of the rise of the West on the circumstances of Russia.

The first manifestation of Western superiority was military power. The Russians felt the pressure of it in the Polish–Lithuanian outposts of Western civilization in the sixteenth century. By the seventeenth century, Western power was strong enough to advance farther afield, and the Turks, formerly the greatest military power in the European theater, began to yield to it. Gathering strength, in the eighteenth century, it challenged the Indians of South Asia. Only in the nineteenth century was the West strong enough to overcome the civilized states in the remotest regions of the earth—China in the Opium War (1839) and Japan in Tokyo Bay (1854).

Of course, the West brought to these places the blessings as well as the curses of its own civilization. It is still too little appreciated, however, how much damage the non-West sustained in this confrontation measured by the index of its wounded self-respect. Like those busybody Athenians of whom Thucydides wrote, the European imperialists, the missionaries, the instruments of the "White Man's burden" and the "*mission civilisatrice*" were "born to take no rest themselves, and to give others none."

Among all of the peoples who experienced the West as an intrusion of aliens, the Russians alone lived practically on the border of the beast, next door to the scourge of the earth. They have had a longer experience of the problem than the other peoples, and in wrestling with what they have demonstrably perceived to be the superiority of the European challenge, they have accumulated more cultural and psychic scar tissue from the struggle than nations initially more remote from the experience.

The Russians addressed themselves to the problem seriously during the reign that constitutes the decisive watershed and the most basic political revolution in their history, that of Ivan III the Great (1462–1505). Ivan was the first great reformer in the history of Russia. The challenge that he faced was formidable. Though the Mongols were no longer the awesome power that they had been, they could still mount serious security threats on Moscow's eastern and southern frontiers.

More serious by this time was the rising power of Poland–Lithuania in the West. Between 1386 and 1569—the Union of Krewo and the Union of Lublin—these two formerly separate principalities were joined into one. By this time, Poland reached from the Baltic to the Black Sea, and it remained until the end of the eighteenth century, after Russia, the second largest state between the Atlantic and the Ottoman Empire.

Moreover, Poland exhibited graphically the Russian problem of the cultural challenge of Renaissance Europe. It is illustrated in the life of Nicolaus Copernicus (Mikołaj Kopernik, Niklas Koppernigk), born in Toruń, Poland, in 1473. He was educated in mathematics at one of the oldest and most distinguished universities in Europe, Kraków, founded in 1364, the center of the Polish Renaissance. He studied canon law and medicine at Bologna, Padua, Rome, and Ferrara, taught in Rome, and went in 1503 to serve as canon at the Prussian cathedral in Frauenburg. There he began work on the treatise that would become the Copernican system of astronomy, largely completed in 1513. In 1526, he wrote, at the request of King Sigismund I of Poland, a treatise on monetary reform, *De monetae cudendae ratione*. His published work on the heavens, *De revolutionibus orbium coelestium*, reached him only on his deathbed in 1543.

Russia, by contrast, was to get its first university in Moscow in 1755. Russia was the last country in Europe to acquire printing presses. At the time when Sir Isaac Newton published his *Principia mathematica* in 1687, Russia was still without the publication of a mathematics textbook.[7]

Obviously, Ivan III faced Western enemies of superior strength and superior material culture. In order to oppose such enemies, he needed a society richer in resources, and a state with more authority to requisition and dispose of them, than the society and the state of Muscovy afforded in 1462. He needed what states in such circumstances have always needed, a great increase of executive power. He needed absolutism, and he set out to found it. The revolution that Ivan accomplished was the great watershed of Russian political tradition. Ivan's statecraft was the great prototype, a classic Russian system of absolutism and militarism under cautious and scrupulous control.

He addressed himself first to the least of his problems abroad. In a series of campaigns in the 1460s, he attacked the Tatars of Kazan, due east of Moscow, sufficiently to keep them at bay while he turned his attention elsewhere.

Thereafter he took up the task of strengthening the internal supports of his power. The Mongol dominion and the institution of the *yarlyk* (right of investiture of a Russian prince) had weakened the institutions of the *veche* and the boyar *duma*. These institutions were not able to challenge Ivan in most of the country. There remained two chief obstacles to the internal centralization of his power. First was the division of the Russian land among a variety of different territorial governments, the *rota* system of princely succession. Fortunately for Ivan, all his father's brothers had died by 1462, but he himself had five brothers with whom to share the sovereignty of his own patrimony (*votchina*).

Ivan evidently aimed to destroy whatever princely power rivaled his own. Judging by the scant historical evidence, he seems to have made very heavy demands of his rival princes, probably heavier demands than he thought that they could bear. Judging by his policy, he must be suspected of deliberately seeking to drive them to resistance, revolt, or treason. Having done so, he marched his army into his brothers' principalities and took possession of them by right of conquest.

Novgorod was a special case, probably the most significant obstacle to Ivan's goals. It was in important ways unlike the other territories of Russia. It long preserved inviolate the free traditions of Kiev. As the northwesternmost area of Russia, it had felt the least influence of the Mongol yoke and the most influence of Europe among Russian principalities. It was a member-state of the fabled Hanseatic League of northern European trading cities. It reflected the bourgeois republican qualities of the city-states of both northern Germany and Renaissance Italy. The *veche* was still alive and well in Novgorod. Its republican and semidemocratic principles contrasted conspicuously with government elsewhere in northern Russia. And it was richer than the other Russian states. Novgorod was naturally attached to its European connections and naturally loath to surrender to the grimmer encroachments and solicitations, not to mention the principles of government, of Moscow. Hence it found flirtation with Lithuania impossible to resist, and Ivan found it treasonous. In 1478, he marched his army into Novgorod, took possession of it, and closed down the operation of the *veche* that had so long represented the attachment of the city to freedom. Viatka suffered a similar fate, as did Pskov in the next generation.

Having in this fashion aborted the operation of the *rota* system, Ivan used the right of conquest to attack the *votchina* system. First he declared large parts of the population in the conquered territories treasonous; then he abrogated their property rights; and finally he engaged in massive transfers of the population so condemned. He moved his victims out of the principality of their traditional rights into any other principality where they had no rights, and he settled them on a new system of land tenure called *pomestie*. A *pomestie* was in effect a fief. In the language of European feudalism, a *votchina* was an allod, land held unconditionally; a *pomestie*, a fief, was held conditionally in a contract of obligations to the prince who granted it. Hereafter, as the *pomestie* system advanced across Russia, Ivan developed an effective lever on the political conduct of the warrior class. The ultimate aim of the system was to place all landholding in Russia in the conditional *pomestie* system of tenure and thereby to place both the property and the people of the entire nation at the disposal of the grand prince as his patrimony. Ivan and his heirs would be the sole proprietors whose possession of land was secure and unconditional, that is, his *votchina*. All others used his land as their *pomestie* at the pleasure of the prince. Stalin would achieve the same result with the collective farm.

Ironically, the fief in Russia worked to centralize power just as it worked in Western Europe to decentralize it. The contrast is explained by the phenomenon of subinfeudation in Europe and its absence in Russia. That is, European feudalism allowed a single vassal to receive a fief from multiple suzerains and thus to contract multiple and conflicting allegiances such as to make a genuine anarchy of the claims of hierarchical order in the system; whereas in Russia there were legions of vassals and one suzerain, the grand prince. In Europe, moreover, the contractual relationship was conceived to be bilateral, while in Russia it was effectively unilateral. Hence, while Russia had fiefs, it did not have conventional (European) feudalism, as Ivan made the system work in a powerfully centripetal fashion. In Europe, the fief conferred elements of freedom and generated anarchy; in Russia, it imposed bondage and brought order.

Ivan III laid the foundations of Russian absolutism. If we compare the free institutions of Kiev and the absolutist institutions of Muscovy, they are utterly antithetical. There was, however, a continuity of consciousness. The policy of Muscovy represents a lesson drawn from Kievan experience. No state afflicted with the geography of Russia— open frontiers and a northern European agricultural economy—could afford the luxuries of freedom and anarchy that had condemned Kiev.

In sum, Ivan III, a consummately cunning and deliberately devious

prince, lacking practical precedents useful to him, devised imagin-
atively original policies and designed persistent essentials of Russian
statecraft. He was the most creative figure in the political history of
Russia. He proceeded by reason and established tradition. The boyars
surrendered much of their freedom inside Russia, but the nation acquired independence of the Mongols in the East and sustained its independence along the Western frontier with Lithuania, already a source
of serious pressure on the politics of Russia. The influence of Ivan's
achievement can scarcely be overemphasized. Adjusted, refurbished,
updated, it was to form the fundamental paradigm of Russian politics
into the 1980s.

Ivan III's son Vasilii III (1505–33) mimicked his father's policy.
Vasilii's son Ivan IV (1533–84) did more. The early part of his reign
(1547–60) was devoted to the same kind of policies, arguably rational
and constructive, that had typified the government of his father and
grandfather. He formed a new style of regiments, the *streltsy* (musketeers) regiments, equipped with firearms of imported foreign manufacture, and manned by the Russian gentry. They were settled on *pomestie*
land (conditional tenure) and required to discharge their obligation for
the land so granted by universal and perpetual service. Here are the
origins of the comprehensive Russian service state. The class of personnel serving the state in this capacity came to be known as court
people, *dvoriane*, after the word *dvor*, court. This new gentry was
designed to supplant the refractory old boyar aristocracy attached, as
aristocracies habitually are, to traditions of freedom. The new gentry
service class was the executive arm of the absolutist state.[8]
    The early work of Ivan IV is recognized in the Muscovite tradition
as rational and constructive. We also know him, however, as Ivan the
Terrible, and especially after 1560, that is what he was. He was pious,
learned, lecherous, sadistic, perhaps mad. He married eight wives and
yet allegedly assaulted his daughters-in-law. In an argument likely
provoked by such an assault, he struck the heir to the throne and
killed him.
    When Ivan's coffin was opened some years ago for a belated post-
mortem, his bones were found to contain abnormally high levels of
arsenic. No one knows why. Terrible as his reputation was, he remains
one of the most popular figures of Russian folklore.[9]
    Ivan had inherited the throne as a child of three years. His mother

ruled rather arrogantly as regent. In 1538, she died suddenly, possibly of poisoning. Ivan was eight years old.

His relations with the old boyar aristocracy in Russia were typical of those west of Russia in Europe as well. The aristocracy had enjoyed freedom and elements of political supremacy in the Middle Ages, and the new monarchies founded their power on the subjugation of the aristocracies and the exploitation of them as an instrument of monarchical power. After the removal, therefore, of the firm hands of Ivan IV's grandfather, father, and mother, the boyars naturally seized the opportunity of a royal minority to engage in various insidious forms of revolt. Ivan reacted with impotent fury, bided his time, and eventually turned the tables with quite a potent fury.

A contemporary chronicle describes a characteristic episode of Ivan's childhood:

> There was at that time much rioting and disorder in the Christian land, on account of our sins, the sovereign being young, and the boyars [being] given to corruption without restraint; and they stirred up much bloodshed among themselves, and they dispensed justice wrongfully, and their deeds were not godly. . . . On the twenty-ninth day of December [1543], Grand Prince Ivan Vasilievich of all Russia could no longer tolerate the boyars' unruly and willful doings, in that they had committed many murders without the grand prince's orders. . . . The great sovereign ordered that their leader, Prince Andrei Shuiskii, be seized and delivered to the dog-keepers, and the dog-keepers took him and killed him . . . and from that time the boyars began to fear the sovereign.[10]

In 1560 Ivan's beloved first wife Anastasiia died, and he suspected foul play. His Livonian War with Poland (1558–83)—a very ambitious attempt to conquer an advantageous position on the Baltic, even to assert a claim to the throne of Poland—began to go awry. It was more than his resources could support, and he soon began to perceive treason all around him. In 1564, Ivan instituted his most notorious creation, the *oprichnina*. The term means something like "land apart." It was a kind of paramilitary police apparatus. The *oprichniki* rode about in black robes on black horses, their saddle horns made of a mounted dog's head, and bearing the curious symbol of a broom. Compounded of treason, vengeance, and perhaps sadism and paranoia, the *oprichnina* attacked the boyar class viciously and bloodily.

In 1570, the *oprichnina* went to perform its vengeance on Novgorod. After the torture and dispatch of the leading males whom Ivan found objectionable, he "ordered their wives and their children of all ages, male and female, even suckling infants, to be brought to the Volkhov bridge and taken up to a tower built for that purpose, with their hands and feet tied behind them, and the infants tied to their mothers; and [he] ordered them to be hurled from a great height into the river Volkhov," where his soldiers waited in boats with weapons to attack anyone who had the misfortune to surface.[11]

Whether the enterprise of the *oprichnina* was rational or not, it advanced the construction of absolutism at a terrible price. Only nine boyar families are found to have survived the reign.[12] It virtually created a civil war in the land—as Stalin, who so much admired Ivan, did in collectivization. It was absolutism run amok, and like Stalin's riot of authoritarian excesses, it left the land out of joint and incapable of adjusting to a civil life thereafter. A Time of Troubles followed both experiences.

Ivan had pursued with unhinged reason excessively ambitious goals of absolutism, the subjugation of the boyars and the gathering of the Russian lands. His policy nearly wrecked both state and nation, and it opened the country to a foreign invasion that for a time made it the pawn of a Catholic sovereign of Poland.

Ivan, having killed his eldest son and heir, Ivan Ivanovich, was followed by his younger son, Fedor I (1584–98), known as Fedor the Feebleminded or Fedor the Bell-Ringer (his favorite pastime). Fedor died childless, and the dynasty came to an end. A national assembly elected Ivan IV's brother-in-law, Boris Godunov, to the throne, and the Time of Troubles (1598–1613) began. The remaining boyar aristocracy fought Boris and each other, the gentry fought the boyars, the peasant serfs fought both of them, and the Poles and Swedes invaded Russia. It was dynastic war, civil war, and foreign war compounded.

In 1610, Ladislas, the son of King Sigismund of Poland, was installed on the throne of Muscovy, and Russia witnessed something like the realization of a national nightmare: itself as the prey of the papacy and the Jesuits. Eventually Russia united against the invaders and drove them out, and in 1613 an Assembly of the Land elected a new dynasty, the Romanovs. Somehow, Russia and absolutism survived.

The violent anarchy of the *oprichnina* and that of the Time of Troubles contributed to the last logical stage in the development of Russian absolutism: serfdom. Until almost 1600, the peasants of Russia were free people. They lived on and worked their own land, or state domain, or the land of large proprietors, including that of the church. From the time of the Livonian War and the *oprichnina*, the burden of taxes and rents on the peasantry weighed as heavily as did that of military service on the gentry. Economic depression set in, and peasants fled their debts to the state and landlords alike. They went to the "wild field," Ukraine, to Poland, or to hide in the woods. A shortage of labor developed, and the service gentry had trouble keeping peasants enough to work its lands while it went about the serious business of war. The problem was exacerbated by the Time of Troubles.

Eventually, in some fashion unrecorded, a tacit bargain was struck between tsar and gentry. We know nothing about its origins or development. No document records it. We know its results. Evidently, the gentry persuaded the tsar that they could perform his service effectively only if he found some means of assuring them a reliable supply of peasant labor.

The process was gradual. For generations past, it had been customary that a peasant family might not move, might not leave its previous place of residence, except during a period of two weeks around St. George's Day, 26 November, after the season's labor was done. Late in his reign, Ivan IV decreed that certain years of special stress were "forbidden years," that is, during such a year the peasants might not move at all. Peasants who did so move were subject to discovery and forcible return. A statute of limitations, however, was placed on the right to search for and apprehend them. By 1600, the time limit was being gradually extended. Finally, by 1649, the new law code, the *Ulozhenie*, forbade peasant movement entirely.

There are several curious features of serfdom. The serf was not the property of the landlord. Serf law (*krepostnoe pravo*) consisted only of the prohibition on moving. Serfdom came to Russia only after it was disappearing in Western Europe. It also came in a different form. In Western Europe, serfdom was a contract between a laborer and a landlord. The serf paid rent on land granted by the lord, sometimes in produce, sometimes in labor on the lord's own domain; the lord provided land and a variety of other forms of capital that the lowly serf could not provide for himself, especially a wine press, a grain mill, and a castle in which to take refuge during feudal combats. It was distinctly reciprocal, and it was emphatically an economic arrangement.

In Russia, on the other hand, it was primarily a legal arrangement, a device of statecraft, decreed, as it never was in Western Europe, by a sovereign prince. Furthermore, there was little of reciprocity about it. The peasant sharecroppers found themselves bound to the land that they had formerly worked, and the state required the landlord to deliver nothing to the serf.

Finally, the coming of serfdom was an inappropriate anachronism. In the roughly seventy-five years between the time when the tacit bargain was struck, presumably some time in the midst of the Livonian War of Ivan IV, and the time when the *Ulozhenie* of 1649 capped the edifice of the ugly device, Russia was engaged in a variety of wars with the Swedes and the Poles, whose military Russia increasingly imitated. The army, then, relied more and more on *streltsy* regiments, mercenaries, and other elements of a modern military machine. Thus the semifeudal gentry cavalry that Ivan IV had impressed into service in 1556, based on the *pomestie* system, had been superseded to a large extent by a salaried standing army. The argument of which the gentry had persuaded the monarchy when the encroachments of serfdom began, then, no longer applied: serf labor was not needed to support an army that was no longer drawn from *pomestie* landholding but was organized and salaried like the standing armies of Europe. And so the serf law of 1649 was both an anachronism and an anomaly. It imposed a rigidly static social order on the bulk of the Russian public. It encouraged the degradation of the defenseless peasant population, as well as the dissipation of the pampered gentry beneficiaries of the corrupt bargain.[13]

It is conceivable in the history of human society to drive enthralled masses in a creative or constructive fashion such as to yield a Great Wall of China or a Pyramid of Cheops, an irrigation system in the great early river-valley civilizations or, arguably, in a five-year plan. Russian serfdom did not do so. It retarded social and cultural development, probably without yielding compensatory benefits, as there is no indication that its immediate beneficiaries, the gentry, profited by it except to indulge themselves.

From this time, as Mikhail Speranskii, the distinguished civil servant of Alexander I (1801–25), put it, there were two categories of people in Russia: the gentry were the slaves of the prince, and the serfs were the slaves of the gentry. In the course of constructing this service state, freedom inside Russia was extinguished. On the other hand, freedom from alien dominion was preserved, and that had been, in its initial conception, the purpose that both gentry military service and serf labor service were designed to support. The future would exact a high price of Russia for the failure to maintain in serf law the rational adjustment of social organization to strategic needs that had been characteristic of the early evolution of absolutism there.

Adam Olearius, a German diplomat, visited Russia during the reign of the first Romanov, Michael (1613-45). He observed at that time the increasing aversion of the Russians to foreigners from Europe and yet the increasing dependence of the government on them. Russian suspicion of Westerners was then evidently fully as apparent as it was during the height of the cold war, yet in the most private audiences of the tsar and foreign delegations, the tsar's own interpreter was Hans Helmes, a German. According to Russian ceremony, in formal audiences the tsar allowed foreign Christian emissaries to kiss his hand. Having done so, however, he then turned to a basin and towel, which he kept nearby in such ceremonies, and in the presence of the emissaries proceeded to wash his hand.[14] Western culture was in this environment a pollutant, but it was an indispensable one, as evidenced by the growing numbers of Europeans received in Russia and employed there.

The chief achievement of the second Romanov, Alexis (1645–76), was the reincorporation into Russia of the eastern part of Ukraine (the left bank of the Dnieper River), that part of the ancient Russian patrimony most intimately in contact with the West and most subject to its influence. Ukraine, unlike Russia, had been administered directly by the Mongols themselves, as distinct from their indirect government of Russia. Around the middle of the fourteenth century, however, Poland had conquered it from the Mongols. For four hundred years, then, Ukraine had been separated from Russia: one hundred years under Mongol rule, three hundred under Polish. When it was returned to Russian rule (1667), it was different in religion, in language, and in its institutions and customs.[15]

The third Romanov was Fedor III (1676–82), who, like his predecessor-namesakes, was not very significant.[16]

The first three Romanovs are not regarded as distinguished sovereigns. Yet the institution of absolutism, which had faltered and collapsed during the Time of Troubles, was nevertheless effectively restored in the course of the seventeenth century. One mysterious institution might have threatened it. The *zemskii sobor*, the assembly of the land, was an intriguing phenomenon, because it was in some clear-and-obscure respects a parliamentary body. The first one was called by Ivan IV in 1566 to advise him on the Livonian War. It consisted of a delegation chosen by the government. The *zemskii sobor* of 1613 was undoubtedly a genuinely representative assembly of the land, one gen-erated by the people in some fashion, and its purpose was to elect a dynasty. It included peasants, and it functioned continuously until 1622, presumably in an advisory capacity. It was convoked again, in what configuration is not clear, in 1632 to consult on an approaching war with Poland and in 1637 and 1642 when relations with Turkey were strained.

Alexis convoked the *zemskii sobor* four times: in 1645 to confirm his succession; in 1648–49 to discuss the law code (*Ulozhenie*); in 1650 to deal with rebellion in Pskov; and in 1651–53 to consider the Cossack imbroglio with the Poles in Ukraine. It was apparently never convoked again. In any event, it disappeared—no Parliament, no Es-tates General, no Diet of Poland or the Holy Roman Empire. Its ap-pearance is intriguing, but its significance is not clear.

By the end of the seventeenth century, Russian absolutism, straining every sinew of its power, had achieved one decisive result that had not always appeared likely. It had sustained the survival of the Russian nation. In its foreign relations, something like a Russian version of manifest destiny, a process long known as the ''gathering of the Rus-sian lands,'' had been operative throughout the Muscovite period. Ivan III had not only thrown off the Mongol yoke; he had also conquered the ancient Kievan patrimony on the Baltic coastline, though it was subsequently lost in the Time of Troubles and had to be conquered again by Peter I. Ivan IV had improved the security of the nation by conquering the Tatar lands of the central Volga basin, Kazan and As-trakhan, in the 1550s. He failed to incorporate the western Russian lands of Lithuania in the Livonian War. In the latter part of the six-teenth century, the eastward movement across Siberia, the rich source of furs, began, and by the end of the seventeenth century Siberia was a Russian province. The left bank of Ukraine was annexed from Poland in 1667. Thus by the dawn of the eighteenth century, the bulk of the ancient patrimony of Kiev had been gathered—in the east a great deal more—and it remained to claim right-bank Ukraine, east central Poland, and the Baltic and Black Sea littorals. The state was poised to embark on a more ambitious career of imperialism. The next Romanov, if we ignore his virago half-sister Sophia, was Peter the Great, and Peter I had the energy to undertake it.

As Russia stood at the threshold of the eighteenth century, much of its familiar modern face was already apparent. The challenges that it faced, the attitudes of the people, its tense relations with the West, and the institutional style of its response had all emerged clearly. The maintenance of the independence of Russia and the gathering of the Russian lands were achieved by the imposition of the absolutist service state, transforming the institutional nature of Kiev yet succeeding in addressing national strategic requirements at which Kiev had failed. The state arrogated to itself the wisdom to govern for the people and to draw up the national agenda of their policy. The degree of its political pretenses and the degree of their political submission were unequaled elsewhere in Europe.

❖ 2 ❖

Politics and Religion:
The Divorce of State and Society

*He surpasses all other kings and princes in the power he
has and uses over his own people.*
Herberstein, *Description of Moscow*, 1557

The state and form of their government is plain tyrannical.
Fletcher, *Of the Russe Commonwealth*, 1591

*Where the people is weak, the state is strong; and where the
people is strong, the state is weak.*
Shafarevich, *Socialism in World History*, 1977

*Russia still reflects what in mature, developed cultures is no
longer possible, . . . the naive metaphysic of the folk.*
Lou-Andreas Salomé, "Das russische Heiligenbild," 1897

*Bitterness, savagery, love of the wilderness, contempt for
hope. . . .*
Nikos Kazantzakis, letters, Russia 1929

From the fourteenth to the seventeenth centuries, the Russian state
invested ever more of its energies in the mastery of the politics of
this world, while the people retreated ever farther from it into the
reveries of an otherworldly religion.

Scarcely anyone who has regarded the history and politics of Russia, traveled in the country, or read the headlines has failed to notice
the huge role in national life that the state has played, and thoughtful

Russians have been as impressed by it as have frightened foreigners. In the nineteenth century, a particular school of Russian historians undertook to explain why the apparatus of their native state occupied such a disproportionate place in national life compared to the politics and statecraft of Western Europe. The exegesis of the political-juridical school (*gosudarstvenno-iuridicheskaia shkola*) is the most compellingly coherent single explanation of the nature of modern Russia.

They begin with an observation of Sergei Soloviev's: in Europe nature was the mother of society, in Russia nature was the stepmother. The north central Russia of Muscovite society was no Riviera. The people of Russia could not raise, as the French around Nice could, six crops of carrots a year. The land was poor. Furthermore, the people were scattered over a vast hinterland without the roads, bridges, and canals of Western Europe. They were largely illiterate. They had no secular educational institutions before the eighteenth century, and the clerical ones outside Ukraine had little quality and little influence. It was difficult to communicate and therefore difficult to organize. In a word, there was little national cohesion.

In the conception of B. N. Chicherin, who is largely responsible for generating the school of thought, the greater the freedom that the mass of people had to roam the land and the more thinly they spread themselves over the vast expanse, the greater was the need for a state that could grasp the dispersed masses, bond them into a stable union, and force them to serve public purposes. It was no simple matter, given the scarcity of resources, the vastness of the wilderness, and the sparseness of the population, to bend the people to the fulfillment of their national duties. They were disorganized, atomized, impotent, and passive. The formation of the state lay, then, at the basis of the evolution of modern Russia.

The crux of this argument is the somewhat familiar one that there was no sufficient order among the people, that they were weak, and that they required a strong state to establish its protection over them. It was precisely the weakness of the people that demanded the strength of the state. In the pithy formulaic imagination of a contemporary Russian and recent dissident, a friend and colleague of Solzhenitsyn, a distinguished maverick mathematician turned renegade historian, "Where the people is weak, the state is strong; and where the people is strong, the state is weak." Igor Shafarevich owes this suggestion to an ancient Chinese sage from nearly the age of Confucius, the author of an authoritarian Legalist tract, *The Book of Lord Shang*.[1]

The irony of this situation in Russia was that it made the strength of the nation depend more and more exclusively on the strength of the state, or it weakened society progressively. As the great Russian historian Vasilii Kliuchevskii put it, the state grew fat and the people grew lean.

The Russian experience was vastly different from that of Europe in several ways. Russian society contained none of those corporate social entities endowed by ancient tradition and Roman law with certain inviolable, inalienable, uninvadable rights and exemptions. Those who fight, those who work, and those who pray were present in Russia, but they had no institutional foundations to protect them, to forbid encroachments on a legal integrity that they simply lacked. We have seen how the prince of Russia could dispose of life and limb as he chose, that he could convert free men, or whole free classes of people, into various categories of thralldom, call them servitors, call them serfs.

In Western Europe in the Middle Ages, the aristocracy and the clergy did persistent combat with the monarchy for rights and privileges. They were perpetual and effective rivals. The English barons required a Magna Carta of King John at Runnymede (1215), and in the celebrated Investiture Controversy—over control of clerical appointments to ecclesiastical fiefs—Pope Gregory VII ruined the power of Emperor Henry IV (1075). The institution of monarchy as the characteristic governing principle of the early modern nation-state eventually emerged from these battles with a qualified upper hand, but it never erased its rivals, and it never converted them into a subservient service class. In Western Europe, it was society and its institutions, supported by tradition and Roman law, that evolved, defined, and, above all, limited the nature of government, the power of the state.

In Russia, the relationship was reversed. Kievan Russia had enjoyed freedom through the rich mixture of institutions, but these, lacking the protection of a robust corporate legal nature, were vulnerable. The Mongols found it to their advantage in the unruly land of the Russians to favor a strong prince, one who could deliver better than weaker princes the enforcement of their demands. Their mistake was not to have observed the calculus of the growth of Russian power and the decline of their own in time. In the meantime, they had dealt roughly with Russian institutions rivaling the prince's power. They nearly wiped the slate clean.

The decisive power and support of the Mongols made the prince of

Russia increasingly independent of the influence of the town council (*veche*) and the council of his retainers (boyar *duma*). Ivan III, then, had only to cripple the claims of his brothers to a share in his power (*rota* system) and render boyar/gentry landholding dependent upon him by overwhelming allodial tenure (*votchina*) with fief-holding tenure (*pomestie*), and nothing stood between him and absolutism. In Russia, it was the state that evolved, defined, and limited society: the fief, new regiments of musketeers (*streltsy*), the new service class (*dvoriane*), the Assembly of the Land (*zemskii sobor*), and serfdom (*krepostnoe pravo*). After Kiev, the first principle of Russian politics and its relation to society was statism.

There was one striking peculiarity in this state of affairs. The people were overfleeced but undergoverned. The strong state consisted chiefly of the army, the *oprichnina* (in its time), the police, and the internal revenue service. It consisted of controlling, ordering, and extracting devices. It did not provide the courts, banks, and justices of the peace of Western Europe, nor the water-control system, civil-service exams, or ever-normal granary of China. The Russian state was "despotically strong but infrastructurally weak."[2] To repeat a previous observation because it is so often forgotten, if the Russians were tormented by their government, it was to spare them a foreign government.

The juridical school gave a name to its conception of the Russian state: the hypertrophic—or overdeveloped—model of statecraft.

Was there really a difference of degree between the absolutism of Russia and that of Western Europe? Was there an absolutism more highly developed than that of Louis XIV, the author of the attitude "*L'état, c'est moi*"?

Russia was by no means alone on the Eurasian landmass in being confronted by stubborn enemies on two frontiers. From the early sixteenth century, France was engaged in the Habsburg–Valois (later Habsburg–Bourbon) rivalry, the Habsburgs of the time occupying the thrones of Spain in the south and of Germany in the north. The Habsburgs of Germany were caught in the same fashion between the French in the west and the Turks in the east. Poor little Prussia, exposed on all frontiers, a trivial state in the sixteenth century, became the power base of Frederick the Great and the cornerstone of the German Empire. Poland was situated between Prussia and Austria in the west and Russia in the east.

The states in this situation that saved themselves from the ravages of their neighbors did so, as Russia did, by the pursuit of absolutism and militarism. By the end of the seventeenth century, the aspirations of absolutism had been decisively defeated in just two major nations. One of them, England, was shielded from the armies of Europe by the English Channel. The other, Poland, succumbed to the carving knives of her three authoritarian neighbors in the course of the eighteenth century.

Still, none of these states was quite so deep in the wilderness of northeastern Europe as was Russia. None was quite so remote as Russia from the sources of dynamic civilization. More important, none of them was without traditions and institutions that served as stable and stubborn impediments to the pretensions of absolutist power.

In other words, among all the states of Europe—unlike Russia— there were traditions and institutions inhibiting the claims of absolutism. In Bohemia, Hungary, and Poland, the kings were elected, and they swore to respect the traditional social-political contracts of the lands where they reigned. They governed with representative assemblies, the Diets, which had ideas of legislative prerogative and the control of taxation. Such an assembly, the Althing, had appeared in remote Iceland in the tenth century. In Sweden, it was the Riksdag; in Denmark, the Rigsdag; in Spain, the Cortes; in the German Empire, the Reichstag; in the *Länder* of Germany, the Landtage. These representative assemblies were composed, like the three estates of France, of the delegates of different classes; in Sweden and Denmark, for example, the nobility, the clergy, the burgers, and the peasants. The idea of a society composed naturally of orders disposing of unequal but inalienable rights was known everywhere between France and Russia as a *Ständestaat* (*Stand* was German for French *état*, or estate). According to one authority, "One would have to travel farther east [of Poland] to Russia to find an independent Slavic state in which there was no assembly equal or superior to the king."[3]

It has been argued plausibly that the notion of a West European absolutism was simply a myth.[4] How could it have been otherwise in a society of orders and law?

The very paradigm, or paragon, of the West European ideal of absolutism was the seventeenth-century France of Louis XIV, but even a cursory comparison shows that absolutism was as real in Russia as it was a vain pretense in France. Seventeenth-century France abounded in institutions of corporate power and privilege and exemption from royal prerogative.

The thirteen *parlements* (law courts) of both Paris and the provinces presumed to pronounce upon what was in effect the constitutionality of royal edicts. The *parlement* of Paris blocked the financial reforms by which the government proposed to deal with the ballooning budget deficit in the late eighteenth century and thereby contributed to the coming of the French Revolution.

In the outlying provinces, the *pays d'états*, the provincial Estates—assemblies of the representatives of the three different estates, the clergy, the nobility, and the third estate—shared in royal government in such a way as both to assist and to obstruct it. These assemblies had the prerogative of appropriating tax revenue. In some of the *pays d'états*, the assemblies also collected the revenue; in others, it was done by royal agents, the *élus*, who had sole responsibility for appropriating and collecting the revenue in the central provinces of the nation, the *pays d'élection*, where no provincial Estates met. There was a conspicuous lack of uniformity in this allegedly absolutist country. In the sixteenth century, provincial Estates had jurisdiction in half of French revenue and more than half of French territory. In the seventeenth century, Louis XIV regularly *negotiated* the tax levies with the *pays d'états*.[5]

A principal source of French revenue was venality of patents of nobility and simony in clerical appointments. It was indispensable to French finances. This business alone is clear evidence of the flagrant incapacity of the French monarchy to gather sufficient revenue to sustain itself. In addition, there were village assemblies, town councils, Assemblies of Notables, and Assemblies of the Clergy. The Notables and the Clergy had national influence, especially in questions of royal revenue.

It is true that Ivan IV established elective bodies of allegedly local government in Russia in 1555, but at the same time he imposed on these assemblies his own choice of executive administrator, the *zemskii starosta*. To the extent that these institutions survived the *oprichnina* and the Time of Troubles, in the seventeenth century they were overwhelmed when a *voevoda* with plenary executive, financial, and police powers was sent out to all the provinces from Moscow.[6]

In France, on the other hand, unlike in Russia, executive power was further diminished by religious schism. The wars of religion of the late sixteenth century had seen two camps of the nobility seize on the issue of religion to bypass or take control of the power of the throne. In the latter 1580s, there were three armed aspirants to the crown of France— the War of the Three Henries. The successful one, Henry IV, was a Protestant who felt forced to convert to Catholicism ("Paris is worth the mass") in order to achieve the pacification of the country. Yet in order to reassure the Protestants, he not only issued a decree of religious toleration but set aside 128 cities, some of them strongly fortified, as Protestant refuges. This state within the state lasted in residual form until 1685. Privileged preserves where the writ of unfettered absolute power was not allowed were inconceivable in the Russia of that time.

The population of France could also find freedom—as Burke recommended, as Kiev exemplified—in the very complexity of the political institutions of the country.[7] The French Revolution recognized the polymorphous diversity of these institutions, the irrational lack of uniformity among them, and began to reorganize them. The job was completed by Napoleon. In nineteenth-century France, no longer remotely absolutist, it was said that the minister of education could confidently state which page of which textbook the schoolchildren of any province of France were reading at a given time.

The population of France never conceded the monarchy plenary arbitrary power. During the wars of religion, Jean Bodin wrote a treatise in which he was searching for means to bring order and justice out of the chaos of civil conflict by fortifying the power of the throne. Still, he defined the powers of the king carefully, and he explicitly stipulated that a monarch did not have the power to invade the property rights of the citizenry, as was the case in Russia. "Royal, or legitimate, monarchy is one in which the subject obeys the laws of the Prince, the Prince in his turn obeys the laws of nature, and natural liberty and the natural right to property are secured to all. Seignioral monarchy is one in which the Prince is lord and master of both the possessions and the persons of his subjects as absolutely as the head of a household governs his slaves. Tyrannical monarchy is one in which the laws of nature are set at naught, free subjects are oppressed as if they were slaves, and their property is treated as if it belonged to the tyrant."[8]

About the same time, a distinguished French jurist, Louis Le Caron, took an even stronger tone. "I believe that the opinion of Polybius is correct, that of the three kinds of government . . . , to wit monarchy, aristocracy, and democracy, one cannot exist alone. Rather the three together, organized and limited, form a true republic." Thus it was in France, he said, where the king governed with the advice of the "peers of France," the aristocracy, and the common people, "through whom is revealed a form of democracy."[9]

As a delegate to the provincial Estates of Normandy explained in 1622, "the fundamental laws of the kingdom neither permit nor authorize anyone, not even the kings, to raise armies or to levy taxes without the deliberation of the public and the consent of the Estates, the three orders of the kingdom being for this gathered together and assembled."[10]

Charles Loyseau, a French theorist of monarchy writing in the early seventeenth century, condemned as unacceptable precisely the kind of government that the juridical school described in Russia: "Seignioral monarchs . . . have both princely power and also full ownership and private *seigneurie* over the persons and property of their subjects, who consequently are not merely subjects but utter slaves, having neither personal freedom nor any *seigneurie* over their possessions, which they hold only as *peculium* [personal property] and by forbearance on the part of their seignorial prince."

Loyseau then cited examples of this wrong kind of monarchy: the Assyrian, the Median, the Persian, the Turkish, the Ethiopian, and the Muscovite![11]

The classics of Western travel literature on Russia have always included the impression that Russian monarchy was qualitatively different from that of Europe. Thus Sigmund von Herberstein (ca. 1530): "All in the land call themselves their prince's *kholopy*, or sold slaves. The Grand-duke exercised his power over both clergy and laymen, both property and life. None of his councillors has ever dared to gainsay his lord's opinion. One and all agree that the lord's will is the will of God, hence what the prince does is divinely inspired. . . . It is debatable whether such a people must have such oppressive rulers or whether the oppressive rulers have made the people so stupid. . . . He surpasses all other kings and princes in the power he has and uses over his own people."[12]

Giles Fletcher was there soon after the reign of Ivan IV (1591): "The manner of their government is much after the Turkish fashion, which they seem to imitate as near as the country and reach of their capacities in political affairs will give them leave to do. The state and form of their government is plain tyrannical." The prince kept "the nobility and commons in an underproportion and far uneven balance in their several degrees, as also in their impositions and exactions, wherein they exceed all just measure without any regard of nobility or people. . . . There is none that hath any authority or public jurisdiction that goeth by descent or is held by charter but all at the appointment and pleasure of the Emperor."[13] The Russian government was for long sensitive to the unflattering characterization of it in Fletcher's work. Its publication was forbidden by Nicholas I in 1847 and by Alexander II in 1864.

Adam Olearius was there in the mid-seventeenth century:

> The Russian system of government . . . is what the political thinkers call "a dominating and despotic monarchy." After he inherits the crown, the Tsar, or Grand Prince, alone rules the whole country; all his subjects, the noblemen and princes as well as the common people, townsmen, and peasants, are his serfs and slaves, whom he treats as the master of the house does his servants. . . . If one keeps in mind the basic distinction between a legitimate and a tyrannical order, that the first subserves the welfare of the subjects and the second the personal wants of the sovereign, then the Russian government must be considered closely related to tyranny.[14]

In sum, early modern French political theorists, European travelers in Russia, and modern Russian historians agree: the alleged absolutism of Europe and the actual absolutism of Russia were incommensurable. Moreover, the French monarchy was understood to have the responsibility of procuring justice for the people of France. The enemy of popular justice was perceived by the people to be the arrogant and abusive aristocracy, not the monarchy. The monarchy was the protector of the people against its abusive seigneurs. From time to time a *chambre de justice* was proclaimed by the king in order to rectify financial abuses of officeholders. Part of its purpose was "to satisfy public opinion." A more imposing institution of the same kind was the so-called *Grands Jours*, whereby the king established a specially convoked court of law at a place of his designation in the provinces where the local courts were not handling their duties in a satisfactory fashion. The *Grands Jours* of Poitiers in 1634 empowered the king's lawyers to examine cases of "murders, assassinations, thefts, kidnappings, abductions, rapes of women and girls, embezzlement of public funds." The *Grands Jours* were designed not only to correct the mismanagement of judicial proceedings but also to clear the dockets of overloaded local courts. Most famous perhaps was the *Grands Jours* of Auvergne, which sat by order of Louis XIV from September 1665 to January 1666. It was commissioned to spare the people the frauds of local judges, collusion between judges and the grand seigneurs. It condemned the extortion of excess seigneurial dues from the peasants, tried 1,360 criminal cases, including rapes and criminal seductions of peasant girls by local nobility, and established a hospital for the poor in which unemployed and vagrant patients were taught a trade, a seventeenth-century version of job retraining.[15] In the undergoverned Russian provinces, there was no extension of such services to the people by the state.

Knowing something of the character of the state, we know thereby something of the character of the people, which the state naturally reflects. If we wish to know the people better, and to form a just estimate of their character, in particular to know them in that most reliable fashion, through their own self-expression, then prior to the flowering of Russian literature in the nineteenth century we must rely on their most characteristic recorded form of such expression, their religion.

In the defiantly difficult business of trying to comprehend Russian religion, we must accept two propositions as axiomatic: that rationalism became an accustomed mode of mental operation in Russia only in the nineteenth-century intelligentsia; and that the empirical methodology of the historian scarcely suffices to capture the elusive mysteries of Russian Orthodoxy. Russians and students of Russia appreciate more easily than others the crucial element of religion in Russian public life, and the Western newcomer to the subject must simply prepare to contemplate what is by his own familiar patterns of thought the nearly inconceivable. If we do not find in the idea that man does not live by bread alone something more than an anodyne cliché, we will never develop the remotest grasp of Russian religion.

The Russian concept of holiness is singular. It is generally thought to be typified by the reverence for the first two saints of the Russian church. Boris and Gleb were sons of that Prince Vladimir who decided in 988 upon conversion. In the wake of his death, a typical struggle developed among his sons over their father's patrimony. Sviatopolk set out to eliminate his rival brothers. Boris and Gleb were aware of his plans. They did not prepare to resist, and they did not attempt to flee. Boris spent the evening preceding his fate in fasting and praying. His assassins found him in his tent and carried out their assignment. Gleb, still a child, appealed to be spared on account of his youth, but in vain.

This is not the martyrdom of the Greek and Latin conception. The Greek word martyr means witness, one who voluntarily accepts death as the penalty for refusing to renounce his faith. Russian has two words for martyr: *muchenik*, one who is tormented; and *stradatel*, one who suffers. Boris and Gleb are known in the church tradition simply as the *strastoterptsy*, the passion-bearers. No heroics distinguished their behavior. Rather, they are revered for *neprotivlenie*, nonresistance, or kenoticism, submission. This curious phenomenon is explored in a recent critical examination of Russian culture certain to be found controversial, even offensive, Daniel Rancour-Laferriere's *The Slave Soul of Russia: Moral Masochism and the Cult of Suffering*,[16] but the documentation of the argument is massive, enough at least to arrest the attention of the skeptical.

In the conception of Russian Orthodoxy, spiritual edification comes not from moral striving or from service to the faithful so much as it comes from innocent suffering. As the great historian of the Russian church, George Fedotov, put the matter: "The evaluation of suffering as a superior moral good, as almost an end in itself, is one of the most precious features of the Russian religious mind."[17] It is associated with a quality of ecstasy (*upoenie, radenie*). Nicholas II and his unfortunate family are beginning to be revered for this reason. The foundation of a new church has been laid on the site of their execution. In the context of this conception of holiness, Solzhenitsyn's by no means ill-founded criticism of the Russian church—that it has never roused itself to protect the body of believers from the ravages of the state—has a quality of almost alien liberal inappropriateness.

From the fourteenth century, Russian holiness was often associated with the inspiration of Byzantine Hesychasm. Hesychasm was a peculiar form of praying in conjunction with breathing in rhythm with heartbeat. The requisite prayer was the "Jesus prayer" of seven invariable words: "Have mercy on me, Lord Jesus Christ." It is believed to have influenced the life of the great saint, Sergius of Radonezh (d.

1392), who founded the leading Russian monastery, the Trinity, at Sergiev Posad (until recently Zagorsk) just north of Moscow. It inspired the leader of the famous Trans-Volga Hermits, Nil Sorskii (d. 1508), who had studied it on Mt. Athos. In the nineteenth century, it was associated with the monastery that Dostoevsky made famous, the Optina Pustyn, and it inspired such prominent spiritual leaders as St. Serafim Sarovskii (d. 1833) and Father John of Kronstadt (d. 1908). SS. Serafim Sarovskii and Sergius of Radonezh were revered in particular for living alone in the woods and sharing their meager fare with bears and other animals. They are said to have preached to the animals. The aim of the Hesychasts was "flight from the world."[18]

One piece of inspirational literature is invariably associated with the Hesychast tradition. *The Way of a Pilgrim* appeared anonymously in 1860: "By the grace of God I am a Christian man, by my actions a great sinner, and by calling a homeless wanderer [*strannik*] of the humblest birth who roams from place to place. My worldly goods are a knapsack with some dried bread in it on my back, and in my breast-pocket a Bible." At a recent church service, the pilgrim had heard the words from St. Paul's Epistle to the Thessalonians, "Pray without ceasing," and he subsequently found these words in his own Bible. They troubled him. He began to think how such a thing was possible, "since a man has to concern himself with other things." He consulted a famous preacher, who advised him to "make up your mind by God's help from to-day to say the Prayer of Jesus twelve thousand times a day." And so he spent his life in wandering and praying and recorded his doing so.[19]

A type of holiness much prized in the Russian tradition, and one for which it has been slightly notorious abroad, is the "fool in Christ" or "God's fool." The Russian term is *yurodivyi*. The idea apparently derives from the first four chapters of St. Paul's first Letter to the Corinthians. St. Paul wrote that the wisdom of the world is foolishness in God's sight. Better it was to be a fool in the world's sight. Thus I Corinthians 4:10: "We are fools for Christ's sake." In the Russian Bible, though the words for fool and foolishness vary, the word *yurodstvo* is used in 1:18 and 1:21.

D.S. Likhachev, the great authority on medieval Russian literature, observes that Ivan IV, pious and brutal as he was, "played the fool to the utmost" (*yurodstvoval vovsiu*).[20] Giles Fletcher described one such fool (1591). "Among other[s] at this time they have one at Moscow that walketh naked about the streets and inveigheth commonly against the Godunovs, that are thought at this time to be great oppressors of that commonwealth. Another there was that died many years ago whom they called Vasilii that would take upon him to reprove the old Emperor for all his cruelty and oppressions done toward his people." This Vasilii was the saint for whom the great landmark cathedral on Red Square is named; the old Emperor was Ivan IV. "They use[d] to go stark naked save a clout about their middle, with their hair hanging long and wildly about their shoulders, and many of them with an iron collar or chain about their necks or midst, even in the very extremity of winter. These they take as prophets and men of great holiness, giving them a liberty to speak what they list without any controlment. . . . Of this kind there are not many, because it is a very hard and cold profession to go naked in Russia, especially in winter."[21]

Leo Tolstoy described a *yurodivyi* in the nineteenth century, "a man of fifty, with a long, pale, pock-marked face, with long gray hair and a sparse reddish beard. . . . He wore a ragged garment which resembled both a kaftan and a cassock; in his hand he carried a huge staff. As he entered the room, he smote the floor with it with all his might; opening his mouth, and wrinkling his brows, he laughed in a terrible and unnatural manner. He was blind of one eye; and the white pupil of that eye hopped about incessantly, and imparted to his already homely countenance a still more repulsive expression."

He walked up to one of the children, Volodya. " 'Aha! I've found you!' he shouted. . . ; he seized his head, and began a careful examination of his crown. Then, with a perfectly serious expression, he left him, walked up to the table, and began to blow under the oil-cloth, and to make the sign of the cross over it. 'O-oh, it's a pity! o-oh, it's sad! The dear children . . . will fly away,' he said, in a voice quivering with tears, gazing feelingly at Volodya." And he began to cry.

His voice was deep and coarse, his movements abrupt and crude, his talk foolish and incoherent, but his tone was sympathetic. His grotesque yellow face assumed at times a distinctly sorrowful expression. He elicited in Tolstoy a reaction of pity, fear, and grief. This was the fool and pilgrim (*strannik*) Grisha.

Who was he? What were his origins? How had he come to adopt such a singular form of life? No one knew. "I only knew that he passed since the age of fifteen as a fool who went barefoot winter and summer, visited the monasteries, gave little images to those who struck his fancy, and uttered enigmatic words which some people accepted as prophecy."

Grisha was allowed to eat at his own table in the family dining room. The children asked their father the meaning of this phenomenon. "I have only one remark to make to you on the subject: it is difficult to believe that a man who, in spite of his sixty years, goes barefoot summer and winter, and wears chains weighing two poods [seventy-two pounds], which he never takes off, under his clothes, and who has more than once rejected a proposal to lead an easy life,—it is difficult to believe that such a man does all this from laziness."[22]

Konstantin Paustovskii saw in Moscow in the fall of 1914 "a God's fool with downcast eyes, clanking his rusty ascetic's chains and trying to ride the trolley without a ticket."[23] *Yurodstvo* is a prominent theme in Dostoevsky's *The Idiot* (Prince Myshkin), Solzhenitsyn's "Matryona's Home" (Matryona), and Vasilii Shukshin's *Snowball Berry Red* (Egor).

Dmitrii Likhachev says that the "most affectionate expression" of the Russian people is "oh, you are my foolish one [*glupenkii*]" or "oh, you are my little fool [*durachok*] . . . the Russian people loves [its] fools . . . not because they are foolish but because they are clever."[24]

Yurodstvo also conferred a kind of immunity from the usual forms of social and political censure. Thus two such fools are alleged to have confronted Ivan IV as he came to Novgorod and Pskov on a mission of political persecution. They provoked him by the offer of fresh meat on a fast day. When he naturally refused, they asked why he was not equally sensitive to the shedding of Christian blood. They were left unscathed.

Examples of Russian concepts of holiness illustrate a common observation. The Russian attitude to religion is one of spiritual radicalism manifesting itself in indifference to the world and its blessings. Spiritual radicalism has been perceived as the basis of Russian hostility to the bourgeois world, which long antedates the advent of Marxism and is characteristic of both revolutionaries and reactionaries. Without any apparent transmission of influence, the Russian attitude approaches the religious outlook of the Indian subcontinent far more than it does that of Western Christianity.[25]

An antiworldly spiritual radicalism was emphasized in sixteenth-century Russian monasticism. "The consequence of this radical monasticization of society was the virtual elimination of secular culture in the course of the sixteenth century."[26] Yet this was precisely the time of Ivan IV and his venerable *oprichnina*.

A common generalization is that Russia inherited Caesaropapism—uncompromising submission of church to state—from Byzantium. This is a disputed assertion. What is important here is that the Russian state, true to the hypertrophic (overdeveloped) model, consistently dominated the church. A variety of religious heresies in the early church centered appropriately enough in the citadel of Russian freedom, Novgorod. Thus there were the *Strigolniki* around 1400 and the Judaizers around 1475. They preached against the corruption of the clergy and the worldliness of the Russian church. Both were destroyed. About the same time a dispute broke out between the followers of Nil Sorskii (1433–1508), leader of the Trans-Volga Hermits of the far north, and Joseph of Volokolamsk (1439?–1515). Nil's party viewed church propertyholding in a fashion characteristic of hermits and encouraged the state to seize it. Joseph's party took the opposite view and, at the same time incidentally, championed a theory of political absolutism. The government took the side of Joseph. In the next generation, Metropolitan Filipp of Moscow admonished Ivan IV for oppression of the people. Ivan had him strangled.

It was only in the mid-seventeenth century that a serious schism developed and persisted in the Russian church. Patriarch Nikon, full of ambition and presumption, examined church texts and ritual for departures from ancient Greek Christianity. He required revisions of texts and reforms of ritual. He perceived these revisions as restorations of purity. His opponents perceived them as the introduction of perversions. He demanded in particular that the sign of the cross be made with two fingers (index and middle finger) and the thumb held together rather than by the usual Russian custom of the two outstretched fingers alone; that the hallelujah in the doxology be chanted twice rather than three times; that the name Jesus should be spelled and pronounced in Russian as *Isus* rather than the customary *Iisus*; that processions in church should move clockwise rather than the contrary; that crosses on churches, tombs, and elsewhere, must have eight ends rather than six or four (two additional crosspieces on the trunk of the cross), and other similar things. It occasioned the largest revolt that has ever occurred in the Russian church. Nothing else in its history illustrates better the superior attachment of the church to issues of ritual rather than to issues of ethics or doctrine.

At the same time, Nikon insisted arrogantly and perilously upon a revolutionary promotion of the power of the patriarchal office. As he argued, "It is clear that the tsar must be lower than the prelate and obedient to him, for I also say that the clergy are chosen people and are anointed by the Holy Ghost. . . . The throne of the clergy has been erected in heaven. Who says this? The Heavenly King Himself: 'Whatsoever you shall bind on earth shall be bound in heaven. . . .' Thus it is the tsars who are anointed by the priests and not the priests by the tsars."[27]

A church council approved Nikon's textual and ritual reforms but rejected his presumption of patriarchal power and retired him from the office. The Nikonian reform exemplified the customary relationship between church and state in Russia, and Peter the Great was to render it more striking yet.

The reform precipitated the great schism of the Russian church. Ever afterward, a resolute minority held unflinchingly, despite sometimes gruesome persecution, to the old way. These sectarians were called Old Believers (*starovery* or *staroobriadtsy*). They impressed impartial observers, chiefly foreign ones, as far more learned in Biblical literature and far more devoted to a demanding moral code than was characteristic of the majority, the real Orthodox.

Western travelers were impressed by the ignorance of the Orthodox clergy. Giles Fletcher recounted a conversation with a bishop who did not know how many gospels there were in the Bible.[28] Learning is not, however, requisite in the Russian Orthodox conception of holiness.

The rational approach to religion of Catholicism and Protestantism would have been found incomprehensible or offensive in the Russian church. For example, Thomas Aquinas raises the question in his *Summa Theologica* "Whether God comprehends himself?" He presents the objections to his position first. "*Objection 1.* It seems that God does not comprehend Himself. For Augustine says, that *whatever comprehends itself is finite to itself.* But God is in all ways infinite. Therefore He does not comprehend Himself." Other objections follow before Thomas enters into his rebuttal.

> God comprehends himself perfectly, as can be thus proved. A thing is said to be comprehended when the end of the knowledge of it is attained, and this is accomplished when it is known as perfectly as it is knowable. Thus, a demonstrable proposition is comprehended when

known by demonstration, not, however, when it is known by some probable argument. Now is it manifest that God knows Himself as perfectly as He is perfectly knowable. For everything is knowable according to the mode of its actuality, since a thing is not known according as it is in potentiality, but in so far as it is in actuality, as said in [Aristotle's] *Metaph[ysics]* ix. . . . Whence it is manifest that He knows Himself as much as He is knowable; and for that reason He perfectly comprehends Himself.[29]

John Calvin's *Institutes of the Christian Religion* equally exemplified a sure confidence in the intellectual exposition of holy mysteries.

Predestination, by which God adopts some to the hope of life, and adjudges others to eternal death, no one, desirous of the credit of piety, dares absolutely to deny. But it is involved in many cavils, especially by those who make foreknowledge the cause of it. We maintain, that both belong to God; but it is preposterous to represent one as dependent on the other. When we attribute foreknowledge to God, we mean that all things have ever been, and perpetually remain, before his eyes, so that to his knowledge nothing is future or past, but all things are present. . . . Predestination we call the eternal decree of God, by which he has determined in himself, what he would have to become of every individual of mankind. For they are not all created with a similar destiny; but eternal life is foreordained for some, and eternal damnation for others. Every man, therefore, being created for one or the other of these ends, we say, he is predestinated either to life or to death.[30]

These are hardly sublimely emotional expressions of spiritual experience.

Thomas's *Summa Theologica* fills three volumes and nearly four thousand double-columned pages of small print. Calvin's *Institutes* fills two volumes. Russian Orthodoxy, on the other hand, is not a bookish religion. There are no great books in its tradition. It has no more important characteristic than the fact that it abjures the presumption of explicating the mind of God. A national debate over the question of God's intentions for his flock, such as Luther perhaps inadvertently initiated in nailing the ninety-five theses to the church door at Wittenberg, is not conceivable in Russia.

The Bible itself is scarcely more important than other Orthodox books. The Psalter alone has been popular among Russian believers.

The Bible was published in several vernacular English translations between that of John Wyclif (d. 1382) and the King James version of 1611. Jacques Lefèvre d'Etaples published a full French version in 1530. The early German translation was the work of Luther, who died in 1546. The Russian vernacular New Testament was published by the Russian Bible Society in part at the instance of Alexander I in 1820. The Holy Synod objected, however, to the publication in Russian of the Old Testament for fear of encouraging Judaic influences. The Bible Society was abolished by Nicholas I in 1829, and the Slavonic Old Testament was for long not allowed in Russian churches. Finally, a Russian Old Testament appeared in 1875. The Bible, however, has never been a principal part of Russian Orthodoxy.

Study of the Russian church since the revolution has been nourished above all by two original and imaginative scholars, both of whom taught at St. Sergius in Paris before World War II and at St. Vladimir in New York after it, and both of whom have shown an interest in Christian socialism unusual for Russian clerics. According to George Fedotov, "Ancient Russia had no theology worthy of the name." George Florovsky began his exploration of medieval and modern Russian religious thought in order to discover, as he describes it, "the meaning of Russia's ancient, enduring, and centuries long intellectual silence."[31] The Russian attitude toward God is one of wonder, awe, and fear. The believer humbles himself and looks up at the mysteriously miraculous. He does not presume to know it. He marvels at it.

There are other differences between the Eastern and Western churches. The veneration of icons is more prominent in Orthodoxy than in Catholicism. Though the cult of Mary, mother of Jesus, is at least as prominent in Orthodoxy as in Catholicism, she is not conceived in the same way in the two churches. In Catholicism, she is designated typically as the Virgin. In Orthodoxy, the attribute of virginity yields to the attribute of motherhood. She is the *bogoroditsa,* the God-bearer, the Mother of God. By the sixteenth century, most of the stylized features of iconography have been dropped from her portrait in the West. In the East, they remain distinct and rigid. The contrast between a Raphael madonna and the Orthodox *bogoroditsa* could hardly be more striking. The Vladimir *bogoroditsa* is a portrait of infinite sadness, the essence of the much-admired attitude of *umilenie,* or the loving kindness of pained sympathy for a suffering people.

How was the body of believers defined? It was everybody. The word for Christian, *khristianin*, is from the word for Christ, *Khrist*; and the word for peasant, *krestianin*, is from the word cross, *krest*, just as is the word for baptism, *kreshchenie*. A peasant is automatically a Christian. A normal mortal is a baptized Russian Christian peasant. When the peasants spoke to each other, the standard term of address was *pravoslavnye*, ye Orthodox (plural). A widow begging alms for her children would say, "O, *pravoslavnye*, have pity on the poor orphans."

Max Weber distinguishes two basically distinct types of religion.[32] The ascetic-ethical is strongly rational and inner-worldly. It is typical of conventional Judaism, Catholicism, and Protestantism. Among Catholics and Protestants, the conception of salvation was influenced by the worldly, legalistic thinking of Roman law, canon law. In the Catholic Church, the institutional vehicle of salvation is the sacramental system as dispensed by the elaborate administrative hierarchy reflecting the idea of apostolic succession. It was powerful enough to challenge sovereigns and to influence believers. In Calvinism, the signs of salvation consisted in the performance of good works measured in material accumulation. The impact upon human society of the ascetic-ethical impulses of Western religion are enormous. These churches organize themselves, the life of the believer, and the world about them with great seriousness, and they acquire great influence in the world.

The ascetic-mystical type of religion is typical of the Krishna cult in Hinduism, of the Tantric Buddhism of Tibet, of the Kabalists in Judaism, of the Sufis/dervishes in Islam, and of the mysticism of the Protestant Reformation and the Catholic Counter-Reformation. It flees from the world, overcomes the world. It is obvious to which type the spiritual radicalism of the *strastoterptsy* (Boris and Gleb), the Hesychasts, and the fools in Christ belong. From the perspective of the quest of the modern Russian state for material and technical progress, Orthodoxy was simply a great tragedy, an impediment, the wrong religion. From the perspective of Orthodoxy, it is the pursuit of the wrong goals that has brought the real tragedy, and this is precisely how many contemporary Russian Christians explain the people's suffering in the Soviet Armageddon: as punishment for forsaking the faith.

So, hypertrophic (overdeveloped) state, hypotrophic (underdeveloped) people, hyperactive state, hypoactive people: a mésalliance? In the midst of a public consciousness of the Russian sort, no other nation needed a strong state to sustain its mere survival *in this world* so much as Russia did. The attitude that typified Russians was not suited either to assist in the enterprise of national statecraft nor to resist such an enterprise should it turn aggressive and abusive. In trying to comprehend the peculiar experience of Russia and the Russians, it is essential to remind oneself constantly of this peculiar relationship of state and people. From the national experience of Russia from the time of the Mongols until the end of the seventeenth century, the state and the people drew different lessons. They developed distinctly different value systems: an aggressively interventionist and controlling attitude on the one hand, a resigned and mystical submissiveness on the other.

Here is a point that must be emphasized because the mind-set of the contemporary West is so little capable of grasping it. In the cultural taxonomy of the ecumene, some societies develop a viewpoint, perhaps first articulated in the Greek conception, that this world is intelligible, reliable, and manageable. Traditional China exemplifies this outlook, but it assumes its most extreme form in the Europe of the Renaissance, the Scientific Revolution, and the Enlightenment. Other societies, on the other hand, most typically those of India and of medieval Europe, exemplify what Weber calls the world-rejecting ideas of ascetic mysticism.

The great fault line in Russian culture opposes these two outlooks to each other in a schizoid fashion. The tradition of the Russian state has been to believe in a conventionally familiar fashion that this world, addressed seriously, was comprehensible and controllable, as successive variants of Russian absolutism insisted. The tradition of the Russian people, on the other hand, finds such an attitude to be nonsense—pride, arrogance, hubris. In a world like ours, such a people has required such a state—and vice versa. And thus national independence required draconian despotism.

Without the implacable insistence of the Russian state, the concept of spirituality taught the Russian people by the Orthodox Church would have made material modernization quite impossible. Peter I was well aware of it. The remedy that he imposed, or inflicted, was Westernization. The results proved a material vindication of his approach, but he aggravated enormously the divorce of state and society as well as the schizoid fissure of Russian culture.

Reason and Progress:
Peter and Catherine

In a well-governed state, rules and principles are needed for everything; they are executed by those charged with the powers of the police.

Frederick the Great, *Politische Testamente*

[The police] dispenses good order and moral admonitions . . . the police is the soul of citizenship and all good order, and the fundamental support of human safety and convenience.

Peter the Great, Statute on Police

[Peter] hoped by means of harsh governmental measures to evoke initiative and enterprise among an enslaved society, and through the agency of a slave-holding nobility to install European learning in Russia.

V.O. Kliuchevskii, *History of Russia*

[Peter] dreamed of a structure of the state as precise and ideal as a clock.

E.V. Anisimov, *Reformy Petra Velikogo*

The outlook of aggressive statism was never better exemplified than in the statecraft of Peter I. He presumed to transform the very nature of Russia by using his own exclusive power to make both state and nation over in the image of Europe. The source of his inspiration he recognized in the European Enlightenment, the Age of Reason.

The eighteenth century was in many respects the climax of modern Western culture, the acme of self-confidence. What the Renaissance initiated and the Scientific Revolution expedited, the Enlightenment consummated. It was the second Enlightenment, after that of ancient Greece, in the Western experience. It was more ambitious, more presumptuous, and perhaps it too nearly aspired to what it has been accused of, ultimately to relocate the Heavenly City of Augustine here on this earth.[1] It was, in any event, the first modern age of social science, and it was not a humble season.

Among the virtues of the Enlightenment was pride, though pride had been in the medieval conception at the head of the list of the seven deadly sins. One principal commitment justified pride in the age of Enlightenment: to be progressive. In politics, there were two standards of progressiveness, and they were located at the two extremities of the corpus of the West. One of them was liberal and republican, and it was best exemplified in the Declaration of Independence and the Constitution of the United States of America. The other was most evident in the great states of East Central Europe, Austria and Prussia. It is known in our textbooks as, and it was occasionally called by its French Physiocrat advocates, Enlightened Despotism. In its own time, it was more commonly known as the *Polizeistaat*. The French knew it by a similar name, the *état policé*. The practitioners of the *Polizeistaat* proposed to use absolutism as the instrument of rationalism in order to achieve Enlightenment and progress. It was alien to Anglo-Saxon politics, which were liberal and had generated the economic and cultural achievements that served as the very standard of progressiveness that the governments of Eastern Europe aspired to emulate. The *Polizeistaat* was a catalyst, a mentor, and a broker of progress. It was a compensatory device to bring backward Eastern Europe up to the level of forward Western Europe. It was not precisely what the twentieth century conceives as a police state, but it was not an illegitimate relative. It was, however, understood to be what it stubbornly presumed to exemplify, *benevolent* despotism. In the age of Enlightenment, both the Anglo-Saxon liberal model and the East Central European autocratic model reflected the presumption of the time that a rational and virtuous form of government sufficed to bring order, peace, and prosperity to human society.

It was the conception of the *Polizeistaat* that Russia in the person of its revolutionary new emperor, Peter I the Great, adopted at the outset of the eighteenth century. It was to be a Western instrument of further Westernization. Russia had flirted with various forms of Westernization earlier. Ivan III had imported architects and ballistics technicians. Ivan IV had sent his agent, a German named Hans Schlitte, to the Hanseatic cities in 1547, to hire a kind of brain trust of skilled technicians. The mission was discovered in Lübeck. In what was perhaps the first Western embargo on technology transfer to Russia, the city government voided all of Schlitte's contracts and threw him in jail. In the early seventeenth century, Patriarch Filaret Romanov, father of Tsar Michael, had taken the lead in forming Western mercenary units in the Russian army. At the court of Alexis Mikhailovich (1645–76), Western theatrical pieces were produced, and several statesmen cautiously foreshadowed what Peter would boldly exemplify. In the second half of the seventeenth century, several thousand West Europeans lived in a special *Nemetskaia sloboda*, foreign suburb, of Moscow. It was largely in this quarter of the city that Peter I grew up, thus acquiring an unconventional informal education that was to be so fateful for the future of his country.

It was not until the time of Peter I (1689–1725) that the massive and persistent Westernization of Russia began. It was deliberate, in some respects systematic, and it included not only the more readily imported elements of material life, especially military technology and technique, but an effort to accustom the nation to a Western mode of thinking as well.

The monarchies of Europe in the seventeenth century, the age of absolutism, had employed the economic doctrines of mercantilism to enhance both the wealth and, thereby, the military power of the state; and they had used the power of the state in a reciprocal fashion to aggrandize their economic opportunities. The wars of Louis XIV in the Low Countries were a good example. War and the collection of treasure were the sport of kings. The aim was glory and power, which were almost synonymous.

The eighteenth-century enlightened despots revised this agenda. Their program was more dynamic, actually developmental, and they proclaimed loud and long the aim of popular well-being, commonweal, both as an end in itself and as a means of strengthening the instruments of state, which served in turn the cause of public well-being. If the revolutionaries of the United States and France found kings to be an obstacle to justice and progress, in Eastern Europe they were recognized as virtually the only hope thereof. Montesquieu, the great theorist of checks and balances, divisions of powers, was concerned in midcentury France to articulate the *thèse nobiliaire*, that is, the rights of the nobility vis-à-vis the monarchy. Without strong aristocracy, no freedom. Even in France, however, the *thèse royale* was asserted, by Voltaire, for example, as the best hope of preserving the freedom of society writ large from the exclusive privileges and abuses of the presumptuous aristocracy.

Montesquieu was the transitional figure between the conservatism of the ancient *Ständestaat* (society of orders, or classes) and classical modern liberalism. His aim was, like that of Aristotle and Polybius, to counterpoise the different classes in society so nicely as to achieve the greatest feasible degree of stability and justice for all.

The idea of the *Polizeistaat* was quite different. In the seventeenth and eighteenth centuries, the French word *police* and the German word *Polizei* had significantly broader meanings than does our modern English word *police*. All three words are related to Greek *politeia*, which denotes polity, policy, or government and regulatory activity more generally. The *Polizeistaat* was based on three assumptions: that the sovereign was an impartial governor; that only an apparatus of government that stood safely and powerfully above the fray of particular interests could hold those interests sufficiently in check to achieve a just and stable society; and that in underdeveloped Eastern Europe only unfettered, unchecked absolutism would have sufficient power to overcome the many obstacles of conservative tradition to the reforms and development that justice and progress required. It was the instrument of rationalism incarnate.

According to François Quesnay, one of the theorists of the idea, "separation of powers is a sinister idea that only leads to discord among the great and to oppression of the small. The division of society into different orders of citizens . . . destroys the general interest of the nation and introduces the dissension of particular interests among the different classes of citizens."[2] The aim here was the opposite of that of Montesquieu and the American Constitutional Convention: it was government efficient and powerful. Adam Smith, whose views were so different, thought that the best statement of this doctrine was found in Pierre Le Mercier de la Rivière's *L'Ordre naturel et essentiel des sociétés* (1764), which was written in close association with Quesnay and endorsed his ideas.[3] Frederick the Great agreed with such views and wrote his *Politisches Testament* (1758) to insist on them: "As little as it would have been possible for Newton to formulate his system of gravity if he had worked in concert with Leibniz and Descartes, so little can a system of politics be formed and sustained if it is not done by a single head."[4]

It was the police on which the monarch was to rely for the execution of his beneficent designs. According to Johann Heinrich Gottlob von Justi's *Staatswirtschaft* (Political Economy, 1755), "all the methods whereby the riches of the state may be increased, in so far as the authority of the government is concerned, belong . . . under the charge of the police . . . the monarchical form of government is far preferable to all others, in consideration of the rapidity with which it can grasp the means of happiness of a state."[5] This form of government he called *Policeywissenschaft*, literally police science. In the currently dissonant but entirely apt characterization of the Prussian monarchy, "the only proper translation of *Polizeistaat* is 'welfare state.'. . . By the eighteenth century the word *Polizei* had become synonymous with *Wohlfahrt* [well-being] or *Gemeine Nutz* [commonweal]. It implied legislative and administrative regulation in the private and public life of the civil community in order to establish good order and security and to advance the common good."[6]

Nicholas de La Mare wrote for Louis XV what is perhaps the great classic on the subject, *Traité de la police* (ca. 1730), in four large volumes. His purpose was to describe "that good order on which the happiness of states depends" and to contribute thereby to the "public well-being." He treated decent morals; the honor of families; good faith in commerce; control of blasphemy, irreligion, heresy; public health; sumptuary legislation; gambling; astrology; sorcery; and virtually everything imaginable, including *"mauvaises filles de joie"* (prostitutes) and conventional relations between the sexes.[7]

The role of the police in the conception of Frederick II was similarly busy. "In a well-governed state, rules and principles are needed for everything; they are executed by those charged with the powers of the police. This includes the security of travelers, the care of the great roads, of the bridges, . . . of the post. . . . In addition, the police must take care that there are fair prices for workers, merchants, and others, that no one plays prohibited games, that the Jews do not take excessive usury, that there are no quarrels in the cabarets."[8] In Prussia, sumptuary legislation specified that the wines allowed at wedding feasts be regulated according to the social class of the celebrants, and dress styles were governed by the same criteria.

Envying their remarkable efficiency of regulation, Maria Theresa of Austria inquired of the Paris police around 1770 how they maintained such an admirable system. They replied in a memorandum, full of pride, that runs to 131 printed pages. They described their control of religion, discipline, health, food supplies, communication, security, the arts and sciences, commerce, manufacturing, servants, the poor. If all goes well in Paris every day, they claimed, "it is owing to the Prefecture of the Police."[9]

Vestiges of this tradition survive on the continent of Europe today, where practices unknown in the Anglo-American tradition continue: a personal identity paper, the French *carte d'identité*, the German *Personalausweis*, the Russian *pasport* (internal); and the registration with the police of residential addresses and tourists in hotels.

Was the hypertrophic (overdeveloped) model of statecraft of old Russia compatible with the *Polizeistaat* model of Peter I's new Russia? The old model formed a satisfactory foundation for the new one because it left no power in the society capable of opposing that of the state. On the other hand, there was a distinct difference in the two ideas. If the hypertrophic model left the people overfleeced but undergoverned, the *Polizeistaat* aspired to govern them with a busybody vengeance. And Peter I had the will and the energy to attempt it.

The legislation that he published relied heavily on the European idea of the "general well-being" of society. The primary political treatise of his reign, *The Justice of the Monarch's Will* (Pravda monarshei voli), drew heavily on the political theory of Hugo Grotius (d. 1645) and Samuel von Pufendorf (d. 1694). Peter's own statute on the police exemplified a similar debt to the practices of Berlin and Paris.

> [The police] dispenses good order and moral admonitions, gives to all safety from robbers, thieves, ravishers, tricksters, and similar persons, drives away disorderly and indecent living, and compels each to work and to honorable industry, makes good householders, careful and good servants, looks after the correctness and the construction of homes and the conditions of the streets, prevents high prices, and brings satisfaction in all that human living requires, stands on guard against all occurring illnesses, brings about cleanliness in the streets and in the houses, forbids a superfluity of domestic luxuries and all manifest sins, looks after the poor, the sick, the cripples and other unfortunates, defends widows, orphans, strangers, according to God's commandments, educates the young in chaste purity and honorable sciences; in short, over all these things the police is the soul of citizenship and all good order, and the fundamental support of human safety and convenience.[10]

Peter's reforms reflected as much of this thoughtful, naive, and ambitious program as his gargantuan military enterprises gave him the respite to undertake. "He dreamed of a structure of the state as precise and ideal as a clock."[11] Peter's thought was characterized by one of his contemporaries: "For, as in a clock, one gear [*Rad*] must be driven by another, so must one department [*collegium*] drive another in the great clock of state [*Staatsuhr*], and insofar as everything stands in accurate proportion and precise harmony, nothing else can follow than that the hands of intelligence will indicate happy times for the country."[12] Peter's experience was to fall somewhat short of this notion, which, however naive, was quite characteristic of the outlook of the age.

He began appropriately by taking a trip through the Europe that he proposed to imitate. He traveled allegedly incognito as Peter Mikhailov at the head of a large suite. It was not easy, however, to maintain the incognito of a decidedly revelrous troop of exotic Muscovites led by a large and imperious personality nearly seven feet tall. The Grand Embassy produced quite a spectacle. Peter visited Berlin, Vienna, Paris, London, and Amsterdam. He saw the Parliament in session in London. In Amsterdam, he worked in the shipyards. He collected several hundred technicians to employ in Russia.

Upon his return, he began to reform with dramatic suddenness. He summoned the gentry about the court, decreed that they must thereafter, on penalty of a punitive tax, put away their Russian clothes and wear English or German styles. At the same time, he brought out a pair of scissors and began cutting off beards. He had a coin minted to read "The beard is a useless burden." Here was an obvious effort to strike not only at the manifestations of Russian culture but at the mentality itself. For the conservatives, Antichrist was not far to seek. Russian believers did not presume to enter heaven beardless, as that was a violation of the image in which God had created them.

The *Polizeistaat* was one of the grand ideas that drove Peter; the other was Empire. Among his reforms, the earliest and the most conspicuous were military. Peter had spent his youth playing toy soldier on a very adult scale, and, as Kliuchevskii wrote, war was the most important circumstance of his reign. Peter's designs in foreign policy were dramatically more ambitious than those of his seventeenth-century predecessors. In fact, he was probably the first Russian ruler of modern times to pursue self-consciously the aim of empire building. At this point, Russian foreign policy began to depart from purely national goals and to reflect the aims and interests of the apparatus of state itself. It was not an entirely unnatural process for a state whose counsel with its people was as remote as that of Russia was.

Peter began campaigning against the Turks on the Black Sea in 1695. In 1700 he entered what was to be the chief military undertaking of his reign, the Great Northern War against Sweden, reminiscent of the similar Livonian War of Ivan IV, except for the results: in Peter's case, Russia won and annexed by treaty in 1721 the coveted territory on the Baltic, where Russian victories had allowed the establishment of the new capital, Peter's "window on the West," St. Petersburg, in 1703.

A massive standing army was recruited by systematic conscription. A conscripted peasant soldier served for twenty-five years, which amounted to lifetime service, as few commoners of the time lived beyond forty or forty-five years of age. The reforms of the seventeenth century, which made the Russian army more and more like the armies of Europe, were extended. Legions of foreign officers and drillmasters were imported. By the end of Peter's reign, the Russian army consisted of 200,000 regular troops and 100,000 irregulars.

Peter was a mariner, too. His naval impulses seem also to have developed from a maverick boyhood impulse—as Churchill said to Stalin, "Russia is a land animal." In childhood, Peter discovered the derelict of an English sailboat in an inland lake, and the Russian high-seas fleet was conceived. In a war with Sweden for the coastline of the Baltic, a navy was useful. It had been useful against the Turks on the Black Sea as well, and it would be more so in the time of Catherine II. By the end of Peter's reign, the Russian navy possessed forty-eight ships of the line, among many others, and enrolled a force of around 28,000 seamen.

When the Great Northern War was over, Peter embarked on an ultimately unsuccessful campaign against Persia. In the meantime, he prepared the expedition of Vitus Bering to explore the coasts of North America, similar expeditions into Central Asia with the idea of reaching India overland, and an expedition to Madagascar that never sailed! Kliuchevskii has calculated that only thirteen months of his reign of thirty-six years were free of war.

Peter's reforms, inspired as they were in great part by the demands of his imperial and military endeavors, reflected a hasty, impulsive,

violent, and sometimes thoughtless and unrealistic version of the program of the *Polizeistaat*. He inaugurated something like modern ministries. A Governing Senate, appointed by him, was to rule in his
absence, during his travels. He changed the incidence of taxation from
the household to the individual and approximately tripled the tax revenues drawn from the land.

When the conservative Patriarch Adrian VI died in 1700, having
protested against Westernization in general and the shaving of beards
in particular, Peter did not replace him. He used the funds of the
patriarch's office to finance his wars. Subsequently he abolished the
patriarchate and established the Holy Synod as the governing body of
the Russian church, thereby making it effectively a department of state.
Russians were scandalized.

Requiring, after the fashion of Ivan IV, universal and lifetime state
service of the gentry class (*dvoriane*), Peter introduced a combination
civil- and military-service system to render the process more rational
and effective. According to this Table of Ranks, civil and military servants were categorized by distinction in one of fourteen grades. It was
an effort to promote state servitors by merit. Anyone of any social class
was eligible to enter the list, and everyone had to enter at the bottom
and work his way up from rank fourteen. When rank eight was reached,
it automatically conferred the distinction of hereditary nobility.

In economic affairs, Peter followed the contemporary European idea
of mercantilism: he raised tariffs to protect native industry, favored
such industry with subsidies and tax breaks, and attached serf labor to
the factories. In mining, metallurgy, textiles, and armaments, he
achieved extraordinary success.

It was characteristic of both the desultory and the impulsive nature
of the reforms that Peter sometimes thought of elementary fundamen-
tals too late to make the results of his work solid and stable. Especially
was this the case in education. Rather typically he established institutions of higher learning before he founded the primary and secondary
schools that could prepare the population for the higher ones. Thus he
formed an Academy of Sciences, military schools for army and navy
officers, a "school of mathematical sciences and navigation," but he never
effectively addressed the question of institutions of primary education.

If we try to assess the significance of Peter's reforms, it seems that
what he achieved was a pseudo-*Polizeistaat* and pseudo-*Ständestaat*
(society of orders) in a form that really monstrously aggravated the old

Russian hypertrophic (overdeveloped) model of statecraft. He invested the church, the nobility, and the enserfed peasantry with a legal status, the status of a pseudo-*Stand/état*. With the single exception of the privilege of the nobility to rise through the Table of Ranks, however, these pseudo-*Stände/états* received no rights. Rather, they felt only the imposition of obligations. In other words, when there appeared in Russia social statuses whose names corresponded in Europe to privileged corporate bodies legally protected from abuse, they arose not from the evolution of tradition, the independence of social institutions beyond the reach of royal prerogative, but from the peremptory power of the monarch's decree. They served thus not as divisions of power, checks on executive authority, but rather, by design, as extensions of the monarch's power, as effective departments of state. Peter's reign achieved the apogee of unconditional Russian absolutism, and this fact explains what was perhaps the one area in which his success was unambiguous: he made Russia virtually overnight into one of the great powers of the world, probably in the eighteenth century the most powerful country in the world.

In all of this activity, Peter proceeded impatiently and brutally. The reasonableness of his reforms was not apparent in the perceptions of traditional Russia. The society whose improvement he sought appreciated his policy conspicuously little. In fact, as his contemporary Pososhkov wrote with scant exaggeration, the tsar pulled uphill with the strength of ten, but the whole society pulled downhill. Relatively isolated and distinctly xenophobic as Russian society was, it objected to Peter's making a mockery of its religion; to forcing women accustomed to the exclusively female society of the *terem*, the women's quarter of the house, to attend men's drinking parties; to shaving and wearing foreign clothes; to submitting to the superior ways of strange upstart foreigners, who from this time began to enjoy a more honored—and suspect—position in Russia than natives; to higher taxes; to the attachment of serf labor to the newly founded industrial enterprises; to the construction of roads, canals, and St. Petersburg itself at enormous cost in human life. And, of course, the perpetual wars and lifetime military service were almost universally detested.

Peter's policies increased the burden and tightened the reins of state service imposed on the gentry by Ivan III and Ivan IV and on the peasantry through the imposition of serfdom. In the freedom-loving, license-loving steppes of Ukraine, resistance was spirited. The Don

Cossacks rebelled in 1707. The *ataman* of Ukraine, Ivan Mazepa, entered treasonous relations with Charles XII of Sweden in 1709. In traditional Russia, the resistance was more muted. Leaflets were found here and there identifying Peter as the Antichrist. The clerical and noble conservatives gathered around Peter's heir, Alexis. Alexis promised upon his accession to the throne to undo all the unwonted reforms of his father. Peter charged him with treason, interrogated him under torture, and condemned him to death. The tyranny of the West in Russian culture would no longer tolerate the defiance of native tradition.

A distinguished contemporary Russian historian, Natan Iakovlevich Eidelman, writing under the recent impression of parallels between the historical roles of Peter and of Mikhail Gorbachev, has just reminded us of one of the most important features of the Petrine era: the Petrine experience, like that of Russia in the time of Ivan III and Ivan IV, was one of revolution from above.[13] One of the most bedeviling features of such a political program, especially characteristic of the *Polizeistaat*, is that the more initiative the state takes, the more the people grow accustomed to leaving public initiative entirely to the state. It is a prominent phenomenon in the history of Russia. Peter was here caught in a contradiction. As Kliuchevskii explained, "He hoped by means of harsh governmental measures to evoke initiative and enterprise among an enslaved society, and through the agency of a slaveholding nobility to install European learning in Russia. He wanted the slave, while remaining a slave, to act consciously and freely."[14] In our time, as we shall see, Khrushchev entertained similarly contradictory and self-defeating expectations, and the inability of the public to shed its habits of deferential docility on demand contributed to the collapse of the Soviet system in the era of Gorbachev.

One of the reforms that succeeded least well in Peter's lifetime eventually became one of the most significant. The educational reform yielded both progress and sedition. In spite of its demonstrably meager results, it would eventually produce a second variety of what has been called a "parting of the ways."[15] We have observed already the divorce of state and society. The introduction of a Western style of education would eventually generate an intelligentsia alienated from both the state and the remainder of society. This split was inchoate at first, and it did not become demonstrably articulate until the nineteenth and twentieth centuries, when we shall see it plainly. It 1917, one camp of this intelligentsia seized control of state and society.

Already in the eighteenth century, however, a painful fissure that has not yet healed began to develop in the mentality of Russia. It was later to be an experience common over two-thirds or three-fourths of the world, but it was first seen on a massive scale in Russia. It is explained in part by Western dominion in world history since 1500. It was elaborated unforgettably by Arnold Toynbee.[16] When the non-Western societies first encounter the West in their own native cultures, there are two characteristic reactions, the party of the Zealots and the party of the Herodians. Toynbee takes the names from two political camps of the Jews as Israel faced the superior might of the Roman Empire in the first century B.C.E. The Zealots were conservatives whose recommended course of action was typical of the history of such problems solved in the Old Testament. The victorious "faithful remnant" had always recalled its wayward brethren back to Jehovah from various forms of apostasy. The apostasy was punished by foreign conquests, Babylonian captivity, and such until the people were properly reminded of the anger of Jehovah and its consequences. When they returned to their proper Judaic traditions, good fortune followed. The Herodians were those dynasts, including Herod the Great (37–4 B.C.E.), the notorious author of the "slaughter of the innocents" and one of the great builders of the age, who advocated submission to and accommodation with the irresistible power of the Romans and became thus vassals of the empire.

We can see these two reactions in culture after culture around the world. In China the Zealots and Herodians were the Manchus and their successors, the warlords, on the one hand, and Sun Yat-sen, Chiang Kai-shek, and Mao Tse-tung on the other. In Japan the Zealots supported the Shogun; the Herodians were the Satsuma and Choshu clans and the leaders of the Meiji Restoration (1867). In India both Rammohun Roy and Mohandas Gandhi contained a confused mixture of the two impulses. In our own time, the two styles are exemplified by Khomeini and the Shah. Ho Chi Minh was a Herodian. The American Indian ghost dance was Zealot. In nineteenth-century Russia, these two parties were the Slavophiles and the Westernizers.

It is difficult for most of the Western world to conceive the painful nature of this cultural confrontation of the West and the non-West, or its non-Western manifestations in the native parties of Zealots and Herodians, though it is more familiar in the provincial mentalities of

Montgomery, Edinburgh, Munich, and Algiers than in the capital mentalities of Washington, London, Berlin, and Paris. For the Russians, as for the other provincials, it was an identity crisis. Those persons within shouting distance of Peter's court soon came to understand that to be purely Russian was to be a bumpkin and that no such person profited in the presence of the emperor. European capacities were prized, and European style. The only way to be an adequate Russian at Peter's court was to be a pseudo-European. The story is told that in the reign of Alexander I (1801–25) one officer asked another what kind of promotion he sought; the latter said that he would be satisfied to become a German.

Of course, Russians saw themselves persecuted and scorned by Europeans for generations, and so the choice of cultural model that Peter forced them to make was totally graceless. In fact, Russia developed from that time a painfully ambivalent attitude to Europe. The xenophobia was old, and the xenomania was new, but henceforth they would always be simultaneous. Here was a new element of schizoid mentality, a love–hate attitude to Europe that joined remarkably compatibly—and aggravated remarkably perceptibly—the old conflict between the hyperactive, world-affirming state and the hyperpassive, world-fleeing people.

A Danish traveler in the 1730s described two prototypes that would become persistent stereotypes.[17] The first was the young Princess Kurakina, a dandy *koketka*.

> She rides out with a coach and six, accompanied by two outriders and four footmen, keeps two dozen maids and as many lackeys, eats luxuriously and always at odd hours, sleeps until noon, dresses like a singer of the St. Petersburg operetta, knows only Russian, but mixes it with so many French and Italian words with Russian endings, that native Russians have a harder time understanding her than foreigners. Her conversation consists for the most part of praises of French fashions and free behavior; she mocks pious women . . . and . . . tries to prove that amorous adventures are possible in Moscow no less than in Paris or London.

Her cultural counterparts were Prince Cherkasskii and his wife. "The Prince asked if I understood Russian. I answered, yes, a little." The Prince then said that since in his travels abroad he had to speak the local language, he must insist on speaking Russian in Russia. "I should like to know, he continued, why the Russian language cannot be considered as being on a level with French and German. I suggested that this might in part be traced to the fact that learning had not yet flourished in Russia, and that therefore the language had not evolved or spread; but also for the reason that foreigners had only recently begun to hold the Russian Empire in esteem, and that, of course, the reputation of a language grew with the power of a state." This answer satisfied the Prince, whereupon "the Princess asked me whether I were a German," at which point the conversation began to turn upon the question of national virtues. The Princess "took off her straw hat, which was made in the English fashion, and asked me whether I thought that such things ought to be imported from abroad. I replied that such a lapse was atoned for by the utility of the article which Her Highness had been forced to buy. But you see, the Princess said, this hat was made by my *muzhik* [peasant] in Moscow, and therefore we need neither the foreigners nor their wares in Russia." She evidently overlooked the point of the foreign nature of its fashion.

Few travelers have failed to report such encounters. The Varangians had returned, and not for the last time. The awkward question of cultural affinity remains unresolved and unrelaxed. It has, of course, rarely been quite so topical and tense as it is today.

Peter had left two other legacies that shook the stability of dynastic politics earlier than did that of the intelligentsia. First, he decreed, in the wake of the execution of the heir, a new law on succession, allowing the sovereign to choose his heir. Second, he formed two favored guards regiments, the Preobrazhenskii and Semenovskii, which soon developed into a kind of praetorian guard at court. Aristocratic factions of the old blooded nobility and the new Petrine nobility attempted through their progeny in the guards regiments to influence not only policy at court but the choice of sovereign itself. These circumstances explain the Era of Palace Revolutions, 1725–62, which might be called with little exaggeration the era of cretins and freaks. There were six nominal sovereigns between Peter I and Catherine II, one of them less than two years old. These circumstances explain, too, the beginnings of a gradual revolt of the Russian nobility that would bear fruit in the reign of Catherine II.

Catherine, born and raised in Germany, was given a French education. She became the child bride of one of those royal freaks who inherited the Russian throne, Peter III. Catherine was as gifted as

Peter III was not, as ambitious and calculating as he was foolish and frivolous. She alleged plausibly that the marriage was never consummated: she bore children, Peter likely never sired any. Empress Elizabeth demanded an heir, and Catherine turned with little reluctance to lovers. There is no proof, but there is every chance that her children were not Romanovs. Nicholas I once asked a historian, "Who are we actually?" His answer: "Sire, it is better not to ask." When the Russians grew as sick of Peter III as Catherine was, she executed a coup, and her partisans executed Peter. As the wits of Europe described the government of eighteenth-century Russia, it was a despotism tempered by assassination.

Catherine's reign would witness a decisive transformation in the nature of Russian dynastic politics. Prudence was required of a foreign woman ruler in eighteenth-century Russia. After all, she had not a shred of a claim by any conceivable law of succession to a throne of which clearly legitimate sovereigns had been repeatedly deprived in the preceding generation. Catherine had undoubted assets, however. She had great intelligence, resolution, and dignity; and the indiscretions of her private life did not remotely match the prevailing undergraduate legends. Catherine was not a tasteless or sexually gross person. Admittedly, she had an insistent appetite for affection.

Her political program was complicated. She obviously aspired to make the Russian state into something more than a police and military machine. Her reign was a veritable laboratory of the prevailing political concepts of the age, more clearly conceived than in the reign of Peter I and given the trendiest progressive spin of the time: the *Polizeistaat,* the well-ordered, uniformly administered, rational pursuit of commonweal; the *Rechtsstaat,* a state governed by law, obliging the consent of the monarchy as well as its subjects; and the *Ständestaat,* the state of distinct, well-defined, and legally entitled social classes. The most up-to-date reflection of the idea of the *Ständestaat* was the most impressive new political treatise of the age, Montesquieu's *Spirit of the Laws* (1748), and it necessarily posed the question of liberalism, that is, sharing the powers of government and limiting the prerogative of the executive. The issues that these concepts entailed were posed early in Catherine's reign.[18]

One of the insistent claims of the *Rechtsstaat* was a published code of laws. The Austrians and the Prussians were to publish codifications of their own national law during Catherine's reign—the Allgemeines

Bürgerliches Gesetzbuch (Austria) of 1786 and the Preussisches All-gemeines Landrecht of 1794. In order to address the same purpose in Russia, in 1767 Catherine convoked with exemplary fanfare an elected Legislative Assembly representing a broad sector of the Russian popu-lation. She prepared her charge in an *Instruction* drawn directly and candidly from the work of the leading judicial thinkers of the day, Montesquieu's *Spirit of the Laws* (1748) and the Marchese di Beccaria's treatise *On Crime and Punishment* (1764). The *Instruction* was somewhat abstract. "The sovereign is absolute; for no other au-thority except that which is concentrated in his person can act appro-priately in a state whose expanse is so vast" (Montesquieu). "What is the purpose of autocracy? Not to deprive people of their natural free-dom, but to guide their actions so as to attain the maximum good" (*Polizeistaat*). "The use of torture is repugnant to a healthy and natural mind" (Beccaria). "Laws ought to be written in the common tongue; and the code that contains all the laws ought to be a book of utmost usefulness and ought to be sold as cheaply as a book of *ABCs*" (*Rechtsstaat*). "Laws may accomplish something useful by enabling slaves to own private property" (*Ständestaat*).[19]

The Assembly itself exhibited a lot of talk and a lot of class conflict, much of it degenerating into desultory futility. Whenever a debate reached a certain level of intensity in a sensitive question, the president of the Assembly would unaccountably turn to another issue or to the demands of another constituency. One such delicate issue, however, revealed the critical features of Catherine's relations with Russian so-ciety. It was the question of the flight of runaway serfs. One of the government's deputies, that is, one of Catherine's own civil servants, suggested that the growing number of serfs deserting their owners was explained by the cruelties of the landlords and the heavy burden of rent obligations. He demanded that legal limits be placed on the power of the landlords over the serfs. The debate at this point naturally grew heated. A noble deputy replied in a speech "coarse and violent [*gross-ier et brutal*]," attributing the problem to the peasants' notorious vices: drunkenness, laziness, vagrancy. Any limitation of noble authority over the serfs, he said, would lead to social instability, disorder, and riots. This point elicited a rejoinder from the noble deputy Korobin, who was, many delegates believed, speaking for Catherine herself. "Sketching a gripping portrait of the wretchedness with which the peasants struggled, he drew from it the conclusion that a serf decided upon flight only as a last resort when his existence under his proprietor has become absolutely unbearable." Korobin attributed the flight of the serfs chiefly to the abuses of the landlords, and he proposed a new law that would grant to the serf a plot of land in full ownership and regulate the rent that the proprietor could demand of the serf.

Korobin's speech provoked excited responses from multiple deputies. The most challenging was the suggestion, the significance of which was too pointed to be missed, that "the absolute power of the proprietor over his serfs corresponded to the absolute power of the sovereign over her subjects, that it could not be limited without the danger of shattering [*ébranler*] the principle of autocracy itself." Prince Shcherbatov said flatly that the real question here was the emancipation of the serfs and that the security of serfdom was the foundation for the security of the monarchy. Korobin responded by hinting that the views that he expressed corresponded to those of the empress herself. At that point, the president of the Assembly interrupted the debates and forbade the injection of the empress's name into the discussion.

The Assembly was badly deadlocked, and a war with Turkey was approaching. The Assembly was dismissed in order to allow the deputies to join their regiments. The most contentious issue that arose in the Assembly was obviously serfdom, and both the fashion in which it occurred and the hints of Catherine's interest in it reveal important elements of her political commitments in the early years of her reign. The concept of the *Ständestaat* (society of orders) required the *civil*, though not the *political*, equality of all citizens; and enlightened despotism/*Polizeistaat* was designed to expedite social and economic progress in Eastern Europe to the level of Western Europe.

It was precisely the condition of backwardness, however, that also obstructed the progress of civil equality of the classes. The state required an educated class for its civil service and officers' corps, the educated class was the nobility, and the loyalty of the nobility could be counted on only so long as it enjoyed conditions of unequal privilege. Progressive government in Russia, then, was feasible only in the hands of a very strong sovereign, which is to say, in the hands of an intimidating native male such as Peter I. The debates in the Legislative Assembly illustrated as clearly as possible Catherine's dilemma: she could not realize the aims of the progressive political programs of the time without jeopardizing her own power. Catherine's prudent private notes and expressions strongly suggest that she wished, at the very least, to do something to improve the condition of the serfs.[20] It was, she wrote, "against the Christian religion and justice to make slaves out of men born free. . . . To [free the serfs] would not make one popular with the landowners, filled as they are with obstinacy and prejudice." When one of her courtiers wrote that "Our base people have no noble feelings," she responded, "Nor can they have under present conditions." Further, "If we do not agree to reduce this inhumanity and ameliorate the unbearable position of the human race, then . . . sooner or later they will do it against our will."[21]

Already in 1765 Catherine had established the Free Economic Society, which announced an essay competition on the theme "Whether it is of greater benefit to society for the peasant to own land or only movable property, and how far should his rights to this or that property be extended?" The winning essays were for peasant ownership of land, and the essay that placed second argued that serfdom was morally wrong. The Society did not publish this essay.

In the question of serfdom, Catherine evidently retreated from her preferred intentions. The serfs, however, would soon make their influence felt, just as Catherine had warned that they would. This is the story of the determining crisis of Catherine's reign: the Pugachev Rebellion.

Emelian Pugachev was an obscure Don Cossack and an eccentric maverick. His life prior to 1773 was a story of military service, desertion, imprisonment, and escape. When free, he wandered over the wild south and east Russian frontier. In the spring of 1773, he was sentenced to be whipped and imprisoned in Kazan for sowing sedition among the already discontented Cossacks of the Urals. He soon escaped, and in September he raised a revolt of Cossacks and peasants east of the Volga River. Uneducated and illiterate, he was to prove a formidably resourceful adversary.

A nearly Gothic tissue of Russian superstition played into Pugachev's hands. He proclaimed himself Peter III. This piece of deception worked near miracles for him. It was attributable to a combination of the facts of Peter III and of Russian folk mythology. The south Urals and north Volga area was full of Old Believers who remembered fondly that Peter III had relieved some of the measures of discrimination against them. The common people also appreciated the fact that he had offended the Russian nobility. He had dressed the Russian army in Prussian uniforms and powdered wigs, scorned its native ways, and held it to standards of Prussomania. More important, Peter had proclaimed (1762), for reasons that have never been fully clarified, the emancipation of the Russian nobility from state service. While this act ought to have endeared him to the nobility, it did not. It suggested to the Russian peasant, on the other hand, the imminent abolition of serfdom. Illiterate and benighted or not, the peasant was no dummy, and his memory perpetuated from generation to generation that tacit bargain struck between 1550 and 1650: the peasants serve the nobility to enable the nobility to serve the state. The emancipation of the nobility from state service was the logical prelude to the emancipation of the serfs from gentry service. Before it occurred, however, Peter III was overthrown and murdered. Aha, the peasants thought, a corrupt bargain!

The peasants did not notice that Catherine disappointed the nobility by not immediately confirming its emancipation; they noticed rather that she disappointed the peasants by not proclaiming theirs. In their folklore, an explanation for this state of affairs was not far to seek. The real sovereign—preferably tsar—was a good ruler. A sovereign not good to his people was not the real one, and so the real one must be found. Peter III must naturally and logically have planned to follow the nobles' emancipation by that of the serfs, and therefore the nobility must have made Catherine sovereign upon her promise not to emancipate them. The survival of Peter III was no heuristic problem: God took care of his own.

This line of reasoning and the rebellion that it produced have been appropriately called naive monarchism or "rebel[lion] in the name of the tsar."[22] It might as appropriately be called rebellion of superior legitimacy. When Nikolai Danilevskii wrote in 1869 that there had never been a political revolution in Russian history, he was not entirely wrong. Rebellion in the name of superior legitimacy is a characteristic kind of Russian revolt. Emelian Pugachev was one of twenty-five Peter IIIs in late eighteenth-century Russia.

Pugachev, in any event, did his work well. He soon controlled the whole Volga basin and a huge area to the east and north as far as the river Yaik (now the Ural River) and the southern portion of the Urals. At the height of his success, his forces were within three hundred miles of Moscow. All of this occurred in the midst of Catherine's desperate first war with the Turks. She was sufficiently alarmed to consider going to the army herself, and she appointed to the command against Pugachev a politically dissident general, Petr Panin. When the Turkish war was concluded (July 1774), Pugachev was defeated (September

1774), but he had illustrated two factors that struck at the stability of the government: the peasantry was rife with discontent, and the provincial administration had collapsed at his mere approach.

The problem of peasant discontent was not amenable to any feasible solution. The strength of provincial administration Catherine addressed in the Law on the Administration of the Provinces of 1775. It was staffed, naturally, by the nobility.

The Pugachev Revolt terminated all signs of Catherine's plans to do something to improve the condition of the serfs. The reform of provincial government depended for its success on the administrative skills of the nobility. It reflected a kind of tacit political alliance between the two parties, throne and noble class. In 1785, Catherine recognized the dependence of her government on the nobility, made the logical move, and conceded it—in the Charter of the Nobility—the emancipation from universal state service that Peter III had decreed and she had previously refused.

Catherine's potential plans for the peasantry had been frustrated by the conflicts in the Legislative Assembly and by the Pugachev Revolt. The Charter of the Nobility represented a compromise between her political aspirations and Russian realities. She had hesitated for twenty-three years, after all, before acquiescing in the nobles' demands. The Law on the Administration of the Provinces and the Charter of the Nobility together effectively left the peasantry at the disposal of the nobility.

These developments had far-reaching consequences for Russia's future. They have been best articulated by Robert E. Jones. "The alliance between the state and the serf-owning nobility consummated in Catherine's Charter was ultimately harmful to everyone involved." The previous understanding between them had contained progressive and rational elements. In return for its privileged position in the state, its virtually exclusive right to own land and serf labor, the nobility was obligated to state service. Under the new dispensation, the unproductive nobility was sheltered by privilege from the reality of self-reliance. Yet it sank irretrievably into a kind of flaccid and dissipated decrepitude: "the protection of the government debilitated the nobility by sheltering it from the challenge of having to exert itself to save itself." What was worse, once the nobility's service obligation was abrogated, the relationship of state and nobility assumed the form of a contract against the interests of the remainder of the nation. Worst of all, "at that point the autocracy ceased to be the progressive force that it had been throughout most of Russia's history." It concentrated instead on a defense of the status quo.[23]

The Charter of the Nobility, then, aggravated the political illogic of Russian social policy. Serfdom was the first element of gross anomaly in that policy, because serf law was consummated at a time when a salaried standing army no longer depended upon servile labor to support the formerly semifeudal *pomestie* cavalry. The emancipation of the nobility aggravated the anomaly by maintaining that support while freeing the nobility of any service obligation to the state, and thus to the society. As Kliuchevskii said it so well: the nobility became a parasite class, more and more pampered and spoiled, more and more incapable of serving either the national interests or its own.

Still Catherine had perhaps not yet surrendered all ideas of progressive statecraft. Another Charter accompanied that of the Russian nobility: the Charter of the Towns of 1785. Catherine had long taken an interest in the development of a Russian third estate, an economically dynamic merchant class, a manufacturing and trading bourgeoisie.[24] In 1763, Chancellor M.I. Vorontsov commissioned a memorandum written by a Frenchman, M. de Boulard, on "the usefulness of a third estate." Boulard remarked that "every power that lacks a third estate is imperfect, however strong it may be." He proposed to create one in Russia by permitting wealthy artisans and merchants of peasant origin to buy their freedom. He assumed that the prospect of purchasing personal freedom would motivate business activity among the serfs.

In 1766, the second prize in the essay contest of the Free Economic Society was awarded to A.I. Polenov, who argued in favor of the rights of serfs to own property. In a second paper, Polenov dealt exclusively with the absence of a middle estate in Russia. He, too, recommended freeing the most industrious artisans and traders from the peasant class and providing schools for their education.

A bolder proposal of a similar sort was made by the Russian ambassador in Paris, Prince D.A. Golitsyn, who communicated it to Catherine through his brother. Golitsyn explained the absence of a large commercial class in Russia by the influence of serfdom. A bourgeoisie was an urban phenomenon, and serfdom was an obstacle to its development. "As long as serfdom exists, the Russian Empire . . . will remain poor." The power to resolve the problem, he stated, was in the hands of the empress.

Catherine's chief advisor in educational matters early in her reign proposed another means to the same end. Ivan Betskoi envisaged the recruitment of orphans and abandoned and illegitimate children in order to educate them at the state's expense in the arts and sciences of a commercial class. "In regenerating our subjects by an education founded on these principles, we will create . . . new citizens."

Denis Diderot, notorious *encyclopédiste*, was familiar with Catherine's interest in a third estate through his acquaintance with Prince Golitsyn. During his much-publicized trip to visit Catherine in St. Petersburg in 1773, he outlined proposals similar to those of Boulard and Golitsyn for the creation of just such a class. The Charter of the Towns—instituting a conservatively elective form of self-government—represents her aspirations for the encouragement of a lively middle class in Russia.

Alas, it was misconceived. Just four short years later, the French Revolution occurred. The French bourgeoisie soon seized the leadership, and the consequences were not what Catherine expected of the business class. The good French middle class set up the progressive invention of Dr. Guillotin and began to take off the heads of those same two categories of people whom Pugachev had attacked in Russia, monarchs and nobles. It was enough to chill whatever residual progressive impulses the lessons of Russian political science had left alive in Catherine. France had been perceived in the seventeenth and eighteenth centuries as the font of all that was civilized and progressive in the European world. Now France began to exhibit an example that the Russian nobility and the frustrated empress who presumed to lead it could no longer tolerate. The third estate arrogated power to itself, stormed the Bastille, and, in the wake of the marauding bands of peasants in the Great Fear of the summer of 1789, abolished the remnants of feudalism. It was all too reminiscent of the Pugachev Rebellion. Catherine and the Russian nobility reacted abruptly. For the time being, it sealed the fate of the process of Westernization and the idea of progress in Russia.

Catherine succeeded in introducing into Russia an element of freedom only for the nobility. The reasonableness of extending it further foundered on the dependence of her throne and her civil and military service on that nobility, her fear of the other classes, and the scare of the French Revolution.

The idea of progressive monarchy is one that American political mythology can scarcely receive. Born as a nation in a struggle allegedly with George III—actually with the Mother of Parliaments—we learn from our earliest days that monarchy is as naturally and inevitably malevolent as it is naturally and inevitably conservative.

In fact, monarchy in early modern Europe, 1500 to 1800, was often progressive. Louis XIV, remembered in the wisdom of sophomore legend as the great archconservative of history, was in fact the great agent of change in the France of his time. In 1661, he scrapped all but the appearance of the formula according to which "the king governs through the *Grand Conseil*." Louis abolished some of the high offices about the throne, reduced the power of others, excluded from royal councils persons formerly entitled by birth to places in them, curtailed the role of the councils themselves, and entrusted prerogative to junior nobility or non-nobles. He thus vastly diminished the dependence of the monarchy on the great families of France. This was both a political and a social revolution. Henceforth, the class preferred in his government was the class of the future, the bourgeoisie.[25]

Monarchy was in the common conception of the time the chief guarantee of justice for the common people, their chief protector against the ravages of the otherwise all-powerful and willfully abusive local magnates of the nobility. The monarchy of France supervised the grain trade for the purpose—sometimes thwarted—of equitable distribution. Henry IV of France is remembered not only for bringing the public destruction of the wars of religion to an end but also for wishing every peasant a chicken in his pot on Sunday. The enlightened despots of Russia, Prussia, and Austria alike instituted religious toleration. Joseph II moved seriously against serfdom in his empire. Louis XV and Chancellor Maupeou struggled against the political dominion of the noble lawyers in the Parlement of Paris. In the governing of Russia that we have reviewed, we find that the monarchy—Ivan III, Ivan IV, Peter I, Catherine II—was the single progressive institution in Russian society.

At the close of Catherine's reign (1796), the distraught Russian monarchy faced an unprecedented and ironic situation. As the French Revolution was illustrating, progress in Europe now brought into the arena of politics an aggressive bourgeoisie that was subversive of the power of monarchies. Therefore, progress in Russia of the European kind, the only kind that Russia had known for the past two centuries, would threaten to subvert the only agency of progress, the monarchy, that Russia had known since the decline of Kiev.

In a world awash in commerce and science, turned upside down by new theories of republican statecraft, generating ambitious new democratic aspirations that made all thought of a *Ständestaat* obsolete, and inflicted upon all of Europe by brash young generals in their twenties commanding the armies of France, would a government of conservative absolutism bring to backward Russia any kind of hope for the future? If Russia could no longer afford the model of progressive monarchy, the near future would show that it could not afford to surrender it either. The Russian Revolution of 1917 had its source in the sterile conservatism generated in the 1790s.

❖ 4 ❖

Reaction and Revolt:
The Imperial Dead End

*Here [in the army] there is order, there is a strict uncondi-
tional legality, no impertinent claims to know all the answers,
no contradiction . . . ; no one commands before he has himself
learned to obey . . . everything has its purpose. . . . I shall always hold in honor the calling of a soldier.*

Nicholas I

*Only if [the tsar] were to renounce his power and hand it
over to a freely elected Constituent Assembly . . . would we
leave him in peace and forgive his crimes. Until that time—
war, implacable war, to the last drop of our blood!*

The People's Will revolutionary organization

Catherine's transition from a cautiously progressive to a studiedly
conservative political outlook took place between 1773 and
1789. By 1790, it was well established. The year 1790, then, may be
taken as a convenient watershed between two distinct Russian styles of
statecraft.

Three Russian emperors governed in this new era of stand-pat politics, all from the same family: Paul I (1796–1801); his eldest son,
Alexander I (1801–25); and his third son, Nicholas I (1825–55). Paul
grew up frightened of his mother, Catherine II, and of her habit of
disposing of her rivals, for example, his putative father, Peter III. The
tension between mother and son afflicted Paul, who regarded his
mother's throne as rightfully his own, throughout Catherine's reign.
He was unusually nervous and somewhat unstable. When he inherited

the throne, he used the levers of power to operate something like a moralizing and crusading *Polizeistaat*, both at home and abroad, that is, in the French revolutionary wars. He was determined to force the nobility, spoiled in his opinion by the pampering of Catherine, to return to the spirit of duty that Peter I had required of it. He flagrantly violated Catherine's Charter of the Nobility, and this fact, as well as the caprice and suspicion that animated his government in general, was more than his courtiers would bear. In March 1801 they murdered him.

His son, Alexander I, was young, twenty-three years old, strikingly handsome, and equally charming. Alexander the Blessed, Our Angel, as he was called, evoked the most euphoric hopes. He was educated in progressive sentiments by a Swiss republican, Frédéric César La Harpe, under Catherine's tutelage, and he gathered about himself, before his accession to the throne, a group of young friends of similar, pro-French sentiments. He shared their distaste for the folly of his father's tyrannical course. He was certainly afraid that Paul suspected him of the regicidal temptation to which in fact that suspicion drove him for his own protection. In any event, he gave his consent to the coup d'état, and it is believed that he was tormented ever after by lingering guilt.

Alexander was the only sovereign of Russia between Catherine and the end of the empire who had genuinely progressive sentiments and harbored enthusiastic intentions of reform. Yet his political program has remained ambiguous and obscure in great part because he could no more than his grandmother embark blithely and thoughtlessly on a course of liberal reform in an empire where the power structure was so saturated in tenacious tradition as Russia's was. It is tempting to think that Alexander's political thoughts were virgin pure and that, in the fashion of the Virgin herself, he confined such thoughts chiefly to his heart, where he pondered on them. In any case, he proceeded cautiously, which required, in Russia, that he proceed secretly.[1]

Two reforms, the granting of a constitution and the emancipation of the serfs, occupied Alexander's political machinations throughout most of his reign. The question of a constitution had been topical in Russia since at least the time when Catherine II's Legislative Assembly served to educate public opinion to some degree and to delineate the fundamental lines of the constitutional thinking of the age. Alexander's reign witnessed an unusual spate of such projects, all of them worded in a strikingly cautious, abstract, and ambivalent fashion.[2] The single most urgent impulse behind the idea was to establish a government of law, a *Rechtsstaat*, one which bound the monarch as well as his subjects, and to discard forever the capricious government of favorites and tyrants who had been so conspicuous in the eighteenth century. Many of the nobles, whose dignity had suffered so painfully the caprices of Paul, felt very strongly about this point and were eager to support what they understood to be the constitutional intentions of the new sovereign.

The question of constitutional reform was complicated, however, by several factors. First, the mere comprehension of the concept of a constitution, not to speak of sentiment in favor of one, was limited to a tiny educated portion of the relatively uneducated Russian population. In addition, the nobility that understood and favored the idea worked fundamentally for its own political enfranchisement and against that of other social classes. Finally, there were different factions and pressure groups among the nobility.

There was the faction known as the Senatorial party led by Alexander Vorontsov. It comprised the Governing Senate and consisted of a group of relatively elderly figures, most of whom had been prominent in Catherine's government. The Senatorial party wished to lodge the prerogatives of the *Rechtsstaat* chiefly in the Senate, where the most distinguished families of nobility held sway.

There was the group of Alexander's "young friends," joining him in the Secret Committee—*Neglasnyi komitet*, the unglasnost committee.[3] They objected to the Senatorial projects of reform because they did not want Russian government to become the captive of the most conservative class in society. They envisaged the Senatorial party's project as the one reform that would kill the prospects of all others. They recognized what was to be a persistent paradox in nineteenth-century Russia, that only unmitigated political absolutism could secure the prospect of liberal reform in the country, could prevail against the socially dominant forces of an inflexible conservatism inspired chiefly by fear and greed.

There was a group of hidebound old conservatives who, attached to the memory of the reign of Catherine as the golden age of the nobility, opposed any revision of the traditionally absolutist prerogative of the Russian emperor. They supported unlimited absolutism right or wrong.[4]

Finally, to confound matters more, there was the conspiratorial group of Paul's assassins. Alexander was understandably afraid of them. He is said to have believed himself for months at their mercy. He never forgot the fate of his father.[5]

If the social base upon which liberal reform might proceed in Russia was narrow, it was all the more important to develop consensus in the only class that could conceivably support it. Yet given the multiple camps into which the nobility was divided, consensus was plainly impossible.

From the very beginning, Alexander's legislation illustrated the fragile nature of his political constituency. Although he confirmed Catherine's Charter of the Nobility, privately he made it clear that he was opposed to it, that he did so only under duress. In September 1802, he issued his long-awaited decree on the reorganization of the government. It lodged grossly ill-defined powers in three laterally configured bodies: the Senate, the State Council, and the Council of Ministers. Essentially it changed nothing—they all tended to work at cross purposes. One authority calls it "contradictory and incomplete," "half-hearted and un-worked out."[6]

In the meantime, Alexander turned his attention to a question that evidently vitally interested him, serfdom. Characteristically, he proceeded very tentatively. He prepared several measures. First was the mere repetition of an old law increasingly ignored, a ban on the sale of serfs without the land on which they lived. He studied a project to have the state treasury buy the freedom of serfs from their owners as well as one to allow a serf family to purchase its own freedom. Rumors of his intentions provoked a rabid reaction among the nobility. His own select Secret Committee of radical young friends objected as well. In the end Alexander was forced to compromise. He forbade the *advertisement* in the press of the sale of serfs without land, and he *allowed* noble landowners to emancipate whole villages of their serfs with land. In different parts of the non-Russian Baltic provinces, various complicated statutes designed to ameliorate the plight of the serfs appeared to leave both the landowners and their chattel dissatisfied. Even so, the nobility was seriously aggrieved over these limited measures.[7]

In 1805, the War of the III Coalition against France intervened to relieve Alexander of the dilemma of reform, as the Turkish war had relieved Catherine of the similar challenge of the Legislative Assembly. When the war was over and Alexander was allied with France against England in the Treaty of Tilsit (July 1807), he turned back to his former intentions. This time, his whole "unofficial committee" was concentrated in a single person, arguably the most able civil servant in the history of Russia, a priest's son who had married an English wife, Mikhail Speranskii. Alexander asked for the project of a constitution, and Speranskii wrote a good one. It projected civil rights for the entire population, political rights for the propertied classes, and a government divided into judicial, legislative, and executive branches. The process of reform was both glacial and dangerous in Russia, however, and when the War of 1812 approached, Alexander, in deference to the good Russian sentiments that the nation at war would require, dismissed the unpopular Francophile Speranskii and the constitution with him.[8]

The peace of Tilsit had divided Europe into two spheres of influence, French in the west, Russian in the east. It demanded no territorial sacrifices of Russia but required an alliance with France to exclude English commerce from Europe, the notorious Continental Blockade. Napoleon hoped thereby to destroy the prosperity of the "nation of shopkeepers" and the financial system that supported the grand coalitions against France.

It was an unpopular and unstable peace. The Russian nobility and merchants suffered the interruption of trade with their natural trading partners in England. Napoleon reneged on his promise to share the partition of the Ottoman Empire with Russia. He continued to abuse the royal house of Prussia, for which Alexander felt a sentimental attachment, and he manipulated the politics of Poland such as to make Russia suspicious of his intentions in a nation formerly under predominantly Russian control.

When the break came in 1812, Napoleon invaded Russia with the *Grande armée*, the army of twenty nations. It was a genuine epic, later commemorated in the works of art of Leo Tolstoy and Peter Tchaikovsky, among others. On the eve of the war, Napoleon inquired of one of Alexander's diplomats, A.D. Balashev, about a good road to Moscow. Balashev sarcastically recommended the road through Poltava, the Ukrainian site where Peter I had destroyed the army of Charles XII of Sweden. Faraway in London, the Russian ambassador, Semen Vorontsov, recommended a strategy. The Russian army would be, he said, formidable in Moscow, terrible in Kazan, invincible in Siberia. Heedless of the difficulties, Napoleon proceeded. The Russian army, not half the size of Napoleon's nearly 600,000 men, retreated. Before Moscow, it made a stand at Borodino. It was Napoleon's most costly victory. Moscow was occupied and burned, and Napoleon awaited a peace proposal that never came. The story of his retreat and subsequent ruin is well known.

Russia emerged as the greatest power on the continent, perhaps in the world, but reform had been interrupted, and, more important, the victory appeared to place a kind of providential seal of superiority on the Russian system. Alexander nevertheless returned in 1815 to the mission for which he apparently felt destined. When one of his conservative courtiers drew up a victory manifesto a part of which lauded the "mutual advantage" of the relationship of noble landowners and serfs, the emperor angrily crossed out the phrase. In newly annexed Finland (1808), Alexander confirmed the traditional Finnish constitution and forbade serfdom. The Congress of Vienna reconstituted a Kingdom of Poland and made Alexander its king. Napoleon had freed the serfs in Poland in 1807, and Alexander granted it a constitution. In 1817, he secretly ordered the preparation of the emancipation of the serfs in the eastern portion of Ukraine. In his speech formally opening the first session of the Sejm (Parliament) in Warsaw in March 1818, he said—in French—that he wanted to establish "legally free institutions" in all the territories entrusted to him by Providence. He had the speech translated and distributed in Russia at once. It was received in Russia as a harbinger of the emancipation of the Russian serfs, and a Russian nobleman reported at the time that "the entire public [read *nobility*] was alarmed by the intention of the emperor to liberate the serfs." Another wrote that it had occasioned "attacks of fear and depression." Soon thereafter, Alexander ordered Nikolai Novosiltsev, an old friend and former member of the Secret Committee of reform, to prepare a constitution for Russia. There is circumstantial evidence suggesting that Alexander's chief interest in Poland consisted in his wish to use it to set a proper example for Russia; and perhaps that he thought of it as an asylum for himself in the event that his emancipation of the Russian serfs should threaten him with the fate of his poor father.[9]

In any event, at length he tired of the struggle. When the temper of society persuaded him of the infeasibility of his plans, Alexander appears to have surrendered to circumstances—and to depression as well. He soon embarked on a genuinely conservative phase of rule, inaugurating, for example, the Ministry of Spiritual Affairs and Popular Enlightenment under A.N. Golitsyn, an irreproachable reactionary who attacked and eviscerated the better elements of Russian university education.[10]

Alexander had dreamt and talked romantically throughout much of his reign of chucking his political duties and abdicating. In the summer of 1819 he spoke of such plans to his brothers Nicholas and Constantine. A review of his struggles for reform and the discouragement to which they eventually led him only lends credence to the mysteriously unresolved story that he faked his death in southern Russia in 1825—he was forty-eight years old—and lived on in Siberia until 1864 as the monk Fedor Kuzmich.

Alexander's experience illustrates one old Russian phenomenon and one new one. The emperor represented that ancient Russian progressive process of reform coming exclusively from above. In this instance, however, Alexander's frustration elucidates with special clarity a new circumstance, suggestions of which can in retrospect be discovered in the several preceding generations. After the demise of Peter I, the Russian nobility succeeded in throwing off the dominion of imperial control over it that had been so solidly imposed by Peter. From the mid-eighteenth century to the end of the empire, conservative social forces frequently wielded power enough to balk the government of what it thought the well-being of the nation required. The reforms of Alexander II in the latter half of the nineteenth century will illustrate frustrations similar to those of Alexander I at the century's beginning.

The next reign began with a mock-heroic revolution. Alexander's father, Paul, had issued a new law on succession (1797), stipulating inheritance by primogeniture in the male line of the dynasty. Paul had done it presumably in order to end the palace revolutions of the eighteenth century, certainly in the hope of sparing himself the fate of his father—but in vain. Alexander died without sons in 1825. Unknown to all but a handful of people, his oldest brother, Constantine, the conventionally legitimate heir by reference to the law on succession, had agreed years earlier, in exchange for permission to engage in a morganatic marriage, to surrender his claims to the throne. Constantine was at his post in Warsaw, Viceroy of the Russian Kingdom of Poland. Nicholas, the younger brother and the actual heir since Konstantin's marriage, was in St. Petersburg. The plot was thickened by the knowledge of the officers' corps in St. Petersburg that Nicholas was a stern taskmaster and that the Polish army received higher pay.

In the event, a group of young army officers who had fallen under French influences during their presence in Paris in 1814 put out the disinformation that Nicholas was trying to usurp, and they mounted a travesty of a move against him, the Decembrist Revolt. Their aim was more or less that kind of conservative-liberal constitutional government, *Rechtsstaat*, that Alexander had initially encouraged but eventually shrunk from. This was the opening gun in the modern Russian revolutionary movement, a somewhat farcical show on Senate Square on 14 December 1825. The conspirators were inexperienced, nervous, unsure of themselves, and their communications with each other were poor. Some of them failed to show up at their designated posts at the crucial time because they had not finished composing their favorite form of constitution. Nicholas, behaving with admirable aplomb throughout the day, was as good as the reputation of his character. The revolt fizzled pitifully. Nicholas cracked down hard on radicalism, and for a generation it virtually disappeared from the Russian scene.

Alexander had been raised in the spirit of his grandmother Catherine in the days before the French Revolution drove her far from her early liberal pretensions. Nicholas, however, was born in 1796, in the last half-year of Catherine's life, and he reflected his father's personality and values. That is to say, he was born to fear, and the events of the day of his accession encouraged the inclination. The most characteristic institution of his reign was the Third Section of His Majesty's Own Privy Chancery, the security police. Nicholas himself described it as the handkerchief with which he wiped away the tears of his people, but they did not view it that way. The "gendarme of Europe" at home and abroad, his duty—duty was his favorite word—was to fight revolution and radicalism wherever he imagined them. The motto of the reign was "autocracy, orthodoxy, nationality." There were more secret committees, but there was no nonsense about development and little pretense of reform.

Nicholas was a fastidious perfectionist and thought fondly of the military because it symbolized the kind of order that he would have liked all of society to replicate. For thirty years, Nicholas presumed to stifle unhealthy, modern influences in Russian society. Someone observed that the main failing of the reign of Nicholas consisted in the fact that it was all a mistake. If so, it was an infinitely smaller mistake than those made a hundred years later.

The folly of Nicholas's political system was illustrated by the intrusion of international affairs, the Crimean War. It was the principal tragedy of the reign of Nicholas, and it exemplifies more tangibly than anything else the central problem of Russia in the nineteenth century.

The diplomacy of the conflict was virtually theater of the absurd. Its indirect cause was the aggressive reputation left in Russian foreign policy by Peter I and Catherine II. A European legend maintained that a mysterious "testament of Peter the Great" laid down the principles that his successors were to follow in order to conquer the whole continent. Statesmen from Napoleon Bonaparte to Harry Truman found in it the sources of Russian/Soviet foreign-policy aims. The *Christian Science Monitor* revived it to explain the Soviet intervention in Afghanistan, though the fraudulent document itself contains not a word of Afghanistan.[11] Catherine's "Greek Project" reflects the same kind of legacy, ambitious plans of conquest—though Catherine's plan was quite genuine—as she and Joseph II of Austria designed to drive the Turks out of Europe and to divide the Balkans between them.[12]

In fact, Catherine's successors Paul, Alexander, and Nicholas rejected her aggressive intentions, but Europe did not notice. When, late in the reign of Nicholas, the Catholic clergy and the Orthodox clergy began to dispute rights and priorities in the Holy Places of Christendom in the city of Jerusalem, ruled by the Ottoman Turks, the disagreement mushroomed into a confrontation personified by Emperor Nicholas I of Russia and Louis Napoleon Bonaparte, Emperor of the French. Napoleon III was not above simply searching for grandeur, which he did as far from French vital interests as Mexico City. Nicholas, on the other hand, was not pursuing Catherine's projects of aggrandizement at the expense of the Turks. He was doing what he usually did, he was doing his duty: the Treaty of Kuchuk-Kainardzhi had assigned Russia the role of protector of Orthodox Christians in the Ottoman Empire. Nicholas was suspected, however, of using the dispute over the Holy Places as a pretext for following precisely in the footsteps of Peter I and Catherine II.

It was one of the axioms of British policy at this time to thwart the spread of Russian power anywhere in that peculiarly British sphere of influence, the seas, in this case in the east Mediterranean. The attitude of the Austrians was similar. Despite having been saved from the Hungarian Revolution of 1849 by the generosity of Nicholas—he sent a Russian army of 300,000 men—they were still not eager for Slavic big-brother influence among the multiple little-brother Slavs of their own intrinsically unstable ethnic mosaic of empire in the Balkans. Britain and Austria therefore stood by Napoleon III against Nicholas.

The diplomacy of the Crimean War makes a very complex story. In brief, the diplomats bungled, sometimes deliberately, and war followed. Having declared war, the Western allies, France and Britain, had some trouble finding a place to fight it. They finally chose the remote Crimean Peninsula, that is, Russian territory as remote from the heart of Russia as from Paris and London. The Russians lost, and, having been suspected of grandly imperial designs that they did not have, they were punished. The most acute portion of the punishment was an item in the Treaty of Paris called the Black Sea clause. It forbade the Russians to fortify their Black Sea coast or to maintain a navy in that sea. In other words, it forbade them to defend their own borders, a stipulation grossly offensive to a great power.

The Crimean War had unimaginably important—and unfortunate—consequences both at home and abroad. In foreign affairs, it persuaded much of the Russian civil service and the patriotic intelligentsia of the ineradicable antagonism of Europe. Only one major power in Europe stood aside, Prussia. The Russians did not forget it. One other power they singled out for their bitterest resentment, Austria, the power that they had rescued from the Hungarian Revolution in 1849. It was the Austrian ultimatum of December 1855 to St. Petersburg—make peace or face an Austrian declaration of war, too—that broke the Russian will to carry on.

The foreign policy of Russia before the war had been in fact conservative. Thereafter it became revolutionary. When the wars of Italian unification began (1859), the Italians undertaking to throw Austrian Habsburg power out of northern Italy, the Russians watched the humbling of Austria with grim satisfaction. When the Prussians turned against Austria (1866) on their way to creating the German Empire, the Russians applauded again.

In 1870, wily old Prince Bismarck offered the Russians a deal that they could not refuse. He was preparing a war with France to complete the German Empire. He had to consider the revenge that Austria, recently defeated, might seek in such a war. He offered to support Russia in the abrogation of the Black Sea clause in exchange for a Russian guarantee of Austrian neutrality. St. Petersburg said yes and made it clear in Vienna that an Austrian declaration of war on Prussia would provoke a Russian declaration on Austria. The Austrians did not move, and Bismarck got his war, his victory, and his empire.

Unfortunately, this empire, which the Russians had contributed so much to constructing, was the empire that destroyed theirs in

1917. And the rancorous antagonism between Vienna and St. Petersburg over empire in the Balkans was the principal immediate cause of World War I.

The Crimean fallout was as serious at home as abroad. Sixty to seventy years of conservative autocracy that shunned development had exacted its price of Russia in the Crimean War. In the War of 1812, the Russian army had been the technological—though not the numerical, strategic, or tactical—equal of the French army, but it was no match for the British and French armies of 1854. The British and French came to Russia in steamships. When they landed in the Crimea, they supplied themselves on railroads that they laid for the purpose. The Russians supplied themselves over a distance of about 950 miles (Moscow to Sevastopol) by horse-drawn carts. They had no railroads south of Moscow. The French army and much of the British army fought with the new Minié rifle, which was accurate at a distance of a thousand yards, while the Russians continued to use muzzle-loading smoothbores, not accurate at more than two hundred yards. It was a decidedly unequal contest.

The Crimean experience and the inadequacy of the Russian performance in it left a dual legacy. On the one hand, there was the sense of moral guilt. Something was rotten in the state of Russia. The war was a providential judgment. Serfdom had been contributing to a sense of guilt since Catherine's Legislative Assembly. Nicholas I had recognized that serfdom must be abolished, but he feared to undertake it. It was his charge to his son.

On the other hand, there was alarm at the gaping technological lag of Russia behind the modern powers of the West. Russia must be modernized in order to be safe. The obvious lesson of the Crimea was that Russia could not afford cultural isolation. From this time, then, Russia was forced to consider a return to a policy of Westernization. Yet necessary as it was, the reasons for rejecting it were no less real in 1856 than they had been in 1789–90. Modernization, as Europe illustrated, inevitably entailed the development not only of that bourgeoisie so apparent in 1790 but a proletariat equally as evident in 1856. Russian autocracy would be seriously threatened by the ideologies of these classes: liberalism, socialism, and democracy. The challenge of modernization, Westernization, appeared to cut two ways. The Russians were damned if they did not Westernize, damned if they did. What they presumed to do henceforth was to import the material dimension of Western culture exclusively and to continue to prohibit its legal and political appurtenances. As Stalin remarked about something else, this idea was tantamount to the conception of iron wood or dry water (he said it about honest diplomacy). The selective appropriation of an alien culture is a trick that has often been tried. As we can see in the experience of Khrushchev, Gorbachev, and Deng Xiao-peng, not to speak of various Middle Eastern potentates, it remains an awkward process beyond the strength of most practitioners.

The sovereign upon whom this daunting duty devolved was Alexander II (1855–81). He is a historical personality full of irony; he defies definition. He was given, by Romanov standards, a very decent education. Among his tutors were conscientious and distinguished men, especially Count Filipp Brunnow, subsequently ambassador in London, and Count Egor Kankrin, the minister of finance. Most of them complained of the dilatory nature of their student. Alexander traveled more extensively both in Russia and in Europe than had been customary among his predecessors. Often marked by a lassitude of will, Alexander exhibited on occasion a stonewall stubbornness. He defied his parents, for example, in his choice of bride, Princess Wilhelmina Maria of Hesse-Darmstadt (Empress Maria Alexandrovna of Russia), whose own parentage was subject to the suspicion of scandal. Later he defied the opinion of the whole court by deserting his faithful wife and bringing to court his mistress, Princess Ekaterina Dolgorukaia, whom he married a mere forty days after the death of the empress.

Alexander enters the annals of history as the Tsar-Liberator, but he was a reluctant reformer at best. On the other hand, in the face of the massive antagonism of the nobility, it was only the rigid insistence of Alexander that broke the resistance to reform. An obscure personality, the character of Alexander eludes us.

Forbidding and treacherous or not, reason, experience, and tradition alike in this case insisted on reform. The most massive, most urgent, most critical issue was emancipation of the serfs. It was likely motivated chiefly by military considerations. A modern army was then an army of universal conscription, relatively short-term service on active duty and long-term service in the reserves, an army such as the Prussian reformers had devised in the wake of their debacle at the hands of Napoleon in 1806. This kind of army was tolerably affordable. Small during peacetime, it could be expanded to all available manpower in wartime. It was the kind of army that the Russians would eventually institute, but they had to overcome one serious reservation before doing so. They hesitated to draft and train in the use of firearms and violence the peasant bulk of the nation's manpower, then to release it into the reserves to take up residence as serfs on noble estates under the traditional administrative supervision of their landlords. In other words, emancipation was an indispensable prerequisite to a modern army.[13]

The emancipation decree was published 19 February 1861.[14] Its two essential features were simple enough. It suspended all the administrative duties over the peasants formerly performed by the nobility for the government, and it allowed the peasants to purchase their independence as well as land from their former lords. Its other features were subject to considerable criticism, especially on the part of the peasants. They were authorized to buy about one-half of the cultivated land, and they paid somewhat more than the prevailing market price for it.

What the peasants had demanded for years was "land and liberty." Though it is a bit risky to try to describe with any degree of assurance what an illiterate, unpolled, and largely unknown peasantry wanted, it seems likely that the emancipation settlement satisfied the peasants' demand for liberty. It did not give them a vote in national elections. There were none. They had and evidently wanted no political role at all. There is no evidence to the contrary. They got economic and administrative freedom from the noble landlord, and that is apparently what they wanted. They remained subject to the local democratic authority of the village commune in which they lived and to the autocratic authority of the Ministry of the Interior. That is not what everyone would call freedom. Apparently the Russian peasant did so.

The peasants' dissatisfaction stemmed rather from the land settlement. They subscribed to their own peculiar economic ethos, a concept that they knew as the "toiling norm," the spontaneous economic ideology of the Russian countryside, a folk faith that the land belonged by right to those who worked it, and in proportion as they worked it, relative to the amount of land available and the number of persons working it. In other words, democratic egalitarian socialism. Their complaint, then, was that they did not get all the land, that half of it remained in the hands of the noble parasites who did not work it. The solution of their economic problem they conceived as possession of all the land.[15]

In retrospect, it appears that in this view the Russian peasants made a basic mistake. The solution to their economic problem was not possession of more land. Given the rate of growth of the peasant population of Russia in the nineteenth century, its natural increase in the course of two generations would have decreased its per capita landholding by 1900, had the peasants gotten all the land in 1861, to the allotment that they actually got in 1861. That was no long-term solution to their economic problem. In fact, the acreage of land farmed per peasant in 1900 was approximately half that of 1861.[16] A solution to the peasants' economic problems depended on the development of modernized agriculture, which is to say upon the development of a scientific, industrial, technological, and social revolution all at once. The peasants' outlook was an illusion, but this illusory conviction of their needs and entitlements left them fundamentally discontent.

The emancipation reform was, then, from the point of view of the peasants, politically satisfactory, economically unsatisfactory. The government could have satisfied the peasants' *wishes* but not their *needs* by giving them all the land, but only at the cost of a revolt on the part of the ruling class, a step no rational government would take. The government had no means at its disposal for devising an emancipation settlement that satisfied the peasants' *needs*. That would have required the dispensation of measures that governments do not have at their disposal. First, a work ethic—in a population whose experience of work had never been rewarding, had never conditioned it to be encouraged to work. Second, birth control. The Orthodox Church did not approve of it, and the industries to produce the means of birth control were not there. They could easily have been built, of course, but in 1995 they are still not there. Third, industrial revolution and scientific, mechanized farming. But that was generations yet in the future.

If the peasants were to be emancipated from the governance of their landlords, then a new means of local government had to be devised, something approximating self-government—but not too much. A decree of 1864 established an institution called a *zemstvo* (land council) at the provincial and the county (*uezd*) levels. The county *zemstvo* was elected by a suffrage weighted in favor of the nobility, and the county *zemstvo* elected the provincial *zemstvo*. The nobility comprised over 40 percent of the county *zemstvo* and nearly three-quarters of the provincial body.

The term self-government here was a bit of a misnomer. The executive arm of the *zemstvo* was comprised of the police, which functioned under the administrative control of the Ministry of the Interior, and the Russian police were not accustomed to taking orders from locally elected officials. The budget of the *zemstvo* was derived from its very limited power to impose a small tax on land. The activity of the *zemstvo*, the expenditure of its budget in particular, shows that it functioned more as an agency of local charity—something like a combination of PTA, United Way, Salvation Army, and county agricultural extension agency—than as government. It spent its meager funds on education, orphanages, hospitals, and, increasingly, the support of scientific agronomists—five thousand of them by 1914.

In a word, the *zemstvo* was more an eleemosynary than a political institution. It was not by any means on that account, however, unimportant. Rather, it developed an importance of a kind that was undoubtedly never foreseen. It attracted particular kinds of social stereotypes from the Russian countryside, modest gentlemen with a restless impulse to be busy in ersatz politics, to social climb, people with a pet commitment to education, to progressive farming, soft-hearted charitable souls who wished to relieve the gargantuan needs of the population around them. It attracted, above all, that peculiar stereotype of nineteenth-century Russian gentleman, the beneficiary until then of serf labor, the "conscience-stricken gentry."

These people soon found that their political prerogative amounted to nearly nothing. That was not their importance. Their importance derived from the fact that they became something like a spontaneously formed class of social workers. They busied themselves in local affairs, and they educated themselves in local sociology and economics. As they did so, they inevitably developed a mentality critical of the status quo and committed to improving reforms. Within a couple of generations, they developed into a well-defined social-political stratum of opinion in the Russian countryside. They were known as the "third element," neither government nor masses, or the "*zemstvo* liberals." In the midst of the agitation that contributed to the Revolution of 1905, they acquired influence in Russia, and in the constitution that the revolution produced, they acquired more. This third element of *zemstvo* liberals began early in the twentieth century to play the role of something like an inexperienced and rather marginal quasi bourgeoisie.

One of the most-needed reforms was judicial. In the time of Nicholas I, criminology was handled largely by the police in a fashion almost purely administrative. It made a notorious mockery of the dispensation of justice. A citizen could be arrested and shipped to a tour of Siberia long enough to amount to a life sentence literally without knowing of what he was accused. Or a person in detention might sit forgotten in a prison cell until no one remembered why he was there.

The judicial reform of 1864 was well conceived. By the criteria that applied in the West, it was simple and good. In brief, it instituted virtually the whole corpus of practices that we know as due process: equality of all before the law, no punishment without a fair trial, independent judiciary, public trials, trial by jury, representation of the accused by counsel. It abrogated that pseudojudicial practice of Nicholas's Third Section—administrative exile and political prophylaxis. Subsequently, in the early 1870s, in the face of the growing provocations of the revolutionary movement, crimes against the state were removed from the jurisdiction of the regular courts and transferred to the higher bodies of government, where they were dealt with in a fashion far more administrative than judicial, a partial return to the system of Nicholas I.

Finally, the military reform was introduced. It stipulated universal conscription, reduced the term of service from twenty-five years to six, and granted partial or total exemption to persons with skills more useful to the nation outside military service than in it. It also instituted primary schooling in the military for all conscripts. This latter measure contributed greatly to an increase of literacy levels, which reached 42 percent of the population by 1914.

These were the Great Reforms. They relinquished some of the formerly near-total initiative of the government in national affairs. They contained elements of liberalism, rather modest elements. They were a demonstration of the government's concern for the well-being of the people, concern about the attitude of the people, and concern for its own survival—in both the domestic and the international perspectives. It seems unavoidable to conclude, however, that they had only an ineffective impact on the more challenging problems of Russia in the nineteenth century.

There was a serious if not intractable dilemma here: if the Great Reforms did not effectively address Russian problems, it is not easy to imagine, even in abstract logic, how those problems might have been effectively addressed. What both monarchy and society needed was economic modernization. The monarchy needed it for the sake of both military power and a less miserable and seditious population, but it would not tolerate, perhaps survive, the changes in the social structure or in the distribution of political power that modernization had brought in Europe. A bourgeoisie and a proletariat that would serve as a new agency of progress would undermine the only old agency of progress that Russia had ever known, the monarchy. The society, on the other hand, was not eager, perhaps not psychologically equipped, to engage in the kind of enterprise from which European modernization had come. Society was doomed to destitution if development did not take place. The structure of monarchical government was doomed by internal forces if modernization did take place and by forces in the brutal arena of international affairs if it did not take place. Damned if they did, damned if they did not.

This dilemma was focused and vastly aggravated by the entrance onto the scene of a newly influential force in Russian society, the intelligentsia and the revolutionary movement that it unleashed. Germinated in the time of Peter I, nourished by Catherine II, and incubated over several generations, it was now ready to assert in national life a role that it would never relinquish.

Nicholas's crackdown on the Decembrists in 1825 had stilled revolutionary stirrings for a time. In the 1840s, the dissident, but subrevolutionary, opposition began to find its voice, although very much *sotto voce*, in reading groups and discussion clubs. When the revolutions of 1848 proceeded across Europe, they frightened Nicholas badly: "Saddle your horses, gentlemen, the revolution is coming." His police struck out and made arrests. Dostoevsky was among them. Sentenced to death by firing squad, he was reprieved while tied to the stake, having already heard the order, "Ready, aim . . ." One of his fellow sufferers went mad on the spot. Dostoevsky spent the next ten years in Siberian exile.

At midcentury, the Crimean War and the Great Reforms introduced a kind of moratorium on active opposition and revolutionary activity. It seemed treasonous to engage in opposition while enemies were at the gate; and during the reforms, many liberals and radicals took a wait-and-see attitude, determined to assess the new measures before deciding upon a course of action.

This moratorium came to an end in 1866. By this time, the opposition was disillusioned with the quality of the reforms. A determined radical, Dmitrii Karakozov, acting alone, approached Alexander II, who was taking a walk near the Winter Palace, and fired a shot at him. The shot missed. It is by no means insignificant that he was apprehended by bystanders, as his angry retort to them indicated: "Fools, I've done this for you." He was delivered to the police, who brought him to the emperor. Alexander asked him, "Why did you do it?" Karakozov replied, "Look at the freedom you gave the people."[17] He was tried and hanged. Thus began the most active phase of revolutionary activities in the nineteenth century.

The most significant force in the nineteenth-century Russian revolutionary movement prior to the coming of Marxism in the 1890s was populism. It took its Russian name, *narodnichestvo*, from the Russian word for the people, *narod*, a word that has no genuine English equivalent. It means the people as an ethnic group, more nation than people, the equivalent of the German word *Volk*. Populism was perhaps not sufficiently developed to deserve the term ideology until the early twentieth century. In the 1860s and 1870s, it designated a vague and naive faith in the peasant, his commune (the *mir*), his folkways, and especially his penchant for grassroots democratic socialism, equal division of the land, equality of opportunity.

As populism gathered its forces, inchoate, awkward, and radical, it infected the student bodies of the major universities. In the winter of 1873–74, almost as if by verbal legerdemain, the students seized on one of those conjuring phrases that Alexander Herzen's opposition launched into the Russian underground from its secure precincts in London: "*V narod*" (to the people). The word spread, and they prepared to respond. The students in the universities had almost necessarily come from classes of people other than the peasants. They came only to a limited degree from that other class prominent in Russian society, the nobility, whose children were educated at home and in the more prestigious universities of Europe. The students were typically a *déclassé* lot. Their parents were from the clergy, the merchant class, the theater crowd, from artists and artisans—in a word from that class of people that Russian often designated *raznochintsy*, people of different rank, or *meshchane*, city dwellers—terms corresponding to the French *déclassé*. They had some cultivation, more pretension, and an enormous amount of ignorant commitment.

In the spring of 1874, they lay down their books to go about a more serious business. "Where are you going?" they were asked, and they answered with real simplicity, "*V narod*, to the people." And so they went, having made clandestine preparations. That is, they acquired and dressed in peasant costume. Unfortunately, if they were going to Ukraine, they often dressed in central Russian or Baltic costume; and vice versa. They did not look like peasants. They looked like impostors. They found the peasants less sensitive to them than the police were. The peasants themselves were not unreceptive to a message of popular justice recognizably like their own. The students told folk tales and gave out "little books" in simple language. The peasants would often nod in agreement. Frequently they said, Oh, yes, if you can get something started down the road, we won't be far behind. But as for staking their own fate on starting it—that was another question. As one of them put it, he simply could not engage in revolt again, because he remembered its previous consequences too well. "One soldier [peasant soldier, of course] stood on one arm, another on the other, and two on my legs. I was beaten, beaten until the earth was soaked with blood. That is how I was flogged. And that did not happen merely once or twice. I was exiled to Siberia, came back, and began all over again; but I can't do it any more."[18] This story was recounted by one of the grand heroines of the adventure, Katerina Breshko-Breshkovskaia, remembered as the little grandmother (*babushka*) of the Russian revolution. Over and over again, the peasants insisted that their plight was the fault of the landlords who were no longer their masters. The tsar they exonerated stubbornly.

This was the "mad summer" of 1874, the "Children's Crusade."[19] Most of the students were eventually rounded up and jailed, and they were at length tried and sentenced. Naive as the experience had been, it taught one unavoidable lesson. Under an autocratic regime lacking in civil liberties, agitation among the public for the formation of a mass movement was not a hopeful mode of carrying on a revolutionary struggle. In other words, the circumstances were stacked against an open and honest form of mass politics; and a democratic form of struggle, which is what the revolutionaries aimed at, was for the time being impossible.

They turned to conspiracy. They tried various forms. In 1875, a revolutionary organizer, Yakov Stefanovich, stumbled on a case of unusually angry peasants in the Chigirin district of Ukraine near Kiev. Several villages there were convinced that they had been denied their fair share of the land apportioned at the time of emancipation. Getting no satisfaction from their complaints to local authorities, they organized a delegation to petition the emperor in person. This delegation was arrested on its way to the capital and returned home under armed guard. One of its number, however, escaped and told upon his return the false story of his interview with the emperor. Alexander II, according to this story, had confessed to being the captive of landholding nobility such that he was helpless to assist his people, and he therefore urged them to seize the land by force.

This story encouraged the villagers, and they refused to sign the documents signifying their acceptance of the land settlement. Soldiers were called in to be quartered on the peasants, and floggings began. Two flogged peasants died, but the others held out stubbornly. At that point, about a hundred of them were arrested and imprisoned in Kiev. Because they received no maintenance, they were released during the daytime to work for their meals. It was thus that Stefanovich made contact with them. He had actually visited one of the insurgent villages, and he represented himself to the others as the official delegate of that village to the emperor. Late in 1875, he left them, promising to return in the spring.

He returned with two gilt-edged documents. The first was an "Imperial Manifesto." In it the emperor declared that the emancipation statute issued to the peasants was a fraud perpetrated by the nobility, that in the real emancipation all the land had been given to the peasants free of charge. The government was, however, powerless to fight the influence of the landlords; therefore, Alexander urged the peasants to take matters into their own hands, organize bands (*druzhiny*), and prepare for an armed uprising. The "Manifesto" coincided perfectly with the folk myth of a good tsar and evil landlords—as well as with the peasants' own wishes and needs.

The second document consisted of the statutes recommended for the organization of the armed bands. A *druzhina* was to consist of twenty-five armed men paying small monthly dues and led by a *starosta* (elder). Betrayal of the organization was punishable by execution. The *starosty* were to elect an *ataman* (commander), who was responsible to a council appointed by the tsar. Both the Manifesto and the statutes bore a large gold seal and the imperial signature. They are believed to have been printed in Geneva.

The impression that these documents made may be easily imagined. "*Druzhiny* sprang up like mushrooms." By the middle of 1877, about a thousand men had been subscribed. The *ataman* embezzled the funds collected, and eventually one of the faithful made indiscreet comments—while under the influence of *horilka*, Ukrainian vodka—that led to arrests and dissolution.[20]

The myth of the "little father tsar"—what has previously been called here naive monarchism or "rebellion in the name of the tsar"—was an open invitation to the use of fraud in the revolutionary struggle. It had already been prominent earlier in the Decembrist Revolt. It would be seen again, and more decisively.

Growing frustration drove the revolutionaries more and more to desperate, systematic terror. Sergei Kravchinskii, alias Stepniak, stabbed to death General Mezentsev, chief of the Third Section (police) in the middle of Moscow in broad daylight. A more sensational episode illustrated the observation that "our women are crueler than we men." The St. Petersburg chief of police, General Trepov, irritated at the behavior of a prisoner, ordered him flogged. The order was contrary to the rules, but the flogging was carried out. Vera Zasulich decided to avenge the victim. She went one morning to Trepov's office as he was receiving petitioners and shot him at close range. He was seriously but not fatally wounded. She threw down her pistol and gave herself up at once. Her attorney at the trial turned the proceeding against Trepov. Though she pled guilty, the jury acquitted her! When Alexander learned of it, he gave orders for her rearrest, but she was surrounded and hidden by friends until she escaped abroad.

The most prominent populist organization of these years, 1876–79, was Land and Liberty. It was small in numbers—estimated membership, two hundred—and in 1879 it split in disagreement over the policy of terror and assassination. The terrorist wing now organized The People's Will. The other wing largely went abroad to Geneva and evolved, under the tutelage of Georgii Plekhanov, into the party of Marxism in Russia. It was not to be important until the 1890s.

The People's Will, on the other hand, set out to make its mark at once. Its long-range objective was to bludgeon the government into the grant of a constitution. Its immediate objective was the life of Alexander II.[21] The Executive Committee of The People's Will passed a death sentence on Alexander II on or about the anniversary of his coronation, 26 August 1879.

The first attempt was a design to dynamite Alexander's train as he returned around the middle of November to the capital from the Livadia Palace at Yalta in the Crimea. Andrei Zheliabov, the most dynamic and forceful personality in The People's Will, took charge of the plan. Early in October, he appeared in the town of Zaporozhe in Ukraine, where the train track passed along the top of an embankment seventy-five feet high. He represented himself as a merchant who intended to set up a tannery in the town. He played the part admirably and hired fellow revolutionaries to assist him.

Dynamite was a new phenomenon in 1879. It had been invented in 1866 by Alfred Nobel, a Swedish chemist who had studied in St. Petersburg. Nobel also helped to develop the world's first great oilfield at Baku in the Russian Caucasus, and he subsequently developed smokeless gunpowder. It was his nagging pacifist's conscience, concern about the future uses of his inventions, that led him to establish the Nobel prizes at his death in Italy in 1896.

The experiments leading to the invention of dynamite had resulted in several unintended explosions and lost lives. The revolutionaries had first imported a sample of the explosive from Switzerland, but it proved impossible to continue to do so. At that point, they decided to manufacture their own. Their designated chemist was Nikolai Kibalchich. He supplied Zheliabov with the materials, including electrical detonators, for the bomb under the train track and taught him to assemble them.

The track was patrolled regularly by watchmen, and the revolutionaries had to work in the intervals between patrols. They were safe from discovery only at night. Zheliabov was at this time suffering from night blindness and had to be led by the hand to the site of the bomb, but he insisted on participating in the work. They especially worried about the coming of snow, as it would disclose their enterprise in footprints. One night they were almost discovered by one of the inspectors. Their nerves began to fray. Zheliabov woke one night screaming "Hide the wire! Hide the wire!"

The revolutionaries had their own spies in the government. They knew that the imperial train was scheduled to pass Zaporozhe on 18 November. They completed their preparations the day before. As the train reached the critical part of the track, Zheliabov closed the circuit. Nothing happened. They subsequently examined their apparatus and could find nothing wrong. They were unable to recover the bomb.

They had laid a back-up plan, however, farther north. In a remote southern Moscow suburb Aleksandr Mikhailov and his putative wife,

Sofiia Perovskaia—she was Zheliabov's lover—had bought a house near the train tracks. They moved in during the last week of September. As they began excavating a tunnel under the tracks, they explained to the neighbors that they were constructing an ice cellar. The neighbors were curious, but the new proprietors played the part of tradespeople well enough. There were icons and small talk. In the event of discovery by the police, Perovskaia was to shoot two bottles of nitroglycerin stored under a bed. They would not be taken alive.

Problems accumulated. Damp fall weather covered the floor of the tunnel with water. A fire in the neighboring house was extinguished before it reached their own. Those working in the tunnel sometimes fainted for lack of air. They were in constant danger of cave-ins. One of them carried poison. Especially for Mikhailov, hardship simply stimulated exaltation.

They fell behind schedule, and so they bought equipment. In order to do so, they had to mortgage the house, which was risky, as it entailed an inspection by a police officer. Finally, all was as ready as practicable. Eighty pounds of dynamite were laid and wired.

The tsar's security arrangements were naturally growing more complex. He traveled in a retinue of several trains and changed trains unexpectedly. The conspirators received a telegram from one of their spies informing them that the tsar was in the fourth car of the second train. At the precise moment, the bomb was set off. It severed the locomotive from the cars following. Several cars were derailed. Crimean produce was strewn about. No one was hurt. Alexander had been in the first train.

The revolutionary newspaper *Narodnaia volia* (People's Will) proclaimed: "Only if he were to renounce his power and hand it over to a freely elected Constituent Assembly . . . would we leave him in peace and forgive his crimes. Until that time—war, implacable war, to the last drop of our blood!"

Stepan Khalturin got a job as a mechanic on the staff at the Winter Palace. He had sleeping quarters in the basement. Originally he had planned to attack the tsar at the first sight of him. Opportunity knocked when Khalturin found himself unexpectedly alone and behind Alexander one day with a hammer in his hand. His resolve failed him. He began to bring dynamite into his sleeping quarters. His objective was the dining room, two floors above the basement. Incredibly, his cache of explosive was not discovered, though he stored it in a clothes chest.

When he could tolerate the fumes and the headaches that they gave him no longer, he decided to set it off. He chose 6:30 in the evening, the imperial dinner hour, 5 February 1880. The blast of a hundred pounds of dynamite killed eleven people and injured fifty-six. The dining room was scarcely damaged, and the tsar was at the time in another part of the building to greet the Grand Duke of Hesse and his son Alexander, Prince of Bulgaria.

A case of nerves afflicted Alexander, his family, the government, and the capital. If Alexander went to the opera, the fear of terror discouraged attendance. Alexander turned to a new minister of the interior, Count Mikhail Loris-Melikov, who instituted the "dictatorship of the heart." He approached dissent mercifully and made concessions. Censorship was bridled. There were a few political amnesties. The reactionary minister of education was dismissed. On 17 February 1881, Alexander signed an order instituting an imperial consultative council elected by *zemstva*, something of a symbolic turning point. Alexander himself confessed, "I do not hide from myself the fact that it is the first step toward a constitution."

In the meantime, a lull occurred in terrorist activity. It gave the impression that the program of Loris-Melikov was achieving the desired results. It was not. Several terrorist operations had simply gone awry without results, and the police had happened upon a godsend of information that they used to good effect. Grigorii Goldenberg, the assassin of the governor-general of Kharkov, was found in Odessa in November 1879 with incriminating evidence in his possession. Under interrogation, he would give no information whatever, but he talked freely to his cellmate, a police plant. Goldenberg was neither clever nor stable. Rumors of the Loris-Melikov "constitution" reached him. His police handlers encouraged him to think that they were the persons recommending such measures, that full political concessions would follow. Loris-Melikov himself twice visited Goldenberg in his cell. He was told that the revolutionaries would have to compromise with the government in order to make the reforms feasible. Goldenberg soon began to see the political salvation of Russia a new way, not without the prompting of the police.

At this point, in February–March 1880, Goldenberg made a full confession and began giving all the information in his possession. Nikolai Kletochnikov, the revolutionaries' agent among the police, was able to keep them apprised of the information given and thus to control some of the damage, but the episode had serious consequences. When Goldenberg realized what he had done, he wrote a hysterical confession, begging forgiveness, and managed to hang himself with a torn towel.

The hardy remnant carried on. They had observed that the emperor often drove along Malaia Sadovaia Street to review a retinue of soldiers on Sundays. In December 1880, they rented a cheese shop on this route and began to tunnel under the street. All went well until they encountered a large wooden pipe. They cut it. It was a sewer and filled the tunnel with stench. They continued. By late February 1881, they had reached the middle of the street and began to place the dynamite. In the meantime, they developed two backup plans. According to the first, Kibalchich, the chemist, would supply four attackers with bombs suitable to throw by hand. According to the second, Zheliabov himself would attack the emperor with pistol and dagger.

The police, however, were making good use of the testimony of Goldenberg. They picked up Kletochnikov, the revolutionary spy in the police office. That was a heavy blow, but worse followed. On 27 February, they arrested Zheliabov. About the same time, the police inspected the cheese shop. Loose dirt lay in covered boxes under a sofa. It would have been inexplicable. The search must have been very perfunctory: nothing was discovered.

These events prompted the party to hasten their attempt before they were wiped out. They worked frantically all night on 28 February to be ready the next day, 1 March. The dynamite was placed, and Kibalchich completed the four portable bombs. In Zheliabov's absence, Perovskaia, his love, took charge. The police dragnet had reduced the organization to a spare nucleus, thinning it of personnel and experience. The four bomb-throwers ranged from nineteen to twenty-six years of age.

The arrest of Zheliabov actually played into the hands of the plotters. The news of it had lifted Alexander's spirits immeasurably. Loris-Melikov begged him not to leave the palace, but Alexander decided to go. He was driven in a light carriage. Although he avoided the cheese shop on Malaia Sadovaia Street, on his way back to the Winter Palace he encountered Nikolai Rysakov and his bomb. The police had not noticed suspicious parcels under the arms of several pedestrians. Rysakov approached the carriage and threw the bomb. Several bystanders were hurt. Alexander stopped his carriage, got out to examine the wounded, and paid no attention as his security guard urged him to get into one of the carriages and off the street. As Alexander turned to go back to his own damaged carriage, Ignatii Grinevitskii approached within two or three steps of him and threw his bomb between the two of them. It severely wounded both on the lower legs and several other bystanders as well. It was about 2:20 or 2:25 in the afternoon. Alexander was driven to the Winter Palace, bleeding freely. He died about 3:40. Grinevitskii died at 10:30 that night.

Within a few days all the participants in the assassination were in custody. Rysakov confessed and informed on his colleagues. Zheliabov and Perovskaia confessed unreservedly and proudly. As they went to trial, Russia's most distinguished philosopher, Vladimir Soloviev, made a public appeal that mercy be shown the defendants. Leo Tolstoy made the same appeal in a letter to Alexander III. Of the six principals, all but one pregnant woman were sentenced to be hanged.

In European Russia, there was only one executioner, a man named Frolov. When he was taken ill before an execution once, the government advertised in the army and the police for another. There were no takers—fifty years later, there were thousands and tens of thousands. On 3 April 1881, the five condemned were led to the scaffold. Frolov was drunk and had not prepared adequately. Kibalchich was first to be hanged. Mikhailov, large and heavy, was second. When he had been hanging about a minute, the noose slipped, and he fell to the floor. The crowd groaned. Frolov remade the noose, and Mikhailov climbed the platform again. When he had been hanging for about a minute and a half, the noose slipped again, and he fell again. This time, the crowd, angry now, tried to fight past the police cordon to reach the scaffold. Mikhailov was this time too weak to stand again, and he was replaced in the noose by Frolov's assistants. He had been hanging this time about three minutes when his weight was rather obviously about to pull the metal ring to which the rope was tied free of the crossbeam overhead. Frolov climbed a ladder and attached a second rope. It held. Perovskaia was third. Zheliabov was also heavy, and Frolov took precautions this time by doubling the knot in the noose. This procedure, however, delayed strangulation and prolonged convulsions. The military doctor expressed his disgust. Frolov cursed him. Rysakov was last. Having witnessed the fate of all the others, he had to be forced.

Both the assassination plot and the revolutionary movement more generally were the work of that radical intelligentsia, the unwitting creation of Peter I's and Catherine II's educational reforms, that was typically to find itself as alienated from the people, the *narod*, as from the government. In the fall of 1879 and the spring of 1880, the government had felt under siege. From the summer of 1880 through the arrest of Zheliabov, the revolutionaries had had little success, and the police had had much. The government felt that matters were improving. When the assassination occurred, panic seized it. Alexander III was more conservative by a good deal than his father. Yet even he hesitated before the demonstrable power of the revolutionary movement and the assumption, greatly assisted by the propaganda of The People's Will, that there was an understanding between the populists and the people. In the course of March and April, it became apparent that the peasants, however hostile they were to the landlords and the government, were loyal to the tsar. At that point, Alexander III found his confidence and embarked on the line of policy that he preferred.[22] The presumption of The People's Will had been a tragic mistake: the assassination of the tsar was not the will of the people at all.

The Russian revolutionary movement was active with transient interruptions from 1815 to 1917. Sometimes it was carried on by a tiny coterie of true believers, as in 1881, sometimes by a great mass of the violently discontented, as in 1917. If we look for the sources of dissatisfaction, three of them are altogether obvious: the nature of the government, the condition of the economy, and the structure and mentality of Russian society.

Probably the most serious problem of the Russian government was that it had lost a comfortable conception of its role. Peter I had such a conception, even if it was a misconception, and he did not hesitate to act on it. Catherine II and Alexander I had such conceptions, even if they were frustrated of implementing them. From the time of the French Revolution, however, the European conception of progressive despotism had been discredited in Russia. Yet by this time it had served as the standard tradition of Russian government for the past one hundred years. The older model of seventeenth-century Russian government was not plausible or appropriate in the dynamic world environment of the nineteenth century, and the governments of Alexander I and Nicholas I seemed at a loss to find any alternative other than the negation of the eighteenth-century tradition. In other words, conservative government became sterile government, to a remarkable extent deliberately so. The watchword of Nicholas's government was "Orthodoxy, Autocracy, Nationality." At least as early as 1826, the government of Nicholas I began to show clear signs of fearing the development of a proletariat in Russia.[23] Yet by the end of the century, modernization, and therefore the power and consideration of Russia in the world, would depend on an industrial class of citizens.

From the time of the French Revolution and the Decembrist Revolt, the impression had steadily gained ground among the intelligentsia that Russian government was both unjust and obsolete. While the government for obvious reasons did not agree with this opinion, it is hard to escape the impression that it was *afraid* that it was true. The great powers of Europe, countries boasting power and prestige in international affairs and a respectable standard of living at home, exemplified one or more of the categories of modern European politics: they were constitutional, liberal, republican, democratic. And socialism was already a powerful contender for the allegiance of the urban masses.

The revolutionary movement illustrates that the government had provoked the opposition of a substantial part of the intelligentsia, although by no means all of it supported the degree of radicalism and violence that The People's Will personified. The tsarist government had betrayed the trust of the conservative nobility in the act of emancipation, and its own post-Reform conservative rigidity increasingly cost it the allegiance of the *zemstvo* liberals. Ironically, perhaps the class of Russians most loyal to the tsar was the peasantry, convinced as it still was—as evidenced by the massive disillusionment of the populists who went to the people to persuade them—that it was only the corrupt nobility and bureaucracy that were responsible for the sad plight of the people. And yet the tsar and his government clearly had not trusted the peasants since the time when they declared for the fraudulent Peter III of the Pugachev Rebellion. Thus the poor beleaguered government was virtually without a constituency, and therefore its chief rationale had become to serve itself. Trusting none of its subjects, it could not dispense with those subjects, and thus it grew increasingly confused about the question how its interests—chiefly self-preservation—were served.

Its problems were compounded by its character. The qualities of the government were very ambivalent. It had come increasingly in the nineteenth century to be staffed by trained and educated professional civil servants. From the Speranskii civil-service reform of 1809, no one was admitted to rank eight of the Table of Ranks without a university degree or the passing of an examination demonstrating commensurate education. The competence, the education, at least the literacy, of the late nineteenth-century civil service was much higher than that of its seventeenth- and eighteenth-century predecessors.[24] The roads to power and influence in this hierarchical elite lay through superior birth and superior education in the most privileged schools, the *Corps des pages* and the schools of law of Moscow and St. Petersburg universities. By midcentury, Russian government had a quarter as many civil servants per capita as did the governments of France and England. Yet it remained a dormant and somnolent giant. The affairs of government proceeded through the corridors of the civil service at a glacial pace. The chief qualities valued in a civil servant were obeisance to the rules, respect for superiors, and civility that bordered on servility.[25] The system seems to have sustained itself by a practice of something like Confucian co-optation.

Yet among all the drones and the sycophants were undeniably brilliant people. One student of this elite has characterized it virtually rhapsodically, reminding us that the class of Russians from which it came "made a contribution to world culture incomparably greater than any of its European equivalents": Pushkin, Lermontov, Turgenev, Tiutchev, Tolstoy, Mussorgsky, Borodin, Rimsky-Korsakov, Rachmaninoff.[26] If only it had been a theater rather than a government! In any event, it contained talented people who worked conscientiously for the betterment of the regime and of Russia.

The government was not only divided from the people. It was also divided against itself, and not only between drones and reformers. From the time of the Russian Enlightenment, two ideas asserted themselves overtly or covertly against the tradition that the tsar's will alone defined the law of the land. These were the ideas of government by law, the *Rechtsstaat*, and government by the constitutional means of popular consultation and/or consent. The idea of constitutional government was more common among the intelligentsia, and the idea of the *Rechtsstaat* was widespread among civil servants.

The upper echelon of civil servants divided into two political camps. One of them was composed of a strikingly expanded corps of trained lawyers, a recent phenomenon, and the growing commitment among them to government by legal norms.[27] Of course, this was in itself no small metamorphosis in Russian politics. By the age of the Great Reforms, the Ministry of Justice was dominated by such people, and their influence in the judiciary reform of 1864 was apparent. It was only natural that their influence caused friction in the government. The new legal profession "impugned the autocrat's claim to be the source and protector of legality." These institutionalists hoped through adherence to stringent legal norms to encourage a government of law and regular political procedure. The other camp, the traditionalists, believed exclusively in the tsar's own conventionally unlimited autocratic power.[28] Alexander II had shown a considerable disposition to defer to the legalists, but his successors, the last two tsars, Alexander III and Nicholas II, rejected their claims.[29]

The civil servants who have been designated as enlightened prepared the reforms of the 1860s. In support of those reforms they mobilized forces that they themselves termed *glasnost* and *zakonnost* (legality) against the forces of *proizvol* (arbitrariness). It must be emphasized that they mobilized these forces *inside the government*, for, in the best tradition of Alexander I's Secret Committee, they were convinced that reform and the future were safe only if they were protected from the force of public opinion—especially the opinion of the serf-owners on the eve of emancipation. For the sake, then, of implementing a measure whose impact was liberal, it was necessary to resort to the most illiberal concentration of arbitrary autocratic power. In this fashion the outlook of enlightened despotism crept silently and half-heartedly back into Russian government.[30]

Members of the imperial family took sides in these conflicts. The Grand Duchess Elena Pavlovna and Grand Duke Konstantin Nikolaevich operated veritable political lobbies. He was an influential publisher and acting Minister of the Navy. She made a conscious effort to influence the reforms, actually convoking conferences of civil servants and other experts who evolved projects of emancipation that were forwarded to the tsar.[31]

Alexander II considered two proposals for a form of institutionalized consultation with elected representatives of the people. The first of these was drawn up by Minister of the Interior P.A. Valuev (1863). Valuev observed the considerable discussion of the advisability of summoning a *zemskii sobor* (assembly of the land), an institution defunct since the seventeenth century, and he suggested that the Russian masses had demonstrated loyalty to the tsar superior to that of the nobility. He called attention to the currency of the idea that "in all

European countries various estates are given some degree of participation in the business of legislation or general administration of the state; and if this is so everywhere, then it should also be the case with us." He proposed that the Council of State, a large consultative assembly of more than two hundred persons appointed by the emperor to help prepare legislation, be expanded to include a group of representatives elected by the *zemstva*.[32] This proposal apparently elicited no response.

Valuev's proposal was repeated in a more cautious form by Minister of the Interior M.T. Loris-Melikov in January 1881. As he wrote, in Russia "it is impossible to organize popular representation in imitation of Western patterns; not only are these alien to the Russian people, but they even could shake its basic political outlook and introduce troubles whose consequences are difficult to foresee. Similarly, the proposal put forth by some adherents of ancient institutions of the Russian state, of establishing a *Zemskaia Duma* [Parliament] or a *Zemskii Sobor* seems to me far from opportune."

Loris-Melikov's proposal was written in so cautious a fashion as to make it opaque and evasive. It seems that he favored convoking commissions like those that wrote the emancipation reform of 1861, the personnel to be both appointed by the sovereign and elected by *zemstva*. The business of the commissions was to be "the preliminary elaboration of the most important questions touching on the life of the nation" in, of course, a strictly *consultative* fashion. This is the document of which Alexander II said that he did not hide it from himself that he had thereby embarked on a course leading to constitutionalism. It was repudiated by Alexander III, who wrote on it: "Thank God that this criminal and hasty step toward constitution [*sic*] was not taken, and that this whole fantastic project was rejected."[33]

The last two emperors, Alexander III (1881–94) and Nicholas II (1894–1917), repudiated both the idea of the institutionalization of legality in government and the idea of regular consultation with public opinion. Nicholas's accession to the throne was accompanied by rumors of constitutional reform, but in fact his attitude toward a constitution was the same as that of his father. As he received a delegation of *zemstvo* liberals known to harbor such hopes, he said bluntly that ideas of a constitution were "senseless dreams." He was to find his commitment in this question beyond his strength.

The economy of Russia was as serious a problem as was the government. The backwardness of the Russian economy is legendary, and it has long been the subject of extensive explanation. The invidious comparison is, of course, with Europe. In fact, the backwardness of the Russian economy is not nearly so remarkable in the world at large as is the forwardness of the European economy.[34] First we must try to understand "the European miracle."[35]

Among the objective factors favoring Europe are the geophysical. Europe has historically experienced a tiny proportion of the world's earthquakes and volcanic eruptions. The European climate is favorable. It is subject neither to the monsoons of India nor to the famines of China—some province of China experienced famine every year from 108 B.C.E. to 1911 C.E.[36] Europe has been comparatively free of the rampant epidemics and epizootics of Asia that are due in part to the use of human sewage for fertilizer, in part to the passage of parasites from animals to men in the conditions of flooded Asian agriculture. Moreover, the public works of India and China were much grander in scale than those of Europe in premodern times, and hence such natural disasters as war and fire made a more limited impact in Europe.

Political and social factors also favored Europe. The absence of nation-states in medieval Europe, the presence there of multiple small political units, limited the damage done by political misfortunes. Caste in India discouraged mobility and innovation more rigidly than the European society of orders did, especially after the birth of that dynamic class not foreseen in the medieval conception, the bourgeoisie. Asia seems to have dealt with Malthus's "positive checks on population"—famine, plague, war—by prolific breeding; Europe, by later marriage and more selective breeding.

Europe exploited invention more effectively. According to Francis Bacon, the three greatest inventions of man were the compass, gunpowder, and printing. All were Chinese in origin; all were European in effective exploitation. And the great explorations were European. They led to what is known as "ghost acreage," that is, the maize, potatoes, and codfish of the New World; and subsequently they led to the dynamism of worldwide seaborne commerce.

How much of this did Russia share? Russia missed most of the liabilities of Asia, though not the Mongols, but missed the assets of Europe as well. As we have seen, in early modern times the Russians struggled with a northerly forested environment, largely landlocked. The plagues of Asia and the inventions of Asia had to cross territory once Kievan before arriving in Europe, but by that time the Russians had moved north. On the other hand, a crude approximation of a caste system prevailed in Russia, a law preempting the movement of the enserfed population, to a large extent preempting enterprise and preempting hope; and the seaborne opportunities (ghost acreage) of Europe were denied the Russians by their geography.

One of the obvious differences between the Russian economy and the European economy of late medieval and early modern times was the extent to which Russian absolutism reached into and influenced economic mechanisms, to some extent paralyzing them. We have seen how the travelers from Europe in the sixteenth and seventeenth centuries found that the prince of Russia disposed with impunity of the life and property of his subjects. One of the most important reasons for the failure of capitalist development in early modern Russia was that the overdeveloped state usurped much or most of the spectrum of economic activity that in other countries fell within the private sphere.[37] Overdeveloped state, underdeveloped economy. The merchants of seventeenth-century Russia pursued their business in an unusually insecure economic environment. Those who were prominent were often co-opted by the state to serve it in various ways, as factors in the fur trade, as collectors of tariffs in Arkhangelsk, Russia's leading port in the trade with Europe before Peter's conquests on the Baltic. They were known as *gosti* (guests). Just as suddenly and arbitrarily, however, they might find themselves the victims of a state treasury crisis. They were subject to extraordinarily capricious measures of taxation extending not only to their income but to their capital as well.[38] In the seventeenth century, only one in four prominent *gosti* families survived with their fortunes intact more than a single generation; only one in fifteen survived more than two.

Peter I apparently preferred, in his quest for rationality, to abolish so impulsive a system of economic administration. He naturally embraced the European theory of mercantilism.[39] Attaching traditional Russian customs of statecraft to European ideas of economics, he commanded his lieutenants to found factories, and he supplied the labor by attaching peasant workers to an industry rather than to land. There was a great spurt of productivity. And then there was a contraction. This is a pattern representative of Russian economics. It follows a comprehensible rule: the greater the perceived need to achieve economic advance quickly, the greater the need to apply the power of the state to achieve it; and the more the power of the state is used to force it, the more is the economic future of the country compromised.[40] In brief, the more the people are forced by the instruments of political economy, the less they learn about the forms of enterprise that benefit them. This pattern becomes a nearly constant Russian conundrum.

Catherine II failed to create a Russian bourgeoisie by fiat. When she and her successors recoiled from the political progeny of bourgeois politics, as exhibited in the bloody reprisals of the French Revolution, when they entered into that self-consciously conservative phase of the 1790s, they simply condemned Russia to be unprepared for the Crimean War. The reformers of the succeeding generation sought progress, and it had to be in part economic.

The most serious part of the economic problem of Russia in the nineteenth century was the combination of two factors: relative economic stagnation and rapid population growth. The Russian population grew from 36,000,000 in 1796 to perhaps 165,000,000 in 1914, and no one believed that economic modernization was matching the pace of population growth. At the end of the nineteenth century, there was a profound consciousness of backwardness and an urgent sense that something must be done about it. A growing sense of alarm was evident on two accounts: the population lived in desperate misery, and economic backwardness was diminishing Russian political influence in the international arena.

Russian industrial output nearly doubled from emancipation to the end of the century, but Russia still ranked lower in the international scale of industrial output in 1910 than in 1861.[41] From 1885 to 1913, the economy grew at a rate of 3.25 percent a year and a rate of 1.7 percent per capita per year.[42] Grain production per unit of land was improving relatively rapidly: from an index figure of 75 in 1860 to 130 in 1911. Still, per capita production of grain declined throughout European Russia between emancipation and the First World War.[43] Per capita peasant income, on the other hand, was clearly rising at the end of the century.[44] According to some findings, it rose from 71 rubles per person in 1861 to 119 per person in 1913.[45] On the other hand, there was crop failure and famine in Russia in 1880, 1885, 1891, 1897, 1898, and 1901. The repetition of famine in a country is a sure sign of its marginal economic condition. Descriptions of the economic plight of the Russian peasants in the tracts of the revolutionaries and in the reports of the emperor's loyal ministers exhibit remarkable agreement about the peasants' desperate condition.[46]

If some of the statistical abstractions show the population improving its condition, others register the misery to which its continuing disposition to revolt also testifies. Around 1910, infant mortality in Russia was 245 per thousand live births, and in some areas it was over 400. At the turn of the century, the population of the empire was 72 percent illiterate. Among the elderly, the rural population, and females, illiteracy was higher, though in the cities it was much lower, and in the Baltic provinces it fell to 22 percent.[47]

The most recent research supports conclusions of cautious optimism. According to Paul Gregory, during approximately the last two decades of the nineteenth century, agricultural output grew (2.55 percent per annum) at twice the rate of population growth (1.3 percent per annum). "In fact, on an economywide basis, Russian agriculture was growing per capita, peasant living standards and real wages were rising, and exports were booming."[48]

Perhaps it is fair to conclude, however cautiously, that the trend of economic developments was upward, that things were getting better, more hopeful. If so, that conclusion depends upon objective data. Subjectively, such a conclusion must depend upon what the people who were experiencing it thought, and that is what we need to know now.

In nineteenth-century Russia, the nation produced for the first time a great literature. It is our most valuable compendium of public attitudes, and it tells us graphically, if unscientifically, what the people thought of the government, of the economy, and of themselves. It informs us, in addition, of another Russian problem: the peculiarly Russian social structure and the singular attitudes of the various classes threatened to deadlock movement in either of the two increasingly critical enterprises of reform or revolution.

❖ 5 ❖

Culture, Character, Psyche:
A Literary Excursion

Who keeps the tavern and encourages drunkenness? The peasant. Who embezzles and drinks up the funds [of] the community, the schools, the church? The peasant. Who steals from his neighbours, sets fire to their property, bears false witness at court for a bottle of vodka? . . . The peasant.

Chekhov, "Peasants"

These good-humored [nobility] looked upon life as . . . an idyll of peace and inactivity.

Goncharov, *Oblomov*

In the "cultured" language of our dear country, employed by former owners of serfs, the word "industrialist" has somehow become a synonym for "swindler," "bloodsucker," "exploiter," and other, no less flattering, definitions.

An industrialist

Wrong a [person] . . . , deny him all redress, exile him . . . if he complains, gag him if he cries out, strike him in the face if he struggles, and at last he will stab and throw bombs.

George Kennan, *Siberia and the Exile System*

Among the ingredients of Russian revolution were the ingredients of Russian society, its culture, character, and psyche. Taking the measure of another culture is an unavoidably tricky business. It is subject to all kinds of cultural bias on the part of the observer.

Fortunately, about the middle of the nineteenth century Russian society itself comes to our rescue on this point. In the course of the nineteenth century, for the first time in the history of Russia, the processes of education nourished a scale of literacy sufficient to generate a mass of self-expression. Russian literature of the nineteenth century is one of the glories of Russian culture. It would be an ornament in any civilization. In this golden age of Russian literature, the Russians began to tell us about themselves, and no people has ever been more critically concerned to describe and define what they were than the Russians of that time.

Russian literature was one of the two most typical forms of the nation's self-expression. The other was its religion. The fullness of Russian religious expression preceded the eighteenth century and the increasingly secularizing spirit of the enlightened government of Peter I and Catherine II. At that time, as we previously observed, Russian religious attitudes were characterized by elements of resignation, mysticism, submissiveness, and unworldliness. It is only natural that the literati of nineteenth-century Russia express quite different attitudes.

Of course literacy was not uniformly distributed among all categories of Russian society. The class whose numbers were dominant in Russia, the peasantry, was itself largely illiterate. In some respects—not in all, as we shall see—this was the most important class. Unfortunately, the peasants did not leave us their memoirs, diaries, and correspondence. The one form of peasant self-expression that eventually became literary was folklore. In the nineteenth century A.N. Afanasiev (1826–1871), among others, collected Russian folk tales of a volume and importance comparable to those collected by his contemporaries, the brothers Grimm, in Germany.

Two standard characters in Russian fairy tales (*skazki*) are Ivan Tsarevich (Ivan the Heir) and Ivanushka Durachok (Little Ivan the Little Fool). They appear like two avatars of the same personality. The single asset of Ivanushka Durachok is his foolishness; but in the world of Russian fantasy, as in the philosophy of the Slavophiles, the last shall be first, and foolishness is the invariable elixir of victory for Ivanushka Durachok: providence always rallies to his cause. Dmitrii Likhachev observes that the most affectionate expression of the Russian people is "ah, my silly one," or "ah, my little fool you" (*akh, ty moi glupenkii, akh ty moi durachok*). "And the fool in the fairy tale turns out to be wiser than the wisest and more fortunate than the most successful. . . . The Russian people . . . loves its fools. The Russian people loves the fools not because they are foolish, but because they are wise."[1]

Ivan Tsarevich embarks on what Joseph Campbell calls a quest, and he is assisted by a variety of magical sponsors. They give him wise advice, and he ignores it. Thus he gets ever deeper into trouble. But his good fairies come constantly to his rescue, and so his history exemplifies the triumph of folly, frivolousness, and bad judgment. The moral of these stories would seem to be that there is none. They exemplify rather a depressingly capricious fate. They do not contain any recognizable conception of responsibility. We look in vain for a reliable relationship of cause and effect. Most significantly, we do not find the familiar idea that, in order to achieve good results, it is necessary to make good efforts. Here is no nomothetic vision of rational men but a society of antinomian whim and anomie.[2] If this aspect of the portrait of the Russian nation is not perfectly identical to that which we find in religious self-expression, it is remarkably compatible.

Apart from their folklore, if we look for depictions of the contemporary reality of Russian peasant life, we must approach it through observers from other classes or observers from other countries. Still, those who observed them and wrote of them are among the most revered names in world literature.

At midcentury, the peasants were so little known as to be called the "dark people" (*temnye liudi*). In what sense were they dark? They were dark because they were obscure; that is, they were an unknown quantity. They were dark because they were ignorant. And they were dark because—as the semantics of the Russian term unmistakably connote—they were evil. That is, they were drunken, lazy, unreliable; yet if aroused, they were capable of great bouts of violent destruction. They were capable of innumerable diminutive Pugachev uprisings. As Pushkin said of this phenomenon, deliver us from a Russian peasant revolt, savage and destructive. In Russian peasant speech itself, the expression *temnye sily*, literally dark forces, is better translated as forces of evil.

Yet about this time, a brilliant new view of them suddenly broke onto the scene. Ivan Turgenev (1818–1883) published in 1852 his *Sportsman's Sketches* (Zapiski okhotnika, literally *Notes of a Hunter*), and for the first time the Russian public found plausible portraits of peasant personalities done with consummate art by someone who obviously knew them intimately.

Here we find Khor and Kalinich. The author was the guest and the hunting companion of a modest landowner, Mr. Polutykin.[3] They called on various of Polutykin's serfs for transport, for shelter, and for meals. The first was Khor, who lived in a hut apart, outside the village of the other peasants.

"Why," [the author asked], "does your Khor live separately from your other peasants?"

"I'll tell you: because he is the clever one among them. About twenty-five years ago his hut got burnt down; so up he comes to my late father and says: 'Nikolai Kuzmich, please may I settle on your land, in the forest beside the marsh? I'll pay you good rent. . . . But you, sir, Nikolai Kuzmich, please don't give me any work to do, but fix any rent you like.' "

"And he's done well out of it?"

"He has. Now he pays me a hundred roubles rent. . . . I have said to him several times: 'Buy your own freedom, Khor, do!' But he, the crafty brute, assures me that he could not manage it; that he has got no money . . . As if he expected me to believe him!"

Next day, as they drove through the peasant village, Mr. Polutykin called on another serf: "Kalinich!"

"Coming, sir, coming," replied a voice from the yard; "I'm just tying my shoe."

Kalinich was the constant companion of his master. Without him Mr. Polutykin did not move. Kalinich carried the game bag, the gun, fetched water, picked berries, brought the carriage, built shelters. He was a person of the "gayest and gentlest character imaginable . . . his attitude to his master was one of fatherly supervision."

One day when Mr. Polutykin had business in town—his neighbor had plowed some of Polutykin's land and beaten one of his peasant women—the author went shooting alone. Toward evening, he decided to pay a call on Khor. They sat down to eat.

"Tell me, Khor, why don't you buy your freedom from the master?"

"And why should I buy it? As things are, I know the master and I know the rent he wants. . . . He is a good master, too. . . . And what am I to buy it with, sir?"

"Well, don't you do a bit of trading?"

"I trade in a small way, with oil and tar. . . . Now, sir, would you like me to harness the cart?" Khor was changing the subject, avoiding the inquiry.

"No, . . . if I may, I'll spend the night here in your hay-shed."

"You'll be welcome . . . I'll tell the women to spread a sheet for you and to put out a pillow. Hey, there, women! . . . Come here! . . . Fedya [his son], you go with them. Women are such fools."

The next three days the author passed in and around Khor's place. Kalinich came, bringing Khor a basket of strawberries.

Khor was a positive, practical fellow, an administrator, a rationalist. Kalinich, on the other hand, belonged to the category of idealists, romantics, enthusiasts and dreamers. Khor understood reality, that is to say, he knew how to get on in the world, how to put money aside, and keep on good terms with the master and the other powers that be; Kalinich went about in plaited shoes and lived from hand to mouth. Khor was the father of a large, submissive and united family; Kalinich had once had a wife, of whom he had been afraid, but never any children. Khor saw right through Mr. Polutykin; Kalinich, on the other hand, idolized him. Khor loved Kalinich and gave him his protection; Kalinich loved and revered Khor. . . . But Kalinich was endowed with advantages that even Khor allowed him; for instance, he knew spells to cure fear, frenzy or bleeding; he could drive out worms; his bees did well, he had the right touch with them. Khor asked him, in my presence, to lead a newly-bought horse into the stable, for luck, and Kalinich carried out the request of the old skeptic with conscientious gravity. Kalinich was nearer to nature; Khor, to people, to human society. Kalinich did not like arguing and believed everything blindly; Khor had risen far enough to take an ironic view of life. He had seen a lot, he knew a lot. . . . He was a man of fairly wide knowledge, by his own standards, but he could not read; Kalinich, however, could.

Another of Turgenev's hunting companions, Ermolai, was a vagabond of utterly idiosyncratic habits. He used a flintlock gun with the kick of a young colt, his right cheek being always swollen out of proportion to his left. The wadding for this muzzle-loader he produced out of the apparently infinite resources of his hat. His peculiar obligation to his master was to bring to the estate kitchen once a month two brace of blackcock and two brace of partridge. Otherwise he was free to do as he pleased. He was considered useless for any sustained work.

"He was a queer fellow: carefree as a bird, talkative enough, absent-minded, and clumsy-looking; a deep drinker and a rolling stone; when he walked, he shuffled his feet and lurched from one side to the other—yet, with all his shuffling and lurching, he could cover [thirty-five miles] in twenty-four hours." Full of misadventures, he spent his nights in the swamp, in a tree, under a bridge. He was beaten up or robbed. He would nevertheless invariably return home with his wits, his dog, and his few possessions about him. "He was not what you would call of cheerful disposition, although he was almost always in pretty tolerable good spirits." He visited his wife once a week, treated her harshly, and she responded generously. "In brief, he was a regular freak."

One day's hunt took them to a miller's residence. They bought straw and bedding to spend the night outside on the ground. They built a fire, Ermolai began to prepare dinner, and the author dozed off. He woke up some time later to find Ermolai and the miller's wife in a subdued conversation. Why had not the miller invited them inside? Ermolai asked.

"He's afraid."

"The great fat lout. . . . Arina Timofeyevna, my love, bring me out a little glass of vodka."

She got up and walked away. Ermolai began to sing under his breath:

"I wear my shoes out heel and toe,

"So oft to see my love I go."

Arina returned with a small carafe and a glass. Ermolai drank and invited Arina to come and live with him, promising to send his wife away.

The author stirred, Arina remarked that the potatoes were done, and Ermolai announced that dinner was ready. The author recognized in Arina the former maid of a neighboring landowner, Mr. Zverkov, and he knew from the neighbor something of Arina's story. She had begged permission to marry. Zverkov refused. She then turned up pregnant by another household serf, the footman Petrushka. Zverkov was infuriated. As he explained, "nothing offends me so much . . . as ingratitude." Something had to be done, however, to rid the house of the embarrassment. At that point the miller stepped in. Arina, like many other household serfs, had been taught to read and write, skills useful in the miller's business. He bought her freedom and married her. Petrushka was sent to the army. The miller was a stern husband.

Ermolai had obviously known Arina for a long time. She was young and pretty, but she was ill. As Ermolai put it, "What else should she be?"

Turgenev's *Sportsman's Sketches* were an instant success. Alexander II confessed that they were instrumental in his decision to emancipate the serfs. Whatever their author's purpose was, they brought the peasants out of the obscure mists of anonymity and invested them with a character at least in part attractive and sympathetic. The impression that it gave of such landowners as Mr. Zverkov was obvious. Sympathy for the plight of the serfs began to grow.

Turgenev lived among the serfs on his mother's estate. He knew them well. Those whom he knew best, however, were those among whom he spent his time, and Turgenev did not, as Count Leo Tolstoy was later to do, work in the fields with the peasants. Turgenev knew those peasants who, for whatever peculiar reasons, had the license to roam the meadows in search of game. He knew, then, the mavericks, the eccentrics, and he wrote in the genre of romanticism dominant in Russia at the time. Turgenev left the impression of the peasant as a charming naïf, a noble savage oppressed by corrupt sophisticates.

Count Tolstoy (1828–1910) also knew the peasants. He knew them as he knew whatever he knew, seriously, solemnly, conscientiously. He observed them, studied them, undertook considerable efforts to school and educate their children, and shared their fieldwork. By Tolstoy's time, the golden age of Russian literature was entering the era of realism, and the works of literature for which Tolstoy is chiefly known, *War and Peace* (1869) and *Anna Karenina* (1874), are monuments of the genre.

Tolstoy's two great novels deal with the peasant only marginally. The work in which peasants take center stage is a play little known outside Russia, and its title returns us to a word with which they were introduced here, *The Power of Darkness* (Vlast tmy, 1886).[4] It is a grim business. Sex was the centerpiece. Nikita was the unreliable hired hand of a wealthy peasant, Peter, who was sick and dying. Nikita was carrying on love affairs with Peter's wife, Anisya, and with an orphan girl, Marina. He was the nearly characterless instrument of the stronger wills of the women in his life, one of whom was his mother, Matryona. His father Akim was a pious simpleton who insisted that Nikita cleanse himself of sin by marrying Marina, the orphan girl. Anisya argued that if Nikita would only wait for the death of her husband, then the two of them could get married, and she pointed out that his material circumstances would be considerably better in that event than if he married the orphan Marina. Nikita's mother approved of this plan entirely. In fact, she was so enthusiastic about it that she brought poison to Anisya and urged her to dispose of her husband at once. There remained only the problem of discovering where Peter kept his cache of cash. When the money was discovered, the poison was administered, and Nikita and Anisya married.

Within the year, Nikita grew tired of Anisya and turned instead to her stepdaughter Akoulina, who was soon pregnant. When the child was secretly delivered, Anisya instructed Nikita to bury it in the basement of the house. He assumed that he would be brought the dead child. He was horrified to discover a live child and thus his responsibility to kill it. He was pushed into the basement by Anisya and his mother, Matryona, and there he crushed the infant between two boards. Soon overcome by remorse, he confessed all to his father. He was arrested and sentenced. His father assured him of God's forgiveness, and he was bound and led away.

The natural question to raise about *The Power of Darkness* is whether we are learning from it about the peasantry or about Tolstoy. Like his novels *Anna Karenina* and *Resurrection*, the play is about the sin of seduction. Like the plot of *Anna Karenina*, the plot of the play was derived from events with which Tolstoy was familiar.

As protean as the art of Tolstoy unambiguously is, we must remember also that he was a moralist possessed. His work consisted to a great degree of homely homilies dressed in the garb of genius. He had many of the instincts of a country parson, and he served sermons well adorned. He passed his life in the bondage of two dreadful obsessions, sex and death, epitomized in the macabre naturalism of "The Kreutzer Sonata" (1886) and "The Death of Ivan Ilich" (1889), respectively, though the former theme is obvious enough in both *Anna Karenina* and *Resurrection* (1899) as well. Tolstoy's work, especially his later work, that following his great religious crisis of the late 1870s, was never free of the insistent advocacy of some form of snake oil. He had, as Isaiah Berlin observed, two souls in his breast: the hedgehog and the fox—Tolstoy complained that he had a whole squabbling tribe. Tolstoy was the Simple Simon of omniscience.

In *The Power of Darkness*, Tolstoy evidently intended to teach several lessons. It is obvious that the women in the play are smarter than the men. They also dominate the scene by the superior power of their will. Nikita's sins are those of foolish instinct and moral weakness, those of the Garden of Eden; that is, he succumbed to the persuasion of women. The really creative sinners in the play are the women. They are motivated by greed, and they do not appear to be forgivable, as Nikita, in the author's conception, patently was.

Tolstoy's peasants are not, in any event, the lovable naïfs whom Turgenev gave us. Which peasant is the real peasant? For help with this question, we must turn to a writer of great reliability.

Anton Chekhov was the prince of realists. Reliability of depiction was his literary profession of faith. "In real life, people don't spend every minute shooting at each other, hanging themselves and making confessions of love. . . . They're more occupied with eating, drinking, flirting and talking stupidities. . . . Life must be [represented] exactly as it is, and people as they are—not on stilts."[5] As he wrote to his editor, Aleksei Suvorin, in 1888, "It is not the writer's job to solve such problems as God, pessimism, etc.; his job is merely to record who, under what conditions, said or thought what about God or pessimism."[6]

Chekhov was the son of a failed petty merchant, the grandson of a serf. He was educated in medicine, and he began to write in medical school in order to support himself and his parents and siblings. All his adult life he divided between his two callings: "Medicine is my lawful wife, and literature is my mistress. When I get fed up with one, I spend the night with the other. Though it is irregular, it is less boring this way, and besides, neither of them loses anything through my infidelity."[7] One of the common observations on his work is that he wrote as if describing surgery.

Tolstoy said of Chekhov's *Three Sisters* that he could not finish reading it, that it was heartless. Chekhov had a very high opinion of Tolstoy, but he did not submit supinely to Tolstoyism. As he said, "Something in me protests. Prudence and justice tell me there is more love for mankind in electricity and steam than in chastity and abstention from meat. War is an evil and the court system is an evil, but it doesn't follow that I should wear bast shoes and sleep on a stove alongside the hired hand and his wife."[8]

In the spring of 1892, Chekhov purchased and moved to Melikhovo, a rural estate of 575 acres fifty miles from Moscow. He was seeking escape from the busyness of city life and the intrusions into a writer's time that a physician had to endure. His literary earnings gave him a tolerable income. He had always been a city person. This was his first resident experience of rural life.

He soon acclimated himself. He won the support of the local peasant population by hiring a cleric to reactivate the abandoned local church. At the same time, he naturally responded to requests for medical care. Evidently he did not enjoy it. It kept him busier than he imagined that life in the country would be. Civic duty drove him to it. Like Tolstoy, though Chekhov was never wealthy, he built and supported peasant schools. Several years of this routine soon taught this most unsparingly realistic recorder of human life the nature of the peasants whom Turgenev and Tolstoy had previously addressed. Perhaps no one not himself a peasant might have been so readily accepted and might have seen peasant life so naturally undisguised as the benefactor that a physician among these wretched people was. The average Russian peasant of the late nineteenth century lived his short life through without any access to the services of medicine.

The literary result of Chekhov's acquaintance with the peasants was a story by that name: "Peasants" (1897).[9] Nikolai Chikildeyev, a waiter in the renowned Moscow restaurant Slavyanskii Bazar, took sick and returned home, with his wife, Olga, and daughter, Sasha, to the village of his relatives to die. He remembered his childhood home as a bright and pleasant place. When he saw it again, he was shocked. Half of the only room in it was "black with soot and flies." The house appeared ready to collapse. And "the poverty, the poverty!" Only one house in the village was in better shape. It was the tavern.

Sasha coaxed the cat, but it did not respond. Why? It was deaf. Someone had hit it. Where, Nikolai asked, was his brother Kiryak? "He works as a watchman for a merchant," his father said. "He stays there in the woods. He ain't a bad worker, but he's too fond of the drink."

"He's no breadwinner," his mother added. "Our men are a poor lot; they bring nothing into the house, but take plenty out. Kiryak drinks, and the old man too knows his way to the tavern—it's no use hiding the sin. The wrath of the Queen of Heaven is on us."

The tea smelled of fish. The sugar was dirty. Cockroaches ran over the bread.

Suddenly there was a cry from the yard. It was Kiryak, calling his wife, Marya. Marya turned pale, a look of terror on her face. Her daughter began to cry. Kiryak, drunk, had simply come home to beat his wife. "Help me, for Christ's sake, good people," she begged. Coming in, he walked up to her and slugged her in the face. She fell down, her nose bleeding. He grabbed her and prepared to proceed before he noticed the guests, which made him hesitate. Embarrassed, he reluctantly left her alone.

Fyokla was the other sister-in-law. Her husband was in the army. She swam the nearby river and spent her evenings with the peasant men on the other side.

Marya had borne thirteen children. Six had survived, all girls, the eldest, Motka, being eight. When Granny found the geese in the kitchen garden, she gave Sasha and Motka a lively thrashing. Sasha appealed to her mother, who told her that it was a sin to complain against one's grandmother.

The new arrivals were soon roundly cursed by the others, as they consumed bread but contributed nothing. As Fyokla said to Nikolai: "You're ready to croak there on the stove, you loafer! The devil has brought you here, you spongers!"

When the local tax-gatherer stopped by to seize the samovar as indemnity for tax arrears, the father lamented that the better order and better prosperity of the time of serfdom were gone forever.

In the fall, Nikolai grew worse and died. Olga and Sasha were forced to become beggars: "Orthodox Christians, give alms, for Christ's sake, as much as you can, and in the Kingdom of Heaven may your parents know peace eternal."

> It seemed as though these people lived worse than cattle, and it was terrible to be with them; they were coarse, dishonest, dirty, and drunken; they did not live at peace with one another but quarreled continually, because they feared, suspected, and despised each other. Who keeps the tavern and encourages drunkenness? The peasant. Who embezzles and drinks up the funds that belong to the community, the schools, the church? The peasant. Who steals from his neighbors, sets fire to their property, bears false witness at court for a bottle of vodka? At meetings of the Zemstvo and other local bodies, who is the first to raise his voice against the peasants? The peasant. Yes, to live with them was terrible; but yet, they were human beings, they suffered and wept like human beings, and there was nothing in their lives for which one could not find justification. Crushing labour that made the whole body ache at night, cruel winters, scanty crops, overcrowding; and no help, and nowhere to look for help.

Such was the life of the peasants as Chekhov knew it. Chekhov was not the only authority to have the privileged access of a medical man to these people. John Rickman was an English physician who lived and practiced in the Russian countryside from 1916 to 1918. He subsequently published his observations in the form of sketches that are factual, not fictional.[10] Returning one winter evening from a medical mission of twenty miles in "eighty-seven degrees of frost," he was engulfed by a driving snowstorm. The driver fell asleep, and the sled turned over against a snowdrift. They righted it and continued, but it happened again. This time, the driver despaired: "We will pray and then die." Rickman did not agree. "At this craven and fatalistic suggestion I flew into a rage and knocked him down, asking how he dared to talk about dying, and besides we were pledged to be back in the hospital at eight o'clock in the morning!" The driver, however, "seemed to have lost his reason. He kept on repeating 'It is foolishness to go on; better die, better die!' Every time he yielded himself to the thought of death my anger was roused afresh; each appeal to resignation was responded to with curses and blows. Under this treatment his view changed; I ceased to be human; it was obvious, he told the Deity, that I was a devil under the protection of Satan." They survived. He later heard that the woman to whose assistance he had gone had died.

A peasant woman whose stomach was distended with fluid came to the hospital. Rickman blindfolded the patient to avert alarm and used a trocar and cannula to pierce the stomach and drain the fluid. Every six weeks or so, the woman returned, and the procedure was repeated. On the fourth occasion, the patient, charmed by medical science, asked to watch the procedure, and she examined the instruments with curiosity. This time she returned to her village with a new knowledge of medical mysteries. When a neighboring wench, accosted by the village gossips with her unmarried pregnancy, denied it, Rickman's patient offered to deliver her from embarrassment. She used a kitchen knife, "and doctor, she lay three days dying."

Gleb Uspenskii was a leading student of the peasantry in the latter half of the nineteenth century. He spent the summer of 1878 in the steppes around Samara, a province that he described as "the richest area that I myself have ever seen."[11] The ratio of grain harvested to grain sown was twenty to one, at least five times higher than the national average. He found beggars there, however. He recommended that they turn to their village commune, but he was told that the commune had refused to help. "The first thing one notices from observing the contemporary rural order is the almost complete absence of moral bonds among members of the village commune." Each commune elected an executive chief, the *starosta*. Merchants, Uspenskii found, bargained with these peasant authorities, paying rent for the right to establish some concession in the village, usually a tavern. It was simply assumed by the villagers that the elders and their cronies would plunder the money thus paid into the village fund, none of which would reach the bulk of the people. On the other hand, the peasants showed no capacity to do for themselves what the merchants were doing for them.

One such merchant leased the village mill. He had built a new house with his profits. He sat at an open window drinking tea. The peasants were flushed with anger.

"[Look at] the red-faced devil drinking tea!"

"Brother, is he drinking tea!"

"I've been counting and counting the cups, but I gave up."

"All he has to do is drink tea."

"That's how he does his business, too."

"You and I, my friend, break our backs to earn a kopeck. But there he is, doing nothing, not dirtying his pretty white hands, and raking in money while he drinks his tea."

If, on the other hand, Uspenskii points out, the question is raised to whom the mill belongs, the answer is that it belongs to the village. It has not occurred to the peasants that the village as a whole or any member of it might have turned the same trick.

Sir Donald Mackenzie Wallace took an interest in the Russian peasant. He was the leading British expert on Russia in his generation. Wallace studied at the universities of Glasgow and Edinburgh in Britain and then went abroad to study law in Paris, Berlin, and Heidelberg, where he received the degree of Doctor of Laws at the age of twenty-six. He worked as London *Times* correspondent in Russia, the Balkans, Turkey, and Egypt and served as secretary of the Viceroy of India in the 1890s. In 1900, he became the editor of the *Encyclopaedia Britannica* (tenth edition). His *Russia on the Eve of War and Revolution* has been considered since its first edition in 1877 "the standard description of the life and institutions of Russia."[12] Wallace spent a considerable part of his time there traveling in the countryside and speaking to the peasantry.

He addressed the question whether the peasants found themselves in a better or worse condition as a consequence of emancipation. He used, in particular, the records on arrearage in the payment of taxes. He found that tax collection continued during the first twenty years of emancipation (1861–81) pretty much as before. During the succeeding twenty years (1881–1901), the arrears of European Russia rose from 27 million to 144 million rubles. In some cases, the arrearage during this period increased by twenty-five times in spite of tax reductions. The decline of the livestock population reflected the same trend.[13]

Wallace repeated some of the observations of Chekhov. "That the peasantry injure their material welfare by drunkenness and improvidence there can be no reasonable doubt, as is shown by the comparatively flourishing state of certain villages of [Old Believers] in which there is no drunkenness, and in which the community exercises a strong moral control over the individual members." The Orthodox Church seemed powerless to encourage such behavior among its own flock.[14]

On the other hand, he noted also, as later historians have abundantly demonstrated, that the peasants were buying land at a rate that would soon put the great bulk of it under their control.

Nevertheless he recorded the peasants' thinking, like the father in Chekhov's "Peasants," like Firs, the former house serf in *The Cherry Orchard*, that life was better before emancipation. "Often I have heard . . . some such remark as this: 'There is no order now; the people have been spoiled; it was better in the time of the masters.' "[15] Foka, a peasant in *The Golovlyov Family*, agreed: "As I see it, Mr. Golovlyov, we were far better off in the old days, when we had masters."

What we Western liberals are hoping to find here is the provident peasant. It is what our counterparts in nineteenth-century Russia also sought. Where is he?

A part of the answer is suggested by agronomists and anthropologists. Aleksandr Chaianov was perhaps the leading Russian agronomist of the early twentieth century. His thorough knowledge of Russian farming and his outlook on Russian agriculture ultimately fell afoul of Stalin's ideological predispositions, and Chaianov died in an unknown fashion in the camps in 1939. His studies of the Russian rural economy explain some of the mysteries of the economic behavior of the Russian peasant.

"In a natural [peasant subsistence] economy human economic activity is dominated by the requirement of satisfying the needs of a single production unit [the family], which is, at the same time a consumer unit." The natural-economy farm family was not acquainted with the concept of wages and other elements of contemporary bookkeeping. "A single glance at the inner structure of the labour unit is enough to realize that it is impossible, without the category of wages, to impose on its structure net profit, rent and interest on capital as real economic categories in the capitalist meaning of the word. . . . Thorough empirical studies on peasant farms in Russia and other countries have enabled us to substantiate the following thesis: the degree of self exploitation is determined by a peculiar equilibrium between family demand satisfaction and the drudgery of labour itself."[16] In other words, the peasant worked until he had grown what he needed, and then he was satisfied. He was motivated by family needs; labour itself he found distasteful. He did not fit any capitalist conception of economics.

The Russian peasant was not unique. The dilemmas and pitfalls that bedeviled his life were characteristic of peasant societies in general. He was mired in what anthropologists call a "paleotechnic"—premodern—as opposed to "neotechnic" agricultural society and economy. Such societies do not practice systematic, scientific crop rotation or plant and animal breeding, do not use chemical fertilizers, do not readily accept new applications of mechanical techniques—Wallace recorded the reluctance of the Russian peasants to accept new agricultural machinery.[17] The traditional practice of "partible inheritance," that is, division of the land each generation among all the members of the new generation, burdens the land with more population than it can support. No land reform or emancipation can long solve the problems inherent in this kind of economy. The solution is industrialization that siphons excess population off the land and, through the application of scientific agronomy, enables those remaining to make both labor and land more productive.[18]

Peasant culture accepts such challenges reluctantly, however. Peasant societies whose livelihood depends upon the cultivation and accumulation of food "favor socialization techniques which render their members dependent on the socializing group, because dependence training will favor the routine execution of routine tasks." Primitive hunting and gathering societies, on the other hand, "are more likely to favor socialization techniques productive of self-reliance and drives toward individual achievement. . . . More precisely still, there appears to be a tendency on the part of extended families to emphasize the dependence of members on the domestic group by indulging their children . . . for prolonged periods of time. This practice rewards the continued seeking of economic support from the family unit."[19]

Peasants are farmers for whom "agriculture is a livelihood and a way of life, not a business for profit." In peasant life, "the market is held at arm's length." When industrialization develops in a society, it is the maverick or the vagabond who is likely to seek sustenance from it; "the landowning peasant, with a way of life already in stable adjustment to many aspects of civilization, is more resistant to industrialization."[20]

Oscar Handlin observed of the way of life left behind by "the uprooted," the immigrants who made their way to America, that in traditional peasant society the "efforts of man were directed not toward individual improvement but toward maintenance of status. It was fitting and proper to exact one's due rights, to fulfill one's due obligations. It was not fitting to thrust oneself ahead, to aspire to a life above one's rank, to rebel against one's status; that was to argue against the whole order of things. . . . The seeds of ultimate change were not native to this stable society. They were implanted from without."[21] These seeds consisted principally of population growth.

E.K.L. Francis and Robert Redfield found the common denominators of the peasant ethos in "the oldest book we have about peasant life," Hesiod's *Works and Days*, from the eighth century B.C.E.[22] "In European history up to very recent times no peasant revolt had revolution for its goal, and . . . the prevailing relation between the peasant and his gentry has not been one of oppressor and oppressed but rather that the peasant has thought that the rich should be generous and the powerful should not abuse their power. . . . Generally speaking, peasantry have been a conservative factor in social change, a brake on revolution, a check on that disintegration of local society which often comes with rapid technological change."[23]

The peasants, then, whether Russian or other, have little capacity to engage effectively in reform, revolution, or self-improvement. If their situation is to be transformed, it will be by outside forces.

Barrington Moore's *Social Origins of Dictatorship and Democracy* speaks directly to this problem. He argues that modern democracy and economic modernization depend upon the gradual dispossession of the peasantry and its removal to an urban environment, where it must become either bourgeois or proletarian. In England, it was the enclo-sure movement of early modern capitalist agriculture that created the unemployment that facilitated the transfer of population, distributing the concomitant suffering over a period of several generations less dramatically than it was done by Stalin later. Where the process was not gradual and spontaneous, sooner or later it was implemented by the application of massive force.[24]

In the peasant class, Russian economic attitudes were as little suited as Russian religious attitudes to contribute to the improvement of the situation of the nation.

Perhaps the other social classes of Russia were better qualified to help themselves as well as the troubled nation. The most obvious place to search for such a prospect is among the nobility, the best-educated and most talented class in the country. It is largely from the nobility that the great writers of nineteenth-century Russia came, and they have given us an abundance of introspective self-portraiture.

Two features of personality are characteristic of virtually the whole nobility that we find in this source. First, as Kliuchevskii pointed out, after their emancipation from state service and so long as the serfs were not so emancipated from service to the nobility, the nobility was a parasite class. It lived on the serf labor of its peasants, and it pro-vided nothing in exchange. It spoiled itself, dissipated its moral re-sources. Second, as the consciousness of the evils of serfdom spread, the nobility developed feelings of guilt. It became, in the term com-monly applied to this phenomenon in the nineteenth century, the "con-science-stricken gentry." Parts of it sought to expiate this burden of conscience by something not unlike social work, and this impulse natu-rally led it to the *zemstvo*, where it began to constitute the "third element" between people and state. A few nobles reacted, as we shall see, more passionately and extremely to the problem of conscience.

Apart from these two characteristics, the personality types of the nobil-ity in Russian fiction fell into three principal stereotypical categories.

The first was Oblomov. *Oblomov* (1858) was a novel by Ivan Goncharov (1812–1891).[25] Goncharov shared with Lenin the same home town, Simbirsk. He was in some respects an improbable dullard who produced an improbable classic. He spent his adult life in the civil service, first in the Ministry of Finance, later in the office of literary censorship. He did little of interest, and he never married.

Oblomov is the name of the hero/antihero. As the novel opens, Oblomov is in bed. He poses the acutely existential question: "Shall I get out of bed?" Some fifty pages later, he does. He goes to his dressing table. There, however, the demands of life overcome him, and he retreats back to his bed. Oblomov is the symbol of Russian lethargy, of the spoiling to which serfdom had led the Russian gentry.

What did the adults of Oblomovka, Oblomov's estate, live for? They never thought about it. No such question puzzled them.

> The whole thing seemed to them at once simple and clear. Had they, then, never heard of a hard life wherein people walk with anxious hearts, and roam the face of the earth, and devote their existence to everlasting toil? No, the good folk of Oblomovka had no belief in disturbing the mind; they never adopted as their mode of life a round of ceaseless aspirations somewhither, and towards an indefinite end. In fact, they feared the distraction of passion as they did fire; and as, in other spheres, men's and women's bodies burn with the volcanic violence of inward and spiritual flame, so the souls of the denizens of Oblomovka lay plunged in an undisturbed inertia which possessed their ease-loving organisms to the core. . . . These good-humoured folk looked upon life as, rather, an idyll of peace and inactivity.

One rare day a letter arrived. In Oblomovka a letter was an unusually dramatic event. "The missive fell to being passed from one person to another; and much guessing and discussion began. Finally the company had to own itself nonplussed." Old Oblomov ordered that his spectacles be fetched. His wife and the servants began to search for them, and over an hour later, they were brought. He prepared to open the letter.

"'Wait a moment,' said his wife, hastily arresting his hand. 'Do not break the seal. Who knows what the letter may contain? It may portend something dreadful, some misfortune. To what have we not come nowadays? To-morrow, or the day after, will be soon enough. The letter will not walk away of itself.'"

So the letter was locked in his desk, and tea was served. It was, however, too curious a phenomenon to be ignored for long. The talk was of nothing else. On the fourth day, when the suspense could be borne no longer, the letter was opened.

It was from a family friend, Filip Matveich Radishchev. He requested the sending of a recipe for a locally brewed beer.

Two weeks went by.

"'Really we *must* write that note,' old Oblomov kept repeating. Where is the recipe?'

"'Where is it?' retorted his wife. 'Why, it still has to be looked for. Wait a little. Why need we hurry?'"

In fact, old Oblomov finally went to his study, closed the door, put on his spectacles and sat down to write. "Everything in the house was profoundly quiet, since orders had been issued that the establishment was not to stamp upon the floor, nor, indeed, to make a noise of any kind. 'The [master] is writing,' was said in much the same tone of respectful awe that might have been used had a dead person been lying in the house."

When he had written the words "Dear Sir," his wife came in. "'I have searched and searched,' she said, 'but can find no recipe. Nevertheless the bedroom wardrobe still remains to be ransacked, so *how* can you write the letter now?'

"And to this day no one knows how long Filip Matveich had to wait for that recipe."

Universal recognition of the common features of this character type in the Russian social landscape quickly led to the coining of the term Oblomovism (*Oblomovshchina*). Literary criticism contributed to rounding out the character. What were the influences, Nikolai Dobroliubov asked, that led to such behavior? Oblomov never undertook anything so independent as pulling on his own socks, tying his own shoes, because he had three hundred servants to do these things for him, and his parents insisted that he defer to the servants. "The feature common to all these men is that nothing in life is a vital necessity for them, a shrine in their hearts, a religion, organically merged with their whole being, so that to deprive them of it would mean depriving them of their lives."[26] Lenin considered Oblomovism one of the most frustrating obstacles to his own plans for Russia.

Ivan Turgenev was the most fertile of the sociographers in fiction of nineteenth-century Russia, and the two principal remaining stereotypes of the Russian nobility are his creation. The more complex and intriguing of the two was the subject of his novella, *The Diary of a Superfluous Man* (1850), but it is much more fully delineated in his other works.

One of these is a striking portrait from *Sportman's Sketches*. The author was on a weekend in the country for a hunt, one of numerous house guests, some of whom he did not know. They were provincial civil servants, local petty nobility, distinguished guests, and others. There was Prince Kozelskii, "that tall man there. . . . You can see at once that he's lived abroad . . . he always arrives late like this." In the author's bedroom at the end of the evening was a remarkable eccentric, a provincial cosmopolite. Both of them had trouble falling asleep, and as soon as each discovered this fact in the other, they began to have a long and extraordinary conversation.

> "I'm surprised," [the roommate began], "that there are no fleas here. Wherever d'you think they've got to?"
> "You speak as if you missed them," I remarked.
> "No, I don't miss them, but I like due sequence in all things."
> I say, I thought to myself, what words he uses! My neighbour was silent again.
> "Would you like to have a bet with me?" he said suddenly, in a rather loud voice.
> "About what?". . .
> "H'm, about what? I'll tell you about what. I'll bet that you take me for a fool."
> "For goodness' sake," I murmured in amazement.
> "For a boor, a wild man from the steppes . . . Admit it . . . "
> "I haven't the pleasure of knowing you," I rejoined. . . . "How you can have concluded . . ."
> "How! Why, by the very sound of your voice. . . . But I'm not at all what you think . . ."
> "If you please . . ."
> "No, if *you* please."

And here began the singular soliloquy of "Prince Hamlet of Shchigrovo."

> In the first place, I speak French no worse than you, and German even better than you; secondly, I have lived abroad for three years; in Berlin alone I spent eight months. I have made a thorough study of Hegel, my dear sir, and I know Goethe by heart; and into the bargain I was for a long time in love with the daughter of a German professor, and got married, at home, to a consumptive young lady, a bald but very remarkable person. So I'm a bird of the same feather as yourself; I'm no bumpkin from the steppes, as you suppose. . . . I too am a prey to reflection, and there's nothing spontaneous about me at all. . . . You're proba-

bly wondering how it was that you never noticed me this evening. . . . Because I hide behind other people . . . I must strike you as a very odd fellow, as what they call an original. . . . We can neither of us sleep . . . so why not talk? I'm in good form, too, which seldom happens to me. I'm shy, you see . . . in the sense of being a man of intense self-esteem. But sometimes . . . my shyness vanishes completely. . . . Now you could put me face to face with the Dalai Lama—and I would just ask him for a pinch of snuff.

Like Pushkin's Onegin with respect to Tatiana, the talkative guest had not declared his love to the German professor's daughter. His bald-headed wife Sofiia he liked best when his back was turned to her or when she was not present. "I have known the poisonous delights of cold despair; I have learnt how sweet it is to spend a whole morning lying motionless in bed and cursing the day and hour of my birth." After several hours of such soliloquy, the author interrupted to ask his name.

"If you positively wish to call me something, then call me . . . call me the Hamlet of Shchigrovo district. There are numbers of such Hamlets in every district, but it may be that you have not come across the others. Therewith, I wish you farewell."

Next morning, he was gone.

The crucial experience in the life of the superfluous man was that he had lived abroad, had experienced Europe, and was educated, probably abroad. The crucial consideration, as suggested by Prince Hamlet of Shchigrovo, was not to be exclusively, and therefore provincially, Russian. The question where he was educated was somewhat less important because education in Russia was unavoidably European education. That was its content, and any other content was inconceivable. It began with Peter I. Moscow University, the first, was established in 1755. By the mid-nineteenth century, there were seven universities in the Russian Empire. To be university educated in Russia was to have an alienating experience. It was to be drawn to the content and the charms and eventually the experience of Europe. Russian students returning to Russian reality from this European point of view invariably had problems of adjustment: liberal European dreams and grim absolutist Russian reality. As Prince Hamlet put it, "Just tell me, what is there in common between [Hegel's] *Encyclopedia* and life in Russia? How can one be expected to apply it to our existence, not the *Encyclopedia* only, but German philosophy in general, or rather German science?"

Those European-educated gentlemen who attempted in any way whatever to introduce into Russia the beautiful dreams that they had dreamt in Europe encountered the fierce disapproval of the state. The English Parliament allowed Englishmen to pursue and find their advantage, political and economic, by the route of loyal opposition—the Chartist movement, for example. Russian absolutism did not. Opposition in Russia was by definition disloyal. Reformist sentiment, unless it came from on high, from the altitude of the monarchy or its minions, was labeled opposition, and opposition in Russia led to Siberia. It led to the demise of one's interests. When the European-educated students of Russia encountered the reaction of the state to their aspirations for their country, they quailed before the prospect. There was no middle of the road in Russian politics. It was necessary to choose, as they recognized, between "trivial deeds" or "senseless dreams," between the route of the revolutionary movement, which required desperate self-assurance and morbid convictions, and the route of the superfluous man. What made them superfluous at that point was the fact that Russia condemned them to a lifetime of meditating on pretty abstractions while retreating from Russian reality. It condemned them to a life of paralytic introspection, the torment of an emasculated ethos, the guilt of defective will. Alexander I spent his life in just this atmosphere, abstraction-mongering. The Decembrists who aspired to supplant his dynasty were too busy, even on the morning of the uprising, finishing the dreaming of their dreams—constitutions—to set seriously about the concrete business of revolt.

Turgenev wrote about the subject well because he knew it as an insider. Most of his life was spent fleeing from Russian reality to Europe, then fleeing from European dreams to Russian home. To make a moral stand was alien to him. Awash in love affairs, he never married, making a practice of confining his affairs to married women. They necessarily gave him more freedom. In one of his celebrated essays, he maintained that all men were divisible into Hamlets or Quixotes, and he admitted frankly what should have been apparent to all: he was a Hamlet. He proceeded by the preconception of principled ambiguity. Here was no Tolstoy, whose Titanic talent, reputation, resolve, and vanity allowed him to challenge both state and church—he was excommunicated in 1901. Encountering one day, while out for a horseback ride, three Romanovs, two in a carriage, one on horseback, all blocking his path, Tolstoy stared at them sternly. The saddle horse stood aside, and the count was able to pass. The horse recognized Tolstoy, he said.

Turgenev's fullest portrait of the superfluous man was in a novel little known outside Russia and Slavic studies, *Rudin* (1856). Dmitrii Rudin wandered one day into the provincial estate of Daria Mikhailovna Lasunskaia, a widow who lived with her daughter and two sons. Her home served as the gathering place of the local educated gentry, and Rudin, hitherto unacquainted there, had come to read to the company an article written by a mutual friend. As the newest person on the scene, he was of some interest. He began to talk, and his talk began to enchant. He was eloquent, lyrical, seductive. When he mentioned his student days in Germany, he naturally excited more interest, and he was asked to describe his university life.

For the first time, his talk fell flat. "His descriptions lacked color. He had no gift for provoking laughter." He soon turned from the particulars of his own student days, however, "to general observations on the importance of education and science, about universities and university life in general. In broad and bold outline he sketched an enormous picture. Everybody listened to him with deep attention. He spoke in masterly fashion, absorbingly, not altogether clearly . . . but that very lack of clarity conferred especial charm on his remarks.

"The very profusion of his thoughts prevented him from expressing himself definitely and precisely." It was not an artful performance; it was inspiration itself. "He did not seek words: they themselves came obediently and freely to his lips, and every word seemed to be poured straight from his soul, and flamed with all the fire of conviction. Rudin possessed what is perhaps one of the highest secrets—the music of eloquence. . . . Something radiant shone out before him." His audience was entranced. " 'Vous êtes un poète,' Daria Mikhailovna declared."

In the fashion of Russian gentlefolk upon whom life made no urgent claims, he stayed on. He charmed some of his hosts, and his very charm offended others. Among those whom he charmed was Daria Mikhailovna's daughter Natalia. She declared her love to him. Rudin, face to face now with "the hollowness of his romantic abstractions," was utterly confused and embarrassed.[27] What would your mother say? he asked. Natalia had anticipated that problem. Her mother had told her not to think such nonsense, but, undeterred, she asked Rudin what were his intentions. "Submit to fate," he said, and he gave the most unromantic reason why it was impossible to do otherwise: he was poor.

There was nothing left for him to do but to flee this unhappy mess. In departing, he wrote to Natalia, of course, a long letter of anemic self-justification. He paid an unsatisfactory visit of self-justification to Volyntsev, a former suitor of Natalia whom Rudin's presence had offended.

Years later, he happened across one of his university friends and gave an account of his recent undertakings. He had tried his hand at scientific agronomy; he had attempted the engineering feat of rendering a small river navigable; and he had become a teacher of Russian literature. He had failed, of course, at all of these enterprises. He had no training or experience in them. Finally, he died on the barricades in one of those innumerable romantic revolutions in Paris.

One of the most characteristic features of the personality type was that he pretended honestly to himself to entertain no nonaltruistic motives. His life was devoted to ideals and to others. Adam Smith's enlightened self-interest he would not have recognized.

The gentry types of Chekhov's plays are relatives of the superfluous man. In deference to the judgment of Tolstoy, who thought *The Three Sisters* heartless, we will rely on what is likely Chekhov's best-known play, *The Cherry Orchard*.[28]

Madame Ranevskaia was a widow whose infant son had drowned. Grief prompted her to flee to Menton, where she spent five years. There she exhausted her financial resources, and she was forced to return home. At home, she found that a part of her estate was to be auctioned to pay her debts. That, she thought, was a great pity because it contained a cherry orchard famous enough to have been mentioned in the Russian *Encyclopedia*. Madame Ranevskaia fidgeted in a frenzy of irresolution. She thought, like Mr. Micawber, that something would turn up. Her brother Gaev, whose management of the estate had helped to bring it to its fate, fidgeted too. Between billiards and bonbons, he suggested that Madame Ranevskaia might marry her daughter to a rich man, that they might suddenly come into an unexpected legacy, and so on and so forth. He made no suggestions as to what he himself might do about the problem.

Their neighbor Lopakhin was a prosperous merchant whose father had once been a serf on the estate. He tried to befriend and advise the besieged family. He was frankly puzzled by their attitudes. He understood neither their tastes in books, which he tried to share, nor their insensitivity to their predicament. In particular he failed to understand why they did nothing but agitate about it. He suggested a solution that seemed to him both natural and full of good sense. If the cherry orchard were cut and the land on which it grew were divided into plots for dachas, then the rental income would amount to 25,000 rubles a year, enough to save the estate. Madame Ranevskaia and Gaev were offended. Cutting down the cherry orchard was a vulgar idea. Only a person without taste could think of it.

Instead, the entire estate was put up for sale, and that same evening Madame Ranevskaia gave a ball. Lopakhin arrived to announce that he had bought the property. As Madame Ranevskaia departed for Paris, she could hear the ax being laid to the cherry orchard in the background.

The lives of these people, and their wills, were saturated to immobility with ponderous trivia. They could neither see nor deal with the vital issues, indistinguishable as they were from the trivia. They had little sense of their interests. Hard as it was for Lopakhin to divert Gaev's attention from billiards onto auctions, it was just that hard for Gaev to give his attention to anything pertinent. His conversation, like that of his class—something that only the writers of that generation could have recorded—was filled with parenthetical irrelevancies. As Lopakhin insisted on the urgency of a decision about the cherry orchard, Gaev launched into a paean of praise of an antique bookcase. "Dear, honored bookcase, hail to you who for more than a century have served the glorious ideals of goodness and justice! Your silent summons to fruitful toil has never weakened in all those hundred years (*through tears*), sustaining, through successive generations of our family, courage and faith in a better future, and fostering in us ideals of goodness and social consciousness."

In the presence of the characters of Chekhov's plays, there is always a faint odor of formaldehyde. They are like ambulatory fossils, relics of a mentality virtually prehistoric. Some of the literary people of his generation Chekhov described as "walking mildew."[29] A St. Petersburg official in "An Anonymous Story" complained that "our generation consists entirely of whimpering neurotics. All we do is talk about fatigue and exhaustion . . . snivelling neurotics and backsliders we are."[30] Superfluous in Turgenev's sense or not, the bulk of these people lacked any positive dimensions of character to contribute to reform or revolution in Russia.

Were these fictional characters real? We must remember Chekhov as a realist, his profession of faith as a writer—"the writer's job is to record"—his reputation of describing his subjects as if he were observing surgery.

Donald Mackenzie Wallace was traveling in Russia in these years, and he met these people, the Oblomovs, the superfluous men, the Ranevskaias, and the Gaevs.[31] "Of all the foreign countries in which I have traveled, Russia certainly bears off the palm in the matter of hospitality. Every spring I found myself in possession of a large number of invitations from landed proprietors." Much of each summer he spent traveling from one country estate to another.

At one such stop lived "Ivan Ivanovich K———, a gentleman of the old school, and a very worthy man of his kind." Here was Oblomov in the flesh!

> If we look at him as he sits in his comfortable armchair, with his capacious dressing gown hanging loosely about him, we shall be able to read at a glance something of his character. Nature endowed him with large bones and broad shoulders, and evidently intended him to be a man of great muscular power, but he has contrived to frustrate this benevolent intention, and has now more fat than muscle. . . . His features are massive and heavy, but the heaviness is relieved by an expression of calm contentment and imperturbable good nature, which occasionally blossoms into a broad grin. His face is one of those on which no amount of histrionic talent could produce a look of care and anxiety; and for this it is not to blame, for such an expression has never been demanded of it. Like other mortals he sometimes experiences little annoyances, . . . but ill fortune has never been able to get sufficiently firm hold of him to make him understand what such words as care and anxiety mean. Of struggle, disappointment, hope, and all the other feelings which give to human life a dramatic interest, he knows little by hearsay and nothing by experience. He has, in fact, always lived outside of that struggle for existence which modern philosophers declare to be the law of Nature.

He lived in the house where he was born. Family connections placed him as an adolescent in a provincial civil-service sinecure. Performing his duty there largely by proxy, he served seven years and retired. Then he married, here again perfectly effortlessly. "The course of true love, which is said never to run smooth for ordinary mortals, ran smooth for him. He never had even the trouble of proposing. The whole affair was arranged by his parents." His wife was the only daughter of a near neighbor, and she brought a handsome dowry. She was exactly suited to him. She had been raised entirely at home, had had a trace of education from the parish priest and a governess. "Between her and her husband there is as much mutual attachment as can reasonably be expected in phlegmatic natures after nearly half a century of matrimony. . . . Under [her] care he 'effeminated himself' (*o-babilsya*), as he is wont to say."

Ivan's daily life was singularly monotonous. In summer, he rose at seven o'clock, dressed with the help of a valet, and sat down before a window to look into the yard, talking occasionally to passing servants. He sometimes wandered out to observe the work in the fields. At nine o'clock, he went to the dining room for morning tea. Then the "head of the house begins the labors of the day by resuming his seat at the open window." A large dinner was served at midday, followed by a long afternoon nap. The peasants might come petitioning. If so, they were dealt with curtly and effectively. There were few books in the house, no magazines or newspapers. There was little in the life of Ivan to break his preference for still equilibrium. Some "may fairly condemn him for his indolence and apathy. But, on the other hand, he has no very bad qualities. His vices are of the passive, negative kind."

The life of his brother Dmitrii, who lived nearby, was similar, but Dmitrii spent most of his time drinking and playing cards with house guests. A little further along, a variation on the theme of the landowners of the old school, was Pavel Trofimych, a landowner who served for years as a provincial judge. He was not distinguished for either probity or corruption, taking modest bribes discreetly, as befitted one of his station.

The landowners of the new school bore Turgenev's stamp. In the neighborhood of Ivan Ivanych lived Viktor Aleksandrych L_____. "As we approach his house we can at once perceive that he differs from the majority of his neighbors. The gate is painted and moves easily on its hinges, the fence is in good repair . . . in the garden . . . more attention is paid to flowers than to vegetables." The house is more carefully furnished. With his wife and daughters he speaks only French. The most notable difference is apparent in "le cabinet de monsieur." That of Ivan Ivanych was careless, neglected. That of Viktor Aleksandrych is comfortable and elegant and evinces more ambition. It contains a remarkable collection of books.

At Moscow University, Viktor Aleksandrych had studied history and philosophy and acquired "many ill-digested general principles, and certain vague, generous, humanitarian aspirations." They led him to believe that he could be a useful citizen in the countryside. He began to read of English and Tuscan agriculture. He soon ordered a series of agricultural implements from England. "The peasants examined them with attention, not unmixed with wonder. . . . One old man remarked in an audible aside, 'A cunning people, these Germans!' " When the master had gone, the peasants stated their opinion. The plows were too big for their little horses, and the threshing machine was useless. These views were borne out by experience.

This course of events made poor Viktor Aleksandrych despondent. He turned to a new scheme. He found in his books that the system of communal property common to Russian peasants was ruinous of the soil, that free labor was more productive than serfdom. He called together his peasants and proposed to dole out to each a family plot and to charge them an annual rent on it. They understood nothing. He tried again. This time they understood that he wanted to break up the commune. This proposal "they regarded . . . as a sea captain might regard the proposal of a scientific wiseacre to knock a hole in the ship's bottom in order to make her sail faster. . . . [Viktor Aleksandrych] began to perceive that it was very difficult to do good in this world, especially when the persons to be benefited were Russian peasants."

Viktor Aleksandrych undeniably had a certain kind of intelligence. "Few men could play more dexterously with abstract principles. What he wanted was the power of dealing with concrete facts." His behavior puzzled the peasants. Was he not comfortable enough as he was? In some of his ideas they detected the aim of increasing his income, but in others they found pure caprice.

He differed from Ivan Ivanych in several significant ways. Unlike Ivan Ivanych, he never went into the field to see how the work was done, and talking to the peasant in whom he took such a humanitarian interest always made him uncomfortable. Though the estate stewards of both men stole from their masters, that of Ivan Ivanych stole only with difficulty, while that of Viktor Aleksandrych stole with ease. "The rough, practical man has a much larger income than his elegant,

well-educated neighbor, and at the same time spends very much less."
One of his neighbors had a low opinion of him. "Look at him! What a
useless, contemptible member of society! In spite of his generous aspirations he never succeeds in doing anything useful to himself or to
others. When the peasant question was raised and there was work to be
done, he went abroad and talked liberalism in Paris and Baden-
Baden. . . . [In spite of all his books], he knows less of farming than a
peasant boy of twelve, . . . and can hardly distinguish rye from oats."

Rudin was here, too. Nikolai Ivanych N_____ talked constantly of
the lamentable state of the country and the government. In fact, he
"more frequently preaches than talks." He contributed frequently to a
progressive periodical. "His stock of positive knowledge was not very
large, but he had the power of writing fluently and of making his
readers believe that he had an unlimited store of political wisdom." He
grew incautious in expression and was arrested and exiled to a provincial town. Since then, he spent his time "in brooding over his grievances and bewailing his shattered illusions." His conversation
degenerated into a monotonous repetition of what Wallace termed "political metaphysics."

The situation of the nobility at the end of the old regime was, of
course, changing. Between the emancipation of 1861 and the end of
the empire, the nobility lost half its landholdings, though the nominal
value of its remaining holdings more than quadrupled. By the latter
date, fewer than 40 percent of noble families owned land at all. On the
other hand, among those who did, nearly 70 percent of them actually
worked their own land. In the meantime, a more entrepreneurial economic ethos was developing in the noble class. A titled nobleman who
had been away from St. Petersburg for some years returned there in the
1890s to a spirit that he hardly recognized. "What is known as Society
no longer existed. One no longer went about as before, simply to
amuse oneself, to see people, to talk and pass one's time pleasantly,
but rather as one goes to market, not for one's personal pleasure but to
do a little business, to sell one's wares and to use one's knowledge,
talents, convictions, and often, alas, one's honor, to the best advantage.
In this market were to be met men who wielded power, great lords,
rich people, men who would be useful but very rarely any real gentlemen. Gentlemen, by birth, of course, were to be found there, but the
spirit was changed." The landowners who had sold their land were
investing their capital in business ventures, real estate, coal mines,

stocks and bonds.[32] The social structure of Russia was changing, but such things change slowly, and the crisis was already at hand.

When the educated Russian student rebounded from his European inspirations, if he did not deteriorate to the moral quality of superfluous man, then his only other choice was that of radical, or, in the terminology of the time, nihilist. In *Fathers and Sons* (1859), this type, too, was defined by Turgenev. Arkadii Kirsanov and his friend Bazarov were returning home from their studies in Germany. They were met and hosted by Arkadii's father, Nikolai, and Nikolai's brother, Pavel. Here was the beginning of a classic generation gap. The point of the novel was that it was also a philosophical gap. Arkadii's father and uncle were typical landowner liberals. They were active, for example, in preparing for the emancipation of the serfs.[33]

Arkadii explained that his friend was a nihilist. What was a nihilist? He was a man "who respects nothing. . . . A nihilist is a man who does not bow down before any authority, who does not take any principle on faith, whatever reverence that principle may be enshrined in."

Bazarov himself explained his principles more impatiently and sarcastically. He was a student of German natural science. "The Germans are our teachers in it." Did he have, then, a condescending attitude to Russian scientific men? "That's very likely." But he accepted the German scientists as authorities, did he not? "And how am I accepting them? And what am I to believe in? They tell me the truth, I agree, that's all." Then he believed only in science? "I have already explained to you that I don't believe in anything; and what is science—science in the abstract? There are sciences, as there are trades and crafts; but abstract science doesn't exist at all." Pressed farther, Bazarov declared that "we act by virtue of what we recognise as beneficial. At the present time, negation is the most beneficial of all—and we deny . . . everything." Which is to say, destroy everything; but one must construct, too, must one not? "That's not our business now. . . . The ground wants clearing first."

Bazarov had equally reductionist views of love and marriage. He found Nikolai reading Pushkin and advised Arkadii to tell his father how foolish it was. As the plot developed, however, it did not bear out the values of nihilism. Bazarov fell in love, declared his passion, and was rejected. He retreated to the Kirsanov home and made advances to Nikolai's peasant mistress, whereupon Pavel challenged him, and they fought a duel. When he left the Kirsanovs, he went home to his own parents, and there, while treating a sick peasant, he contracted typhus and died.

Turgenev seems to have taken some cheap liberties with his plot here. Though he admired the resolve of the sons, his real sympathies were with the fathers.

Fedor Dostoevsky's (1821–1881) reaction to nihilism was characteristically more intemperate. He grew up in the family of a physician assigned to a hospital in a very poor region of Moscow. Mental illness was rife in the area. His father gave up his hospital post, moved to the family estate, behaved more and more eccentrically and tyrannically, and was murdered by his serfs. It is perhaps natural that Dostoevsky filled his novels with an atmosphere of tormented reality and a population of the sick and the perverse. Nevertheless, his account of nihilism in *The Possessed* was in some respects remarkably prophetic.[34] It is a kind of dystopia of amoralist ideology, inspired by Bakunin's *Catechism of a Revolutionary* and Sergei Nechaev's revolutionary conspiracy based on complicity in the murder of a colleague. Complex, dreary, and fantastic, prior to the Stalinism of the 1930s, it may have seemed utterly hysterical.

The nihilist brings us unavoidably to a more considered characterization of the Russian intelligentsia. This is not a class. Rather, it is a phenomenon, an extraordinary one. The scope of the term is quite indeterminate. It is applied to different scales of educated society in different contexts—from those vaguely liberal to the hard core of the radicals. The radicals were drawn from the congenitally discontent, from those without prospects, from the radically conscience-stricken gentry, from sources likely and unlikely. The intelligentsia's sole source of power and influence—both of which it desperately sought—consisted of ideas and its willingness to resort to radicalism in pursuit of them.

The Russian intelligentsia has always attracted the strikingly disproportionate attention of Western intellectuals for reasons partly manifest: it takes ideas pure and undiluted—and it takes them seriously. This is not the common reaction of the Western public to the purveyors of ideas, the professors, writers, editors in our world. There is a superficially more obscure reason, too: the Russian intelligentsia began with no power and influence and at dramatic moments—by dint of the pure force of ideas and will power—came into plenary possession of both.

There is an element of envy here, and there is cause for caution. Western intellectuals are accustomed to think, quite erroneously, that they and their ideas have no influence.

One of the fundamental assumptions of the Russian intelligentsia was that the culture, society, and politics of the past were repugnant and evil. As Bazarov put it, construction was not their contemporary task, "the ground wants clearing first." This fictional line was likely inspired by the anarchist Mikhail Bakunin's quite real observation: "the passion for destruction is also a creative passion." The past and the present were dirt, and the despised present must be destroyed.

It must be evident by now that the term nihilist was a great misnomer. These people did not believe in nothing. They believed in a radically, rationally reconstructed future, and they were eager to sacrifice what was bad, and willing to sacrifice much that was good in the present generation for the sake of that radiant future.

That part of the Russian intelligentsia that would not be satisfied with a superfluous role in society, being denied a middle-of-the-road route of loyal opposition, had no alternative to disloyal opposition. It necessarily became revolutionary. It joined the cause—to use the term a little loosely—of nihilism. It dedicated itself to the destruction of the evil old order in anticipation of a better one.

For the bourgeoisie of the European world, revolution was a means to an end.[35] It was an instrument for the attainment of justice. For the nihilist element of the Russian intelligentsia, revolution was a near apocalyptic end in itself. In the opinion of Nikolai Berdyaev, the nihilist intelligentsia resembled a monastic sect. Impassioned and sectarian as it was, it lacked all but the thinnest social constituency, and it did not pursue interests, because no substantial social categories shared interests with it. Rather, it pursued ideological goals. It was genuinely *déclassé*, rootless, isolated from people of substance by its radicalism and from the peasantry by its education. The *intelligenty*, as the individuals comprising the intelligentsia were called, had every prospect of professional promise, provided only that they were willing to seek it. They did not, because they rejected collaboration with a system erected on injustice, oppression, and misery. In the opinion of some of their contemporary critics, "A certain other-worldliness, an eschatological vision of the City of God, of the coming kingdom of justice (under various socialist pseudonyms), and an urge to save mankind—if not from sin then from suffering—constitute [their] immutable characteristics."[36]

Their motives were impeccable. Considerations of self did not enter their heads. They dedicated themselves to the people. Or, better, they dedicated themselves to what they imagined the people to be or ought to be. While making a veritable totem of the people, at the same time they distrusted the people just as the state did. The state distrusted the people's intentions. The intelligentsia distrusted the people's capability to comprehend and to pursue their own interests. Thus deification and condescension at the same time. The people were an altar to which the intelligentsia brought their ideas. Ideas were the ultimate reality. The conception of politics as the art of the possible smelled of corruption. Compromise was betrayal. Liberty and legality interested them less than equality.[37] These people were the purest of the pure, and as callow and jejune as pure.

Alexis de Tocqueville found some of these characteristics in those eighteenth-century intellectuals who inspired the French Revolution,[38] but the Russian intelligentsia had the habit in aggravated form. How is it to be explained that a sectarian minority isolated itself from government and society alike and pursued its own *idée fixe* with consequences ranging from individual martyrdom to social Armageddon?

This question was posed in a yet more pointed form by a contemporary nobleman. As F.V. Rostopchin, governor of Moscow in 1812, put the matter on his deathbed, "I can understand the French bourgeois bringing about the Revolution to get rights, but how am I to comprehend the Russian nobleman making a revolution to lose them?"[39]

The best answer is suggested in Martin Malia's study of Alexander Herzen. As Herzen himself put it, "In Russia people subject to the influence of the mighty Western wind did not develop into historically meaningful individuals, but into eccentrics. Foreigners at home, foreigners abroad, idle spectators, spoiled for Russia by Western ideas, for the West by Russian habits, they were a kind of intelligent futility." Malia comments: "They displayed only the destructive effects of the emancipation of the gentry. Their liberty was too complete and there was nothing to do with it." They had no compelling needs, no urgent problems. Their elegant education prompted them to reject trivial deeds without providing outlets for their energy commensurate with their talents.

"It has often been noted that the farther east in Europe one goes the more abstract and general political ideals become." Political struggle in England centered on particular historic rights of Englishmen. The

French Revolutionary Declaration of the Rights of Man was abstract and universal. The Germans thought of freedom in terms of Hegelian absolutes. The relative authoritarianism of the state in Europe grew as one moved east just as did the abstractness of political ideas. "For where the entire order of the world, in every detail of its organization, is an affront to the dignity of the individual, the formulation of a specific set of grievances is impossible, and the cry of protest can only find expression in generalizations. . . . Early socialism is largely no more than the demand for democracy made shrill and insistent through frustration. And the Russian intelligentsia affords the purest example of a socialist commitment founded on general frustration rather than on specific class interest."

Lenin himself discounted the class consciousness of the workers. The protest of the workers was specific, particular, and reformist. It reflected concrete grievances and pragmatic remedies. The vision of socialism was primarily the concern of the intellectual, and it was the function not merely of his education but of his frustration.

> Because the protest of socialism is general rather than specific, it tends to sweeping eschatologies as the only expression adequate to frustrations— and aspirations—so vast. . . . Since under [Russian] circumstances democracy could not be realized by any conceivable concrete institutions, to approach politics pragmatically was in effect an abdication of hope, if not downright collaboration with the existing order. Therefore the only thing left to do was to think in terms of general principles; and principles, the longer one lives with them, without any possibility of application, become increasingly pure, ideal, sweeping and, most crucial of all, uncompromising. The reformer turns intransigent and will settle for nothing less than the complete destruction of the "old," corrupt world and the creation of a totally "new" one, or socialism.[40]

In sum, there was an inverse, ironic, but logical relation between the political experience of oppressed intellectuals and their political aspirations. They sat manacled in their thoughteries and designed ever more cosmic regeneration.

We have sufficient concrete particulars to make Malia's own slightly abstract generalizations credible. One single story provides many of them. George Kennan, born in 1845, worked from age twelve in his father's office, Western Union Telegraph, in Norwalk, Ohio.[41]

During the American Civil War, he was employed as assistant chief operator for Western Union and as military telegrapher for the Associated Press in Cincinnati. In 1864, Western Union, having failed to lay a trans-Atlantic cable in order to establish telegraph communication between Europe and America, decided upon an alternative plan: to construct a line through Alaska and Siberia to Europe. Kennan applied for work on the project and was accepted. He was then nineteen years old. He and three companions landed on the Kamchatka Peninsula to explore, cut poles, and hire construction workers for the expedition that would follow. In the meantime, the trans-Atlantic cable was successfully laid, and all of Kennan's endeavor came to naught. He returned to the United States through European Russia, having traveled six to seven thousand miles by horse-drawn cart and dogsled.

In the United States, he turned to journalism and capitalized on his exotic Siberian adventure. When asked for his educational credentials, he simply responded, "Russia." In 1882, he gave to the American Geographical Society a lecture much reported in the press. Based on his extensive travels in Siberia, he thought the reports of the cruel repression in the Siberian exile system much misrepresented and exaggerated. Moreover, he thought the revolutionaries who were chiefly responsible for the spread of these stories were of an unreliably anarchist type. In his own words, "all my prepossessions were favorable to the Russian government and unfavorable to the Russian revolutionaries." *Century Magazine* then hired Kennan to make a more particular investigation of the question. His attitude was well known to the Russian government, which, accustomed as it was to a relentlessly hostile foreign press, was delighted to find an authoritative and friendly advocate. The minister of the interior in St. Petersburg was thus glad to provide him with an official document that opened the doors of the Siberian system such as to allow him both to enter and to exit.

What he found there changed his mind utterly. The prisoners went the two to three thousand miles to their places of exile by horse-drawn cart, by riverboat, and on foot. When proceeding on foot, they commonly walked seventeen to twenty miles a day for two days and rested the third. Those in the most heavily penalized category walked in five-pound leg irons. The annual mortality rate in the Tiumen Forwarding Prison was 30 percent.

One typical victim of this system was Konstantin Staniukovich, a young naval officer who had been on the staff of Grand Duke Alexander when the latter visited the United States. Judging by his collection of visiting cards, he had been widely received in good society in the United States. His father was an admiral, and he himself was an officer of great promise. He had literary ambitions, however, and resigned his rank in the navy. He wrote novels and plays and became the editor and owner of a prominent magazine. In 1884, he spent the summer abroad, left his wife and family in Baden-Baden, and started home. He was arrested at the frontier and incarcerated in the Peter-Paul Fortress of the capital. When his wife got no response to her letters to him, she telegraphed his office. The office staff assumed that he was still in Baden-Baden. Alarmed now, his wife went straight to St. Petersburg, where, however, she could learn nothing of his whereabouts. She was therefore advised to turn to the police. She did so and discovered that her husband was a prisoner. The police had been for some time intercepting his correspondence. He was found to be in touch with a well-known revolutionary in Switzerland. Their correspondence concerned the business of the magazine exclusively. Nevertheless, Staniukovich was arrested as a person whose activity was "prejudicial to public order." In 1885, he was sentenced by administrative process—that is, without judicial proceeding—to three years in the west Siberian town of Tomsk. The magazine had to suspend publication, and Staniukovich was ruined financially. As Kennan observed, "If the Russian Government deals in this arbitrary way with men of rank, wealth, and high social position in the capital of the empire, it can be imagined what treatment is accorded to authors, physicians, students, and small landed proprietors whose presence is regarded as 'prejudicial to public order' in the provinces."

Another victim was a Mr. Borodin, who was arrested and sent to Siberia when the police found upon a search of his premises an article that he had written on the economic condition of Viatka province. While in Siberia, he read his article in a prominent journal. The Ministry of the Interior had sent him to Siberia for an article that the St. Petersburg committee of censorship had certified as harmless, allowing it to be published without any editorial revision in a magazine of mass circulation.

A Mr. Y was banished to Siberia because he was a friend of Mr. Z. Mr. Z was waiting for trial on charges of political conspiracy. He was acquitted. In the meantime, however, Mr. Y was exiled by administrative process for his acquaintance with his innocent friend.

Mr. Lazaref was arrested in 1874 and charged with carrying on revolutionary propaganda. He was acquitted. He studied law and practiced in the Volga town of Saratov. In 1884, he was called to the office of police there and informed that he was to be exiled by administrative process to eastern Siberia for three years.

"May I ask your high excellency for what reason?"

"I do not know. I have received orders to that effect from the Ministry of the Interior, and that is all I know about it."

He was later able to learn that he was sentenced "because you have not abandoned your previous criminal activity"—of which, of course, he had been acquitted.

Kennan was one day discussing the exile system with one of its alumni. Mr. Volkhofski showed him a large collection of photographs.

> That is Miss A——, once a teacher in a peasant school; she died of prison consumption in Kiev three years ago. The man with the full beard is B——, formerly a justice of the peace in N——; he was hanged at St. Petersburg in 1879. The thin-faced girl is Miss C——, one of the so-called propagandists; she went insane in the House of Preliminary Detention while awaiting trial. The pretty young woman with the cross on the sleeve of her dress is Madame D——, a Red Cross nurse in one of the field hospitals during the late Russo-Turkish war; she was sentenced to twenty years of penal servitude and is now at the mines of Kara. The lady opposite her on the same page is Miss E——, formerly a student in the Bestuzhev medical school for women in St. Petersburg; she cut her throat with a piece of broken glass, after two years of solitary confinement in the fortress.[42]

As Kennan observed, "Wrong a [person] . . . , deny him all redress, exile him again if he complains, gag him if he cries out, strike him in the face if he struggles, and at last he will stab and throw bombs. It is useless to say that the Russian Government does not exasperate men and women in this way."

For such people as these, it is not hard to imagine that "the entire order of the world, in every detail of its organization, [was] an affront to the dignity of the individual," and thus that "the formulation of a specific set of grievances [was] impossible, and [that] the cry of protest can only find expression in generalizations."

The kind of temperament that such experience developed in these people is only too natural. Their exploits in the assassination of Alexander II testify to it. Their expression and behavior as they awaited execution do, as well. Aleksandr Mikhailov, known among his friends as a "poet of organization," said that he knew of no one to whom fate had given so lavish a happiness as to him. "Everything great that has existed in the Russia of our times has passed before my eyes. For some years my most wonderful dreams have come to life; I have lived with the best men and have always been worthy of their love and friendship."[43]

N.I. Kibalchich had taken part in the "To the People" movement of 1873–74 and had spent a long term in prison. One of his friends noticed a change in him. "Prison had had its effect on him. I can see two Kibalchiches in front of me, one before and the other after prison. True, he had never been a cheerful youth, and he was always a systematic person. But before prison he loved taking part in discussions; perhaps he dreamed of guiding the others. Afterwards I remember nothing of him except handshakes and a friendly and affable smile. . . . Even the jokes of his friends he answered only with a smile. . . . He studied chemistry in a small scientific laboratory and had one firm purpose: to provide the Russian revolution with dynamite."[44]

Salomon Vittenberg, sentenced to death for revolutionary activity, confessed that he did not want to die. In his last hours, he remembered "that the highest example of honour and sacrificial spirit was without doubt shown by the Saviour. Yet even he prayed, 'Take this cup away from me.' And so how can I not pray also?" If he could not be spared, however, then "let our blood be shed [for socialism] and flow to redeem humanity. . . . Forgive them, for they know not what they do. . . . Their mind has been obscured." He turned down a plan of escape because it involved risk for his guards.[45]

There was in the makeup of these people a kind of moral absolutism hypertrophic in its own way, a counterpart of the nature of their state. Catherine II, Alexander I, Alexander II on the one side; the Decembrists, The People's Will, eventually the Bolsheviks on the other—on neither side could anyone find a way to approach the other side, or the problem of political change at all, except through the medium of conspiracy. Between people and state, there was only one small chance of a moderating relationship.

Donald Mackenzie Wallace's countryside character who reflected the personality of Rudin was said to hate "what he calls the *bourgeoisie*— he is obliged to use the French word, because his native language does not contain an equivalent term." This is an important point. If the language does not contain the term, then the society likely does not contain the phenomenon. In Russia, that was almost true. The Western bourgeois is a phenomenon for which there is a word in every Western European language, all of them based on the root *bourg/burg/borg:* *bourgeois* in French, *Burger* in German, *burger* in Dutch, *burger* in English, *burgués* in Spanish, *burguês* in Portuguese, *borghese* in Italian, *borger* in Danish, *borgare* in Swedish, and so on.

Henri Pirenne has sketched a brief biography of what we might take as the prototype bourgeois, Godric of Finchale. Born of poor peasant stock late in the eleventh century and apparently turned out of the indigent home at an early age to fend for himself, he resorted to a common practice of the time: he became a beachcomber scavenging for shipwrecks. With one or two lucky finds he put together a peddler's pack. He worked hard, traded shrewdly, and became a rich merchant.[46]

The first bourgeois were peddlers. Later, town life generated artisans or small-scale industrialists and soon added the category of bankers and moneylenders. The history of the bourgeoisie has been written at great length. In the Whig interpretation of history, the bourgeoisie is the repository of political virtue. Among the socialists, it is a class of exploiters. Even in the accounts of the bourgeois historians of culture, the bourgeois are often the exemplars of philistinism, the acolytes of filthy lucre. The novelists have been unsparing of them.

For good or ill, in the scale of macrohistory, in both its temporal and spatial dimensions, the bourgeoisie has almost certainly been throughout the past millennium the single most progressive force in world history. It either orchestrated or played an indispensable role in the Italian Renaissance, the commercial revolution, the agricultural revolution, the industrial revolution, the French Revolution, the revolutions of 1830 and 1848, the unification of Italy and Germany, the imperialist revolution, the democratic revolution. In the nineteenth century, it fairly sat astride power and influence, in varying forms, throughout the world. The bourgeoisie of Europe had been the midwife of those reforms and revolutions that appear in retrospect to have been irresistible. If it has grown in the twentieth century socially and politically conservative, it remains economically and technologically progressive—the communications revolution is only the most recent example.

If Russian then lacked the word, and Russia lacked the phenomenon, Russia, living on the border of the European lair of this great bourgeois beast, was in deep trouble. Russia was not without a commercial class, but it differed in nature, temper, scale, wealth, and politics from its European counterpart. The modern Russian Marxist term for bourgeoise is *burzhuaziia*, an obvious adoption. The nearest native Russian term in the nineteenth century was *kupechestvo*, merchant class. A merchant was a *kupets*, a buyer, like his German counterpart, *Kaufmann* (the French *négociant* is a bit different). To maintain seriously the proposition that there was no Russian bourgeoisie requires some honest qualification. The merchant class in Russia was more conspicuous around the Baltic, where it was to a high degree German, the western (Polish) provinces of the empire, where it was notably Jewish, and the Black Sea—Odessa especially—where it tended to be Jewish, Italian, and Greek. In central Russia, it was to a high degree religiously dissident, that is, it consisted of Old Believers. If they were ethnically Russian, in religion they were not fully so. Of course, there were Russian merchants who were Orthodox, too. Many merchants of the country were not, however, really merchants of the nation; and even those merchants who were fully Russian suffered from a distinct lack of the respect that their counterparts had for some time past been accorded in Europe.

The merchants were the most passive and submissive class in Russian society. They shrank from demanding from the state the economic and social reforms that would have given them the status of their counterparts in Europe. The merchant family was authoritarian, and respect for authority in the family was transferred to respect for authority outside it. Their operational axiom was that of Solomon: "The wise see misfortune and seek cover; the naive march forward and are punished."[47]

Rounding out what we might call less inappropriately the middle class were the professions. The professionals—physicians, lawyers, professors—were the intellectually active part of the rising Russian middle class. They had formidable brain power. They lacked the financial power of the English bourgeoisie of the seventeenth century, the period during which the issue of the dominance of Parliament or monarchy in England was decided.

Given their problem of acceptance and respect as a class, it is not strange that we do not have many portraits of the type in classical Russian fiction. Two authors are usually cited to give us the exceptions.

The leading satirist in Russian fiction, Mikhail Saltykov-Shchedrin, was said to have drawn his portrait from the personality of his mother. *The Golovlyov Family* (1880) depicted the stereotype.[48] Even so, some qualifications must be made here, too. Satirist though he was, this novel was not satire. It was unvarnished realism or naturalism. Admittedly it was, we must hope, in some respects caricature. The aggravated foibles of these people were sometimes funny while they were tragic. The family Golovlyov was not really a merchant family, either. Rather it represented a merchant mentality. What it traded in was land; more precisely, family members traded in the cunning acquisition of each other's birthrights. The very names by which they called each other tells us something of their spirit: Stepan was Stepan-Blockhead; Porfirii was Little Judas, Bloodsucker, and Mr. Goody-goody; Uncle Mikhail was Misha-the-Bawler. Come to the father's deathbed to take their leave of him, his sons were told, "Come to judge the publican, have you? Get out of here, you Pharisees! Get out!" One brother, finding the other habitually sleeping off a drunk, liked to fill his mouth with dead flies. The champion cheat among them, the one who eventually conned all the others, Porfirii, habitually spouted, in the fashion of Tartuffe, the most banal moral platitudes and extensive quotations of scripture. Yet, according to Saltykov-Shchedrin, "he was a hypocrite of the purely Russian variety. That is to say, he simply had no moral standards and the only truths he recognized were copy-book precepts. He was a dreadful ignoramus, a pettifogger, a liar and a windbag; and, to crown it all, he feared the devil." The great historian and critic of Russian literature, D.S. Mirsky, said of the Golovlyov family that "the reign of brute matter over human lives has never been portrayed with greater force. . . . The [Golovlyovs] are an unrelieved wilderness of animal humanity."[49]

One Russian author, little known in the West, was identified with the persistent portrayal of the merchantry. This was the playwright Aleksandr Ostrovskii. If we consider the merchant family in *It's a Family Affair*,[50] we find themes reminiscent both of Molière's caricature of M. Jourdain in *Le bourgeois gentilhomme* and of Denis Fonvizin's caricatures of Russian Francomania in the time of Catherine II (*The Brigadier*). Lipochka was a daughter who aspired to rise above the level of her own family, which she referred to as "kopek-pinching merchants." She declared that she would "never marry a merchant. . . . Why, I learned French, I play the piano, and I can dance!" The matchmaker characterized the family in a candid moment: "Her father . . . traded in leather mittens without linings on the

Balchug. . . . And her mother . . . just barely made it into the striped skirt class. . . . They put together some money and crawled out into the merchant class." In the end she married one of her father's servants, who had cheated his master out of his property, leaving him in bankruptcy, and the happy couple refused to come to her father's financial assistance, thus landing him in Siberia.

The character of these figures does not inspire much hope that a Russian middle class could intervene successfully to mediate a civil style of politics between the ever more rigid government and the ever more rigid intelligentsia. Moreover, the most important feature of the Russian merchant class, from the point of view of what it might contribute to Russia's future, was its status of inferiority at home and its passive acceptance of that status.

This attitude, however, like many others in Russia, much to the dismay of the conservative forces, was changing. Literacy was growing, and the reading public was consuming a conspicuous quantity of how-to-succeed-in-business books. The Old Believer merchants and a few Orthodox intellectuals of central Russia were articulating a work ethic and an ethic of philanthropy as well. They were demonstrating attachment to a European style of liberal values, civil rights, and the rule of law. Pavel Tretiakov, among others, was patronizing the arts and assembling his own impressive collection, which in 1892 he donated to the city of Moscow—the present Tretiakov Gallery. Other patrons, such as Savva Mamontov, Ivan Morozov, Nikolai Riabushinskii, were less in evidence, but the success of the *Peredvizhniki* (Society of Traveling Exhibitions) owed much to the support of these wealthy merchants. They hired architects to fashion residences commensurate with their budding pretensions.[51]

On the other hand, the national organization of the country's merchants and manufacturers, the Association of Industry and Trade, complained much of the arbitrariness with which government regulations hamstrung economic development in the country, referring to it as "state socialism."[52] As a spokesman for the iron industry put it in 1905, "In the 'cultured' language of our dear country, employed by former owners of serfs, the word 'industrialist' has somehow become a synonym for 'swindler,' 'bloodsucker,' 'exploiter,' and other, no less flattering, definitions. And the industrialists? They kept quiet, keep quiet, and apparently intend stubbornly to keep quiet forever and ever, as if to confirm the correctness of our kindhearted public opinion."[53]

Though the social structure of Russia was changing, "what clearly distinguished Russia [from Europe] was a strongly felt, clearly formulated, and widely held antipathy to the functioning of the market economy."[54] Gorbachev and Yeltsin would experience the same problem.

Forming and beginning to flex its muscles though a Russian bourgeoisie may have been, the revolutions of the early twentieth century would reveal its weakness beyond a doubt.

If the material ingredients for a revolution—population growth, economic stagnation, political rigidity—were present in abundance, the psychological ones were clearly wanting. Neither nobility, nor peasantry, nor middle class was prepared for it. In the nineteenth century, the proletariat was not yet a significant factor. Where would the forces of political dynamism come from? Where was the resolution necessary for either reform or revolt? While the intelligentsia worked for revolution, the state took up once more the question of reform.

Part II

The Revolutionary Experience

❖ 6 ❖

Reform or Revolution, 1900–1917

The farther east one goes in Europe, the greater become the political weakness, cowardice, and vileness of the bourgeoisie, and the greater become the cultural and political tasks that fall to the lot of the proletariat.

Russian Social-Democratic Party Program, 1898

A Russian rebellion, mindless and merciless, will sweep everything away, will crumble everything into dust.

Count Sergei Witte to Nicholas II, 1905

As the reign of the last emperor of Russia, Nicholas II, began in 1894, it was obvious to everyone that there was something rotten in the state of Russia. In retrospect, it is equally as obvious that the social resources with which to address the crisis were meager. Other resources had to be found. The state, in traditional fashion, had to look to itself.

Modern (post-Petrine) Russia, the Russia of literacy, reflection, of European consciousness of its status in the world—and of the deficits of that status—has formed two general approaches of political philosophy to explain the comparative inadequacy of Russia relative to its great-power neighbors.

One of these schools of thought was called the Westernizers. Its ideas, given its name, are unsurprising enough. What was wrong in Russia, according to the Westernizers, was that it was not sufficiently like the West. According to the founder of the school, Petr Chaadaev (1793–1856), Peter I had once tried to show the Russians the path of civilization, but they, armored in their stubborn obscurantism, had eventually undone his best efforts. Since his time, according to Chaadaev, not a single useful idea had grown in the sterile soil of the fatherland.

By the late nineteenth century, an adequate replica of the West entailed images of liberalism, democracy, and socialism. The Russian radicals and nihilists, committed as they were to a thorough metamorphosis of the nation, a virtual apocalypse, were dedicated to egalitarian socialism of a kind so remote from contemporary reality as to be hard to imagine in a mode either liberal or democratic. There was a peculiarly Russian quality of messianic crusade in their pursuit of aims that in the West had been nurtured by the temperament of bourgeois liberalism. There were in their outlook contradictions of ends and means of which they were unaware.

The other school of thought imagined itself—wrongly—to be more traditional. It was rather devoted to a more *exclusively* Russian tradition. This school had resisted the best efforts of Peter I, but it had had neither organization, nor coherence, nor even a name until a philosophy contrary to its own was defined by Chaadaev. It was the school of the Slavophiles, the lovers of Slavdom. What was wrong with Russia, according to the Slavophiles, was that it was too Western. The conflicts of modern Russia stemmed from the dissonance introduced into Russian society by the alien ideas of the West. The dominant feature of Western culture was rationalism; the dominant feature of Russian culture was spiritualism. In the conception of Konstantin Aksakov, the foundation of the state in the West was characterized by violence, slavery, and hostility; and the foundation of the Russian state by free will, liberty, and peace. Only Peter I interrupted and corrupted this marvelous harmony.

The highest principle of social organization in Russia was represented by the peasant commune, which Aksakov described as a "moral choir," and the aspiration of the Slavophile school was to form a political nation after the fashion of the commune writ large.[1] Unbiased observers might not have recognized in the commune as they knew it the fantasies of Aksakov, but the Slavophile idea in ever so many permutations has persisted in a lively fashion in Russia, whether imperial, Soviet, or post-Soviet.

The Slavophiles were Toynbee's Zealots, and the Westernizers his Herodians. In the modern world, it is the Herodians who have taken the upper hand, as they were to do in formulating the reforms of the last generation of the Russian Empire. In fact, in contemplating the selection between the two traditional Russian impulses, it appears that the Russians had little real freedom of choice. Russia had become in the time of Peter I a part of the European international state system. Quite self-consciously Russia had entered under his direction onto the road of expansion, imperialism, competition for territory and empire. In that generation, the bulk of the initiative in the interaction between Russia and its neighbors had been taken by Russia. On the other hand, it is questionable whether Russia could have in the long run avoided entering the European system of international relations. This system that Peter I embraced on his own initiative had been brought forcefully to Russia a hundred years earlier by the invasion of the Poles and the Swedes (the Time of Troubles), when the Russians had had more than enough difficulty at home to deter them from foreign adventures. Napoleon I and Napoleon III would repeat the challenge later. By the end of the nineteenth century, the great age of imperialism, Europe had generated a system of international relations rarely, perhaps never, equaled for restless competition and relentless conflict. No great nation involved in this system could afford to lag in the race forward to the modernity that conferred power, prestige, and security. The choice of the Slavophiles, however romantically gratifying, culturally comfortable, and familiarly reassuring—as well as dirt- and disease-ridden—offered nothing but martyrdom to Russia in the European international system.

It was the Westernizers who would prevail. Yet for the reasons manifest in an examination of the structure and the character of Russian society, no replication of the Western experience was possible. The West had, by definition, never Westernized. Premeditated Westernization was not real Westernization at all, still less one driven by the only engine capable of driving it in Russia—the all-embracing state. If Russian society could not do the job for itself, then liberalism, socialism, and democracy were scarcely to be anticipated in Russia. The Russian state set out to match, in a distinct order of priority, the military, imperial, and industrial achievements of the West while avoiding the social, political, and cultural order that was the indispensable instrument of those attainments in the West. The achievements were essential to Russian imperial survival. Yet the achievement of them was difficult without dispensing with the imperial instrument of achievement—autocracy. And therefore the very pursuit of Westernization, accompanied as it inevitably must be in Russia by the social and political ideas of the West, put the empire itself at risk. As Livy had observed of the late Roman republic, so it was in late nineteenth-century imperial Russia: the regime could tolerate neither its own vices nor their remedy. Once again, damned if they did, damned if they did not. A modern industry would bring a socialist proletariat. An immodern agrarian society would invite colonial subjugation—the Germans in 1917.

The first of several bold conceptions designed to divert Russia from its rendezvous with the destiny of revolution or decay was that of Count Sergei Witte. Witte was born of a Dutch family in the Caucasus, educated in Odessa, and trained in the railroad business around the Black Sea. He became minister of finance in 1892, and that is where Nicholas II found him in 1894. Witte had conceived and implemented a plan that relied implicitly on the vigorous autocratic will of Alexander III. Nicholas lacked the will of his father, whom he admired, and so he allowed the plan to proceed, though without giving it the stubborn support that his father had given it.

Witte's idea was both original and relatively simple.[2] He was the grand pioneer of the idea of planned industrialization. He augmented the state's revenues by drawing more heavily on excise taxes on staples of common consumption and on tariffs on the Russian frontier. The monies that he thus collected he used to grant tax exemptions and subventions to Russian industrial enterprise. At the same time, he invited far more massive foreign investment in the Russian economy. It was logical, given his background, that he emphasized growth in railroads. The Trans-Siberian was his brainchild, one of his chief claims to fame. Railroad enterprise was logical in other ways. It required the support of other industries that naturally lay at the base of serious industrial revolution, coal and the metallurgical branches of the economy in particular. The tariffs on the frontier served with similar logic to protect infant Russian enterprise.

The advantages of the plan were easy to see. Most obviously, Russia would be modernized and strengthened, would be a more robust competitor, a more reliable survivor, of the Darwinian struggle that the age understood international relations to be. Somewhat more subtly, the plan held out the promise of stabilizing an increasingly unstable society. The grand trick turned by the industrial revolution in Europe was population transfer, the removal of excess population from the overly crowded agrarian economy of the countryside to the eager new industries of the cities. In other words, to move indigent peasants from the environment of their ever bleaker prospects onto a new means of making a living—urban factory life. To put the matter in a somewhat summary fashion, that is what the industrial revolution accomplished in Western Europe in the course of the nineteenth century.

The process had not proceeded without problems, however. Marx remarked that the industrial revolution entered the world dripping blood from every pore. In the novels of Dickens, Hugo, and Zola, in the sketches of Hogarth, Daumier, and Doré, in the reports of the British Parliament's committees of investigation of the condition of the working class, it is easy enough to appreciate the import of Marx's observation. In the initial stages of such population transfer, the most immediate consequence was not so obviously to relieve the condition of the oppressed as to concentrate their misery and thereby to magnify the impression of it. Their very numbers depressed the price of labor, and the concentration and proximity of the miserable catalyzed discontent and facilitated organization. On the continent, the early results of the population transfer and of the initial stages of industrial revolution are most readily visible in the political revolutions of 1830 and 1848.

All of these European factors were complicated in Russia by one other. Whereas in Europe the human force driving the process was the spontaneous self-interest of the bourgeoisie, in Witte's plan it was the autocracy, which was thus called on to create social classes hostile to itself, a small bourgeoisie and a large proletariat.

The success of the program, judged by the measure of raw industrial output, was little short of sensational. During the eleven years of its implementation, the Trans-Siberian Railroad was all but completed, coal production doubled, iron production tripled, oil production grew proportionately, and Russian industrial output as a whole doubled.

Problems, however, were not far to seek. The new taxation fell most heavily on the class least able to bear it, the peasantry, and Witte's critics attributed the peasant revolts of 1902 directly to his tax policies. To tax more heavily an already indigent population, the critics said, was to destroy the purchasing power of the consumers on whom the development of a Russian market depended. Worse yet, concentrating as it did on heavy industry, it produced little to benefit the population of consumers. Was the state to be the chief producer and the chief consumer at once? If so, what kind of curious future was to be foreseen for an economy the like of which had never before been contemplated?[3]

Most seriously, the aggregation of the industrial proletariat in the swelling Russian cities began to reveal the impact that the process had earlier had in Western Europe. It posed the problem of revolution. By 1900, the working class was being increasingly subjected to the propaganda of various revolutionary socialist parties, including Marxist parties, and the government was naturally alarmed about it.

It was an effort to address precisely this problem that led indirectly to the Revolution of 1905. A Russian police official more imaginative than most, Sergei Zubatov, conceived a plan called "police socialism."[4] The idea was to form something awkwardly akin to labor unions, which were illegal in Russia, under the auspices of the police. The police would serve as the founders of one big company union, though in this instance the company was the imperial Russian government. Obviously, some little element of disguise was necessary. The organization had to be headed by someone who was not a police official. Zubatov found his man in an Orthodox priest.

Father Georgii Gapon was a sensitive and volatile personality, sometimes nervous and unstable. He was known to give his kopecks, articles of his clothing, whatever he could spare, to the suffering people about him. He was as loyal to the autocracy as he was charitable to the people, and he was convinced that when an appropriately dramatic moment came, the emperor would reveal his "true self," listen to his people, and dedicate himself to their welfare. He appeared to be an ideal collaborator for Zubatov.

Gapon was naturally suspicious at first. His own views did not entirely accord with those of Zubatov, but he was interested, as he was made an offer that provided him a rare vehicle of influence for a modest Russian priest. After a variety of misadventures, the St. Petersburg Assembly of Workers was formed under the leadership of Gapon. Gapon never made a secret of his contacts with the police, but he himself was apprehensive of them, and his intention was to free his organization of police influence.

The St. Petersburg Assembly diverted the impetus of the workers' movement into community recreation halls, schools for literacy, lectures, and other activities not subversive of autocracy. It was an awkwardly discrepant organization, as for example when foreign factory owners objected to the presence of an illegal union only to discover that it was sponsored by the government.

The Assembly had formed against the background of the disgraceful failures of Russia in the Russo-Japanese War. One of the unfortunate consequences of Witte's Trans-Siberian Railroad was that it made war with Japan feasible. It did not suffice, however, to make the fighting of such a war effective. When the negotiations of the two countries over division of the imperial spoils of Manchuria and Korea deadlocked and as the Russians contemplated with equanimity "a nice victorious little war,"[5] the Japanese attacked without warning (February 1904). The Russians' response was, like that of the Crimean War, comic and tragic. They went from defeat to defeat. Eventually Witte was called on to make peace under the mediation of Theodore Roosevelt at Portsmouth, New Hampshire (September 1905).

Disgrace sullied the prestige of the Russian government and played a role in the events of the Revolution of 1905. In its inception, however, politics were not involved. In December 1904, the management of the largest industrial enterprise in the capital, the Putilov Iron Works, fired four workers on the grounds of their membership in Gapon's St. Petersburg Assembly. The Assembly demanded the reinstatement of the four and the dismissal of the offending foreman. The management refused. On 2 January 1905, the Assembly declared a strike until its demands were satisfied.

In the course of the week that followed, what began as a conventional labor dispute mushroomed unaccountably into events of revolutionary proportions. Evidently, this was the occasion for which Gapon had been waiting. In the fall of 1904, he had begun the preparation of a petition that would give the tsar the appropriate opportunity to reveal his genuine goodness to his people. By Thursday, 6 January, Gapon had completed the petition and was circulating it. What it demanded departed so far from the labor grievances that precipitated the dispute as to make the original issues scarcely recognizable. The petition was published in the press on Friday, 7 January. At the same time, Gapon announced that on Sunday, 9 January, the workers would march en masse to Winter Palace Square to present it to the emperor. By this time, 150,000 of the city's 175,000 workers were out in support of the strike.

It is obvious that by the end of this fateful week several unpredictable factors had entered the situation. One was the volatile personality of Gapon. Another was the old Russian folk myth of the "little father tsar" who always addressed himself to the well-being of his people. Still another was that element of irrational excitement so familiar in the presence of unhappy crowds in the twentieth century.

The content of the petition was quite startling, not consistently coherent, but remarkably challenging to the entire old order.[6] "We, the workers and inhabitants of St. Petersburg . . . come to Thee, O SIRE, to seek justice and protection. . . . We are suffocating in despotism and lawlessness." They had been refused negotiations with their employers on the grounds that they lacked such a right in law. They complained that they did not "possess a single human right, not even the right to speak, think, gather, discuss our needs and take steps to improve our conditions. We are enslaved, enslaved under the patronage and with the aid of Thy officials." The document revealed the influence of Marxist doctrine, attributing much of the plight of the people to "capitalist-exploiters of the working class and officials" of the Russian state. "Raze the wall that separates Thee from Thy people and rule the country with them. Thou reignest in order to bring happiness to Thy people, but this happiness is torn out of our hands by Thy officials, and there is nothing left for us but grief and humiliation." The inauguration of national happiness was envisaged through nothing less than elections to a constituent assembly and the writing of a constitution.

There followed a list of other specific demands. Some of them were purely political: an immediate political amnesty, the introduction of full civil liberties—"freedom of speech, press, association, and worship"—universal free compulsory education, the principle of ministerial responsibility—a cabinet dependent upon a legislature—a government bound by law, equality of all before the law, and separation of church and state. Others were economic: abolition of indirect taxation, introduction of a progressive income tax, "gradual transfer of the land to the people," and termination of the war. These were followed by "measures to eliminate the oppression of labor by capital": workers' committees in the factories, freedom for labor unions, an eight-hour day, state insurance legislation for workers. The petition concluded with a warning: "if Thou withholdest Thy command and failest to respond to our supplications, we will die here on this square before Thy palace."

The extraordinary motivation of the workers under Gapon's spell is suggested by the account of one of them. "Everyone said: Let us go to the father and tell him how we suffer from those who fleece us. We will tell him: Father, hear us out. We came to you; help us, your children. We know that you would gladly sacrifice your life for us, and that you only live for us, but you do not know how we are beaten and how we suffer. . . . And we also said: Why, even in the New Testament it is said that the father took back his prodigal son, and we are not prodigal."

In order to leave no room for misunderstanding, Gapon delivered to the minister of the interior on Saturday, 8 January, a letter clarifying his intentions. He and the workers, he wrote, wished to meet the tsar on Sunday, 9 January, at 2:00 P.M. "The Tsar has nothing to fear. . . . Let Him, as a true Tsar, come to His people with a courageous heart" and accept the petition. "This is essential for His own welfare, and for the welfare of all the inhabitants of St. Petersburg and the Fatherland. Otherwise the moral bond that binds the Russian people and their Tsar might be broken." A copy of the petition was enclosed.

On the same day, having been duly warned what to expect, the government convened a council to consider how to respond. It decided that Nicholas should leave town—he went to Tsarskoe Selo, the imperial residence several miles beyond the suburbs. Authority in the capital was vested in the grand dukes, and the police were given orders to disperse the crowds of marching workers before they reached the Winter Palace. The government obviously did not appreciate at all realistically the stubbornness of intent of the workers' organization.

In St. Petersburg in January, it grows fully light around ten o'clock in the morning, and it darkens noticeably by four in the afternoon. The marching workers had a short day during which to carry out their intention. Their carefully considered plan was to gather in different working-class districts of the city, to form columns, and to converge on the Winter Palace at two o'clock. They began to gather well before light. They carried holy icons and portraits of the tsar. Spirits were high, and hopes were high. As they set off late in the morning, they sang the national anthem, "God Save the Tsar!"

Echelons of police were stationed somewhere across the line of march of each of these columns. What happened varied little from column to column. As the workers approached the police lines, from a distance of several hundred yards, the police ordered them to halt. They did. The police then ordered them to disperse. They did not. The police threatened—no result. The police fired several warning volleys over the heads of the workers. Still no result. Eventually, the police fired into the crowd. Typically, the workers absorbed one or two volleys, perhaps incredulously, and broke and ran upon the third or fourth.

Bloody Sunday was over, and the Revolution of 1905 had begun. The numbers of dead and wounded have always been controversial, perhaps around a thousand taken together. One powerful element of Russian folklore did not survive: a little father tsar Nicholas II was not.

In the spring and summer of 1905, there was a great deal of agitation and activity among emerging political parties, most of it without serious consequence. In the early fall, developments grew consequential. On 7 October, the railroad workers went on strike. They were soon followed by their fellow workers. The general strike, long powerful as myth in the working-class movement of Europe, was pioneered by the miniscule Russian proletariat. Not only did it paralyze the government. More significantly, it detained the tsar's all-important army in Siberia far from the madding crowds. The government appeared to be at the mercy of the revolutionary movement.

When Witte returned from Portsmouth, Nicholas asked his advice. Witte, always a strong monarchist, said that if Nicholas were unable to establish a military dictatorship, then he must grant a constitution. On 17 October, Nicholas issued a document known as the October Manifesto. It promised three unprecedented concessions: a full regime of civil liberties, a popularly elected legislature called a Duma, and no future legislation without the approval of the Duma. Russian autocracy came to an end, and the Revolution of 1905 soon withered and died—not, however, without fateful consequences. It left behind a constitution.

In the meantime, on 13 October, workers' committees in St. Petersburg constituted an inconspicuous organization with a conspicuous future: the St. Petersburg Soviet of Workers' Deputies, soon to become the Soviet of Workers' and Soldiers' Deputies. The term soviet (*sovet*) is Russian for council, counsel, advice. In its origins, it had little to do with Marxism, which simply adopted it later. It slowly grew somewhat systematic, and the deputies were elected presumably to represent approximately equal numbers of constituents. On 6 December, Witte had it arrested, and it disappeared until 1917.

Father Gapon went abroad and was celebrated. In the spring of 1906, he returned to Russia and went to work for the first time, for reasons entirely unknown, as a paid agent of the police. He was detected by Yevno Azev, one of the slickest intriguers in the history of the genre. Azev worked for the police and the revolutionaries simultaneously, faithful probably only to himself. He distrusted and feared other double agents, and he decided to get rid of Gapon. Knowing Gapon's reputation among the workers of the city, however, he was bound to hesitate. He was eventually able to arrange a conversation between Gapon and a double agent whom Azev trusted. Several hidden former associates of Gapon in the St. Petersburg Assembly were concealed to overhear the conversation, which clearly revealed the truth. They hanged him in a little hut so small that they had to sit on his shoulders to finish the job.

In a serious break with tradition, Russia entered the constitutional era. It was granted a cautious regime of civil liberties. It was expectantly destined, in the opinion of so many observers at home and abroad, to repeat the happy experience of Europe. Of course, its progress was measured by European standards, though its circumstances were entirely different. Political harmony was not to be attained so miraculously.

The councils of government, under the leadership of Sergei Witte, spent the winter of 1905–6 spelling out the details that the October Manifesto lacked. The Fundamental Laws of the Russian Monarchy were published in April 1906. The promised Duma was duly sanctioned. The electoral franchise was remarkably generous, including virtually all males in the empire of twenty-five years of age. On the other hand, the franchise was indirect, weighted heavily in favor of presumably reliable classes. The vote of one nobleman counted as much as that of fifteen peasants or forty-five workers. Though the October Manifesto had implied a unicameral legislature, the Fundamental Laws established the Duma as the lower of two houses. The upper house was the State Council, half appointed by the tsar, half elected by a franchise so restricted as to make it *plus royaliste que le roi.*

Of the two major variants of modern Western constitutions, the presidential system that prevails in the United States and France and the parliamentary system that characterizes Britain and Germany, the Fundamental Laws reflected the former variety. The division of power between the executive and legislative branches was more rigid by far than that in the American constitution. Not only was there no consideration of ministerial responsibility—common to the parliamentary system and the demands of the liberal Russian parties—but the legislative branch lacked the right of advice and consent in the selection of ministers. The executive depended on the legislature only for budgetary appropriations, in fact only for part of those. In addition, it possessed powers of emergency decree in Article 87.

The conservatives of the country were dismayed at such a derogation from traditions of autocracy. A cautious liberal party calling itself the Octobrists pronounced itself satisfied with the constitution. A more left-leaning liberal party, the Constitutional Democrats (Kadets), presumed to use the constitution to work toward a parliamentary system. The socialist parties initially regarded the new constitution largely as eyewash.

The first Duma was elected and convened in April 1906. It was stridently radical. It proposed parliamentary government and ministerial responsibility, abolition of the State Council, a broad political amnesty, land reform based on the expropriation of large estates, and abrogation of the indirect electoral system in favor of equality of franchise. Nicholas naturally rejected this whole program, and he dissolved the Duma in July.

The second Duma was elected and convened in February 1907. It was considerably more radical than the first because the socialist parties that had scorned and boycotted the elections to the first now saw the enormous advantages of publicity in the institution and duly ran. It naturally proved even more unacceptable to the government than the first, and it too was soon dismissed.

By this time, a man of an altogether new type of vision and strength had been appointed premier of Russia, Petr Stolypin. On the day of the dismissal of the second Duma, 3 June, Stolypin issued under Article 87 an emergency decree radically altering the electoral law of April 1906, excluding large parts of the peasant and working-class population from the franchise and guaranteeing a far more conservative third Duma than the first two had been. This move had two vitally significant results. First, it produced a relatively moderate Duma with which the government could to a limited degree work, one that conceived and passed some constructive legislation. Second, the new law was utterly illegal as judged by the Fundamental Laws themselves. The constitution provided that legislation issued under Article 87 must be approved by the succeeding Duma. In fact, a Duma qualified to consider such legislation was abolished by the new law itself, and the decree was never submitted to the illegally constituted third Duma.

This development poses the question which consideration is more important: the somewhat encouraging and constructive relations between the third Duma and the government, on the one hand, or the fact, on the other hand, that these relations were brought about only by the most flagrantly illegal violation of the constitution. Perhaps only philosophers and the bookkeepers of heaven may render authoritative judgment on the question; still it is interesting to consider it in light of what the Duma accomplished.

The third Duma was certainly the best opportunity of constitutionalism to deliver the Russian old regime from its travails.[7] It is to a great extent a story of two personalities who presumed to cooperate in order to make the system workable. Stolypin tried to find a modus vivendi with the Duma and thereby to tutor his sovereign in the virtues of constitutional government. His counterpart in the Duma was Aleksandr Guchkov, the leader of the Octobrist Party, the more cautious of the two liberal parties, and the most influential figure in the third Duma. The very name of his party signified its attachment to a conservative constitutional monarchy. Guchkov was an ardent patriot and a staunch advocate of reform to improve the effectiveness of Russia's armed forces.

Stolypin and Guchkov undertook several pieces of legislation. The government asked for large appropriations to restore the Russian navy, decimated by the Japanese in the recent war. Guchkov was naturally sympathetic, but he insisted that the government's customary scheme of promotion of senior officers by reference to family patronage networks be replaced by a system of Duma review of promotion. The government refused to relinquish prerogative of appointment. A bill on religious liberty failed because of division of opinion in the Octobrist Party itself. Stolypin attempted to extend the *zemstvo* system to the western, non-Russian provinces of the empire, where it had not been instituted in 1864. He thought that he had an agreement to that effect with Nicholas, but the State Council blocked the measure. Stolypin, sure that it would not have dared to do so without Nicholas's tacit approval, stormed, implied that Nicholas was deceitful, and threatened to resign. Nicholas consented to discipline the State Council, and Stolypin insisted on implementing the measure in his own way: by proroguing both the State Council and the Duma for three days, during which the bill was decreed under Article 87. Having done so, he found that he had offended the Duma, which insisted that his procedure was illegal. The Octobrists broke off their cooperation with him at this point.

On two pieces of legislation the third Duma was more fortunate. It authorized funding for plans drawn by the Ministry of Education to provide four years of universal, free, compulsory primary education by 1919; and it authorized a measure on workers' health and accident insurance.

The fourth Duma was dominated by more extreme parties of both right and left and accomplished little of significance before the outbreak of the war.

Evaluating the import of the constitution for the problems of Russia, 1906 to 1914, is fraught with ambiguity. The constructive third Duma was illegal—as was the fourth. The brave efforts of Stolypin and Guchkov to render government more competent and effective through cooperation of the executive and the legislature began with some element of promise but in the end largely failed. In the starkly pessimistic, but by no means implausible, argument of Theodore H. von Laue, it was precisely the coming of the Duma that condemned Russia to revolution. It was industrial growth, he argues, that Russia needed both to sustain its international position and to stabilize a volatile society.[8] Given sufficient support from autocratic authority, Sergei Witte could achieve awkward elements of an industrial revolution by decree, but, failing such support, the State Council was most unlikely to tax the nobility, and the Duma was equally unlikely to tax the common people, in order to implement such a program.

It has often been pointed out that the Russian constitution of 1906 inhibited the power of the people so thoroughly as not to allow popular government a chance to work. The truth of this observation is obvious, but it ignores the difficult question whether untrammeled popular sovereignty was the way to solve Russia's problems. What might the people have done for the crisis had they been handed a parliamentary constitution with direct and equal electoral franchise? The bulk of them, the peasants, would have looked to their own interests, ignorant as they were of international affairs and national interests. They would have had little patience with industrial policies like those of Witte, costly in taxes yet providing little or nothing for peasant consumption. If peasants had governed Russia, they would almost certainly have demanded radical land reform without compensation of the large landowners, and that would have precipitated a civil war of peasants against landlords, government apparatus, and at least large parts of the army—the nonpeasant parts of an army whose peasant soldiers had never hesitated to fire on peasant rebels in the past. The more one considers the question what real popular sovereignty might have accomplished in Russia, the less obvious is the answer—are we not witnessing a similar dilemma at the present time?

One difference the Duma regime clearly made. It focused national attention on the government such as to reveal its flaws more clearly than had been possible in the old days before a constitution and civil liberties. The unsatisfactory nature of the constitution of 3 June 1907 is as clear as it is unclear what positive influence a constitution of genuine popular sovereignty might have had.

A third measure directed at combating revolution was addressed to land reform. Principally the conception of Petr Stolypin, it was stimulated in part by the shock that the government experienced at the fact that the peasants had not voted conservatively in the Duma elections. Why might peasants have been expected to vote conservatively? Because they had done so in the recent European experience. In the elections to the French Constituent Assembly of the spring of 1848, it was the peasant electorate that overwhelmed the socialist republicans of Paris and provoked the uprising that served as a prelude to the triumph of Louis Napoleon Bonaparte and the coming of the Second Empire. As Otto von Bismarck extended the universal manhood suffrage of Prussia to the south German states in 1866, on his way to creating the German Empire, the results fully justified his confidence. If European peasants voted conservatively and Russian peasants did not, what was the explanation?

The question was too obvious to be avoided, and the most obvious difference between the two peasantries was in their property relations. The peasants of Europe were private proprietors, and the property of Russian peasants consisted of collective holdings in that fabled institution known as the commune—the *mir* or *obshchina*.

Before emancipation, it was the *mir*, that is, the village community, the township, the collective, that dealt as a unit with the landlords who owned the peasants and the civil servants who taxed them. It was the *mir* that managed landholding in the peasant association. After emancipation, the landlord was excluded from the question, but the function of the *mir* with respect to the government and to peasant land tenure remained the same. The *mir* conducted its business in a form of spontaneous Russian democracy. Each household was an electoral unit in village affairs, and the deputy for the household was the eldest healthy adult male or, failing one, female. Should the *mir* accept the offer of a local merchant to open a tavern or a teahouse, to lease property to the village or from the village? These questions were decided by gatherings of the entire village at which the household elders debated and voted.

More important for the new conception that Petr Stolypin was about to apply, landed property in the village belonged not to individuals or to households but to the village as a whole. More peculiarly yet, in those parts of central Russia where the land was rich and productive enough to make it the most important capital asset in the economy—elsewhere, in the north, for example, cottage industry and seasonal employment in regional cities was more significant—the *mir* undertook upon a village vote ever so often to redistribute the use of its land to the households comprising it. The objective of this exercise was equality of opportunity. Metaphorically speaking, the total units of land belonging to the village were thrown into a common pot and counted, and the total number of able-bodied individuals in the village into another and counted. The latter number was then divided into the former in order to determine the size of one unit of land for the current repartition, as the process was called. Each household in the village then received as many units of land as it contained able-bodied persons to work it. The procedure took place on the average about every twenty years.

The object of this intermittent repartition was the peasant concept of the "toiling norm." It was defined by the rule that the land should belong to those who worked it and in proportion to their capacity to work it relative to the amount of land and the number of people in the village. Of course, the quality of land belonging to a village varied, and therefore it was the value of land rather than the unqualified quantity of it that the *mir* was concerned to parcel out. The holdings of a given household might vary quite a lot from one generation to another, and the consideration of quality and value of land required that a household must be assigned a bit of the better, a bit of the mediocre, and a bit of the worse. In fact, the holdings of a family were likely to number two to three dozen strips widely scattered over a distance of several miles, many of them only several feet in width.

Stolypin attacked the commune on two grounds. On economic grounds, it was disincentive enshrined. No peasant in the system had any rational motive for engaging in capital improvements in land that he might lose at any time. Manuring and the use of legumes were discouraged by the system. On political grounds, Stolypin found in the system the source of the electoral radicalism of the Russian peasant. It constituted the most obvious economic difference between the politically conservative peasant of Europe and the politically radical peasant of Russia.

Consequently, he decided to dissolve the commune. He was convinced that he would both achieve a more productive agricultural economy and eventually develop in the countryside a stable constituency of prosperous peasants on whom a conservative constitutional monarchy could count. He sought to create a class, in his own words, of "the sober and the strong." He proceeded in two phases. In phase one, collective communal tenure was simply abrogated and the peasant household was given clear legal title to its scattered strips. In phase two, under the auspices of teams of government surveyors, a complicated process began of trading the strips of one family against the strips of other families such as eventually to provide each family a consolidated single unbroken piece of property, one, if possible, on which the family hut was located.

Here was a plan that to economic rationalists and Western entrepreneurs contained all the elements of good sense and faced none of those disadvantages that even sympathetic observers might foresee in Witte's industrialization or in the constitution. The results are fascinating.

The program was implemented midway through 1907; for obvious reasons it was interrupted by the dislocations of the war after 1914. The number of households embracing the program and leaving the commune during these years is as follows:[9]

1908	508,344
1909	579,409
1910	342,245
1911	145,567
1912	122,314
1913	134,554

What proportion of Russian peasant households do the sum of these figures comprise? By 1917, 24 percent of households had separated from the commune and received clear title to their landholding, and 9 percent had achieved the consolidation of their holdings into one unified plot.[10] What is more curious is that the progress of the program experienced a serious slowdown after 1909, that is, in the course of its third year of implementation. Also significant are the categories of peasants seeking separation. The program was typically embraced by the richest and the poorest peasants.[11] The poor sold to the rich and moved away. The rich aggrandized themselves and began to embody that class of the "sober and the strong" on which Stolypin had counted. Equally as interesting is the fate of Stolypin's truncated reform in the revolutionary year 1917, when liberty and chaos descended on the Russian countryside and the peasants did just as they pleased. They forced the reconstitution of the *mir* wherever it had been dissolved, and, where individual peasants had separated, they were forced to rejoin, sometimes by the application of violence. In one instance in the Volga, for example, the communal peasants rounded up separators, tied one of them to a stake, and beat him to death with clubs. The other separators then consented to rejoin.[12]

Obviously there was something in the mysterious ethos of the Russian peasant that was seriously resistant to considerations of rationalism and to Western conceptions of economic efficiency. Here the reasonableness of reform was not equal to the truculence of tradition.

The results, then, of the three reforms that had been performed on the body of Russia had not led to effective modernization. What were their results on social stability? Neither historical method nor social science possesses any secure index of social stability. We have figures that are suggestive rather than conclusive.

The strike movement in the cities diminished significantly after the revolution of 1905, declining from 1,108,406 strikers in 1906 to 46,623 in 1910. From that point, however, it began to gain its former momentum, growing from 105,110 strikers in 1911 to 1,337,458 in 1914. This latter figure is all the more significant as the bulk of strikes in 1914 occurred during the first six months, that is, before the outbreak of World War I.[13] The number of workers on strike per month in early 1914 was thus running nearly as high as in the Revolution of 1905.

The record of peasant revolts is also significant. In a fashion similar to that of the strike movement, it bottomed out in 1909 and then began to climb again:

1908	154
1909	80
1910	147
1911	113
1912	160
1913	146

There were ninety revolts in the first half of 1914, the period before the outbreak of the war.[14] The number per month, then, exceeded that of any year since the dissipation of the Revolution of 1905.

Obviously the crisis of revolution had not been mastered. Neither, as the war would show, had the crisis of modernization.

The Russian role in the coming of the war was a large one. Imperialism was a way of life among the great powers of Europe, and the Russian government was afraid to fall behind in the race. In the generation after the Crimean War, the Russian quest for compensation and resuscitation was directed chiefly to the Balkans. It contributed to the unification of Germany, and it brought one frustration after another to the drive for dominion in the Slavic lands of southeastern Europe. In the 1890s, Russia turned its attention to its remote, non-European frontier, the Far East. In the Russo-Japanese War, the results were worse yet. So it was back to the Balkans in 1908. When Serbian students assassinated the Archduke Franz Ferdinand, the multinational Austro-Hungarian Empire decided that it must suppress Serbian nationalism as an intolerable catalyst of its own inherent ethnic instability. The Russians supported Serbia, and, as Sir Edward Grey put it, the lights began to go out all over Europe, not to be lit again in that generation.

The demands of modern war imposed an insupportable strain on the ramshackle economy of Russia. Manpower went to the front. Agricultural acreage was lost. Russian industry, never equal to a modern war, shifted with as little lethargy as possible to military production, leaving the already deprived consumer in worse condition than before.

To make matters worse, the Russians fought, as they had against Japan, remarkably incompetently. In the opening battles in East Prussia (Tannenberg, 26–30 August; the Masurian Lakes, 6–15 September), the decisive German victories owed much to the fact that the Russian military units communicated with each other by unciphered messages over field radio. From this time, the Russians lost the military initiative, and their ability to persist in the war is explained chiefly by the superior attention that their German enemies gave to the western front.

The government conducted itself more fatuously than ever. In 1915, in an effort to shore up morale, Nicholas named himself commander-in-chief and departed Petrograd (as the capital was renamed at the outset of the war in order to avoid its previously German name) for general headquarters at the front. In the capital he left affairs under the malign influence of Empress Alexandra and her mentor Grigorii Rasputin, "our friend" and "man of God," who, she believed, was alone able to control the hemophilia of the heir, Alexis, the only son of

Nicholas. Rasputin drank, seduced, and raped his way around the city. The imperial family was disgraced. Too late, in December 1916, a conspiracy, including Romanov relatives who were attempting to save the dynasty from itself, despatched the "holy devil" to his rest.

Wartime naturally concentrates political power in executive offices. As the crisis deepened, however, the formerly quiescent fourth Duma grew aggressive. It formed a Progressive Bloc, which demanded a "government enjoying the confidence of the nation." Pavel Miliukov, a leading liberal, read in the Duma a litany of the government's failures and asked ominously, "Is it stupidity, or is it treason?" Alexandra was a German princess, and Rasputin was known to have pro-German sentiments. Nicholas failed utterly to comprehend the nature of the threat that faced him.

The crisis broke, at first inconspicuously, in the last days of February 1917. There were bread riots before bakers' shops. Strikes followed. The crowds began to appeal to soldiers in the garrison. A Cossack, long a merciless defender of law and order, was seen to wink at the crowds. From this time the cause was lost. Nicholas sent instructions from the front that the disorders should be quelled and the Duma prorogued. It was not possible. The Soviet reappeared. The Duma established a Provisional Committee, soon to become a Provisional Government. Its deputies went to the front and persuaded Nicholas to abdicate.

Nicholas conferred legitimacy on the Provisional Government. The Soviet, however, was the seat of more popular influence and prestige. There was a system, as Leon Trotsky dubbed it, of "dual power." The political parties, legitimized for the first time in 1905, now began with greater opportunity a frantic struggle for dominion and power.

The Octobrists had had their great chance in the third Duma. Their nearest rivals, the Constitutional Democrats, headed by Pavel Miliukov, sought a parliamentary government of the English style. Both parties possessed much talent, much brain power, the capacity for organization and articulation, and these initially were great advantages. In the long run, however, in circumstances of genuine popular sovereignty, neither party had a chance to preserve its influence for long, because Russia was not a country dominated by a liberal, professional, or industrial bourgeoisie. The liberals were destined from the outset of 1917 to be bypassed.

The Russian future belonged to socialism. There were two sources of socialist ideology in Russia. The one more familiar abroad was the party of Marxism. Marxism is a hybrid of German idealist philosophy and English economic history. The Hegelian conception of the dialectic—the theory of the union of opposites, thesis, antithesis, synthesis—was borrowed as the engine of history. It was supposed to respond, however, to material influences in a determinist fashion.

Marx conceived of society in two strata. The substructure consisted of material "modes of production." It determined the character of the superstructure, which is what the anthropologist recognizes as culture, that is, opera and ballet, property law, religious beliefs, rituals of greeting at cocktail parties, and so forth. History had thus far witnessed four modes of production characterizing four periods of history: primitive communism (precivilization), classical slaveholding society (Greece and Rome), feudal society, and bourgeois capitalism. The future was pregnant with the fifth stage—proletarian communism.

The political dimension of Marx's doctrine of revolution contained two essential tenets. First, all history was the history of class struggle, and the apparatus of state was always only an instrument whereby the dominant class exploited the dominated class. Second was the Law of the Progressive Accumulation of Capital and its corollary, the Law of the Progressive Impoverishment of the Proletariat. Capitalism, the fourth stage of history, functioned axiomatically such as to concentrate capital progressively in fewer and fewer hands and to multiply both the quantity and the quality of the misery of the masses. Society gravitated, then, to two extremes of more and more miserable proletarians and fewer and richer capitalists. Eventually, the force of numbers would lie entirely on the side of the proletariat, and when the masses could tolerate their misery no longer, they would rise up and "expropriate the expropriators." At this point, they would establish the "revolutionary democratic dictatorship of the proletariat."

If we grant Marx's premises that government is an instrument of exploitation and that capitalism drives society to two extremes, then his doctrine of revolution was both perfectly logical and perfectly democratic. There is no contradiction in the idea of a "democratic dictatorship." It was conceived to represent the overwhelming majority, and it was dedicated to destroying the formerly exploiting minority. The concept was illiberal; it was not undemocratic.[15] The historical task of the democratic dictatorship was, of course, to destroy the bourgeoisie. Once that was done, the alleged "withering away of the state" would begin. In a society of a single class, a government whose job description is the exploitation of one class by another has no role to play.

What does the doctrine of Marxism have to do with Russia? Nearly nothing. The economics of Marxism and the five stages of history related with some degree of verisimilitude to the experience of Europe, but they were decidedly Eurocentric. They applied to Russia only slightly less awkwardly than to Indonesia and Tasmania. Russian economics had never been remotely English. Russia in the nineteenth century or Russia in 1917 did not fit plausibly into any historical period described by Marx.

Such considerations did not deter the coming of Marxism to Russia. The Russian intelligentsia, as we have seen, took ideas more seriously than reality. Marxism, in what has been called its "magnificent presumption," offered the seductive potion of comprehensive explanation of the past and a true-believing guide to the future. Nothing could have been better calculated to intoxicate a party of Russian intelligentsia.

The party of Marxism in Russia had split into two factions. From the disputes of their London party congress of 1903, the Mensheviks and the Bolsheviks emerged. The Mensheviks are best understood as classical Marxists, that is, faithful students of the master. They took the logical position in the Soviet of 1917 that it was premature to attempt to implement Marxism in the Russia of that time for the obvious reasons that capitalism had not matured there and thus that there was no proletarian majority. Their position in the struggles of 1917 was therefore naturally passive, and it condemned them, in Trotsky's taunt, to the dustbin of history.

The Bolsheviks, on the other hand, under the leadership of Lenin, were the soul of revolutionary impatience. Lenin was the perfect embodiment of a philosophical principle antithetical to Marxism: not a determinist, he was a voluntarist. It is what real revolutionaries must infallibly be. Lenin had spent years constructing the reasons why Marxism, for all its exclusive applicability to advanced capitalist countries with large proletariats, was not unsuitable for poor, backward Russia. Two such reasons provided the bulk of the argument.

First was the "theory of the vanguard." The masses, Lenin maintained, were incapable of class consciousness. They were capable only of "trade-union consciousness," that is, of considering higher wages and shorter hours rather than politics in general—the contemptible crumbs from the larders of the captains of industry. If they were to appreciate their real interests, that is, revolution, they would have to be led by a vanguard of full-time, professional revolutionaries—intellectuals, of course, intelligentsia.

Marx never maintained such an idea, but Marx was at home in the more advanced parts of Europe, while Lenin grew up on the Volga. Lenin's idea was not so unnatural in a Russia that lacked civil liberties, possessed a plethora of police powers and an army that was in his generation fit chiefly for use against Russian civilians, a Russia with its traditionally mute masses. The vanguard theory was an ideal instrument of conspiratorial revolution in an autocratic country. It was not, however, either determinist or democratic.

Lenin's second revision of Marx he owed substantially to Trotsky. It was the idea of "telescoping two revolutions into one." The two in question were the bourgeois and the proletarian revolutions. Trotsky had pointed out the weakness of the Russian bourgeoisie, a natural consequence of the fact that Russian industry was nurtured more by Witte and autocracy than by a native middle class. The Russian proletariat, then, was proportional to Russian industry, while the Russian bourgeoisie was, relatively speaking, underdeveloped. For this reason, when the bourgeois revolution began—February 1917?—the bourgeoisie would prove too weak to resist the power of its relatively stronger adversary, the proletariat. Thus the bourgeois revolution would serve simply as the tocsin of the proletarian revolution, and it would be unnecessary to anticipate a significant interval for the development of capitalism—as the Mensheviks maintained—between the two.

These ideas were only half muddled. Lenin was not entirely wrong about the political consciousness of the Russian public. Witte and Stolypin agreed with him. He was not wrong about the state-capitalist nature of Russian industry and the relatively greater strength of the proletariat by comparison with the bourgeoisie. The half that was muddled was, however, the critical half: Russia was a peasant country. A democratic proletarian government would be conceivable in Russia only generations in the future. And a vanguard theory, however practical for underground revolutionaries in an oppressive autocracy, was inconsistent with demands of democracy before or after revolution. In short, no recognizable form of Marxism was applicable in a country of Russia's social and economic structure—backwardness—and Leninism was a recipe for dictatorship without democracy.

There was one other socialist party on the scene, and it was in intriguing ways more promising because it was more Russian—the Socialist Revolutionary Party. It was the heir of the *Narodniki*/populist tradition of the 1860s and 1870s. In those days, the populists were more inclination than party, a disparate phenomenon, haphazardly organized. Their success in the assassination of Alexander II provoked a police crackdown that left them in the 1880s in total disarray. In the 1890s, they began to regroup. At that time, however, they encountered unaccustomed rivalry, the competition of the Marxist parties. In the many varieties of the student/nihilist soirées of the time, the populists encountered studious, serious, articulate Marxists who possessed what they themselves did not, a comprehensive world outlook, a real *Weltanschauung*. The Marxists were well prepared. The *Narodniki* were not. They experienced a crisis, and like good Russian *intelligenty*, they set out to create a theory of political reality, an ideology to serve their needs. The task was assigned to Viktor Chernov, who emerged as the party ideologist. Naturally, his work was a reaction to the challenge that had provoked it, a reaction to Marxism. It was in fact an adaptation of Marxism. In the early twentieth century, armed with their own ideology, the populists emerged as a genuine party, the Socialist Revolutionaries. The Socialist Revolutionaries (SRs) were a party of democratic peasant socialism. To their credit, their ideology was a more realistic reflection of Russian reality than was Marxism.

SR ideology differed from Marxism in several basic points.[16] It differed in questions of historical causation. As the Marxists believed in economic determinism, or the exclusive influence of environment in historical causation, the SRs believed in the influence of both objective and subjective factors. They did not deny the great force of economic and environmental factors, but they insisted as well on the contribution of human will and historical ideas and ideals.

Second, the SRs had a different conception of the class struggle. They championed the real Russian masses, the peasants. They found the peasant, however, in his benighted and dark condition, to be unpromising material for revolution. They were convinced that he would require the leadership of the intelligentsia to show him his proper interests.

Third, the SRs were convinced that the widespread presence of the commune (*mir*) among the peasantry, and its clearly socialist character, would enable a revolutionary Russia to pass straight from what Marx would term feudal stage three of history to the socialist stage five without the trauma of the capitalist stage four usually conceived as an essential transitional era between the two.

Obviously Lenin's revisions of Marx and the SRs' revisions of Marx had a lot in common. Lenin and the SRs reckoned carefully with Russian society and arrived at eminently realistic conclusions about revolutionary tactics. In matters of revolutionary tactics, Lenin was practically an unconscious SR. His ultimate political goals, however, remained Marxist. The basic problem for Leninism was that any early seizure of power by the proletariat would abort all considerations of democracy—and thus Marxism—in backward, peasant Russia.

The SRs' numbers and popularity and the large role of peasant revolts in the Revolution of 1905 forced a change in Lenin's thinking about the tactics of revolution. He embraced the idea of a revolutionary dictatorship of the proletariat *and the peasantry*, emphasizing the poor peasantry. Lenin recognized that the small Russian proletariat alone could no more maintain power in Russia than could the bourgeoisie alone. It needed an ally. The ally that he proposed was the poor peasantry.

Trotsky, too, recognized the proletariat's need of an ally in the Russian Revolution, but the ally that he proposed was the European proletariat. Both designated allies were to prove pure illusion.

Lenin by this time had become a kind of curiously Slavophile Marxist, anticipating the breakthrough of the socialist revolution in backward Russia. Relying now on socioeconomic metaphors for the analysis of revolutionary prospects, and mixing metaphors frightfully, he proclaimed Russia "the weakest link in the chain of capitalism"; Russia would provide the "spark from which would come the flame" of European revolution. On such wordplay was the future of the revolution staked.

The Provisional Government was early dominated by liberals, as Stolypin's skewed electoral franchise had given them a strong position in the Duma. Both the populace as a whole and the Soviet in particular, however, soon grew dissatisfied with liberal government. Two issues arose that defied liberal resolution: land and peace. The liberals in the government, Miliukov and Guchkov, were committed advocates of great-power imperialism. They wished to prosecute the war to a victorious conclusion and to annex the Turkish straits. Similarly, they were advocates of property rights, and hence they could not countenance radical land reform without compensation. On both issues, they squirmed but found a plausible pretext for postponing decision until after the convening of a Constituent Assembly. Yet in circumstances of universal suffrage and equal franchise in Russia, urban liberals did not stand a chance of winning an election; hence they postponed the elections to the Assembly.

The public tired of this position, and demonstrations brought down the liberal cabinet in the spring. The new cabinet incorporated deputies from the Soviet. In fact, the dominant influence in it was that of the SR Party. The prime minister, Aleksandr Kerenskii, was an SR, and the SR leader himself, Viktor Chernov, became the minister of agriculture. Now, here was opportunity itself. The masses of Russia and the government of Russia found themselves on the same wavelength.

The SRs spoiled it. They lacked the necessary party discipline that Lenin described in the vanguard theory. On the two key issues that increasingly agitated the desperate Russian public, land and peace, the SRs could find no agreement among themselves at the center, and hence they temporized. One faction wanted peace at any price. Another pointed out that the German imperialists were no friends of socialist revolution, which would therefore not be safe with the German wolf at the gate. These were the "defensists." Other factions wavered and generated subtler ideas. On the question of land, the SRs in the government, being persons of European education, wanted a solution that was legal and hence suggested that it must await the Constituent Assembly. It is not hard to imagine how much of that reasoning was understood by the Russian peasant. The SRs in the provinces turned their backs on the government and encouraged the peasants to seize the land. The peasants in the army heard about it, deserted the front, and brought their rifles home to insist on their share. In sum, the SRs, the only party on the scene with a chance at genuinely popular democratic revolution, squandered their opportunity.

One party was left to make a play for power, the Bolsheviks, the party that had appeared early in the year, both in its numbers and in its ideas, to be the only party that was genuinely absurd.

When the February Revolution occurred, Lenin was in Switzerland. He was contacted, transported home, and provided funds by the German Foreign Office in the hope that he would have in Russia precisely the impact that he did have. His first political statement in Russia is known as his "April Theses." He demanded a second revolution at once. He relied on two propaganda slogans: "All power to the Soviets" and "Land, Peace, and Constituent Assembly." He counted on taking control of the Soviets and thus both manipulating them and putting a facade of at least urban democracy over the reality of vanguardism. His colleagues, more Menshevik in mentality than they wanted to admit, hesitated, but they did not oppose him. The force of Lenin's personality was formidable, and those close to him did not antagonize him willingly.

In July, a large demonstration was mounted by workers and soldiers in the capital. It demanded that the Soviet overturn the government. It was put down. In August, a coalition of generals attempted a right-wing coup d'état. It was put down. On this latter occasion, however, Kerenskii was forced to rely on the Bolshevik Red Guard to defend himself, and from that date, it was just a matter of time before the Bolsheviks asserted their power in the capital.

When the first Congress of Soviets had met in June, the Bolsheviks accounted for only 11 percent of the representation. In September the Bolsheviks achieved a majority of deputies in both the Petrograd and the Moscow city Soviets. By the fall, the tide of opinion was running heavily in their favor. They were alone among the political parties in promising what the people were demanding, and the people responded. In the second Congress of Soviets, 25 October 1917, the Bolsheviks achieved a majority. Simultaneously, they unleashed the revolution. In fact, they encountered scarcely any opposition. For all the vaunted vanguard theory, the mood of the masses was very likely in advance of the resolution of the party at this point. As Fedor Chaliapin sang "Don Carlos" at the Bolshoi, the Bolsheviks mounted what is somewhat grandly termed an assault on the Winter Palace. Kerenskii had escaped. The remaining ministers of the government were having dinner. There were seven fatalities in the revolution in the capital. This was the Great October Socialist Revolution: Bolshevism had come to power.

As the elections to the Constituent Assembly were subsequently to show, in urban Russia the Bolshevik Revolution was a remarkably democratic affair. Sentiment in the countryside still favored the SRs. Even there, however, thanks to the newspaper *Soldatskaia pravda* (Soldiers' Truth), published by Lenin largely with the funds of the German Foreign Office, the soldiers coming home from the front contributed to the good repute of the Bolsheviks.

Their success was based, however, on deception. Not only did they deceive their own public following. Above all, they deceived themselves.

❖ 7 ❖

The Awkward World of Leninism, 1917–1928

The final victory of our revolution, if it were to remain alone . . . would be hopeless. . . . Our salvation . . . is an all-European revolution.

Lenin, winter 1917–18

We are for the Bolsheviks, but we are against the Communists.

Russian peasants, winter 1920–21

What did NEP mean? The New Exploitation of the Proletariat.

Workers' slogan, following 1921

I have a presentiment that, thanks to the perplexity and flabbiness of all the others, our party will one fine morning be forced to assume power. . . . Whoever is put into this awkward position is irrevocably lost.

Engels, correspondence and *Peasant War in Germany*

The deception that the revolution inflicted on Russia was not altogether surprising. If Marxism was utterly unsuited to the backward social and economic environment of Russia, it was wonderfully adaptive to Russian culture. It was an intellectual elixir, an ideological philosopher's stone for the intelligentsia, a faith, a secular church to whose altars sacrifices—the forces of greed and obscurantism—must be brought, blood sacrifices if necessary. Marxism was compatible with the collectivism of Russian life, of the peasant commune (*mir*) and the commercial cooperative (*artel*), of that in-

stinctively informal authoritarian democracy beyond the reach of appa-
ratuses of state, omnipresent in the *kollektiv*. The dictatorship of the
proletariat, democratic or not, was strongly reminiscent of the ancient
overdeveloped (hypertrophic) model of statecraft or Peter the Great's
updated enlightened despotism, the *Polizeistaat*. One of the more sub-
tle but powerful and effective attractions that Marxism brought to Russia was a new mode of relating to the West. The West had long been
regarded in Russia with love and hate, with xenophobia and xenomania. Marxism had now brought out of this schizoid mentality an
integrated attitude. Imported like so much of modern Russian thought
from the West, Marxism was a Westernizing instrument of opposition
to the West. It was to be both a defense against the West—if Germany
had won World War I, Russia would certainly have become a German
colony—and a superior form of the West against an outmoded form of
the West.

Given the multiple ways in which Russian attitudes and Marxist
tenets meshed, perhaps it is not so strange that for a time the doctrine
exercised a deeply seductive influence in Russia in spite of the gaping
disparity of socioeconomic profiles between the lands that Marx envisaged for his revolution and the land that Russia was. If religion was, in
Marx's outlook, the opiate of the masses, Marxism was, as Raymond
Aron observed, the opiate of the intellectuals, at least of many of them.

Now, for the first time in the history of the world, Marxist socialists
were in command of a government. The uses that they would make of
this power would constitute a powerful precedent for all subsequent
followers. The mere fact of the considerable discrepancy between
Marxist theory and Russian reality would make of the deeds of the new
government material of unusual interest.

The most compelling need of the Bolsheviks on the morrow of their
victory was to organize their power. They began at once the construction of a hierarchy of government modeled on that of their party. The
Second Congress of Soviets elected a Central Executive Committee
composed entirely of Bolsheviks and their only allies, a fraction of the
SR party that broke away from the main body, the Left SRs. The
Council of Commissars, in effect the executive cabinet, consisted, at
Lenin's insistence, of the same political composition, though it was
more exclusively Bolshevik. Two of the Bolsheviks, Lev Kamenev
and Grigorii Zinoviev, argued that the Marxist theory of democracy

required a genuine coalition government consisting of all working-class parties. Lenin would have none of it. Executive power was to be almost purely Bolshevik. By the spring of 1918, it was entirely so.[1]

Having organized the government, their next compelling need was to preserve it. This they did largely by fulfilling what might be called the campaign promises of 1917—land, peace, and Constituent Assembly.

By a decree of 8 November 1917, Lenin simply nationalized all land. By a decree of 19 February 1918,[2] he placed the land at the disposal of local soviets for distribution. These were paper decrees. They changed nothing. They simply recognized, legitimized what the peasants had done for themselves in the course of 1917.

Viktor Chernov objected that Bolshevik land legislation was in fact the SR land program. He was right. Lenin must have laughed. Lenin owed his seizure of power to his willingness to promise the people what they wanted. He owed his tenure of power to his fulfillment of those promises. The point that Chernov made, however, was important, and it would become more so, for Lenin and his party had no intention of leaving the land settlement in the long run in its short-term condition. The Marxist vision of agriculture had nothing to do with small-scale landholding. Rather, it envisaged large farms with large mechanization, and eventually it envisaged what would be called "factories in the field," farms operated by what was in effect proletarian wage labor. That is the program to which the Soviet government moved in 1928. It was not at any time popular among Russian peasants, and hence it would have been impolitic in 1917–18, before the new government was stabilized, to do anything but precisely what the peasants wanted. The copying of the SR land program was, then, in a sense democratic. It was also deceptive. It fulfilled a promise until such time as the government acquired the strength to violate it.

The revelation of deception in the issue of the Constituent Assembly came more quickly. On the morning of 8 November 1917, *Pravda*, edited by Stalin, appeared with the assurance, "Comrades, by shedding your blood you have [guaranteed] the convocation . . . of the Constituent Assembly." Lenin dissented. Now that he had power somewhat securely in his hands, he no longer wanted to gamble it on risky elections. For one of the few times in his life when he was present to argue his case, Lenin was outvoted in the Central Committee. The elections were then duly held in December. As they were proceeding, Lenin turned characteristically to his weapon of last resort: he published a pamphlet, "Theses on the Constituent Assembly." He stated flatly that proletarian democracy was a naturally higher form of democracy than bourgeois democracy. If the Constituent Assembly proved amenable to Bolshevik power, well and good. Otherwise, "the crisis in connection with the Constituent Assembly could only be solved by revolutionary means." The Bolsheviks won 25 percent of the vote. The SRs won 59 percent. On 18 January, the Assembly convened. It elected Viktor Chernov to preside. It talked until late the following morning, when the Bolshevik security guard complained of fatigue and asked for a suspension until the following day. The delegates voted to adjourn. When they returned the following day, they found the hall locked, boarded up, and guarded by armed force.

The third campaign promise, peace, was more complicated. Lenin attempted to decree it as he had decreed land settlement. He broadcast over shortwave radio a decree calling upon the belligerents to convene a conference whose fundamental principle would be peace "without annexations and indemnities." There was no response. Lenin then asked the Germans for negotiations. A conference was convened at Brest-Litovsk. Trotsky, sent to negotiate, invited the German proletariat to overthrow the German imperialists. The Germans demanded the cession of all Russian territory of which they were in occupation, a considerable amount. Lenin and Trotsky were embarrassed, as the admission of the German demand would have appeared to confirm the report that Lenin came to Russia as a German agent. They stalled, and the German army marched unopposed. The Bolsheviks then decided to capitulate. Lenin was convinced that continuing the war had cost the two previous governments their lives, and he was determined to avoid the same mistake. The Bolsheviks signed on 3 March 1918. It was a punitive peace, far more so than the peace of Versailles of which the Germans complained so bitterly later. The Bolsheviks gave up Finland, the Baltic states, Poland, Ukraine, and more, territory comprising 62,000,000 people. In exchange, they got what the population demanded, peace. They counted, of course, on relief to be brought soon by the European proletariat. In fact, it came from Woodrow Wilson, the Fourteen Points, and the Peace of Versailles.

By the first week of March 1918, then, the government had been organized, the campaign promises had been delivered, and all issues of immediate urgency had been resolved. There was no organized opposition on the scene. The Bolsheviks experienced a welcome respite. It was then that the most conspicuous features of a political honeymoon became evident. They had power securely in their hands, and they had the time and the opportunity to reflect upon what to do with it.

Perhaps the most surprising thing about the period from March to July 1918 is that the Bolsheviks did nearly nothing. In particular they did not engage in any systematic nationalization of industry. Even the banks were left alone until they refused to appropriate money for the new government. Such nationalization as took place was largely retaliation of this kind. Were these Marxist revolutionaries not eager to use their power to effect the happy transformations for which they had worked and suffered so much?

In Lenin's mind, the spring of 1918 was a time of waiting. He was waiting upon one of two events without which he could proceed no farther. Either there must be a revolution in Europe that would bring the European proletariat to the rescue of its Russian fellows otherwise isolated by a peasantry in whose alliance the Bolsheviks evidently had little faith; or they must wait until the slow work of modes of production, of economic determinism, transformed the substructure of Russia such as to allow its government to legislate a superstructure, a state and society, reflecting the ideals of Marxism. To put the matter in a nutshell, they found themselves in an embarrassing position, one allegedly impossible according to the tenets of their doctrine: the superstructure, that passive reflection of the substructure, had in fact outdistanced the substructure, and an advanced socialist government sat atop a primitive capitalist society. It is little wonder, then, that Lenin waited. It would be interesting to know whether, as he waited, he reflected upon the anomaly of his achievement.

By late spring and early summer, challenges developed. These constituted a transition to civil war. The first problem to arise was bizarre. An army of about fifty thousand Czechs took over Siberia. What did Czechs have to do with Siberia?

By the end of the nineteenth century, several nationalities in the multiethnic Austro-Hungarian Empire had been seeking the opportunity for independence. When World War I broke out, many of the Czech soldiers in the Austro-Hungarian army deserted to the Russians. They fought there in the hope that their contribution to an allied victory would bring their nation the benefit that they sought. It did—in 1919— but in the summer of 1918, they were still deep in the territory of Russia, which by this time was at peace. The Czech Legion, as it was known, sought an exit to the western front, and the British and French were eager to receive it, as Brest-Litovsk had allowed the transfer of masses of German troops to the western front and Americans, having entered the war in April 1917, were in the spring not arriving in numbers sufficiently reassuring. Given the political confusion and complexity prevailing among Russians red and white, Germans, and the variety of nationalities along the western frontier of the former empire, it was first planned to transport the Czechs from Vladivostok in allied ships to France. The Czechs were then duly dispatched along the Trans-Siberian Railroad. The French soon intervened, however, to arrange for a quicker route of transfer through Arkhangelsk in the Russian northwest. In the meantime, the mere presence, the coherent organization, and the arms and discipline of the Czech Legion made it the only formidable fighting force left in Russia, and that fact made the Bolsheviks nervous. When a brawl of drunken Czechs broke out somewhere on the western reaches of the Trans-Siberian Railroad, local authorities arrested several of them. Their fellows freed them. At that point, Trotsky, commissar of war, gave orders to disarm and intern the Czechs. It was not a prudent order, as no force at the disposal of the Bolsheviks had the strength to carry it out. The Czechs declared a revolt, and, as they controlled the Trans-Siberian, they controlled Siberia, which is to say, three-quarters of Russia. The importance of this somewhat unlikely series of developments was that opposition to the Bolsheviks now had a huge and safe asylum in which to gather and organize.

In the meantime, the Left SRs had been intolerably offended by the territorial sacrifices of the Peace of Brest-Litovsk. They contacted their former fellow party members and plotted revolt. On 6 July, Left SRs employed by the Cheka, the first Soviet security police, called on the German embassy and said that they would like to speak to the ambassador, Count Mirbach, in order to inform him of a plot on his life. He appeared, and they were the plot on his life. They shot him and bombed the embassy. Their hope was to provoke a renewal of the war with Germany. They failed. The Germans had their hands full on the western front, where the numbers of Americans were now substantial, and Lenin made humble apologies.

Simultaneously, however, the SRs staged armed uprisings in some two dozen central Russian cities. These also failed. On 30 August, as Lenin returned to his car from a factory where he had spoken in Moscow, a woman fired three shots at him at close range. Two of them struck him. One was a harmless wound in the arm. The other was a dangerous wound in the brain. He bled heavily, lost consciousness, and his pulse grew faint, but he survived.

His assailant, Dora Kaplan, was said by the Cheka to have had SR associations. She explained her motivation. Lenin, she said, had betrayed socialism in dissolving the Constituent Assembly and signing Brest-Litovsk. She had allegedly cut cross marks on the three bullets and filled them with the South American Indian poison, curare. Evidently it had lost its strength.[3] She was executed, and a red terror was unleashed to discourage others.

The sum of these events was to precipitate among the Bolsheviks a mentality of extreme emergency. From the summer of 1918, they were engaged in civil war.

The opposition to the Bolsheviks consisted of the monarchists, the nobility, the officers' corps, and most of their rival political parties. The White armies had more military talent, and they procured more foreign support and supply. They suffered, however, from equally important disadvantages. Their four armies, located in Siberia, in southern Ukraine, around the Baltic and the White Seas, had scarcely any access to the old industry of central Russia. Moreover, they were unable to coordinate their strategic movements, no two of the four ever joining flanks. Their politics were crude and self-defeating as well. They spoke of the Russian Empire monarchist and indivisible. They offended the minority nationalities. And they promised restoration of newly redistributed land to its former owners.

Of course, foreign armies intervened in Russia, too, the British, French, American, and Japanese. In the beginning, the primary motivation was the restoration of the eastern front against the Germans. For a time, the allies were undecided which Russian side to choose, the Bolsheviks or their opponents. Lenin favored, if the allies made a sufficiently attractive offer, "accepting arms and potatoes from the bandits of Anglo-French imperialism," as he put it. When no such offer came to save the Bolsheviks from the German demands, they signed Brest-Litovsk, and the allies then turned to the enemies of Bolshevism. When intervention continued after the armistice of 11 November 1918, it can only be explained by an anti-Bolshevik motivation. Winston Churchill and Marshal Foch were among its chief advocates.

After the briefest of honeymoons, then, the Bolsheviks found themselves besieged by what was on paper a formidable array of foes. In fact the war-weary populations of the allied coalition did not long allow further adventures in faraway Russia. To the Bolsheviks, however, it seemed as if they were alone in a hostile world. It may well be, as has been suggested, that allied intervention in Russia enhanced the antagonism of Bolshevism to the capitalist world, but that antagonism was inherent in the ideology itself. Hence the first blow struck in the struggle came from the Bolsheviks. Just how transient the roots of the cold war that began in 1917 were is obvious in the haste of its disappearance around 1990. Antagonisms rooted in material interests do not disappear so quickly.

In order to master the crisis, the Bolsheviks formulated for the first time since their seizure of power a coherent series of policies identifiable as communist. The most important and notorious of them was applied in agriculture: grain requisitioning. They seized grain from the peasants without payment. They had nothing with which to pay. The currency was inflated and without value. Industrial production was diverted to military matériel. Grain requisitioning was not a policy that Lenin preferred. He did it, he said, in order to feed the cities and the armies and to beat the landlords and the capitalists. It was rough on the peasants. The Bolsheviks had first given them land, then they had stolen their grain. The White armies requisitioned grain, too; yet they promised to do worse, to take back the land that the Bolsheviks had given. As evil as Bolshevik grain requisitioning was, it was a lesser evil.

In industry, the Bolsheviks applied now for the first time massive and systematic nationalization. By November 1920, it had been extended to shops employing as few as five to ten persons. At the same time, they outlawed free trade and attempted to direct all exchange of goods into government channels. Labor, too, they conscripted and regimented—the militarization of labor. Perhaps most offensive to the ethos of proletarian communism was the fact that the Bolsheviks were forced to use the technical and managerial experts of the former regime for lack of qualified experts of their own—just as they used old tsarist officers in the new Red Army.

In sum, the Bolsheviks tried to control the production and distribution of all industrial goods and the distribution of all labor and agricultural produce. In the chaos of civil war and War Communism, they did not attempt seriously to collectivize peasant farms—that was an agenda for the future.

The nature of War Communism was debated at the time and has been debated ever since. Was it Marxist policy, or was it a natural reflex response to military emergency? In favor of the pragmatic military explanation was the fact that all the belligerents of World War I adopted similar policies and that the Bolsheviks adopted such policies only upon the development of the civil war. In favor of the ideological explanation is the fact that they continued the policies long after the civil war was over.

The civil war had been largely won by the end of 1919, yet the most stringent policies in industrial nationalization were decreed late in 1920. Of course, a Polish war intervened from April to October 1920, but War Communism continued after its end as well. The best evidence suggests that it was military emergency that motivated War Communism in the first place but that in the course of time it generated an ideological fervor and commitment independent of military considerations on the part of many Bolsheviks. In fact, just as it had required a crisis to generate the policy, so did it require a crisis to terminate it.

The crisis of 1921 reveals Bolshevism in the fullness of its error. In fact, there were several concurrent crises the sum of which amounted to an emergency as grave as that of the summer of 1918.

One of them was foreign in origin. It was the lack of a revolution in Europe. Lenin had said it over and over again: without a revolution in Germany, the Russian Revolution would not survive. Why? Because it would leave the Bolsheviks face to face with that huge mass of dark people, the peasantry whom Lenin presumed so light-headedly to include in his democratic dictatorship. Lenin's attitude toward a revolution in Germany was an open admission of the contradictions in his doctrine of revolution. How could a Russian proletariat of perhaps 2 or 2.5 percent of the population presume to implement a policy of progressive socialism in a country dominated by what Marx had called "the idiocy of rural life"?

A revolution in Germany was not a pure will-o'-the-wisp at the end of World War I. Both the allied blockade and the loss of the war weighed heavily on the German population, as did the deception practiced upon it by the Kaiser's government about the imminent prospects of victory when they were long gone. On 9 November 1918, the chancellor, Prince Max von Baden, announced (without authorization) the Kaiser's abdication and invited the Social Democrats Friedrich Ebert and Philipp Scheidemann to form a provisional government. Thus the party that took over the reins of power in Germany only a year after the Bolshevik victory claimed the legacy of Marxism, too. It was, however, more committed to democracy than to any other element of ideology, and it did not satisfy Lenin in the least. He instructed the Soviet embassy in Berlin to serve as a school of revolution. There was an abortive attempt at communist revolution in Berlin in January 1919. A Soviet regime in Bavaria lasted for two weeks in April 1919. Another endured for five months in Hungary. In March 1921, the German party made another desperate effort at revolution, this time resorting to the bombing of its own headquarters as a deceptive act of provocation in order to excite the workers. It failed, and Lenin's revolution remained alone.

The other elements of the crisis of 1921 were domestic problems. The first was the development of opposition in the party. The Workers' Opposition demanded an end to the employment of noncommunist experts in industry and objected to the increasingly centralized authoritarian management of both the party and the trade unions. The Democratic Centralists emphasized the violation of democratic procedures in the party. These were embarrassing criticisms, as the critics stood squarely on principles of Marxist democracy. They received a full hearing at the Tenth Party Congress of March 1921.

More dangerous by far was the new mood of the peasantry. During the civil war the peasants tolerated as well as they could the devastation of grain requisitioning. After all, grain requisitioning alone was less evil than grain requisitioning plus the return of the landlord class, which is what a White victory threatened. When the civil war was won, however, and the grain requisitioning continued, the peasants took a grimmer view of the Bolshevik government. The operative slogan of the time expressed their attitude: "We are for the Bolsheviks, but we are against the Communists." The Bolshevik Party had begun to use the name Communist Party. The peasants were for the party that gave them land, but they were against the party that stole their grain. In the winter of 1920–21, the grain-requisitioning detachments encountered unprecedented resistance. The resistance was mainly local, but it multiplied and was eventually widespread. A myriad of jacqueries amounted nearly to a national uprising, though it was entirely without national direction. In the Tambov region, Aleksandr Antonov raised a peasant army of 20,000 men to resist War Communism.[4]

The peasants' new mood was abetted by demobilization of the army that had now won the civil war. Demobilized peasants were better trained in violence, and they sometimes managed to bring their arms home with them. They succeeded much better than previously in withholding their grain from requisitioning. They were abetted by the weather, as the snows of the winter were unusually heavy and blocked rail transport over large parts of the country.

The antagonism of town and country was clearly focused here, and the terms of engagement suddenly favored the countryside. The cities were faced with starvation. Here was the ironic fate of revolution predicated upon the juggling of metaphors—Russia as the "weakest link" in the chain of capitalism, the "spark from which shall come the flame" of European revolution—of Lenin's democratic dictatorship of the proletariat and the peasantry.

It was the third element of the crisis of 1921 that was the most immediately dangerous—the Kronstadt Revolt. Kronstadt was the largest Russian naval base, located twenty miles west of Petrograd in the Gulf of Finland. In 1917 it came to be called with pride "Red Kronstadt," home to the workers and peasants who comprised the enlisted corps of the navy. Trotsky had often gone there to orate and receive a hero's welcome. In 1921, they called him "Traitor Trotsky." What had happened?

Part of the explanation is that Kronstadt reflected the discontent of the Workers' Opposition and the Democratic Centralists. Another part is that after the civil war many of the sailors went on furlough to their peasant homes, and they were shocked at what they saw and heard of grain requisitioning. The ill temper of Kronstadt grew.

In the meantime, nearby Petrograd fell victim to serious shortages of both grain and fuel. People sat in their unheated apartments and waited for malnutrition and exposure to the elements to do their ugly work. A graphically realistic account of this experience, a kind that the writer of fiction can represent better than can the historian, is Evgenii Zamiatin's story, "The Cave." The opening lines describe an apartment house: "Glaciers, mammoths, wastes. Black, nocturnal cliffs, vaguely like houses; in the cliffs—caves." In one such apartment sat Martin Martinych and Masha. On her nameday, Martin stole firewood for the "short-legged rusty-red, squat, greedy cave god: the iron stove." It roared and spat, the last glow of warmth that she was ever to experience. When it was over and the room returned to normal, Masha could endure no more. She reminded Martin of the little blue medicine bottle.

"Mart, darling! Give it to me!"

"But you know, Masha, there's only enough for one. . . ."

"Mart, if you still love me . . . Please, Mart. . . ."

He gave her the bottle.

"Now . . . Go and take a little walk. I think the moon is out. . . . Don't forget to take the key. You'll slam the door to, and without a key . . . Who will let you in?"[5]

The heroic proletariat of the cradle of the revolution grew restive at such benefits of its handiwork. In February 1921, the workers began to demonstrate. The party boss of the city was Lenin's old friend Grigorii Zinoviev. He ordered out the police. The police fired on the demonstrators, and there were fatalities.

Reports of these events found Kronstadt in an already excited condition. A delegation of sailors was designated to go to the city and investigate. It returned with a full account. On 28 February, a mass meeting was held on the battleship *Petropavlovsk*. It adopted a series of demands known as the *Petropavlovsk* Resolution:

1. new elections to soviets, since their present composition did not reflect the will of the workers and peasants;
2. freedom of speech and the press for all workers' and peasants' parties;
3. freedom of assembly for trade unions and peasant organizations;
4. political amnesty for all political prisoners of socialist parties, of workers, peasants, soldiers, and sailors;
5. full peasant freedom over the land and its produce;
6. abolition of the privileged position of a single party.[6]

Kronstadt was a very dangerous problem. There were fifteen thousand armed sailors on the base. Their mood appeared faithfully to reflect the discontent of the masses in the country, both worker and peasant. The resolution of their demands exemplified perfectly the canons of socialist democracy. They were asking for the implementation of the policies in whose name the revolution had been made.

Kronstadt was dangerous in other ways. The Gulf of Finland was still frozen, and it was possible to walk to Finland over the ice and thus to communicate with émigré groups. On the other hand, the ice would soon melt, and the ships icebound there could sail away to bring back what kind of support only Bolshevik alarm might imagine.

These are the contours of the crisis of 1921. They were addressed at the Tenth Party Congress of March 1921.

There was nothing further to be done about revolution in Germany. Lenin and his colleagues had done all that they could. So they made peace with the capitalist world and established diplomatic and commercial relations with it. The domestic dimension of the crisis they addressed more aggressively.

The simplest problem was the smallest, that of opposition in the party. It had been directed especially against Trotsky's practice of the regimentation and militarization of labor. The congress made concessions to the opposition in this practice, and at the same time it passed what was called the "ban on factions." Although the principles of democratic centralism continued to prevail in theory—there might be free discussion of any issue until a vote was taken on it, after which no criticism of it was allowed—henceforth it was forbidden to form organized factions in the party in order to lobby for or criticize any position.

The most immediately dangerous problem, Kronstadt, had to be dealt with as quickly as possible. When the ice on the Gulf melted, Kronstadt would be quite beyond the reach of Bolshevik armed force for at least eight or nine months. Assault troops were selected carefully, brought up from remote corners of the land, places where it was hoped the infection of Kronstadt had not spread. Fifty thousand were assembled and dressed in white for a night attack. The congress was rushed to conclusion in order to allow delegates to enlist in the assault. It was a murderous business, as the guns of Kronstadt were formidable. Artillery bursts opened holes in the ice through which many attackers slipped forever into the frigid waters of the Gulf. The job was done thoroughly, however, and the threat of Kronstadt disappeared.

The largest problem was the peasant revolt. It was approached with both carrot and stick. The stick was the Red Army. It was assisted, especially in the Volga basin, by a famine that perhaps did more damage than the army itself. The carrot was the scrapping of War Communism, of grain requisitioning. In its place came the New Economic Policy, or NEP, as it was called. In agriculture, the "tax in kind," amounting to 10 percent of harvest, replaced grain requisitioning. It was precisely what the peasants had been demanding, a legally and publicly recognized percentage of their harvest in taxation. At the same time, industry was largely denationalized, returned to private ownership and management. Only the strategically important industries, what Lenin called the "commanding heights," were retained in nationalized form. And the free-enterprise system was restored both in the distribution of goods and in the labor market.

Lenin called it a "retreat, a breathing space." It was also known as "the peasant Brest-Litovsk," the kind of concession to the Russian peasants that the treaty with Germany had been to the foreign imperialists. Lenin's revolution was still caught uncomfortably between the antagonism of the foreign capitalists and the distrust of the native peasantry.

Lenin referred several times to the NEP as a return to the policy of the spring of 1918, to the honeymoon period.[7] Thus it was a policy of waiting—for the revolution in Germany and the transformation of the Russian economic substructure such as to make a legislative organization of socialism feasible.

The ironies of the NEP were as painful as they were obvious. The NEP was frankly liberalism in economics decreed by communists in politics. The NEP was the golden age of the modern Russian peasantry. Having taken power in the name of the proletariat, the Bolsheviks now governed in the interest of the peasant at the expense of the proletariat. After all, the commodity most in demand in the country in 1921—in the wake of world war, revolution, civil war, and famine—was grain, and in the conditions of the New Economic Policy, the peasants controlled both the supply and the price of it.

The predicament in which the NEP left the proletariat was aptly characterized by E.H. Carr.

> It was only gradually that the industrial worker became conscious of the lowered status which NEP conferred on him in the Soviet economy. He had at the outset profited by the relaxation of tension and the general economic recovery which NEP had initiated. He had been freed from the bogey of labour conscription; his wages rose steadily throughout the greater part of 1922; and his standard of living, though wretched enough even when compared with that of 1914, had risen well above the starvation level of war communism. It was only in the winter of 1922–23 . . . when a balanced budget and a stable currency became the

lodestars of financial policy, and concern for the peasant became the keynote of every official speech of the principal leaders, that the industrial worker became slowly conscious of his changed position. Everywhere acclaimed under war communism as the eponymous hero of the dictatorship of the proletariat, he was now in danger of becoming the stepchild of NEP.[8]

The worker's status as stepchild was conferred by hard facts. In 1922–23 his real monthly wage was approximately half that of 1913; in 1924, unemployment rose as high as 18 percent; unemployment compensation ranged from 13 to 45 percent of the average wage; and in conditions of high unemployment, he was subject to much more stringent labor discipline. "There had been no time since the revolution when discrimination was so overtly practised against him, or when he had so many legitimate causes of bitterness against a regime that claimed to govern in his name." One manifestation of his bitterness was a new name attached to the initials NEP. What they really meant, the workers were overheard to say, was the New Exploitation of the Proletariat.[9]

This flagrant travesty of the goals of Marxist revolution was the natural and inevitable product of Lenin's revisions of Marxism, the vanguard theory and the combining of bourgeois and proletarian revolutions into one. An infant revolution made in the name of a minority constituency, a revolution before its natural time, could maintain itself in power only by serving the interests of the majority constituency. All of this had been foreseen long in advance by the most authoritative of experts on Marxist politics.

> I have a presentiment that, thanks to the perplexity and flabbiness of all the others, our party will one fine morning be forced to assume power. [In that event, the party would be] constrained to undertake communist experiments and perform leaps the untimeliness of which we know better than anyone else. In so doing we would lose our heads . . . a reaction sets in, and until the world is able to pass *historical* judgment on such events, we are considered not only beasts . . . but *bêtes* [fools]. . . . In a backward country . . . which possesses an advanced party . . . , the advanced party must get into power at the first serious conflict and as soon as *actual danger* is present, and that is, in any event, ahead of its normal time. [Such an event would be] the worst thing that can befall a leader of an extreme party . . . to be compelled to

take over a government in an epoch when the movement is not yet ripe for the domination of the class which he represents, and for the realization of the measures which that domination implies. . . . In a word, he is compelled to represent not his party or his class, but the class for whose domination the movement is then ripe. In the interests of the movement he is compelled to advance the interests of an alien class, and to feed his own class with phrases and promises, and with the asseveration that the interests of that alien class are their own interests. Whoever is put into this awkward position is irrevocably lost.

The author of these lines was Friedrich Engels. He was writing in the 1850s.[10]

The NEP was a return to an SR program for the peasantry. It was also virtually a replica of a pamphlet published by the Mensheviks in 1919, one that they had the temerity to entitle "What Is to Be Done?"—the title of Lenin's best-known work, the one in which he in 1902 propounded the vanguard theory. This state of affairs was too embarrassing for the Bolsheviks to tolerate. Soon after the introduction of the NEP, therefore, they took steps to eliminate the remnants of the Menshevik and SR parties—and all others.

Thus the NEP was an awkward combination of economic liberalism and political dictatorship. To paraphrase Lincoln's characterization of American government at Gettysburg—government of, by, and for the people—the NEP was dictatorship *of* the party *for* the peasantry *over* the proletariat. A grander travesty of the ideals of Marxism—or of democracy—would be hard to devise. The flaw in the Russian Revolution was not introduced by the malevolent caprice of Stalin. It was in the foundation. It was congenital. In Marxist terms, it derived from the premature nature of the revolution: proletarian democracy was not possible in a country where economic backwardness required a vanguard theory and the telescoping of two revolutions into one in order to introduce a fraudulent Marxism called Leninism. Considered without the skew of Marxist blinders, the experience of the Russian Revolution demonstrated the fallacy of the doctrine, for Marxist theory did not allow, as Engels pointed out, the possibility of a proletarian revolution in a backward peasant country.

If the Bolsheviks had reckoned honestly with their predicament in the crisis of 1921, they would have admitted that their revolution was a grave mistake, and they would have resigned. That would have been a politically unnatural act, of course. Their continued possession of power would entail yet other unnatural acts. They presumed ever more desperately to make the recalcitrant reality of Russian substructure conform to their voluntarist fantasies, and the nation would pay a terrible price for the party's persistence.

There was one other dimension of the crisis of 1921. It was for serious party members bitterly disillusioning. They had to climb down from the heights of lofty idealism into the slough of tawdry realism. They had stormed the citadel of the Winter Palace, won against what seemed great odds in the civil war, and prepared their grand assault on the evil asylums of world capital. Suddenly they were charged with resurrecting private property, stabilizing the currency, facilitating the work of the peddlers—they were called "bagmen" or "Nepmen"—while their government signed trade treaties and went to diplomatic receptions with the bourgeois gentlemen of Britain and France.

What were sometimes called the "grimaces of NEP" were portrayed with the lively ambiguity inherent in them in Yurii Olesha's 1927 novel, *Envy*. The hero was Andrei Babichev, the director of the Food Industry Trust, embodiment of the new Soviet man of the NEP, supremely, offensively self-confident and corpulent, generous, and condescending. Or, as one of the wastrel protégés whom he has rescued from the gutter, Nikolai Kavalerov, described him, "sausage maker, pastry man, and cook." Is not Andrei Babichev the conscious NEP counterpart of George Babbitt? Can the similarity of surnames be an accident? Sinclair Lewis's novel appeared in 1922, and Russian translations, *Mister Bebbitt: roman*, appeared in 1924 and 1926.

Perhaps the most unvarnished and unambiguous account of the disillusionment of the NEP is in Ilya Ehrenburg's *Memoirs*. He had gone abroad in the last weeks of War Communism. He was astonished when he saw Moscow again. "Ration cards had disappeared. . . . Administrative personnel was greatly reduced and no one was working out grandiose projects. [Proletarian Culture] poets had ceased writing on cosmic subjects. The poet Mikhail Gerasimov said to me: 'It's right, but it makes me sick.'"

A typist whom he had known, "a red-haired girl whom for some reason we used to call Cleopatra, had long forgotten 'October in the Theatre' and [Director] Meyerhold's screams. She stood in the Petrovka near the arcades and sold brassières." Old workers and technicians were restoring production. Consumer goods were appearing. The peasants were bringing chickens to the market. "From the point of view of the politician or the production expert the new line was correct; we know now that it produced what it was intended to produce. But the heart has its reasons: NEP often seemed to me to have a sinister grimace." A sign in a Moscow café simply read "Stomach." The old restaurants had reopened. "The waiters wore dress clothes (I never could find out whether these tail-coats had been made for them or had been preserved in trunks from pre-revolutionary days). At every corner there was a noisy beerhouse with foxtrotting, with Russian choirs, with gypsies, with balalaikas, or simply with brawling."

The communist form of address, "comrade," was not always used. Smart carriages stood near the restaurants waiting for customers. As in the old days, their drivers would call, "Your Highness, can I take you anywhere?" There were beggars and homeless children in abundance. Casinos opened, and millions were won and lost.

The new songs described "better than anything else 'the grimaces of NEP.' There was a philosophical one: 'Chicken roasted, chicken steamed, chickens also want to live. I'm not Soviet, I'm no Kadet, I'm just a chicken commissar. I cheated no one, and I shot no one, I only pecked the grain.' " Or the bandit song from Odessa: "Comrade, comrade, my wounds are aching, comrade, comrade, what did we fight for, what did we bleed for—the bourgeois are feasting, the bourgeois are gloating."

An actress had managed to keep a whole apartment to herself. She had lots of guests. "They danced the foxtrot solemnly, as though performing a rite. At midnight a young man arrived, dressed in a tight-fitting bright ginger suit, and explained patronizingly that in Moscow people were unable to distinguish between the foxtrot and the onestep. He had lately returned from a mission and seen how they danced in Leipzig. Everybody listened attentively. Then the gramophone was put on: the same tunes as in the *dancings* of Paris and Berlin: 'Yes, we have no bananas.' "

The Nepmen were a mixed breed. "I knew a poet who [had previously] read semi-Futuristic verse at the Domino. Now he was peddling French scent and cosmetics and Estonian brandy. A former worker at Goujon's factory, a veteran of the Civil War, was prosecuted: he had stolen a vanload of textiles and was caught by accident—he got drunk and smashed a mirror, and they found eight million roubles on him."

At a railroad station, a peasant woman carried a sack of grain into a first-class coach. The conductor corrected her unceremoniously: "Where d'you think you're going? Get out! This isn't nineteen-seventeen!"[11]

Lenin suffered a stroke in May 1922. Late in the year, he returned to work on a half-time basis. In January 1923, he suffered another stroke, but he soon recovered sufficiently to work at home. In March 1923, he suffered a further stroke, from which he never recovered. He died in January 1924. After his first stroke, he was well enough to work and exert some influence on political life only during most of the period of six months from December 1922 to May 1923.

During this period, he developed uncharacteristically serious conflicts with his colleagues in the party, above all with Stalin. Stalin was by no means the most prominent of Lenin's lieutenants. He owed his growing importance in great part to his relative inconspicuousness and to his willingness to perform in a temporarily self-effacing fashion a variety of perfunctory administrative duties that the more heroic and presumptuous vanity of his better-known fellows disdained.

For a long time, the bulk of the party's organizational, administrative, and personnel work had been carried around informally in the head of Yakov Sverdlov, who died unexpectedly in 1919. His death caused the party to take account of the informality of its procedure, and three new bodies were established to do more systematically what Sverdlov had done. The Politburo became the executive cabinet of the party. The Orgburo was assigned to all the organizational work of the party. The authority of the Secretariat, vaguely defined, evolved by practice. It was subsequently given responsibility for preparing the agenda of Central Committee and Politburo meetings and of establishing liaison among all the higher bodies of the party. Its authority was aggrandized as it evolved. Its future importance as the single most critical body in Soviet society was not initially recognized.

The first general secretary (or first secretary, as the position would become) was Nikolai Krestinskii. In 1921, he became a principal figure in the Workers' Opposition, and it damaged his position in the party. In April 1922, at a time when Lenin was alive and well, Stalin was selected to replace Krestinskii as general secretary. It has always been surmised that Lenin approved of Stalin's appointment. Within a short time, he came to regret it.

Several issues precipitated conflict between them. First was the

"Georgian question." In the tsarist Transcaucasus, one of three major nations was the Georgian. Stalin was a Georgian. He had been identified by Lenin since before the revolution, because of his non-Russian ethnicity, as a suitable party expert on the nationalities question. He was then appointed in November 1917 as commissar of nationalities, a post that he held until he became general secretary of the party. As commissar of nationalities, Stalin disposed of considerable authority in the borderlands where the national minorities lived, and perhaps he took a special interest in Georgia.

When the revolution dissolved the Caucasus into disparate political entities, the Georgians, having long shown a special taste for Menshevism, organized a Menshevik democratic republic. In February 1921, Stalin planted in Tbilisi, the capital, a Bolshevik uprising that invited the intervention of the Red Army, which Stalin duly dispatched. Stalin then presumed to serve as something like Bolshevik viceroy in Georgia. He conducted himself arrogantly and insensitively, he was insulted, he grew angry. He left two companions, Sergei Kirov, a Russian, and Sergo Ordzhonikidze, a Georgian, in charge. Ordzhonikidze lost his temper on one occasion and struck a party comrade in the face.

When these proceedings were, with considerable difficulty, brought to the attention of Lenin, he reacted strongly. He consulted Trotsky, and together they prepared what Lenin described, according to Trotsky, as a "bombshell" for Stalin at the Twelfth Party Congress of April 1923. Fortunately for Stalin, Lenin had his third stroke in March and was disabled before the congress convened.

Apparently, once Lenin's suspicions of Stalin were awakened by the Georgian issue late in 1922, he began to examine the activity of his former protégé more critically in other areas. One of the concessions made to the Workers' Opposition and the Democratic Centralists at the Tenth Party Congress had been the establishment of a government body called the Workers' and Peasants' Inspectorate. It was charged to work as a kind of auditing commission of the personnel of government, to determine that the reins of the chariot of state were held by ideologically proper people, that the machinery of state did not grow insensitively bureaucratic. Designed to weed out bureaucracy, the device simply multiplied it. It was cumbersome and lackluster work, none of the leading lights of the party hierarchy wanted the duty, and Stalin was made its commissar.

In December 1922–January 1923, during the last flurry of his energetic political activity, Lenin wrote a pamphlet against the Workers' and Peasants' Inspectorate. He wrote that it was not possible to find a worse body of Soviet government. He did not mention Stalin by name, but everyone in the know knew what and whom Lenin had in mind.

In the meantime, some of the conflict between Lenin and Stalin reflected a state of friction between Lenin and the Politburo itself. It was to some extent the natural irritation between a busy Politburo and the remote meddling of an ailing patriarch. The Politburo had better things to do than to serve as the secretary of a crotchety invalid. In addition, the Politburo unambiguously assumed, in perfect Leninist tradition, the responsibility for Lenin's health. It prescribed, in consultation with the doctors and not without some difficulty and testy protests from the patient, Lenin's medical regime. In order to handle this duty, the Politburo appointed a liaison person to communicate between itself and Lenin, his physicians, and his secretaries. Fatefully, it chose Stalin.

It was a position of enormous risk and enormous opportunity. Not only did Stalin as general secretary have all the documentation of party business in his hands; he also had the authority to manage and discipline party members. Lenin's several secretaries—one of whom was his wife, Nadezhda Krupskaia, and one of whom was Stalin's wife, Nadezhda Alliluyeva—were party members. In the Georgian question, in order to reduce risk to himself, to Lenin's health, or to both, Stalin ordered that certain documents be withheld from Lenin. Lenin, however, was a hard man to deny. Krupskaia deferred to Lenin. Stalin discovered it. He telephoned Krupskaia in December 1922 and called her what the documents record only as an indecent name. Lenin learned of it. He summoned Stalin to apologize, threatening otherwise to break off all personal relations with him. Stalin wrote an apology and thereby registered his guilt, though the letter has never come to light.

About the same time, in his last winter but one, Lenin dictated that famous Testament to the Central Committee that was to resonate so loudly only in the history books. He feared the instability of a split in the party between its two most outstanding personalities, Stalin and Trotsky, which might reflect an implicit split in Soviet society between workers and peasants. In order to avoid such a danger, he recommended recruiting new members for the Central Committee—perhaps he forgot that any selection of new Central

Committee personnel was likely to be heavily influenced by Stalin as general secretary. Lenin said that he would not characterize the other members of the Central Committee; then he proceeded to do so. He referred to the episode of October 1917 when Lev Kamenev and Grigorii Zinoviev had betrayed the party's plans for an armed uprising to the Menshevik press, although, he observed, it should not be held against them. He called Nikolai Bukharin the ablest theorist in the party, yet observed that he had never understood something so elemental as the dialectic.

On 4 January 1923, after the clash between Stalin and Krupskaia, Lenin added a postscript. "Stalin is too rude, and this fault, entirely supportable in relations among us Communists, becomes insupportable in the office of general secretary. Therefore, I propose to the comrades to find a way to remove Stalin from that position."[12]

Adam Ulam has made the point that the Testament was not the manifestation of a lucid mind.[13] Rudeness was a trivial flaw in a revolutionary personality called upon to face what Bolsheviks had to face in the world that Lenin left them. Stalin was guilty of worse flaws: duplicity, dishonesty, intrigue, and latent megalomania.

Lenin left the party one other literary legacy over which it paused somewhat more attentively. In this article, "On Cooperation," Lenin stated in boldface type that he was forced to admit a radical change in his entire view of socialism. Before socialism could be successfully introduced in Russia, a cultural revolution must take place in the minds of the people. They must be educated to the advantages of a cooperative movement. Lenin was convinced that the NEP would have to endure for a long time, perhaps for two decades.

"On Cooperation" was no more lucid a document than was the Testament. Had Lenin given up his faith in communism? He was clearly now putting the cart of culture consciously ahead of the horse of economic determinism, as he had in 1917 put political will ahead of social and economic conditions. What the ultimate outcome of Lenin's perhaps agonizing reappraisal of his life's work might have been had he lived longer we cannot know. He evidently died in painful disappointment and confusion.

When the Testament was read to the Central Committee after Lenin's death, it was received by a leadership already deeply involved in a struggle for the deceased leader's political primacy, and the chief candidates for succession to his mantle made the mistake of fearing

Trotsky more than Stalin. They wished to preserve Stalin as a part of their team. Ignoring Krupskaia's protests, they suppressed the Testament. Those who spared Stalin would not be spared by him.

Lenin's death was a serious loss for the party because none of the candidates who fought to succeed him had both Lenin's confidence in himself and the confidence of the party as well. His death was a loss for Russia because none of the candidates who aspired to succeed him was regarded by the Russians as Russian.[14] One was a Georgian, the others were Jews. The Jewish question is always important in Russia, as a common folk saying suggests: "Bud zdorov, bei zhidov!"—Be well, and beat the Jews. The fate of the country under Bolshevism would allow future generations of Russians to say that the revolution was the product of a legendary "Jewish–masonic conspiracy" against Russia. That was not true, although the Jews had few reasons to be sympathetic to Russia. Rather, the revolution was a tragedy of dogmatism imposed on the nation by the mentality of the Russian intelligentsia.

Among Lenin's heirs, four were prominent enough to aspire to his power and to struggle with each other for it. In order of their prestige, as understood at the time, they were Leon Trotsky, Grigorii Zinoviev, Lev Kamenev, and Joseph Stalin.

Trotsky had been at the time of the October Revolution the president of the Petrograd Soviet and hence the de facto chief of the Red Guard. At the time of Brest-Litovsk, he was commissar of foreign affairs. During the civil war, he was commissar of war. Thus he was the man who had led the uprising in Petrograd that brought the Bolsheviks to power and the man who led them to victory in the civil war. More credit than that was hardly available in the Bolshevik order. But Trotsky had more. He was a distinguished orator in a party that prized talent with words. He was an astonishing author. In spite of a busyness of commitments that would have daunted several ordinary men, Trotsky had published the history of the revolution in three volumes and the history of the civil war in three volumes.

Zinoviev was chairman of the Petrograd—soon to be Leningrad—Soviet, first secretary of the party there, and chairman of the Communist International, the organization of communist parties of the world, the "general staff" of world revolution.

Kamenev was first secretary of the Moscow party organization, chairman of the Moscow Soviet, a member of the Politburo, and, in

1922, first deputy chairman of the Council of Commissars. His status benefited as well from his closeness to Lenin. In addition, he was thought to have a stauncher, less versatile integrity than Zinoviev.

Stalin, it is true, possessed many offices, but they were not the ones that in 1924 conferred prestige. He was perceived as a bureaucrat, and the title was not flattering.

An index of liabilities, on the other hand, places the four in the same order. Trotsky had long been a Menshevik. He had subjected Lenin's vanguard theory to the criticism that it was dictatorial. No one else had said so many things critical of Lenin, and it was easy enough to dig up these quotations and to fling them in his face at a time when reverence for the departed leader had quickly become the touchstone of political reliability.

Trotsky's very strengths were liabilities. He was too independent. He was argumentative. His sharp tongue stung too bitingly and embarrassingly. He was cast in a heroic mold, a titan among commoners. Most materially, he was still commissar of war, and thus he had military power with which to urge his candidacy should he choose to use it. For habitually historically thinking Bolsheviks, he was the one of the four most likely to become the Bonaparte of the Russian Revolution.

Both Kamenev and Zinoviev had one indelible stigma on their records. On an ill-fated day in October 1917, they had objected, in the interests of Marxist democracy, to the Bolshevik decision to seize power alone, without the coalition of the other socialist parties; and they had taken their protest, and thus the betrayal of Bolshevik plans for armed uprising, to the Menshevik party press. Trotsky did not let them forget it.

Stalin had the same quantity of liabilities as of assets: none. When the "literary debate" broke out among the other three antagonists, he could stand clear of it all, satisfied in the damage that they were doing each other.

Kamenev, Zinoviev, and Stalin initially formed a bloc against Trotsky, the "triumvirate." Trotsky headed the Left Opposition. Early in 1925, Stalin propounded the new theory of "socialism in one country," and it eventually drove Kamenev and Zinoviev to break with him and to join Trotsky in the United Opposition. By that time, Stalin had gained considerably in strength. Otherwise, he would not have risked offending and losing the support of Kamenev and Zinoviev.

Apart from personal antagonism and rivalry, several serious questions of ideology and policy were at issue here. The one that arose first was that of democracy in the party. Trotsky complained bitterly that the party was being manipulated against him. He was right, of course, but the abuse of party democracy was a problem that he noticed only when he began to suffer from it. Until then, no one else had been more summary and abrupt in the use of authority. In the civil war, he was notorious for severity and impatience.

A second issue was the one that had chased Kamenev and Zinoviev from Stalin's side to Trotsky's: socialism in one country. Stalin had formulated it to take issue with Trotsky's doctrine of permanent revolution. Trotsky was the ideological architect of the idea of combining the bourgeois and proletarian phases of the Russian Revolution, then carrying the struggle without interruption straight to Europe, without the assistance of whose proletariat neither he nor Lenin initially believed that the Russian Revolution could survive. In the mid-1920s, Trotsky continued to insist that socialism could be built in backward Russia only after the revolution had occurred in Europe. Otherwise, Bolshevism, caught between the hostile peasantry at home and the hostile imperialists abroad, would never find the resources both to protect itself and to build socialism at once. This position was known in the party as the theory of permanent revolution. Trotsky had initially called it "uninterrupted revolution," a term that described the idea more accurately, but Stalin preferred "permanent revolution." As Isaac Deutscher observed, after world war, two revolutions, civil war, and the crisis and famine of 1921, the revolution was tired, and the name "permanent revolution" gave offense. Since it was the idea of his rival, Stalin preferred it.

Stalin emerged in 1925 for the first time in his life in the guise of theorist. In a line of reasoning more readily comprehended by simple people than Trotsky's more sophisticated argument, he made the commonsensical point that, since the European revolution had failed and a socialist government existed only in the Soviet Union, it made sense to get on with the business of building a properly socialist economy and society. Trotsky's position, Stalin suggested, was unpatriotic, as it betrayed a lack of faith in the Russian peasant. For Kamenev and Zinoviev, socialism in one country was a retreat from world revolution and from Leninism, so they joined Trotsky.

The merits of the dispute over socialism in one country are characterized appropriately by Donald Treadgold.

Trotsky declared that it was impossible to build socialism in Russia because the peasants did not want it; that it would be possible to do so if the workers of the West revolted, and he was right. Stalin declared that it was impossible to wait for the Western workers to revolt before building socialism, because they were not likely to revolt in the immediate future. Therefore socialism could be built in Russia only if the Party used the peasantry, and he was also right. However, that the Western workers were not Communist, Trotsky could never admit; he could only assert that they would be soon. That the Russian peasants were not Communist, Stalin could never admit, but he could try to compel them to be. As a result Trotsky retreated into utopianism, while Stalin proceeded to establish a minority dictatorship built on terror.[15]

The third issue concerned the pace of industrialization. Stalin in the mid-1920s adhered to the policy of the NEP. Trotsky and the Left Opposition, impatient with the slow pace of growth that the NEP necessitated, were eager to scrap it and to proceed with planned industrialization. The chief economic theorist in their camp was Evgenii Preobrazhenskii. He proposed a radical version of what Sergei Witte had inflicted on the peasantry. The ominous nature of his plans was readily apparent in his reference to the peasants as an "internal colony" that would have to be subjected to "unequal rates of exchange." The adherents of the NEP warned that such an approach would lead to a new civil war, this time with the peasants.

Of course, there were contradictions in the positions of both Trotsky and Stalin. A fast-paced industrial program moved in the direction of socialism in one country, and adherence to the NEP did not. It was not, however, the merits of the arguments of the two sides that weighed decisively in the outcome of the conflict. If it was true, as Trotsky alleged, that "the greater the sweep of events, the smaller was Stalin's place in it,"[16] it was also true, as Stalin alleged, that "Trotsky's strength reveals itself when the revolution gains momentum and advances; his weakness comes to the fore when the revolution is defeated and must retreat. . . . He was equal to herculean, not to lesser labours."[17] The atmosphere of the time favored Stalin's personal style and qualities rather than those of Trotsky.

Stalin had another advantage. He felt the mass mood more sensitively, and in an exoteric medium he was a better communicator. As Deutscher suggested, Stalin reformulated a religious style in party affairs. When Lenin died, Stalin read a litany of loyalty to him in public.

Stalin was the prime mover of the construction of the Lenin Mausoleum on Red Square, the principal shrine of the new cult. When expulsions from the party began, those of Trotsky, Kamenev, and Zinoviev, in 1927–28, they took a form not unlike excommunication, and they were soon followed by recantation and readmission for those who were willing—Kamenev and Zinoviev. As Trotsky said, Stalinism was "the philosophy of a priest endowed with the powers of a gendarme."[18] Stalin's favorite novel was Victor Hugo's *Ninety-Three*, that is, 1793 of the French Revolution. Its hero was Cimourdain, a revolutionary priest.[19] When the party dissolved the power of the Russian church, Stalin constructed a new orthodoxy for the new faithful.

The most decisive factor in the outcome of the struggle was the growing power of Stalin in the administrative apparatus of the party. By 1927, he was firmly in control of party affairs, and his opponents were hopelessly outmaneuvered. Their defeat was simply a matter of course.

At that point the real Stalin emerged, first appropriating the program of his opponents, then carrying it farther than anyone could have imagined. The multiple frustrations that Russian reality imposed on Bolshevik politics had deceived the expectations of Lenin and his party utterly. In the 1920s, the revolution's only beneficiaries appeared to be those peasants whom the party so despised. As the mantle of leadership passed to Stalin, he was to deceive the peasants and the party alike.

✤ 8 ✤

The Brave New World of Stalinism, 1928–1953

We are fifty or a hundred years behind the advanced countries. We must make good this lag in ten years. Either we do it or they crush us.

Stalin, speech of February 1931

Force is the midwife of every old society pregnant with a new one.

Marx, *Capital*

It took a famine to show them who is master here. It has cost millions of lives, but the collective farm system is here to stay. We have won the war.

Soviet official in Ukraine, 1933

I heard the children . . . choking, coughing with screams. . . . And I persuaded myself. . . I mustn't give in to debilitating pity. We were realizing historical necessity. We were performing our revolutionary duty. We were obtaining grain for the socialist fatherland. For the five-year plan.

Lev Kopelev, *Education of a True Believer*

The regime of reason was about to unleash its ultimatum. Stalin set out to make Soviet Russia an unpeasant country and to do so on a crash basis. What the Soviet Union was during most of its life it became in the decade following 1928. The First Five-Year Plan and the purges that followed it laid the foundation of Soviet civilization.

Various efforts were subsequently made to reform the Stalinist substance of the Soviet system. In the end, reform failed, and the creation itself had to be abandoned.

The developments that Stalin initiated in 1928 are appropriately regarded as "the second revolution." The first, that of October–November 1917 and the Soviet victory in the civil war, was a thorough political revolution. The face and nature of government changed beyond recognition. These events were, however, only a partial social revolution. While they chased out the nobility and scotched the church, the mass of Russia's class structure, the workers and the peasants, remained much the same. None of these upheavals constituted an economic revolution. The honeymoon period of the spring of 1918 left the bulk of the old order deliberately intact. When the civil war was over, the NEP returned the economy to the situation of the spring of 1918. It was a good deal more damaged than it had been even in 1918, but it recovered its former condition before the end of the NEP. The second revolution, Stalin's Five-Year Plan, completed the social revolution. It supplanted the old bourgeois managers and technicians with new ones educated in Soviet schools to Soviet goals and ideals. It transformed the nature of both the peasantry and the working class. The economic revolution was equally as thorough. By the end of the 1930s, the Soviet Union was an industrial power great enough to pit its military-industrial complex against that of Germany and to win.

It is no mystery why the forced pace of planned industrialization was adopted in Soviet Russia: to make Russia strong, modern, and Marxist. Why it happened precisely in 1928 is a more complicated question.

The most obvious reason for the Five-Year Plan is that that is how economics was done in the Russian tradition. The science of political economy was more political in Russia than elsewhere. Economic growth and progress, like political reform, in Russia alternated between trivial deeds and senseless dreams. The private practice of persistent modest efforts in economic life was devoted primarily to surviving, not to expanding; and those who expanded, whether seventeenth-century merchants or twentieth-century kulaks, risked coming to the attention of a government always attentive to opportunities for its own rapacious aggrandizement.

It obviously never occurred to the party not to engage when opportune in deliberate industrialization. The advantages foreseen in such a plan were plain, though ranking them in an order of priorities would be sheer guesswork. High on the list, in any event, was the motive to prepare the country for war. After all, Bolshevism had declared ideological war—the only kind that it had the strength to fight at the time—against world capitalism, and it was not to be imagined that the enemy would turn the other cheek.

Moscow perceived in Great Britain in the 1920s the leader of the capitalist camp. The British had established commercial relations with the Soviet Union in 1921 and diplomatic relations in 1924, but the relationship had never been untroubled. In May 1923, the "Curzon ultimatum" complained of Soviet propaganda in the Middle East and especially in British India. In the summer of 1926, in the midst of the general strike in Britain, the Soviet government approved the transfer of large funds to support the strikers. In April 1927, the police in Beijing raided the Soviet embassy and found evidence of Soviet revolutionary activity in China, a subject to which the British were sensitive. In May 1927, the Conservative government of Britain ordered a police raid on the Anglo-Russian Trade Delegation in London, an institution enjoying diplomatic immunity, and found what was alleged to be evidence of Soviet subversive activity. At this point, the government broke diplomatic relations with the Soviet Union. This development was portrayed in the Soviet press as the "war scare" of 1927. Stalin took a special part in expounding on the danger.

Stalin was to justify the Five-Year Plan by reference to war in a famous speech in February 1931. Old Russia, he said, was beaten by the Mongol khans, the Turkish beys, the Swedish feudal lords, the Polish Pans, the Anglo-French capitalists, the Japanese barons—curiously, he did not mention the Germans. "We are fifty or a hundred years behind the advanced countries. We must make good this lag in ten years. Either we do it or they crush us."[1] The quest for strategic security was one of the fundamental motives of the plan.

Another was to proceed with the building of socialism in one country. This aspect of the plan had important underlying corollaries, the most important of which was to establish a secure supply of grain. Both major crises precipitating the two major shifts of policy to date had been associated with this problem. In the summer of 1918, war communism was designed, through grain requisitioning, to procure a grain supply. In the spring of 1921, it was a new problem of grain supply that forced the abolition of War Communism and grain requisitioning and the inauguration of the NEP. Toward the end of the NEP, it was a repetition of precisely this problem, grain supply, that forced another dramatic change of political course.

There was another corollary of socialism in one country: a secure grain supply depended absolutely upon a reversal of power relations between countryside and city. The NEP had been an open admission of the superior economic power of the peasantry. Given such power, the peasant could do what he would about grain distribution, and the urban government, in the circumstances of the NEP, had to adjust, to accept the terms that the peasant offered. In the long run, playing the role of dependent vis-à-vis the peasantry was intolerable to the Bolsheviks, and herein lay the prospect of a terrible struggle.

The condition of Soviet agriculture in the 1920s was not in any case an adequate base to support modernization of the country. Both Marxist doctrine and objective research are agreed on this point. According to Marxism, agricultural efficiency required large-scale mechanization in place of the old Russian commune. No one who has studied Soviet Russian agriculture in the 1920s thinks that the egalitarian small-scale landholding, which the peasant revolution established and Bolshevik legislation sanctioned, was capable of feeding the country on a scale that would make a modernized, and thus largely urban, society feasible.

It is possible that the Five-Year Plan was a response to pressure from the proletariat. Unemployment in Moscow stood in 1926 between 14 and 20 percent, and police reports record talk among the workers of a general strike. At the same time, prostitution was rife, the city streets were awash with wild orphan kids (the *besprizorniki*), and a few of the posh bars and restaurants of the city sported casinos and all forms of offensively decadent bourgeois high life.[2]

Collectivization had always been, unknown to the unsuspecting peasant of 1917–18, an implicit part of the agenda of Bolshevism. The peasant commune (*mir*) of old Russia was a collective organization. The new Soviet collective farm (*kolkhoz*) was a collective organization. Why, then, did peasants devoted to collective forms resist departing from the one form and entering the other? The answers are not far to seek. First, the peasant was deeply suspicious of urban government and its meddling in the countryside. Second, the peasant himself was in control of his commune, and he realized clearly that the meddlesome urban government would be in control of the collective farm. And, of course, that government intended to use the collective farm in part as an instrument of exploitation of the peasantry.

The August version (1928) of the Five-Year Plan drawn by Gosplan, the state economic planning commission, made four assumptions about the near-term economic future of the Soviet state: (1) there would be no serious crop failure; (2) there would be an increase in world trade; (3) there would be an increase of efficiency of production; (4) there would be a decline in national defense expenditures.

As it turned out, the Russians, unfortunate as usual, were to realize none of these expectations. There was a famine, if not exactly a crop failure, of the planners' own making. World trade was devastated in 1929 by the crash on Wall Street and the world depression. The contraction of world trade depressed the prices of commodities drastically; hence Soviet grain exports brought far smaller profits than planned. The regime responded by increasing grain exports, further depressing prices, requiring yet more exports, and so on, in a vicious cycle. Meanwhile, efficiency of production suffered heavily from the tumultuous reorganizations that both agriculture and industry underwent. And the Japanese conquest of Manchuria on the Soviet Far Eastern frontier in 1931 forced an increase of national defense expenditures.

In any event, the Five-Year Plan did not conform to any expectations or anticipations. Its development was subjected to the merciless intrusion of a series of economic events altogether unforeseen. The origins of the problem are to be found in 1925.

At that time, the more prosperous peasants—kulaks—were demanding, in their incipient prosperity, three concessions: unrestricted hiring of labor, abandonment of price ceilings in the grain trade, and reduction of the agricultural tax. In April 1925, the Council of Commissars issued decrees giving them what they wanted. Here was the high tide of the NEP, and, ironically, it was precisely in the deceptive generosity of these concessions to the kulak that the origins of a new conflict lay.

The 1925 grain harvest was 25 percent greater than that of the preceding year, and yet grain deliveries to the state, at preestablished prices, were 40 percent below those of the preceding year. The peasant quite naturally chose to sell his grain on the free market at high prices rather than to the state at controlled prices. The shortfall of deliveries to the state was so serious that grain had to be imported to satisfy urban demand. By December 1925, at the Fourteenth Party Congress, the mood of the party had swung decidedly against the favor that it had recently shown the kulaks.[3]

In the spring of 1926, then, the government lowered the price ceilings on grain that it purchased from the peasant. These purchases were called procurements (*zagotovki*) and these prices, procurement prices. At the same time, it continued to allow free-market sales at higher free-market prices in grain that it did not purchase from the peasant. Thus a dual pricing policy prevailed in the country. The lowering of the procurement prices intended to punish the profiteering impulses of the kulak naturally led to more withholding of grain from procurement deliveries.

Finally, in December 1927, the government revised taxation on the peasants upward on a graduated scale, taxing the kulak more heavily than the other peasants.

If the government intended the lower price ceilings on grain to save expense in feeding the cities and the higher taxes to increase revenues, the consequences were, naturally and rationally, quite different. For neither lower price ceilings on procurement grain nor discriminatory taxation on the more provident producers obtained what the government sought, that is, more grain at cheaper prices.

One other factor contributed to the problem. In the early days of the NEP, agriculture had recovered its productivity much more quickly than the wrecked industry. The prices of agricultural produce then fell much more quickly than those of industrial goods. When the peasant complained of both the scarcity and the price of industrial goods, the government took measures to lower the prices. These goods were then bought up at relatively low prices by the urban consumers nearest to their output and resold, if at all, to peasants farther away in the villages. The artificial pricing of industrial goods did not in the long run benefit the peasant, causing what was known as the "goods famine." Had he had more industrial goods to buy, the peasant would have sold more grain in order to purchase them.

In fact, these policies, irrational as they were, gradually provoked another grain-supply crisis. Both the total harvest of grain in the country and the proportion of grain delivered to the state in procurements began to decline. The crucial factor was the volume of procurements, which fell from 1926–27 to 1928–29 by about 20 percent. By the winter of 1927–28, the leadership was in a bit of a panic, fearing the effects of this state of affairs on the morale of the army and the prospect of being forced to cut wages and raise food prices.

The same trend threatened its premeditated industrialization. In 1927–28, the grain in the internal market was only half that of 1913, and the grain available for export was only 5 percent of that of 1913. Since grain had long been the staple form of surplus capital in Russia, the staple form of export, if the country could not export grain, then it clearly could not finance industrialization.[4]

The problem of 1928 derived partly from production, partly from supply. The peasants had responded to the policy innovations of 1926 and 1927 in several ways that precipitated the crisis. When faced with price ceilings on food crops, they shifted production to other crops. When a kulak was subjected to higher taxation as a large producer, he began to produce less in order to earn the benefit of lower taxation. When faced with the opportunity to sell to the state at low controlled prices or on the free market at high prices, he withheld from the state. This naturally raises the question how the state procured any grain at all, why any peasant at all sold disadvantageously to the state. The only logical surmise is that the more improvident peasants lacked what the anthropologists call "withholding power."[5] The pressure of debt and the lack of storage capacity forced them to sell immediately. Presumably some of them could rely on immediate and convenient government transport.

The kulak, on the other hand, had the capacity to store his grain, to purchase grain for storage from other peasants, and to withhold both during flush seasons and wait until spring and summer, when the depletion of the previous season's harvest typical of peasant economies bids up the price of grain. Toward the end of the NEP, the state was forced, in order to avert disaster in the food supply in the cities, both to purchase grain abroad and to meet the kulak's high prices.

In sum, the government, through its dual price policy, had maneuvered itself again into a direct conflict of economic interests with the peasantry. The question posed here was in effect who had the power to tax whom. Was the government going to tax the peasant or vice versa? If, as the American jurist John Marshall observed, the power to tax involves the power to destroy, the potential consequences of this conflict were fateful. At the least, the peasant was in a position to wipe out those reserves of revenue that the government expected to use to finance the industrial dimension of the Five-Year Plan. At worst, the peasant threatened to starve the government. Thus, in 1928, as in 1918 and 1921, the peasant, with his potent control of the most important commodity in the nation, grain, again challenged not merely the policy choice but the very existence of the Bolshevik government.

By this time, Stalin had sufficiently consolidated his power to put his own personal imprint on the government's response. Just as Stalin had drawn on one stage of his education, that of a priest in a Georgian Orthodox seminary, to invent the tactic of orthodox persecution of heresy in order to deal with the ideological challenge of his opponents in the Left Opposition in 1926–27, so in 1928 he drew on a later phase of his education to deal with the recalcitrant peasants.

From 1925, Stalin had a personal librarian who recorded for the archives the boss's reading and notes. We know, consequently, that Stalin took a considerable interest in Vasilii Kliuchevskii's interpretation of tsarist absolutism as a system in which the nobility was bound to state service through a bureaucratic order. In addition, he followed quite closely a debate between Trotsky and M.N. Pokrovskii over Pavel Miliukov's interpretation of the overdeveloped (hypertrophic) model of statecraft in the history of Russia. In the course of this debate, Pokrovskii quoted in italics, as applicable to Russia, Marx's comment on the uses that the European powers made of the discovery of the New World in transforming themselves into capitalist states. "These methods all employ the power of the state, the concentrated and organized force of society, to hasten, hothouse fashion, the transformation of the feudal mode of production into the capitalist mode, and to shorten the transition. Force is the midwife of every old society pregnant with a new one. It is itself an economic power."[6]

What did Stalin learn? He learned that Russia, "isolated in a hostile encirclement of foreign states, had sought to build a strong state capable of defending the national territory and gathering Russian lands held by external foes. . . . He saw history's relevance to the current situation of Soviet Russia isolated in *its* hostile foreign encirclement, and drew the inference for policy: that it was imperatively necessary to build a mighty industrialized Soviet Russian state in a very short time."[7]

With these ideas in mind, Stalin took the initiative against the peasants. In the winter of 1927–28, he commandeered a train, loaded it with units of the police, and departed for Western Siberia east of the Ural Mountains, where the grain harvest was known to have been especially good and where state grain procurements were running dangerously behind schedule. The state had cut procurement prices during the year by 20 to 25 percent, and the peasants had cut deliveries by more than a third. What Stalin did in this area was to resort to the forcible grain requisitioning that had been practiced in War Communism. The practice came to be called by the euphemism "the Urals–Siberian method." Later in the year, he resorted to the same device in the North Caucasus.

The Urals–Siberian method was a considerable intensification of the conflict between government and peasant. It was not the beginning of the struggle. Rather, it was the third step. Step one had been the lowering of procurement prices and the discriminatory taxation. Step two had been the peasant response of withholding from the state. By the time of the application of the Urals–Siberian method, the two antagonists were locked in a combat in which there could be no compromise. There could only be winners and losers. A retreat on the part of either side would be an act of utter submission. The state, in particular, had experienced this threat enough to know that the Five-Year Plan and its own future depended on a victory. What followed the Urals–Siberian method was a series of attacks and counterattacks, first by one side, then by the other, in an ascending spiral of escalation that could only eventuate in the triumph of one and the ruin of the other.

The peasants responded with their customary tactics: underplanting, hiding grain, and destroying grain. The state came into possession of statistics indicating that the collective farms and state farms, which comprised 2 percent or less of Soviet farming, were releasing 55 percent of their grain for procurements, while the peasant communes were releasing only 12.5 percent. The numbers pointed to a solution: Stalin ordered "full-scale collectivization." This was the fall of 1929.

The peasants responded desperately. They began at once to slaughter and consume, cooked if possible, half-raw if necessary, the livestock of which collectivization would deprive them. The few contemporary visitors to the countryside who have left their accounts speak of the best-fed peasants whom they had ever seen, pot bellies and bloody faces. It was a race to beat the state to the punch. The peasants within a matter of months managed to reduce the livestock population of the Soviet Union by half, and this in the midst of a campaign designed by the state to multiply the capital resources of the country.

Stalin countered with dekulakization, that is, he blamed the resistance on the class antagonism of the rich peasants, the kulaks, rounded them up, expropriated their property—a huge capital windfall for the industrial sector of the plan—and shipped them off to detention and labor camps in trains lacking heat, plumbing, or food and water. Those who survived were set down in the far north and far east in camps that could scarcely accommodate them; or they were driven in herds into the arid steppes of Central Asia, where they gathered around signs designating Settlement No. 1, Settlement No. 2, and so forth. This work was done by units of the police, units of the army, and a host of party enthusiasts who were summoned to leave the workbench and answer the party's needs. Only twenty-five thousand were called, and seventy thousand responded. They were given pistols and sped on their way. Many of them suffered at the hands of their victims grim fates like those that they inflicted.[8]

We have some first-hand accounts of the process. According to the chairman of one collective farm, "when we were told of collectiviza- tion . . . I liked the idea. So did a few others in our village, men like me, who had worked in the city and served in the Red Army. The rest of the village was dead set against it and wouldn't even listen to me. So my friends and I decided to start our own little cooperative farm, and we pooled our few implements and land." They got started, but one day an order came from the local administrative center. It required a hundred more families in the collective. Only a dozen could be persuaded to join. That did not satisfy the county party committee. It "had orders from Moscow, long sheets saying how many collectives with how many members they had to show on their records." After a long and futile argument with the committee, "I called a village meet- ing and I told the people that they had to join the collective, that these were Moscow's orders, and if they didn't, they would be exiled and their property taken away from them. They all signed the paper that same night. . . . And the same night they started to do what the other villages of the U.S.S.R. were doing when forced into collectives—to kill their livestock." The party committee was, however, satisfied. When the chairman reported the attitude of the peasants and the killing of livestock, it was a matter of utter indifference.[9]

Another chairman told a similar story. Two party members came to the village and summoned the peasants to a meeting. There someone distributed a leaflet against the collective farm. The meeting dragged on without result for two days. Later two more party members arrived.

The meeting lasted until dark, at which point someone threw a brick against the lamp, "and in the dark the peasants began to beat the Party representatives, who jumped out the window and escaped from the village barely alive." Next day, the militia arrived and made arrests, and the collective was formed.[10]

By March 1930, the application of such force had placed about 55 percent of the peasantry on collective farms. At that point, something entirely unexpected happened. Stalin made a speech over the radio, subsequently printed in the papers, in which he said that it had come to his attention that excessive enthusiasm and even force had been used in the collectivization campaign, a consequence of fanatics who had grown "dizzy with success." The gates were thrown open, and more than half of those collectivized decollectivized themselves within a matter of months. The peasants carried copies of the newspapers reporting the speech as protection from the local authorities. These papers were so much in demand that their prices multiplied several times.[11]

What was the meaning of this sudden reversal? Why retreat when the corner had been turned? We know of two reasons. First, the bulk of the peasantry sympathized distinctly with the kulaks undergoing dispossession and deportation, especially with the afflicted children, and they gathered around the homes of those designated for expropriation to protect them. Second, the leaders of the Red Army informed Stalin that its use in dekulakization had put its reliability at risk, that Soviet intelligence had reports that Polish intelligence was following Red Army morale closely and considering an attack on the USSR.[12]

Within a matter of months, the process of decollectivization was reversed, this time more gradually.

We have had unimpeded access to the archival record of one Soviet province from the revolution to the outbreak of World War II. In 1941, the government of Smolensk failed to carry out the usual orders either to evacuate the archive or to destroy it, and it was captured by the German army. In 1945, it fell into the possession of the American army, and it is now part of the U.S. National Archives. Among its more interesting features are unpublished letters of peasants to local newspapers protesting collectivization. A poor peasant described it as robbery and eternal slavery. "Collective life can be created when the entire mass of the peasants goes voluntarily, and not by force. . . . I beg you not to divulge my name, because the Party people will be angry."

"Say something against collectivization, and you're put in prison." Only half a percent of the peasants, he maintained, favored collectivization. "It's better to hang yourself than to join the [collective]; it's better not to be born."[13]

By the end of 1932, the level of collectivization of March 1930 was again attained. Resistance had not, however, ended, and the ultimate phase of government escalation was now prepared. This was the famine of 1932–33. The resistance to collectivization was especially stubborn in Ukraine. Stalin obviously tired of it. He surrounded Ukraine with an embargo, siphoned grain out of it, and did not allow shipment of grain into it.[14] Meantime, as the man-made famine developed, Soviet grain exports from 1930–32 were approximately double the level of the best years of the 1920s.[15] The consequence was the starvation of an untold number of peasants. The toll in lives taken by dekulakization and the famine together is often estimated at five to ten million. When the census of January 1937 was taken, the actual population count fell sixteen and a half million persons short of what the demographers had projected, and the purges had at this date not reached serious numerical proportions. Stalin resolved this embarrassment by having the official responsible for the census purged. As an official told a Ukrainian who later defected, the 1933 harvest "was a test of our strength and their endurance. It took a famine to show them who is master here. It has cost millions of lives, but the collective farm system is here to stay. We have won the war."[16]

The tension in the country, especially in the party, was reflected in Stalin's own family. One night in November 1932, at a soirée of party bigwigs in the Kremlin, Stalin's wife, Nadezhda Alliluyeva arrived without her husband, obviously in an ill temper. Stalin came later in a similar humor. She made some remark about the pained condition of the rural areas. Stalin cursed her. She left the gathering. He soon followed her. The following morning she was dead of a gunshot wound. It is generally believed that she shot herself.

One of the more remarkable, and painful, phenomena in this scarcely comprehensible process was the strength of the catechism of those who did the job. Maurice Hindus, an American writer born in Russia, recounted a conversation suggesting the force of this revolutionary conviction. A skeptical citizen was objecting to a party stalwart the unjust treatment of an ordinary peasant. "Listen what has happened to N_____." He was a hard worker, a good producer. For the sake of securing his family in the event of a crop failure, he hid ten sacks of rye. An envious neighbor denounced him. The party official engaged in grain collection "confiscated the hidden rye, the man's best horse, his best cow, his best calf, a mowing machine, ten sheep, seventeen geese, and even the fiddle which the poor fellow had inherited from his grandfather." He was expelled from the village retail cooperative without the refund of his membership fee and denied all salt, kerosene, and dry goods. In addition, his name was listed in public disgrace. "I waited for the Party man to say something, but he only smiled. He seemed unperturbed by the recital of this story. Clearly, he was a man beyond pity and forgiveness, and beyond repentance."[17] Of course, the fate of N_____ was only, relatively speaking, mildly unfortunate, reflecting an early and gentle stage of collectivization.

Vasilii Grossman relates in fiction a considerably more vicious example. It was the fate of kulak families. The fathers had already been arrested. It remained to deal with wives and children. The GPU/police "would threaten people with guns, as if they were under a spell, calling small children 'kulak bastards,' "—legislation forbade offering mercy to children designated kulaks—"screaming 'Bloodsuckers!' And these 'bloodsuckers' were so terrified they had hardly any blood of their own left in their veins. They were as white as clean paper. . . . And there was no pity for them."[18]

In his aptly entitled *Education of a True Believer*, Lev Kopelev confessed in fact his participation as a party activist in just such processes. "I heard the children echoing . . . with screams, choking, coughing with screams. And I saw the looks of the men: frightened, pleading, hateful, dully impassive, extinguished with despair or flaring up with half-mad, daring ferocity. . . . And I persuaded myself, explained to myself. I mustn't give in to debilitating pity. We were realizing historical necessity. We were performing our revolutionary duty. We were obtaining grain for the socialist fatherland. For the five-year plan."[19]

The Soviet novelists have taken more interest in the subject than Soviet historians, even those of the age of glasnost, who are more cautious and conservative.[20] Vasilii Belov's novel of 1989 is titled after one of Stalin's speeches, *The Year of the Great Change* (God velikogo pereloma). The reference is to 1929. A party activist, Shilovskii, was dispatched to the countryside. He was given a pistol, and he discovered that he was to be an executioner. One of his early victims was a woman. She did not understand why she was being brought to this confrontation. When she realized it, she panicked, thought fast, tore open her shirt to bare her breasts, and wrapped her arms around him. She was young and pretty. He was terribly confused. But he recovered and did his duty. Meantime, the kulaks in the churches that served as their transit stations contracted dysentery and died like flies.[21]

According to Boris Pasternak, what happened in the Russian villages that he saw in the early 1930s did "not fit within the bounds of consciousness." Another Soviet writer said that he should write a book about it but that he did not have the courage, for "I would have to relive everything again."[22] The Russian peasants have not forgotten. They are not eager to be privatized. Perhaps they fear another change of course.

The collective farm turned out to be after all less productive than its creators had imagined. In fact, collectivized Soviet agriculture was notorious the world over for its inefficiency. Imperial Russia was one of the leading grain-exporting nations of the world, and Soviet Russia became one of the leading grain importers. Of course, the population has grown, and productivity has not kept pace with it. In the Western world, the simple explanation of the low level of proficiency of Soviet Russian agriculture is that it is socialist. While this explanation may contain elements of truth, it is not very particular, and several particulars are more effectively explanatory.

Natural conditions are an important factor. Canadian conditions are, of course, in many respects similar, and Canadian wheat production is considerably better.

While Russians are everywhere known for their durability, they are nowhere known for a positive work ethic. This observation especially applies to the peasants. It may be that the potential is there, but it has never been rewarded, and experience has taught them the wisdom of cynicism. Serfdom, War Communism, and collectivization are poor tutors of provident work habits.

Perhaps the most powerful explanation of the low productivity of Soviet agriculture during the Stalin era is the fact that the economy of the collective farm was never intended to be the subject of capital investment but the object of capital extraction. It is perfectly true that the rural economy as a whole was the beneficiary of huge capital

Table 1

Harvest Distribution in 1939 (in %)

Deliveries to the State in percentage of harvest:	
Compulsory procurements	14.3
Payments to Machine-Tractor Station	19.2
Return of seed loans	4.0
Total	37.5
Collective requirements and reserves:	
For seed	18.2
For feed	13.9
For aiding those in need	0.8
For other expenditures	2.7
Total	35.6
Sales to the State and in free market	4.0
Distributions per workday	22.9
Grand total	100.0

Source: Lazar Volin, *A Survey of Soviet Russian Agriculture* (Washington, DC: U.S. Department of Agriculture, 1951), 180.

accumulation during the 1930s. The tractors and combines were dispatched in large numbers. It was all arranged, however, to control the harvest and to extract capital in its most accessible Russian form, grain, for the benefit of industry and the military. If we remember that the NEP introduced a tax of 10 percent on the peasant's harvest and compare his statistical fate in 1939, admittedly a very stringent and tense year as Moscow faced the threatening international developments in Europe, then it is plain what price the peasant paid for the revolution in agriculture, even after dekulakization and the other painful elements of early collectivization were over (see Table 1).

The Machine-Tractor Station (MTS) was a pool of mechanized equipment that the collective farms hired. The farms themselves did not own their machinery in the Stalin era. The combined seed reserves and seed loans indicate that the crop produced barely four times the quantity of seed grain, one of the most pathetic yields in modern agricultural history—England was producing a ratio of harvest to seed grain of eight or ten to one in the eighteenth century. It is not clear what the disposition of the 4 percent of the harvest sold to the state above the quantity of compulsory procurements, or on the free market, or both was. In any event, if all of the proceeds in this category were distributed to the peasants, which was most unlikely, then their part of the harvest would amount to that 4 percent plus the nearly 23 percent distributed in "workdays." A workday was a unit of distribution reached by dividing the total number of adult workdays expended during the year into the quantity of harvest left after all collective obligations were met, in this case 22.9 percent, perhaps plus 4. The formula used was "to each according to his work," not "to each according to his needs." That latter formula was reserved for the future. Even after the residual portion of the harvest was divided among the peasants, the authorities insisted on patriotic forced loans of various kinds.

Another factor of considerable but incalculable importance was a degree of centralization in planning and administration such as to be inflexible and insensitive to locally variable needs and conditions. The best examples that we have are from the experience of the collective-farm chairman Fedor Belov. One spring the crop-dusting plane came late, and there was thus no crop. One spring, the party ordered the planting of sugar beets on a particularly early schedule. Belov and his agronomist knew from their studies that the beets should be planted only when the soil reached a temperature of twelve degrees Celsius, and that time was several weeks away. They objected to the party's schedule but in vain. So they planted early, and the planting failed and had to be done again later at considerable cost in money and labor.

A more curious example was provided by John Scott, an American metallurgical worker at a Soviet factory, who used a vacation to have a look at a collective farm. He found there twelve tractors from a nearby MTS, only three of which were working. The chairman was away on business. With some German engineers, he plundered parts from three of the twelve in order to put nine of them in working order. When the chairman returned, he panicked. He could explain to the police, he said, twelve tractors most of which did not work, but for the three that had been put entirely out of commission, he would be held accountable for wrecking and sabotage.[23] In these various examples, excessive centralization preempted a rational degree of local flexibility and contributed to the failure of collectivization as a system of agricultural economy.

It must not be imagined, however, that collectivization was a rank failure in the broader perspective of either economics or politics. It was the crucial element in giving the state control of the majority population of the country, the peasantry, and control of the agrarian economy, a control that the peasantry had exercised during the NEP. Without

Table 2

Indices of Production (in %)

National income	+25
Industry	+50
Producers' goods	+120
Consumers' goods	−15
Agriculture	−20
Retail trade	−20
Rural per capita income	−45
Urban per capita income	−55

Source: Adapted from Naum Jasny, *Soviet Industrialization 1928–1952.* (Chicago, University of Chicago Press, 1961), 67.

collectivization, the spectacular short-term successes of the industrial dimension of the Five-Year Plan would not have been possible.

The elusive elixir of instant industrialization that the Five-Year Plan long appeared to have discovered has in fact very earthy foundations. The peasant population on the state institution of the collective farm, surrounded by instruments of control—the police, the party, the local governmental apparatus, the Machine-Tractor Station—was forced to submit to whatever degree of exploitation the state required of it. The state controlled agricultural production, the distribution of the harvest, the price paid for it to the peasant, and the price that it charged other consumers for it. Similarly, the state controlled industrial production, distribution, and prices. The real key to the success of the Five-Year Plan is seen in these factors. It was what Naum Jasny called "the strangulation of consumption." Controlling as it did all distribution and all pricing, paying what it would, charging what it would, the state naturally came into possession of enormous sums of revenue. During one period of four years, for example, while average wages doubled, the cost-of-food index quadrupled.[24] Here was likely the most fantastically lucrative monopoly in the history of economics.

Stalin had achieved a scarcely credible reallocation of economic resources. A summary of the growth and decline of indices of production compiled by Naum Jasny shows the dramatic results (see Table 2).

Further figures amplify these findings. From 1928 to 1955, agricultural production increased by about 50 percent, approximately the rate of the growth of population. Industrial production increased nearly sevenfold, heavy industrial production twelvefold, and expenditures on the armed forces twenty-sixfold.[25]

Jasny concludes: "The Bolsheviks came on the scene as fighters for socialism and against exploitation, for a great improvement in the well-being of everybody. What they achieved was a great increase in the rate of exploitation, reducing the people's share of the national income to an extent nobody had believed possible. . . . One can only be amazed at the strength of the dictatorship, which persisted in holding down personal consumption to such astoundingly low levels."[26]

A recent study agrees in general terms with the findings of Jasny. Capital investment increased in the period from 1928 to 1940 from 12 percent to 49 percent of GNP. Defense expenditures grew from 1.7 billion to 45 billion rubles; deliveries of military matériel increased 18.4-fold. Livestock products fell in 1933 to 47.4 percent of the 1928 level.[27]

An American worker in a Soviet factory provided one of the most authoritative close-up portraits of the 1930s in industry. Magnitogorsk, the "magnetic mountain," was a huge metallurgical complex built on the great ore deposits of the southern Ural Mountains. John Scott—later an editor of *Time*—told of skill and dedication, slave labor, ignorance and a stubborn commitment to the acquisition of technical education, and primitive and severe living and working conditions.[28] An American student has recently given us an update on the city. "The largest assembly of obsolete equipment in the world," it distributes airborne pollution at forty times Western standards and causes respiratory problems in commensurate proportion, but the demand of fulfilling the plan never allowed it the respite for renovation.[29]

Sabotage and wrecking were not rare in either agriculture or industry. Iron rods were found driven into grain fields to put the combines out of order. Arson was a frequent occurrence. Anti-Soviet leaflets were often left in the wake of such deeds. Severe chairmen of collective farms were murdered. Sand was found in the bearings of Diesel engines. Slowdowns expressed rebellion against industrial speedups.[30] Charges of wrecking and sabotage, thrown around so loosely during the purges, were not purely imaginary.

Stalin had turned the corner in creating the Soviet economic system. It remained only to keep the lid on two elements of dissatisfaction. The peasantry was obviously one such element. The party was the other. Stalin turned his attention to the party.

Stalin made mistakes, and he was evidently determined to eliminate the possibility of their recognition. In the eyes of many party members, the largest mistake charged to his account was collectivization.

In 1930, the police identified an organized association of dissidents among local party secretaries, especially strong in the Caucasus. They objected to what they called the authoritarian regime in the party, the reckless regime in the countryside, and economic adventurism in industry. Such an organization was, of course, a violation of the old 1921 ban on factions, and Stalin was able to break it up.

In the summer of 1932, a similar but apparently somewhat more imposing group emerged. It gathered around a document of about two hundred pages known by the name of its author as the Riutin Platform. It stated that the Right Opposition had proved correct in its criticism of Stalin's economics and the Left Opposition in its criticism of his dictatorial regime in the party. It called him the "evil genius" of the revolution.

Stalin attacked this organization with a conventional, traditional party purge. That is, he procured the expulsion of more than a million people from the party. The new style of blood purge that was approaching was to engulf all the leaders of the Riutin group before the end of the decade.

In January 1933, another such group was exposed, more conspiratorial in nature, as it appeared that there was no legal way to oppose Stalin effectively. It called for revision of the unbalanced industrial schemes, dissolution of most of the collective farms, subjection of the police to party control, and independence of the trade unions.

Stalin tried to get Politburo approval for death penalties of the leadership of these last two organizations, but for the time being he failed.[31] Obviously, he did not forgive, forget, or concede the point in the long run.

A lesser degree of the attitudes of these three groups apparently prevailed throughout much of the party. The mood of the time is described as one of battle fatigue, one in favor of a more liberal period of policy. Stalin himself was attentive to it and soon took an opportunity to enunciate it. In his speech to the Seventeenth Party Congress of February 1934, he made several significant points. The worst was over—"life is better, comrades." The party had proved, he said, that there were no heights that Bolsheviks could not storm. Most significantly, he said that there were no enemies left to fight. It sounded reassuring to a battle-weary party.

In the admittedly grim—and what may be the perversely stubborn—opinion developed here, given the premises and the goals of Soviet power, collectivization was not a mistake. Collectivization was the indispensable, unique way in which the party could hold on to power. It was the single most crucial development in the history of Bolshevism. It saved the power of the party, and it doomed traditional old rural Russia. Of course, the whole plague of the Soviet tragedy was a mistake, but it was made in 1917. The flaw was in the foundation. Given the premises and goals of the party and the social and economic conditions of Russia, the juxtaposition of Leninist theory and Russian reality, all that followed inside Russia from the revolution of 1917 through 1934 was not only not mistaken but not avoidable. At every critical phase of its extraordinary development, the party of the revolution did what it must in order to retain power and thus to be in a position to force its abstract vision on reluctant Russian reality.

In 1934, with urban socialism firmly imposed on rural Russia, the lockstep of no alternatives was broken, and the element of pure caprice entered. Hereafter there were choices, and Stalin made them. Half of Soviet civilization was formed by the unavoidable Five-Year Plan. Stalin's whims formed the other half. In either of its two basic phases, the period of inevitability prior to 1934 or the period of arbitrariness thereafter, the Soviet experience is a scarcely equaled historical tribute—for better or for worse—to the power of ideas. The conflict between what the Marxists called the substructure and the superstructure was a very one-sided battle. Culture and consciousness won a near-total victory.

Stalin's other alleged mistake was a real one. As the noncommunist Left put it in Germany after 1933, "Ohne Stalin, kein Hitler"—without Stalin, no Hitler. This is a more complex issue.

When the Bolsheviks seized power in 1917, their expectations in foreign affairs were more than naive. They assumed that one revolution would trigger others, the "theory of the spark," and thus there would be no foreign affairs. Of course, there was the ugly necessity of Brest-Litovsk. Trotsky, informed that he would at least temporarily be commissar of foreign affairs in order to deal with the Germans, was asked what his foreign policy would be. He answered flippantly that he would issue a few revolutionary slogans and close the shop. The Marxist idea was that nationalism and all of its trappings, national frontiers, diplomatic missions, and so forth, were a kind of bourgeois eyewash thrown in the face of the proletariat to seduce its loyalty to the leadership of an alien class. Brest-Litovsk ended the illusion of no foreign policy, and the Bolsheviks emerged from it with an embassy in Berlin.

They did not so quickly surrender, however, the idea of world revolution. In the period from 1917 to 1921, they evolved what has been characterized as a dual foreign policy, one dedicated to overthrowing such bourgeois governments as they had the power to overthrow while at the same time conciliating those governments powerful enough to threaten their own. The latter policy, diplomacy, they conducted through the conventional device of the Commissariat of Foreign Affairs. For the implementation of the former policy, revolution, they developed a new institution, the Communist International, or Comintern. During most of the period prior to 1921, they gave distinct priority to the Comintern.

This latter dimension of their policy, a foreign policy of ideology and revolution, was unique in the world at that time. They presumed to conduct their policy across national boundaries, to establish a claim on the loyalty of proletarians everywhere, one superior to that which the working classes gave to their own national governments.

Unique though it was at that time, the historical precedents of such a policy were plain. The Athenians in the aggressively democratic Delian League were accused of such a policy in the fifth century B.C.E. Elizabeth I of England and Phillip II of Spain had conducted a similar policy as captains of the Reformation and the Counter-Reformation in the sixteenth century, trying desperately to control France and the Low Countries or to partition them. Generations later, the most adept practitioner of this mode of foreign policy was Napoleon I, who set up a series of satellite states with ancient Roman names over Italy, Switzerland, and the Low Countries.

In 1921, when domestic policy turned right in the NEP, so did it in Soviet foreign affairs. The Comintern had to be restrained, and diplomacy and the Commissariat of Foreign Affairs took precedence, at least in Europe. The Comintern then turned from the first of what Lenin termed "two tactics of social democracy," that of armed uprising, to the second, that of "united front." The idea of the united front was that it was suicidal to assault the bourgeoisie of Europe when it was strong and stable. It was smart rather to ally with one or another of the leftist or centrist elements—sometimes parties, sometimes trade unions—in society in progressive but not radical causes and to bide time until the political situation ripened for more aggressive action.

The tactic was a temporary one, of course, one suitable to Marx's fourth period of history, the period of bourgeois dominance. Lenin described its ultimate intent graphically. We support the bourgeois elements of society, he said, as a rope supports a hanging man; we merge with them as a hungry man merges with a piece of bread. Still, the Comintern was condemned in Europe in the 1920s to a policy of patient waiting for a new revolutionary opportunity.

In Asia, on the other hand, the same tactic in a more underdeveloped part of the world, was revolutionary, although the revolution that it supported was, again temporarily, the bourgeois one. The best example was China, where the Communist Party formed a bloc with the Nationalist Party of Sun Yat-sen and Chiang Kai-shek against the reactionary warlords and, indirectly, against foreign imperialism, principally Japanese. It was a risky business, given Lenin's none-too-secret attitude toward communist allies. The Bolsheviks' Chinese ally, Chiang Kai-shek, had been trained in revolution in Soviet schools in Moscow, and he was not ignorant what fate the communists planned for him. He used them and turned on them before they did the same to him—in the Shanghai massacre of April 1927.

From the Soviet point of view, international affairs in Europe during the 1920s were not, in spite of suspicious sensitivity, unduly alarming. At the end of the decade, that situation changed, as the Great Depression destabilized Germany dangerously.

Ironically, Stalin's policy in the Comintern contributed to the disaster. The Sixth Comintern Congress convened in Moscow in August 1928. For reasons that may always remain mysterious, it announced an enhanced Comintern struggle against the established order while not yet embracing armed uprising. The congress professed to foresee a "further development of the contradictions of capitalist stabilization," one that would "increasingly shake that stability and lead inevitably to the most severe intensification of the general capitalist crisis,"[32] a prediction that appeared to be borne out on Wall Street the following year. The Comintern then prepared to take advantage of the opportunity. The chief enemy was identified as the Social-Democratic Party.

The Russian Communist Party had felt a peculiar sense of antagonism to the German Social-Democratic Party since 1918. As the Social Democrats had assumed the mantle of power in Germany when the Kaiser abdicated, they cooperated with the German army in putting down communist uprisings. From that time, the party of Lenin regarded the party of Ebert and Scheidemann with unmixed distrust.[33] The resolutions of the Sixth Comintern Congress simply stated this attitude in a somewhat sharper form. "From a shamefaced defence of capitalism, social-democracy has turned into its active supporter. . . . The social-democratic and reformist trade union leaders in the imperialist countries are the most consistent representatives of bourgeois State interests," often joining in the support of fascist projects. Social Democracy itself "not infrequently plays a fascist part."[34]

This tactic placed the Communist Party of Germany squarely on the side of the enemies of the Weimar Republic. The constitution of Weimar had established a parliamentary system of government, and the legislature, the Reichstag, contained seven major political parties. An executive cabinet had to command a majority in the Reichstag. As no single party among seven could win a majority, it was necessary to form a coalition cabinet of several different parties, usually three of them. The situation was intrinsically unstable.

Prior to the depression, the Nazis, the National Socialist German Workers' Party, had in the last election (1928) won 2.8 percent of the vote. They were a negligible quantity at that time. When the depression hit, it fractured the center in German politics, sending it searching desperately for remedies in the more extremist parties of both right and left. In the Reichstag elections of July 1932, for example, of the 550 seats, the Communists won 95 and the Nazis 230. By definition, parties on opposite extremes of a political spectrum do not coalesce to form a cabinet in parliamentary systems, and the delegation of these two parties together comprised more than a majority in the Reichstag. Not all the other five parties between them together, should they all have been able to agree, which was unlikely, could form a coalition cabinet with majority support in the Reichstag.

The most powerful party was that of the Nazis, and it is not hard to see how it frightened sober political figures. As they pointed out, a barrier to Nazi success was available, a coalition of Communists with Social Democrats, the German Democratic Party, and the German People's Party. It depended upon the Communists, which is to say, it depended upon Stalin. Stalin said no. Finally, the patience of the president of Germany, Field Marshal von Hindenburg, gave way in January 1933, and he called on the man from the gutter, whom he so despised, to become chancellor of Germany and to attempt, through dissolution of the Reichstag and the calling of new elections, to form a majority cabinet. It worked. Hitler allied with the Nationalist Party. The Nazis won 44 percent of the vote, and the Nationalists won 8. Together they had a majority and a reasonable facsimile of a legitimate democratic victory.

This is the explanation of the saying "without Stalin, no Hitler." As the imperial Russians helped to create in the 1860s the Second Reich that destroyed them in 1917, so the Soviet Russians helped to create in the 1930s the Third Reich that nearly repeated the performance in 1941.

We know nothing of any direct criticism of Stalin on account of his botched policy in Germany. There is in any event nothing so massive as the criticism of his collectivization. Yet it is impossible not to infer that several of the sophisticated Old Bolsheviks, who had spent as much time before 1917 in European exile as in the Russian underground, must have understood the nature of this mistake and its impending consequences. Those instrumental in the Comintern would have known. Nikolai Bukharin could not have not known. Karl Radek would have understood it instinctively. There were probably several dozen such people, maybe more. It is very likely that Stalin's old enemy, Mikhail Tukhachevskii—each blamed the other for the failure to capture Warsaw in the Polish campaign of 1920—the chief of the Soviet general staff, who was in the company of his European counterparts frequently, understood it perfectly.

We know, in any event, of prominent people who were passionately anti-Nazi. They include Bukharin, Sergei Kirov, whose wife was Jewish, Maksim Gorkii, and the whole of the general staff and high command.[35] None of these people survived the purges.

At the same time, we know that Stalin had a kind of fascinated admiration for Hitler. Hitler conducted his own blood purge, the Night of the Long Knives, as it was known in Nazi legend, on 30 June 1934. The German army had given him the word that it would not tolerate two armed forces in Germany, that he must choose between it, the regular army, which had been limited by the Peace of Versailles to 100,000 men, and the *Sturmabteilung*, the paramilitary organization of perhaps two million Storm Troopers that had helped to intimidate law and legitimacy in Germany and to bring Hitler to power. Hitler realistically elected to curb the *Sturmabteiling* (SA), and he did so by the sudden assassination of about two hundred persons, chiefly in its leadership. Stalin's reflection on this episode was a remark that he made in the Politburo: "*Molodets.*" This word means something like "attaboy." It is a term of colloquial approval. Stalin continued: "[Hitler] knows how to treat his political opponents."[36]

For some time after the Nazi victory in Germany, official Moscow disdained to worry about it. The Comintern's attitude was "After the Nazis, it will be our turn." Evidently regarding Nazism as the sickest symptom of capitalism, Stalin and company failed utterly to appreciate it properly. In February 1934, the Stavisky riots in France threatened to repeat the Nazi victory of January 1933 in Germany. The French Communist Party and the French fascists attacked the Republic simultaneously. It survived, but the episode frightened much of France, and the French party began to explain insistently in Moscow the close brush with disaster.

A few months later, when Hitler's Night of the Long Knives (30 June 1934) illustrated the stabilization of his power, Stalin relented and inaugurated the "popular front" line, a broad version of the united front from above, including all antifascist parties. At the same time, however, he began to feel the pressure of his mistakes, real and imagined. At the Seventeenth Party Congress of February 1934, there was a substantial vote against his election to the new Central Committee, a fact that one of his henchmen suppressed. Sergei Kirov, one of Stalin's lieutenants known to be skeptical about the continuation of the harsh regime in the countryside, was applauded noticeably more enthusiastically at the congress than Stalin himself was. Yet the following day's record of his speech in *Pravda* omitted what the Soviet press usually published faithfully, all reference to the applause.[37]

A full-dress meeting of the Central Committee scheduled for the first week of December 1934 promised a dramatic confrontation. There was a *sub rosa* move afoot to replace Stalin as general secretary by Kirov.

Kirov was first secretary of the Leningrad party organization. On 1 December, days before the convening of the Central Committee meeting, he was shot and killed in his office. Even now, in the heyday of glasnost, not all the facts of the matter are known. It is believed that his assassin, Leonid Nikolaev, was arrested several times during the few days preceding the assassination and was found to be in possession of a pistol and a map showing the way to Kirov's office, yet he was released each time. Stalin came to Leningrad to head the investigation of the crime. Kirov's bodyguards and the chiefs of the Leningrad police came to mysteriously morbid fates almost immediately. In 1961, Khrushchev said flatly that Stalin inspired the assassination, and he promised an inquiry and full details that we do not yet have. In any event, Kirov was both a close and loyal colleague of Stalin and a dangerous political rival, and he had become by December 1934 a plausible person behind whom to rally an attempt to unseat the evil genius of the revolution.

The year 1935 was a time of preparation. The dramatic developments began in 1936. This is a relatively familiar story. The first big show trial took place in August 1936. Its illustrious victims were Kamenev and Zinoviev. Yurii Piatakov and Karl Radek and company followed in January 1937. The turn of Bukharin, Khristian Rakovskii, and Aleksei Rykov came in March 1938. In the meantime, Sergo Ordzhonikidze and Mikhail Tomskii had shot themselves, and in June 1937 the high command, Tukhachevskii at its head, was tried and condemned for treason in closed proceedings. Subsequently, about half the Red Army's entire officers' corps was purged. From their very different perspectives, both Hitler and Churchill thought the purge of the military to be utterly mad. The experience of 1941 suggests that they were right.

Those who appeared in the three public trials confessed to fantastic and absurd crimes. A script was written for the trials and recited with occasional errors—premature answers to yet unasked questions. The victims were broken by torture, degradation, and sleeplessness—also the utter hopelessness of not cooperating. They were left with a shred of hope that their full cooperation might mitigate an otherwise nearly certain death sentence. And they were warned that if they did not cooperate, the members of their families would be shot along with them. Bukharin had recently married a very pretty young wife—she is still alive and still pretty—and had an infant son. Some of their final pleas for mercy, all containing a full admission of guilt, have only recently been published in the Russian press—Bukharin's, for example, in *Izvestiia*, 13 October 1992. His widow's memoirs have appeared, too. They are called *The Unforgotten* (Nezabyvaemoe).

Most of the accused were executed at once, and most others died, some by execution, in the camps.

This was one style of the Stalinist purge. It took perhaps seventy–eighty victims. The other style was a much more massive affair of largely anonymous people. These were perhaps real, but chiefly imaginary, enemies of the regime. The prisons were full, and the camps grew large. As in the time of George Kennan, the prisons were among the most distinguished institutions of learning and collections of talent in the country. The camps were different. Unlike nineteenth-century places of exile, the conditions there did not allow for the luxury of learning. Uncertain estimates of the number of persons who fell victim to the process range up to multiple millions. A substantial but still undetermined proportion of those purged were executed, and a greater proportion died of exposure and malnutrition.[38] Around 70 percent of the 1934 Central Committee was subjected to the purge. We now have a large autobiographical literature on the subject, and the recitation of one initially scarcely credible horror after another leads eventually to numbing monotony.

There are several plausible explanations of the purges. Probably their most immediate purpose was to remove all of Stalin's potential rivals. In addition, they provided scapegoats for the failures of the plan. They were intended to persuade the people that Stalin's mistakes, collectivization in particular, were not mistakes. They were intended to make it possible, to keep open the option, to make a deal with Hitler should that be necessary—the Nazi–Soviet pact of 23 August 1939 that lulled Stalin into another mistake, a false sense of security. And they supplanted a pre-Stalinist intelligentsia, even though it was already partially a Soviet intelligentsia, with a Stalinist one that owed everything to "the boss"—*khoziain*—as he was called. The Gulag provided cheap labor in remote places where living conditions were severe and where it would have required large sums of capital to procure labor in civil conditions.

Stalin was in many respects, like his counterpart Hitler, a brilliant autodidact. Neither had much formal schooling; Hitler had less, and Stalin made more conscientious efforts on his own. Both worked to a considerable extent by instinct rather than by the rational assimilation and organization of information, though Stalin, constrained by the matrix of Marxism, had to make gestures of rational accommodation with the doctrine. Both were masters of their native political environments. Both lacked the experience of the world conventionally required of statesmen. Hitler's instincts in foreign and military affairs were, for a time, distinctly superior to Stalin's.[39]

Stalin's closest students acknowledge that he mined and mimed Lenin, his teacher, patron, promoter, ultimately his critic, and nearly his political executioner, and plagiarized Lenin's interpreters—one Ksenofontov, in particular, whom he then exiled to the wastes of Central Asia—manipulating the malleable material of the dialectic such as to make a synoptic catechism comprehensible to the unsophisticated. It is plausible to think that he looked upon the teachings of Lenin as the lodestar of his course throughout his life.

What Stalin knew of agriculture was what he had read of it in Marx. Marx taught the advantages of large-scale, mechanized agriculture over "the idiocy of rural life." It is entirely plausible, though by no means demonstrable, to think that Stalin genuinely believed in the validity of the future of collectivization. He managed it from afar with instruments of intellectual abstraction, and his henchmen managed it at the grass roots with instruments of blood and thunder. There is no reason to doubt that Stalin saw beyond the barrier of kulak obscurantism the cornucopia of Bolshevik dreams.

The person, the motives, and the conduct of Stalin are not nearly so mysterious after Robert Tucker's biography of him. He functioned by fear, by lack of confidence in himself, at least early in his career, by jealousy and envy of Trotsky, Bukharin, and others, by suspicion, and by sadism, too. Less obvious is the question why the Russian nation provided him so many willing assistants in the destruction of its composure, its culture, and its life itself. There can be no question that among great masses of the Soviet population Stalin enjoyed the popularity of a demigod, the grandest luminary in the firmament. In this respect, too, he was like his nemesis Hitler, who at times enjoyed elements of popularity approximating that of Stalin. Part of the historical problem of Hitler and Stalin is the enigma of popular judgment.

Why did so many Russians cooperate in the destruction of large parts of their nation and ultimately, in many cases, of themselves? As it has been put so tartly by the Russian writer Tatiana Tolstaia, among the dramatis personae in the story of the purges "is not just the butcher, but all the sheep that collaborated with him, slicing and seasoning their own meat for a monstrous shishkabob."[40] We will probably never have an adequate understanding of this question, but we have intriguing suggestions. Part of the answer is that people believed in what they were doing, as Lev Kopelev did, for example. As many believed at the time, so others believed for all time. We now have a convenient compendium of these attitudes in what amounts to the memoirs of Viacheslav Molotov, Stalin's faithful gofer and foreign minister, who late in his unjustly long life tried to reach Mikhail Gorbachev and Eduard Shevardnadze in order to explain to them the folly of their course.[41] Such was the faith of many party members in their cult that some of them persisted in prison and the camps in believing in their own guilt, though they did not know what it was. If they were arrested, they thought, there must be a reason. Others believed that the party had made an honest mistake.[42] Some wrote letters to Stalin to inform him what crimes were being committed without his knowledge. In fact, Stalin sent personal observers to the grander executions and relished the stories of undignified conduct on the part of some of the victims.

Vasilii Grossman has given us a brief taxonomy of the "Judases."

"This is Judas the First. . . . During his interrogation he behaved badly. Certain of his acquaintances have even stopped greeting him on the street. The wiser among them are polite when they happen to meet but do not invite him to their homes. Those wiser still, more generous and profound of heart, invite him to their homes, but keep their hearts closed to him. . . . He was an ordinary person. He used to drink tea, eat scrambled eggs, and . . . chat with his friends. . . . On occasion he was kind and generous. True he was high-strung and nervous, and he had no self-assurance."

The interrogators put him through a terrible ordeal, too. They beat him, did not allow him to sleep, fed him salt herring and refused to let him drink. Eventually he committed an awful crime: he gave false evidence against an innocent person. They then sentenced him to twenty years of hard labor, though he was not guilty of the charges against him. "He returned just barely alive, broken, a pauper, on his last legs."

Judas Number Two never went to prison. He was a silver-tongued devil who sent many people to the camps and their destruction. He made it a practice to have confidential chats with his friends, and he reported their opinions to the police. No one pressured him to do so. He himself took the initiative, and he was clever in leading his companions to speak about dangerous subjects. Some of those on whom he reported never returned from the camps. Some of them were shot. Those who returned came back with injuries and illnesses that left them crippled for life.

The informer himself in the meantime grew fat, literally and figuratively. He ate well, developed a reputation as a gourmet and a connoisseur of Georgian wines. He worked in the fine arts and collected rare editions of old poetry.

What motivated him? "Since childhood he had been frightened out of his mind. His father was rich and in 1919 had died of typhus in a concentration camp, and his aunt had emigrated to Paris with her husband, who was a general, and his elder brother had fought for the Whites. . . . His mother had . . . trembl[ed] before all authority. . . . Each day and each hour he and his kinfolk had been made to feel their class inferiority and their class depravity."

His emotional apparatus was simply no match for the test. "A spell was cast on him by the might of the new world. [He was] like a small bird hypnotized by a snake, . . . he so much wanted to become a part of it. . . . And just how was he to cope with a power that had caused half the world to bow down?"

Judas Number Three was self-assured and a master of life. His record was perfectly pure. He came from the poor proletariat. In 1937 he wrote without any hesitation more than two hundred denunciations, all of them against people loyal to the Soviet regime, party people, veterans of the civil war, activists. "His particular specialty was Party members of a fanatical frame of mind. He slit their eyes eagerly with a lethal razor blade." Very few of his victims returned. Some were shot immediately. Others died of illness or were executed in the camps.

"For him 1937 was a year of triumph. He was sharp-eyed, not-very-well-educated. It had seemed to him that every one around him was stronger than he, both in education and in terms of a heroic past. Previously he hadn't a hope of ever scoring a point against those who had carried out the Revolution. But all of a sudden, with a kind of fantastic ease, he was able to mow down by his mere touch hundreds of those who wore haloes of revolutionary glory." He climbed swiftly. He did not understand what he was doing. He was not settling personal accounts, but he was subject to a vague instinctive envy of those better placed. "How can he be accused when others wiser than he could not tell truth from falsehood, when even pure hearts could not in their impotence tell good from evil?"

Judas the Fourth was a simple philistine, greedy for possessions. He grew rich. And he understood perfectly well what he was doing.[43]

Of course, this is only fiction, but the historians have not dealt with the subject so penetratingly as have the novelists.

By the end of the 1930s, Stalin had created the ultimate instrument of vanguardism—though it was now the police rather than the party—that reacted as with one will from its top to its bottom. The use to which he put it was tragic. By trusting Hitler, by ignoring defense-in-depth, by stationing the Red Army in forward positions within easy reach of deep penetration, by forsaking the old and genuinely formidable line of fortifications, partly dismantling it, and advancing to a new line along the new frontiers of the Nazi–Soviet pact, where the fortifications would require years to complete, by eviscerating the officers' corps, by ignoring the imminence of attack, Stalin consummated the tragedies of collectivization and the purges and made one of the most colossally costly blunders in history. If collectivization took millions of lives and the purges of 1936 to 1941 and 1945 to 1953 millions more—all figures on the subject are still educated guesses—more authoritative estimates on the number of fatalities suffered in the war by the stronger country, the Soviet Union, range from 27 million to 40 million.[44] Of all the enemies of the people, Stalin was by far the greatest.

On the other hand, the job that he did required a lot of torpid acquiescence and willing assistance.

The ironies of Operation Barbarossa were gargantuan. In the conflict of these titans, the Soviet Union had far the greater potential strength. It had superior manpower and material resources to apply to any campaign, either offensive or defensive, and it had the obstacles of climate and space to apply to a defensive campaign. Yet it was by far the more fragile of the two powers. Why?

The evils of Nazism were reserved principally for non-Germans, and the remarkable stability of Hitler's regime demonstrated its stubborn persistence until it was physically liquidated by its foreign enemies. Oddly enough, it was the ethos of Prussian militarism in the army that generated both the most conspicuous resistance to Hitler and the most pragmatically humane attitude to the many ethnic groups overrun by his armed forces.

The evils of Stalinism were distributed more indiscriminately over the whole population, native Soviet as well as foreign. The remarkable fragility that the Soviet system exhibited in the 1980s was even more vibrantly present in the late 1930s and the 1940s. Ready to break apart upon the first approach of foreign war, the preservation of the system was achieved only by its worst enemy, Nazism. There were two sources of destructive discontent in the Stalinist system: the collectivized peasantry and the minority nationalities, and especially the two together in the second largest Soviet nation, the Ukrainians. The German army did all that it could to capitalize upon these opportunities, but the Nazi Party ideologues and the Führer frustrated its intentions and it failed. The best efforts of the best Germans were devoted to two goals simultaneously: the destruction of both Hitler and Stalin. They failed, too, and in the end it was the evils of Stalin that supplanted those of Hitler in most of Eastern Europe.[45]

After VE Day, Stalin's government faced enormous tasks of reconstruction. Economic reconstruction was achieved in the traditional mode, by emphasizing heavy industry, though it profited by one new wrinkle, the plundering of the new satellites of Eastern Europe.

No less significant was cultural reconstruction. Soviet prisoners of war and forced laborers deported by the Germans to Central Europe numbered around five million persons at the end of the war. Nearly a million Soviet soldiers sought deliverance from Stalinism by enlisting to fight for Hitler; unfortunately for them, and for himself, Hitler disdained to make serious use of them. By the war's end, most of the Red Army had advanced beyond Soviet frontiers into a formerly forbidden zone where Stalin could not control perceptions. All of these people required reeducation. The camps that had shrunk in wartime to provide military manpower now expanded again.

A cultural purge was put in the charge of Andrei Zhdanov. Zhdanov denounced the satire of Mikhail Zoshchenko, the poetry of Anna Akhmatova, the music of Dmitrii Shostakovich. The world-famous Soviet cinematographer Sergei Eisenstein denounced his own "worthless and vicious film" (*Ivan the Terrible*, part two).

In 1949, a purge in Leningrad appeared to be directed especially against those who might have developed habits of independence when the city had been encircled and partially cut off from conventional communication with the government in Moscow during the siege of World War II. In the winter of 1952–53, the press described a "doctors' plot" to engage in the medical assassination of Soviet leaders. They had allegedly killed Zhdanov, for example, in 1948. This affair had heavily anti-Semitic overtones, most of the accused having recognizably Jewish names.[46] In addition, it obviously threatened Stalin's two most prominent lieutenants, Georgii Malenkov and Lavrentii Beria, as their names suddenly disappeared from their previously prominent place in the press.

Before the doctors' plot matured, Stalin died in March 1953. His body lay for several days in state as long lines of mourners passed it in review. When the body was removed, thousands who had not yet seen it rushed the coffin, and in the stampede several hundred people were crushed to death. Even his ghost was dangerous.

Those whom it had lately threatened now undertook to exorcise it. They attempted to purge the system of its Stalinist excresences while maintaining the essence of the Leninist legacy. They tried reform, and the consequences were unimaginable.

❖ 9 ❖

Reform or Revolution—Again, 1953–1991

I have great pity for the Russians, because they have Algeria within their own walls.
Charles de Gaulle to Otto von Habsburg

A country that craves the benefits of modern industrialization without possessing among its inhabitants the necessary motivation and self-discipline is headed for endless misery.
Theodore H. von Laue, *Why Lenin? Why Stalin?*

If our conscience does not awaken, no economic reform will save us.
Alexander Solzhenitsyn

For all of his stumbling and bungling, his peasant boorishness, crude braggadocio, and rash impulses, his facial warts and his indelicate girth, Nikita Khrushchev has gotten too little credit for his role in Russian life. He was not a mere peasant buffoon out of his element. In fact, he must be taken seriously. As Catherine II planted ineradicably the idea of the evil of serfdom, Khrushchev cultivated the idea of a more decent and civil way of life for the Soviet people. The reformers around Gorbachev—the *shestidesiatniki*, men of the sixties—looked upon him frankly as the harbinger of their own ideas.

Having entered the party in the lifetime of Lenin and before the heyday of Stalin, he evidently wished to return it to the vision of Leninism that he imagined as decent. He wanted to purge Stalinism from Soviet life and to devote the government to the realization of what socialism had promised the workers and peasants. He knew the common people as Stalin had not. He made a point of spending time among them. He meant to achieve détente, to bridle the military machine, to reverse the Stalinist priorities of light and heavy industry, and to bring material abundance to the people.[1]

Glasnost had its trial run under Khrushchev. He is best remembered for one dramatic episode. At the Twentieth Party Congress of February 1956, he shocked his audience and the world along with it in the famous "Secret Speech" denouncing the crimes of Stalin. It was the beginning of a sustained campaign of de-Stalinization. De-Stalinization was to be the leitmotif of Khrushchev's government, characterizing virtually his entire collection of policies.

Already in the wake of Stalin's death, the party had implemented a liberalization of controls in the arts. It was symbolized and christened by Ilya Ehrenburg's novel *The Thaw* (1954). In 1961, the poet Yevgenii Yevtushenko was able to publish "Babii Yar," memorializing the Soviet Jews who perished at the hands of the Nazis near Kiev in 1941. In 1962, he warned in "Stalin's Heirs" of the survival of the dictator's spirit. At the same time, the party leader himself approved the publication of Solzhenitsyn's *One Day in the Life of Ivan Denisovich*.

Some of the liberties taken by the artists, on the other hand, offended Khrushchev. He denounced particular works as obscene, using the earthiest obscenities himself to describe them, and he threatened once that "only the grave straightens the hunchbacked." Artistic expression entered a new era, but it fell far short of freedom of expression.[2] Still, it nourished an aspiration that never ceased.

In material life, Khrushchev's most immediate objectives were evidently to turn some of the achievements of the iron age that preceded him into benefits for the population, to inaugurate an era of affluent socialism. The accumulated record of his social legislation was impressive: reduction of the work week from forty-three to forty-one hours; extension of paid maternity leave to 112 days; the liberty to change jobs without permission; abolition of tuition fees in secondary and higher education; large improvements in pension and disability benefits; more and cheaper medicines; and massive housing construction.[3]

As he turned to the depressed consumer economy, it was logical that Khrushchev should direct the bulk of his attention to the agrarian sector. The deficiencies of Soviet agriculture were notorious at home and abroad, and Khrushchev was of peasant birth and had been for some time the party's leading expert on the peasant economy. He was not alone in recognizing that the key to better consumption lay in better agricultural production. To cite one typical example the like of which might be multiplied almost ad infinitum, in 1962 the Soviet Union had nearly ten million more hogs (66.7 million) than the United States but produced just over half as much pork.[4] In quest of better performance, Khrushchev embarked impatiently on an ambitious agenda of reforms.

The essence of Stalin's approach to the agricultural economy had been minimal investment and maximal exploitation. The collective farmers were paid miserably for their labor, they were paid miserably for their produce, and they were expected to generate the bulk of new investment from their own already overstressed economy, chiefly through forced loans and ostensibly voluntary contributions to community capital funds.

The intense exploitation to which Stalin had subjected the peasant was reversed. Khrushchev raised the prices paid for agricultural produce sufficiently sharply as nearly to equalize the formerly discriminatory terms of trade between urban and rural production. In addition, he supplemented the old system of division of the remnants of the harvest among the peasants by a new system of cash wages.[5]

Perhaps more important, he reduced taxes on the private plots, and he initially allowed the expansion of the privately cultivated area. The Stalinist system had made this important concession to the collective farmers, that they were allowed to hold about one acre of land per family for their own private use. Khrushchev knew from his own experience how important was the contribution that these plots made to the national economy. The private plots accounted for less than 3 percent of the cultivated area of Soviet agriculture and yet produced 64 percent of the potato crop, 42 percent of all vegetables, 42 percent of meat, 40 percent of milk, 66 percent of eggs, and 20 percent of wool. This sector consumed about 40 percent of agricultural labor and produced about 30 percent of the total value of agricultural output. Unfortunately for the productivity of Soviet agriculture, Khrushchev soon reversed his policy on the size of private plots. He found them to be an excessive diversion from conscientious work in the collective fields. In addition, as Mao Tse-tung implemented the "people's communes" of the Great Leap Forward (1957), Khrushchev evidently felt that the private plots were an ideological embarrassment to socialism.[6]

In 1958, with characteristic impulsiveness, Khrushchev decided to sell the equipment of the Machine-Tractor Stations to the collective farms that they served. The theoretical advantages of such a move are easy to imagine. It would unburden the state of a substantial responsibility and a substantial expense. It would realize a windfall of cash for a stretched budget. It would presumably encourage better maintenance of the machinery, as it would establish a more direct connection between its condition and the well-being of the collective farmers. The reason most often mentioned in the Soviet press at the time, however, was different. The critics of the Machine-Tractor Stations objected to the fact that they represented, along with the collective-farm administration, a second boss in the field, a fragmenting of administrative unity.

In addition to implementing the sale, Khrushchev forced the completion of the payment for the machinery in the course of a single year. The consequences were not happy. It required the cessation of all other forms of collective-farm investment. Many of the Machine-Tractor Station mechanics and technicians refused to live on the farms and moved away to the cities, and most of the farms lacked the facilities either to house or to service the machinery properly.[7]

With similar impulsiveness, Khrushchev grew enthused, after a visit to the corn belt of Iowa in 1959, about the prospects of corn. Ignoring the climatic and other differences between the American Midwest and the Soviet agricultural regions, he implemented, in a typically impetuous fashion, the planting of seventy million acres of corn, most of which failed. *Kukuruznik*, they called him, cornball (*kukuruza*, corn). So he changed panaceas: he found a new promise of agricultural abundance in the production of large quantities of chemical fertilizer.

He tried new administrative approaches to agriculture as well. Khrushchev had long been convinced that the bureaucrats in the administration of economic policy in Moscow were too far removed from, and hence too ignorant of, the subject of their work. He therefore decided to displace the centralized ministries by 107 regional economic councils nearer the grass roots. These were subsequently amalgamated into seventeen larger councils. Somewhat later, he decided to divide the party itself into industrial and agricultural units. Some of the party territorial jurisdictions did not conform to the government's regional-council territorial jurisdictions, however, and the result of these administrative reforms together was confusion incarnate.

By far the most ambitious of Khrushchev's agricultural reforms was the celebrated "virgin-lands program." Here was a previously marginal agricultural region that, the party hoped, large investment would render sufficiently productive to overcome the serious Soviet shortfall of food supply. The chief problem in most of the area, Kazakhstan, was the scant and irregular rainfall, ranging from ten to sixteen inches a year. Already in the works at the time of Stalin's death in 1953, this controversial program was expanded by Khrushchev to encompass over 100 million acres of previously uncultivated land, of which approximately 65 percent was in Kazakhstan and the remainder in Western Siberia and the Soviet Far East.[8] Of course, the capital required to move a population, housing, and mechanized equipment to what had been nomadic wilderness was enormous. The weather in the area was quite volatile. It was an enormous gamble, too. The agronomists and meteorologists estimated that the program might realize one good harvest in three years, perhaps two in five years. In years of harvest failure there, both the program in general and Khrushchev himself came in for severe criticism. In general, however, the results justified the risk. In good years and bad, the new virgin lands boosted the Soviet grain harvest by approximately 50 percent.[9]

Several of Khrushchev's programs were extremely expensive—the increased remuneration for the collective farmers, the higher prices paid for their produce, the large-scale production of chemical fertilizer, the cuts in tuition, the construction of new housing, and especially the virgin-lands program. They obviously demanded a reallocation of revenue; there was only one feasible source of financial transfers on the scale required—military spending—and cuts in military spending depended upon easing international tensions and developing better relations with the capitalist world. Immediately after Stalin's death, the new government took some initiatives in this direction: the "thaw" in cultural policy, the "new course" of liberalization among the satellite regimes of Eastern Europe. The Austrian State Treaty, stipulating the evacuation of Soviet troops from eastern Austria, where they had been since 1945, contributed materially to détente. The de-Stalinization campaign of 1956 also made a good impression abroad.

The anti-Stalin campaign and the new course in Eastern Europe, however, led to problems. In 1956, Hungary declared independence of the Soviet bloc, Poland threatened to follow, and Soviet intervention preempted in Budapest what Gorbachev would willingly countenance all over Eastern Europe in 1989. The embarrassment inflicted serious political wounds on Khrushchev, and he scarcely survived in power.

He soon made a remarkable comeback. By the end of 1957, the promise of his program seemed undeniable. Soviet defense spending was down to 9.1 billion rubles from a 1952 level of 10.9 billion rubles. The grain crop was up from a 1953 level of 82.5 million metric tons to 141.2 million metric tons, the virgin lands having provided the entire new increment.[10] The annual growth rate in GNP was 9.9 percent. In the meantime, in October 1957, the Soviet Union had lofted Sputnik, the world's first artificial satellite. Khrushchev, too, was flying high.

There was one ugly flaw, however, in this pretty picture. The Soviet military-industrial complex was unhappy about its diminished share of economic allocations, and it worried loudly and criticized not very obliquely. Was it safe to cut military preparedness in a world of rapacious imperialist powers led by the United States? The question obviously served the vested interests of the military, and it played well in the context of a culture until recently thoroughly Stalinist.

At this point, we must infer and project a bit, imagine what we have no hard information to demonstrate. The next development in the Khrushchev saga was a series of Berlin crises. What is the rationale for a Berlin crisis in this constellation of circumstances? The concentration of foreign power that the Soviets always took most seriously was NATO. They worried in particular about a resuscitation of Germany. Khrushchev must have looked the situation over and found just one genuinely unnatural sore spot or potential flash point. At Berlin, American, British, and French troops faced Soviet troops virtually eyeball to eyeball one hundred miles inside the Soviet bloc. If only a bit of diplomatic surgery could be applied there, then his approach to world affairs might be vindicated and the force of his critics' arguments would be considerably blunted.

Khrushchev bristled, orated, and blustered. He would sign a treaty with the German Democratic Republic and cease to give a Soviet guarantee of Western access to West Berlin. It was an ominous threat. Probably Khrushchev hoped to bring the West to a negotiating table in order to work out a deal more acceptable and equitable than that contained in his public threat, but that was not apparent at the time. The West met his bluster with rigid insistence on the sanctity of the previous agreements.

This turn of events vindicated the arguments of his critics: the United States does not take us seriously. Khrushchev scrambled, looking for a solution. In 1959, he came to the United States, toured Hollywood and Iowa cornfields, and visited President Eisenhower at Camp

David. Back at home he spread the image of President Eisenhower as a man of peace.

In May 1960, on the eve of a summit meeting in Paris, an unfortunate event virtually exploded Khrushchev's whole program. An American U-2 spy plane was downed over Sverdlovsk. This development embarrassed Khrushchev deeply. He said publicly that he was willing to believe that President Eisenhower had known nothing of it.[11] Taking the cue, Eisenhower at first said that he had not. That statement made NATO chiefs nervous, however, and Eisenhower thereupon admitted that he had dispatched the plane. Khrushchev was furious. He then had to deal with the image of his partner in peace as someone both more belligerent and less truthful than he had suggested to his public.

Apparently, the Soviet military was delighted by these events. This particular U-2 flight began in Pakistan and was scheduled for a destination in Norway. It likely had the assignment to bring back the latest intelligence on Soviet missile deployment prior to the Paris summit, a rational kind of inquiry if it did not lead to a fiasco. In fact, the U-2s had been overflying the Soviet Union with impunity for years. Soviet antiaircraft missiles could not reach the plane's altitude, and it was a very sore point with the Soviet military suffering Khrushchev's budget cuts.

The downing of the U-2 naturally spoiled the summit meeting. Worse than that, it spoiled Khrushchev's grand plan for détente with the West and affluence at home. He had to make concessions to his critics. Soviet military spending began to rise sharply, and Soviet economic performance slipped proportionately. In 1962, defense spending rose to 12.7 billion rubles, and the Soviet growth rate fell to 2.2 percent.[12] Khrushchev's program was virtually gutted.

In January 1961, a new American president took office, John Kennedy. The following summer, he and Khrushchev decided to get acquainted. They met in Vienna in June. Khrushchev's manner was never elegant, and at Vienna he was on his worst behavior: he was the senior statesman, he had more political experience, he was gruff and unaccommodating. He promised more trouble at Berlin. Upon Kennedy's return, Congress passed an additional U.S. defense appropriation, and the garrison in Berlin was reinforced.

In August 1961, as the Twenty-second Party Congress convened in Moscow, there was a concurrence of dramatic developments. The Berlin Wall was built. The Soviet Union detonated a record 100-megaton nuclear weapon over the Arctic. Khrushchev denounced Stalin again.

Comrade D.A. Lazurkina reported to the congress that she had sought Lenin's advice on the legacy of Stalin: "Yesterday . . . it was as if he stood before me alive and said: 'I do not like being next to Stalin.' (*Stormy, prolonged applause.*)" Khrushchev obliged Lenin and Lazurkina and expelled Stalin's coffin from the Lenin–Stalin, henceforth the Lenin, Mausoleum. More ominously, the wiliest of Chinese communists, Chou En-lai, demonstratively walked out of the congress, laid a wreath on Stalin's new grave, and flew home to an official airport greeting by Mao Tse-tung and the entire Chinese Politburo. The Sino–Soviet conflict had gone public for the first time.

In the fall, Khrushchev came to the United Nations. As British Prime Minister Harold Macmillan asked what kind of proletarian paradise required a wall to keep its people at home, Khrushchev waved his shoe defiantly at the challenge—he was never forgiven at home this demonstration of boorishness. In the spring of 1962, there were riots over increased food prices in at least half a dozen Soviet cities. In Novocherkassk in the North Caucasus, troops fired on the demonstrators, and the KGB reported twenty-two people killed and eighty-seven wounded.[13]

His program all but ruined now, Khrushchev launched in October 1962 a wild and desperate gamble to salvage what he could. He put missiles into Cuba. If he had succeeded in keeping them there, he might have realized two advantages. He could have faced his military with a substantial and very inexpensive improvement in Soviet defense posture. More dramatically, he could have faced the United States with an offer to remove these missiles from Cuba in exchange for what he had planned to demand in Berlin had the United States consented to negotiate there. What he had wanted to propose, it is believed, was that, if the United States would remove all of its nuclear weaponry from West Germany, he would guarantee that none would ever be deployed in the territory of his Chinese ally. After Chou En-lai's walkout of the Twenty-second Party Congress, such an offer was out of the question.[14] Khrushchev had turned to Cuba, then, in quest of a quid pro quo to substitute for the now unavailable Chinese one. It failed because his bluff was called in a maritime theater of operations too far from home for the plausible projection of Soviet power. His critics won again. In October 1964, a decent interval of time after the Cuban debacle, he was fired. The burden of the charges against him: "harebrained schemes." Sadly, for all of his brave efforts at home and abroad to improve the life of his people, in spite of an undeniable increment of decency introduced into the life of the nation, the charges were not unfounded. At home he was unappreciated. Abroad he was misunderstood.

Leonid Brezhnev was perceived as a professional managerial type, a leader who would shun the impulsive fantasies of Khrushchev and turn to reliable convention to deal with Soviet policy at home and abroad. He apparently inaugurated more regular consultations of the hierarchy in decision-making processes. He put enormous sums of money into Soviet agriculture and was able thereby to promote a better standard of living, even if not one commensurate with the magnitude of investments required to achieve it. He cracked down hard on the level of permissiveness of expression that Khrushchev had countenanced in literature and the arts, and he thereby provoked the dissident protest known as the democratic movement. From time to time, it was reported and feared that he would announce a kind of formal rehabilitation of Stalin. He never did. His policy was nevertheless viewed by the intelligentsia at home and by his counterparts abroad as an attack on a civil political order.

In foreign and defense policy, his achievements were formidable. By the end of the 1970s, it became apparent that he had resolved from the outset of his accession to power to achieve military parity with the United States, never again to tolerate the kind of humiliation that Moscow had to endure in the Cuban missile crisis. By common consent, parity was achieved, and controversy sometimes suggested Soviet military superiority. Through the intervention against the "Prague Spring" in 1968 and the subsequent announcement of the "Brezhnev Doctrine"—the Monroe Doctrine of socialism—he brought Eastern Europe under a tighter degree of control than had prevailed there since 1953. In the meantime, taking advantage of the new dimensions of Soviet military power—a high-seas fleet, a large new air-transport logistics component, divisions of paratroopers, and a rapid-deployment force—as well as the U.S. quagmire in Vietnam, Foreign Minister Andrei Gromyko perfectly plausibly claimed equality with the United States in foreign affairs. As he so often put it, no political problem in the world might any longer be addressed without consulting Moscow.

Alas, much of this achievement was illusory. In retrospect, it seems that the military spending beggared the economy generally. About ten years into the Brezhnev tenure of office, in the latter part of the 1970s, the economy took a downturn that soon appeared to progress to a tailspin. In the meantime, the intervention in Afghanistan (December 1979) began to operate in Soviet affairs in a fashion similar to that of Vietnam in American affairs earlier. It was the first instance of Soviet intervention in any area not previously regarded as a Soviet sphere of interest, and it thus provoked understandable alarm about Soviet policy the world over. It especially cost Moscow support in the Islamic world. It drained military and economic resources in a battle in which total military superiority failed to yield victory.

In the late 1970s and early 1980s, the deployment of SS-20 (Intermediate-Range Nuclear Forces: INF) missiles inside Warsaw Pact countries had given the Soviets a clear claim to military superiority in the European theater, and it raised the question, as it was so well calculated to do, whether the commitment of the United States to the defense of Europe was equal to risking a nuclear Armageddon over an area not initially involving American territory. Moscow relied heavily, and not implausibly in this battle of nerves, on the vibrancy of the European pacifist movements. The subsequent successful deployment of the new Pershing-II and cruise missiles in Europe turned the struggle into a serious Soviet defeat, however. It also led to protests in Warsaw Pact countries that feared their own vulnerability as the reputedly very accurate Pershing-IIs were targeted on SS-20s deployed in their backyard.

The consummation of Soviet troubles was a development that promised to undo Moscow's vaunted military parity: President Ronald Reagan's announcement of the Strategic Defense Initiative or "Star Wars." The proud military achievement that had required the sacrifice of the prospect of every other branch of the economy now seemed vulnerable to the leapfrog of a generation of American military technology.

By this time, the early 1980s, the Brezhnev program was notoriously a shambles. What is now known as the period of *zastoi* (stagnation) is perhaps best characterized by a Soviet joke. Stalin and company were on a train when it broke down and ceased to run. Stalin's remedy: "Shoot all the engineers." The train did not respond. Stalin died, and Khrushchev came aboard. Khrushchev's remedy: "Rehabilitate all the engineers." The train did not respond. Khrushchev departed, and Brezhnev came aboard. Brezhnev's remedy: "Pull the curtains and pretend that the train is going." Shades of Nicholas I.

Toward the end of his life, nearly the whole Soviet establishment was making jokes about the senile incompetence of the Brezhnev "gerontocracy." The Leningrad magazine *Aurora* published a facetious allegory of a kingdom whose sovereign was secretly dead. The KGB itself took the liberty of exposing the illegal traffic in diamonds between Brezhnev's daughter Galia and a mafia figure in the Moscow circus known as "Boris the Gypsy."

An insider dissident, Andrei Amalrik, in his provocatively titled book *Will the Soviet Union Survive until 1984?* left the most authoritative analysis of the politics of reform in the Brezhnev era. The title notwithstanding, the contents of the work are by no means obsolete. The "paradox of the middle class" explained its relative impotence. On the one hand, in spite of its privileged status, it was the class most discontent both with the scant prospect of a better standard of living and with the undignified absence of civil liberties. It was also the class best educated and best able to conceive what was wrong in Soviet society and what was necessary to correct it. On the other hand, it was precisely the class with the most to lose by agitation for reform, and that fact intimidated it. Here was the old superfluous man in its modern Soviet variant.

The paradox of the middle class was matched by the "paradox of the regime." The regime could better address its problems by appointing to its ranks the best talent in the country. Yet such talent would uncover its own mediocrity and threaten its sinecures. Hence it preferred to live by the principle of "unnatural selection," co-opting docile sycophants into the apparatus.[15] Thus the nation drifted aimlessly, no improvement in sight.

From the early 1980s, it was apparent that two problems might well in a generation or two pose serious threats to Soviet stability. One of them was economic. The formerly impressive economic model of progressive authoritarianism was looking more and more anemic. There are two persuasive explanations. Although the method of the Five-Year Plan was well suited to a crash program of building the industrial foundation of modernization, it was very ill suited to manage the complex needs of a developed modern economy. In addition, authoritarian central planning and administration, the command-administrative system, discouraged and stultified individual and local enterprise. In effect, it held out disincentives and taught dis-economics.

The other problem was ethnic. Nothing is more obvious in our time than the renaissance of ethnic consciousness. From western Britain through the Middle East to the Central Asian crescent of crisis, and all over Africa, ethnic conflict challenges all conventional rules of national order. The process would eventually spill over into the Soviet ethnic mosaic. Two seasoned veterans of ethnic conflict had foreseen this challenge in 1962. As one of them, Charles de Gaulle, said to the other, Otto von Habsburg, "I have great pity for the Russians, because they have Algeria within their own walls."[16]

So long as the two problems, the economic and the ethnic, could be kept separate and dealt with in isolation from each other, neither had the capacity in the short run to precipitate a dangerous crisis. In the long run, it was hardly possible to keep them separate. The crisis would come when the question was posed how to apportion economic deprivation among the nationalities. Both of these problems were aggravated by political decay, the patent inability of the Soviet government to handle contemporary problems with the energy and decision that had characterized it in the past.

As the gerontocracy of the Brezhnev generation limped into paralytic senility, a luminous constellation of Russian specialists gathered at the Center for Strategic and International Studies of Georgetown University—"thirty-five men and women from seven disciplines, twenty colleges and universities in the United States and the United Kingdom, seven private research organizations, two journals, and the Library of Congress"—to formulate an expert prognosis of the Soviet future. Their forecast: "All of us agree that there is no likelihood whatsoever that the Soviet Union will become a political democracy or that it will collapse in the foreseeable future, and very little likelihood that it will become a congenial, peaceful member of the international community for as far ahead as one can see."[17]

The slightly more tempered judgment of Seweryn Bialer, one of the most insightful analysts of the Soviet Union in the United States, was a degree less categorical: "Time is not running out on the Soviet system. The regime still possesses enormous reserves of stability, but adjustments have to be made if the system is to remain effective. . . . Should actual Soviet growth and energy shortages in the 1980s fall within the range of the most pessimistic projections, the Soviet Union, without [a] reform and a successful one at that, is condemned not simply to a process of 'muddling through' but a process of 'muddling down.' "[18]

This was the unhappily stable state of affairs that Mikhail

Gorbachev inherited. No one foresaw the catalyst that his intervention would introduce into the situation.

In time of crisis, Russia had habitually relied on two traditions to which Gorbachev could turn: authoritarian initiative of the central government and imitation of the progressive dynamics of the West. In fact, Russia had usually relied in one degree or another on both of these practices at once. In the eighteenth century, both reason and tradition had recommended them. The last quarter of the eighteenth century, however, had witnessed a metamorphosis of Russian policy. The spectacle of the French Revolution, aggravating that of the Pugachev Revolt, frightened Catherine, and she and her immediate successors retreated from the policy of Westernization. The Crimean War forced a reconsideration, and the government compromised, attempting to facilitate technology transfer while avoiding the appurtenant contamination of political ideas. By the century's end, it was obvious that this system was not delivering satisfactory results, and the government tried again. Witte and Stolypin used the instruments of state to generate industrial, political, and agricultural progress controlled such as to make it compatible with monarchy and empire. The war and the revolution rendered history's verdict on their efforts.

During the first period of the Soviet regime, the civil war and the conflict of interest between Bolshevik urban socialism and peasant rural socialism led to a political standoff and a virtual economic standstill in the ancient Russian problem of development. The crisis of 1928 was precipitated in part by the realization that Russia had experienced a decade and a half of stagnation while the Western world had continued its demonically happy ways of infinite economic expansion and technical innovation.

Stalin addressed the problem for approximately a decade by the massive importation and imitation of Western technicians and Western technology. By the end of two Five-Year Plans, the Soviet Union had generated its own body of scientists and engineers, and those imported from the West were sent home. In the mid-1950s, Khrushchev recognized the need to reanimate an increasingly sclerotic system by reforming within it, but the combination of inertia in the system and an irrepressible increment of hare-brained elements in his approach defeated his effort. Brezhnev eventually chose by and large to enjoy his power and to ignore the problem. By the end of the 1970s, however, it was plain that the job done in the 1930s had proved unable to sustain itself. That rhythmical Russian atavism of crisis and cultural cross-breeding arose again. If Brezhnev ignored it, Gorbachev was persuaded that he could not.

There was from the first a distinct parallel between the systemic crisis of the aging Soviet Union—in the time frame in which empires come and go, it had aged remarkably rapidly—and a similar one of which the Russian Empire had died in 1917. To the government of Nicholas II, it seemed obvious that both economic and political reform were required to secure the long-term survival of an increasingly ill-adapted system. Yet the reforms that were devised, particularly the Witte program of planned industrialization and the awkward constitution of 1906, aggravated in the short run a situation that they were designed to alleviate in the long run. Thus the remedy magnified the jeopardy of the system.

Gorbachev faced a similar dilemma, a similarly ugly choice: either what has been described as Ottomanization—the slow, inexorable slide into decline or eclipse, the kind exemplified by the Ottoman Empire from 1699 to 1919—or, on the other hand, the high risks of radical reform.[19] Tocqueville observed long ago that the most dangerous moment in the life of a bad government was the moment when it began to improve. It was once again Livy's dilemma of the Roman republic: the society could tolerate neither its vices nor their remedy. Robert Jones has defined a crisis in Russia as "a problem so serious that the risks of doing something about it that might not work are smaller than the risks of doing nothing."[20] Damned if they do, damned if they do not. The Russians were about to illustrate the experience for the second time in this century; Gorbachev was a bold spirit, and he did not hesitate to choose reform.

The soundest element of Gorbachev's program was his candid articulation of one of Khrushchev's inspirations without the blustering, nearly tragic, confusion that Khrushchev had caused. "New political thinking" denoted innovations in foreign and defense policy. Gorbachev and Eduard Shevardnadze early sought relaxation in international affairs. They were undoubtedly moved by several reasonable considerations.

They understood, first, that nothing in foreign affairs in 1985 threatened the country so immediately and vitally as it had been threatened in 1613, 1812, 1854, 1914, 1941, that much of the tension in the international system of 1985 had been initiated by Soviet Russia; hence the simplest way to relax it was to take initiatives of conciliation.

Second, they understood that Ronald Reagan had challenged the Soviets to an arms race that they could not only not win; they could not even afford to enter the race. They would have lost the claim to military parity that the readjustments of the balance during the Vietnam syndrome and the Brezhnev–Carter era had allowed them, and at the same time they would have seen the collapse of the domestic economy. Especially charismatic and effective, terrifying in fact, from their point of view, was Star Wars. It conjured images of American scientific magicians achieving generations of technological leapfrog.

New political thinking promised other benefits. In broadest terms, it would relieve the Soviet government of the burden of what Paul Kennedy called "imperial overstretch," the characteristic economic inadequacy of empires in decline to shoulder the grand panoply of their strategic commitments.[21] In Eastern Europe, the Soviet bloc initially behaved in a docile and cooperative spirit, surrendered economic assets, and enhanced military security. By the time of the Brezhnev era, it was subventioned, pampered, and virtually bribed for obedience, while it thumbed its nose at Moscow with varying degrees of impunity and impiety—or sport.

Last and most obviously, new political thinking and its military corollary of "reasonable sufficiency" promised to save money, to relieve an overstressed budget of its irrationally oversized military component. New political thinking made good sense.

It had only one drawback. It would seriously offend one ancient tradition. It would damage the pride and ego of the nationalists and militarists grown addicted to great-power presumption best symbolized by Foreign Minister Andrei Gromyko's previous boast that no problem in world affairs could now be resolved without the participation of the Soviet Union. This political camp is now bitterly reciting a litany of problems addressed without such (Russian) participation: Grenada, Panama, Iraq, Somalia, and the former Yugoslavia. Fortunately, the nation at large seems much more concerned about problems closer to home.

At home, everything was more intractable. At every step, the reform was dogged by traditions as obstructive as its rationale was constructive. One impeccably good idea was the antialcohol campaign, and it soon demonstrated how compelling realities limited the choice of desirable alternatives. Both foreign and (unpublished) Soviet research had shown for years the high cost of alcoholism in health care, absenteeism from work, accidents, and crime. It was estimated that alcoholism diminished labor productivity by 10 percent and that in 1976, for example, nearly forty thousand people died of acute alcohol poisoning—or something similar, that is, the use of alcohol substitutes, brake fluid, antifreeze.[22] No one could have plausibly impugned the idea of addressing the problem.

The first year of the campaign, however, cost the Soviet budget 45 billion rubles of revenue—at a time when falling world oil prices were depleting the largest Soviet source of hard-currency earnings. The shortfall of revenue forced the government to accelerate deficit financing and contributed to preempting sound economic choices when better economic managers—such as Egor Gaidar—were brought onto the scene later. In the meantime, determined Russians transferred distilling from state facilities to private ones, and the production of *samogon* (white lightning) ballooned to such proportions that sugar simply disappeared from the consumer economy. At that point, the government was compelled to use its diminishing reserves of hard currency to enter the world sugar market, where it spent over a billion dollars to buy 2.2 million tons of sugar that Cuba could not supply.[23] At the same time, the proletariat in the vineyards of the Caucasus and Moldavia and in the distilleries elsewhere objected to the threat of unemployment. The proletariat everywhere complained of the scarcity of vodka. Gorbachev was compelled to retreat. The experience of wrestling with the alcohol problem was a powerful lesson. Soviet problems could not be isolated and addressed separately from each other—they interacted.

According to initial appearances, Gorbachev had better luck with glasnost. Glasnost was necessary to ferret out crime and corruption in the government, to encourage good civic behavior, to enhance faith both in government and in the public media. It was eminently reasonable.

At first glance, it also seemed a shocking reversal of tradition. In fact, here and there in the Russian past, there were timid experiments with candor of expression. Catherine II had encouraged the idea modestly and cautiously as an appropriate element of Westernization before the French Revolution provoked her imposition of rigid press controls. A perceptive visitor of the 1830s, the Marquis de Custine, understood perfectly the rationale of the censorship. "The more I see of Russia, the more I agree with the Emperor when he forbids Russians to travel and makes access to his own country difficult for foreigners. The political system of Russia could not withstand twenty years of free communication with Western Europe."[24]

The Great Reforms of Alexander II did little to liberalize control of publishing. The Revolution of 1905 and the ensuing constitution necessarily brought a change of policy that the Revolution of 1917 did not instantly reverse. Between 1905 and 1928, then, there was a good deal of free and experimental expression. Stalin, of course, killed it. Khrushchev decided quite deliberately to run a careful and controlled version of the risk that Custine warned of. When Brezhnev cracked down on it, the dissidents organized the "democratic movement." It generated several thousand political documents unpublishable under Soviet conditions, including the *Chronicle of Current Events*, which catalogued illegal transgressions of KGB activity and the victimization of civil libertarians. Brezhnev eventually wiped out such dissident activity. Gorbachev intended to give it free rein.

While glasnost recalled the policy of Khrushchev, it was altogether revolutionary in its scope. It was both novel and amusing, and yet it was deadly serious. Glasnost served a constant fare of lurid revelation. As a saying current in Moscow had it, it had become more interesting to read than to live. All of the banned classics of Soviet Russian literature were published, including Solzhenitsyn's *Gulag Archipelago* and Pasternak's *Doctor Zhivago*. *Moscow News* reported that the Soviet Union ranked between fiftieth and sixtieth in the world in per capita standards of consumption, that the country had only a third of the medicines that it needed. Stalin was held responsible for bringing Hitler to power, for the brutal repression of forty to fifty million victims of collectivization and the purges, and for the defeats of World War II.

Soviet truth–telling was welcome and reassuring, but it produced a boomerang effect, too. The constant revelations of the "blank spots" (*belye piatna*) of Soviet history—so much scandal, dirt, and blood, so much crime against the people—contributed to discrediting the government, to raising questions of its legitimacy. How could such a government plausibly claim the loyalty of the population? Consider the news of the mass graves at Kuropaty. "Over the course of four and a half years, they shot people here every day. . . . They shot about two hundred fifty thousand people here."[25] The document in which Stalin ordered the execution of twenty thousand Polish officers at Katyń and other sites in 1940 has now been published in photostatic copy bearing his unmistakable signature.[26] But impassioned communists and nationalists prefer an unblemished account of their history and a government that can suppress historical embarrassments.

Glasnost collided not only with tradition but with elements of reason as well. It contributed to inflaming the unrest among the nationalities and the conflicts between them, most obviously in the Caucasus, where the combat of the Armenians and the Azeris was followed by that among the Georgians, the Abkhazians, and the Ossetians; in the Baltic, where there was tension between the native Latvians, Lithuanians, and Estonians and the immigrant Russians; and in Moldova, where the native Romanian majority wanted to do business in its own language.

Changing the tone of a controlled press in an authoritarian country, however risky, was not a difficult trick to turn. A more demanding challenge by far was perestroika. Like glasnost, perestroika was not utterly devoid of precedent. Khrushchev had experimented with alternative modes of party supervision of the economy. Both he and Aleksei Kosygin, Brezhnev's partner as premier, authorized the economic reforms of Evsei Liberman, who advocated financial accountability of firms and greater local freedom from central planning. Andrei Sakharov tried unsuccessfully to persuade the Soviet leadership that without the free flow of information the economy would not be able to maintain a respectable national level of achievement. In the remoteness of Novosibirsk, the capital of the Siberian division of the Academy of Sciences, Abel Aganbegian and Tatiana Zaslavskaia drafted the "Novosibirsk Report," which advocated for the first time what the document called "perestroika."

Perestroika was a frightfully formidable undertaking. As experience had shown, the so-called command-administrative system in the economy was not utterly unsuited to storming the heights of almost instant industrialization in an atmosphere of urgent necessity. On the other hand, it was not so suitable to the more conventional management of an already developed semimodern economy. By the time of Stalin's death, economic development had reached a level of complexity that central planning could not adequately manage.[27]

To deprive the economic managers, however, of their entrenched powers and privileges was not so simple as deciding upon a change of policy and administrative style. It threatened managerial turf, material advantages, and ingrained habits; and the capacity of local administrators to engage in passive resistance to the center had long been clear.

Gorbachev received little assistance from those best placed to give it, as they were the ones most exposed to the losses that perestroika would entail. This was the category comprising what had been designed to be "the new Soviet man." He was supposed to have represented some imaginary compound of Poor Richard, Samuel Smiles, and the Boy Scouts, a kind of Calvinist communist imbued with the ideals of socialist construction. This personality type had not only failed; it also blocked the path to perestroika.

Gorbachev was forced to broaden the scope of the struggle by enlisting the support of the masses. He needed a popular ally to lever the bureaucracy from below while he levered it from above. He turned to *demokratizatsiia.*

For the purely political element of Gorbachev's agenda, three important revolutions constituted a precedent: those of Ivan III (1462–1505), Peter I (1689–1725), and Stalin. They all share two features in common. First, they were revolutions from above.[28] Second, they sought the attainment of Western ends by non-Western, traditionally Russian, authoritarian means.

Gorbachev's revolution began in the traditional Russian fashion. He was soon forced, however, to depart from the precedents. The governmental and party apparatus of the Soviet revolution had grown complacent, self-satisfied, attached to its privileges; in a word, it was hostile to revolution, even to more than modest experimentation. In casting his lot with the public against the entrenched apparatus, Gorbachev thereby sought to use revolution from above as an instrument of destroying the device itself, of putting an end in future to the need for revolution from above. In other words, he sought to use traditional Russian authoritarianism to transfer the locus of power to the public.

The embrace of the idea of democracy, although no national government of Russia had ever looked on such a thing with favor, was not so unnatural an act as it seemed. Democracy has never been so rare in Russian life as we imagine. The rarer bird was liberalism. Democracy was present in the commune (*mir*), in the coop (*artel*). There was a quasi democracy, sometimes pseudodemocracy, in the government of apartment houses.[29] There was democracy in the soviets of 1905 and 1917 before it was snuffed out first by Witte and then by Lenin. There was democracy in ancient Novgorod and in modern Kronstadt.

One of the most fascinating and purely spontaneous forms of Russian democracy can be observed in the city bus. In some fashion mysterious to the alien itinerant, the motley transients in the bus evolve a tacit consensus instantly comprehensible to every native. They conceive and impose a requisite order. Silence is broken to discipline the not-infrequent drunks or the citizen who fails to pay his fare and to accommodate foreigners and rustics unfamiliar with the system as well as overburdened *babushki* in need of an already occupied seat. Each city bus contains quite a distinct government. In spite of the fact that part of it departs the scene and a new part enters at every stop, the character of the government remains noticeably stable and uniform. The city bus manifests in its most cantankerous form that busybody interventionist impulse that J.R. Talmon has termed totalitarian democracy. Russian democracy was not, then, purely a figment of a disordered imagination.

Judging by what he appeared to anticipate from the intervention of the people in Soviet politics, Gorbachev must have looked into himself, found himself both reasonable and virtuous, and projected his own self-image onto the people whom he fancied that he knew. He did not know them. Gorbachev evidently imagined that a government turned virtuous would elicit a generous response from a naturally virtuous people. But the people of his conception turned out to be purely imaginary. If power had corrupted, as Lord Acton suggested that it does, the Soviet bureaucracy, then impotence had corrupted, as Studs Terkel suggests that it does, the people. The Soviet/Russian people had had the worst of these two experiences, that is, the juxtaposition of unlimited power in the government and unqualified impotence in the people. Civic virtue was not there, only civic cynicism. A republic of virtue was not within human reach. Too much idealist, too little realist, Gorbachev should have taken counsel with more hard-bitten students of human nature—Thomas Aquinas, Machiaveli, H.L. Mencken, for example. The Marquis de Sade would have informed him that the evil of humankind is as natural as wisdom and virtue are. As one of Gorbachev's party aides and supporters confessed, "Gorbachev's main failing is that he's too intellectual, too rational. He does not understand ordinary people well enough—what makes them tick."[30]

Democracy did not save him and his reform. Rather, it helped to condemn them. The attempt to transfer power to the people was the source of problems unanticipated. There was initial enthusiasm among them for democracy. After all, in all the languages of the earth, the word has now acquired conjuring power. It is considered one of those unambiguous things, a blessing. The Russians understand democracy, however, not as majority rule but as popular justice. Glasnost had fed the appetite of the people to punish the abusive fat cats whom they had always resented and to capture a share of their privileges. But when the consequences of real perestroika were experienced, it chilled their enthusiasm.

Gorbachev was to find among the people a reluctance to support perestroika—not unlike that among the managers and the party bosses, though it had different sources. The bureaucracy fought the loss of power and privilege. The people fought the loss of living standards caused by the removal of price controls and producers' subsidies. Moreover, there was talk of unemployment. Among the benefits that Soviet government had brought the people, job security and price predictability were staples.

Another source of popular misgivings was explained by habit and custom. We must recall Alexander Gerschenkron's economic corollary of the hypertrophic state: the more political instruments are used to attain economic advancement, the more the economic future of the country is compromised. It was the natural function of the state-controlled economy to beggar the mentality of the people. The great tutelary authority that was one of the chief functions of the eighteenth-century *Polizeistaat* and Stalin's similar apparatus of state had served in fact to disinstruct and to de-educate. The people grew accustomed to the idea that they would be told all that was expected of them. Apart from the minority of peasants working their miniscule private plots, the only independent economic enterprise of the masses in the conventional Soviet economy had consisted of cheating the superstate of whatever was essential to their survival, that is, of the commodities of which it had cheated them. When Gorbachev invoked democracy in the presence of perestroika, therefore, he shifted from confrontation with the bureaucracy to confrontation with the whole people, and his popularity ratings soon began to reflect the fact.[31]

Gorbachev's problem—the problem of Witte in 1895, of Peter I in 1700—was the "staggering challenge of matching the spontaneous civic cooperation prevailing in Western society." But the secret of the success of the Western model, "the ceaseless industrial advance promoted by individual self-interest subconsciously socialized into collective cooperation," was not present and not instantly available; and "a country that craves the benefits of modern industrialization without possessing among its inhabitants the necessary motivation and self-discipline is headed for endless misery."[32]

It is part of American mythology, perhaps communicated now, alas, to the bulk of the planet, that democracy is by definition progressive. Russian democracy had other habits. We may remember Tolstoy's disappointment at being rejected when he offered his serfs emancipation, the often-heard peasant remark late in the nineteenth century that times were better before emancipation, and Stolypin's experience with the dissolution of the *mir*. According to Stolypin, "The Russian peasant has a passion for making everyone equal, for reducing everything to a common denominator, and since the masses cannot be raised to the level of the most capable, the most active, and the most intelligent, the best elements must be brought down to the level of understanding and ambition prevailing among the inferior, inert majority."[33] Russians' attitudes have been described as a "culture of envy."[34] Alexander Zinoviev has suggested their voluntary self-enserfment. It is, in a sense, self-dekulakization. Philip Hanson calls it "totalitarianism from below."[35]

The peasants were glad to see free prices for their produce, but they feared privatization. The ghost of Stalin lingered, and the personality of Gorbachev might not (Gorbachev, somewhat illogically, did not favor private ownership of land). The farmers taking advantage nowadays of privatization to leave the collective farms are few, and they are having a hard time. They are refused the use of farm machinery by the collectives, which resent their leaving. They often face, as they did in the day of the Stolypin reform, the threat of arson.[36] They are carrying guns into the fields to protect their crops. Many collective farmers say that, if privatization occurs, it will have to come from central legislative initiative.[37] One advantage that they do not want to surrender is the opportunity to steal from the collective. A January 1993 poll found only 15.4 percent of peasants in favor of the sale of land to private proprietors.[38]

The workers, on the other hand, have had to suffer the higher prices, and the population of Russia today is about 75 percent urban. The social category that has lost the most is that large group of people in retirement. The pensioners comprise 20 percent of the population. Their occasionally supplemented pensions do not suffice. Aging grandparents formerly provided financial assistance to young parents. At present, the flow of assistance has reversed.

The attitudes of the population toward perestroika ought not to occasion excessive surprise. Life became more uncertain, more difficult, and more stressful than before. The demographic trends reflect the trauma. The birthrate is down, and the death rate is up. In parts of Russia, the death rate has for years now exceeded the birthrate.[39] At present, the population of Russia is shrinking. According to Murray Feshbach, our leading demographer of Russia, life expectancy of Russian males declined by three years last year![40]

Somewhat more puzzling was another attitude toward democracy generated by the reform. With the exception of the intelligentsia, which has hungered for civil liberties since Catherine II imposed rigid censorship in the time of the French Revolution, what we perceive to be gains in democracy the bulk of the Russian public has perceived as losses of freedom. They think of themselves today as less free than formerly. Freedom is not everywhere defined identically. In the words of Edmund Burke, "If any ask me what a free government is, I answer, that, for any practical purpose, it is what the people think so,—and that they, and not I, are the natural, lawful, and competent judges of this matter."[41] Now let us add a reflection of Raymond Aron. "I imagine that a Russian who has been given a scholarship, secondary and then higher education, who has risen in the social scale, who today [1969] has a profession, which brings him advantages, feels that he is free. . . . Opportunities for social advancement can give rise to a feeling of freedom when other kinds of liberty are lacking."[42] At the present time, this style of liberty has disappeared in Russia except among those few fortunate and rapacious entrepreneurs lucky enough to live, in the opinion of their fellows, at the expense of their victims. The majority live today more nearly in a Hobbesian state of nature, where life is at best nasty, brutish, and, in fact, increasingly short.

After the heady days of 1985 to 1988 or 1989, most Russians clearly grew more dissatisfied with the kind of freedom and justice that they were experiencing than they had been in the days of Brezhnev. The intelligentsia says that the people prefer Stalin with bread to Gorbachev or Yeltsin without bread. A 1992 public-opinion poll in Moscow found that 69 percent of the people preferred a restoration of the old Soviet Union to the Russian Federation in which they then lived.[43] Consider a recent article in *Literaturnaia gazeta* in which a former KGB operative, the chauffeur for the British ambassador, described how he was recruited. His father had worked for the "organs," and the son was proud of it and eager to carry on the family tradition. He was invited for an interview in a hotel room, and the conversation there proceeded in a fashion described in his words as "comfortably, naturally, professionally . . . reasonably and democratically" (*spokoino, estestvenno, professionalno . . . pedagogichno i demokratichno*). This man was attaching his fate to agencies of freedom.[44]

In sum, one of the great obstacles to the reform has been the feeling that it has cost the people their conception of freedom and justice. This is not at all to say that they are not more free by our standards; rather, that they do not feel themselves to be so by their standards.

The last obstacle posed to the reform by democracy is one that it has shared with glasnost: democracy has provided the actual freedom to engage in conflict of opinion, and the range of opinion in Russia is to us almost unimaginably great, as great as is natural in a country where the exercise of unorthodox opinion has been traditionally banned. There are real communists, and there are real monarchists—and sun worshippers and eskimoes, vegetarians and theosophists. In an empire where variety of opinion is so multifarious and conflict of opinion is so deep and impassioned, good order does not benefit by permissiveness or freedom. There is ideological conflict, ethnic conflict, religious conflict. Consider for the sake of comparison the political instability of France, 1789 to 1962 (the end of Algérie française), a country relatively uniform in ethnicity and religion (i.e., none), where the conflict of opinion gathered almost exclusively around the political axis. Not until the Fifth Republic were the disputes and antagonisms of the revolutionary era digested and mastered.

With the wisdom of hindsight, we can observe that Gorbachev probably failed to connect with two of his three most promising constituencies—the first, the intelligentsia, served him for a time as well as it could. Although his early antialcohol campaign turned into an economic fiasco, it enhanced his popularity with housewives considerably. Furthermore, Russian women are more practical, reliable, and responsible than the society as a whole—they are also more sensitive and humane.[45] Their potential contribution to society is undervalued at home and abroad. Of course, any kind of formal bloc with a gynocracy in so misogynist a society as Russia—"if the hair is long, the mind is short"—would have required skilled political gymnastics. Gorbachev was much criticized in conversation for showing his wife excessive, inappropriate respect. Still, inebriated men will often admit that "only the women work."

The other untapped constituency was the church. Much was made in conversation of the fact that Gorbachev had been baptized as an infant by his mother. He was clearly not a believer, but on the eve of the millennial celebration of the Russian church, he had an interview with the patriarch and publicly regretted Soviet crimes against the church—all duly reported on the front page of *Pravda*. Throughout this period, Dmitrii Likhachev—we may regard him as the patriarch of the intellectuals—said repeatedly that no social or economic perestroika was possible without a preceding *moral* perestroika. In the fall of 1990, Gorbachev held a meeting with "Soviet cultural leaders." Likhachev was the first to speak. He repeated his usual line, and he added, as if to tutor his leader in the futility of Marxism, that society was guided by consciousness (*soznanie*), not by material being (*bytie*).[46] Solzhenitsyn said in an interview with *Izvestiia* in the fall of 1992 that "if our conscience does not awaken, no economic reform will save us."[47] Given the prestige—and the Orthodoxy—of these two figures, surely some kind of rapprochement useful to a humane reform was possible with the church.

Probably Gorbachev's whole conception of reform was doomed in any event. In retrospect, it is clear that it was a tissue of contradictions. Three of them were fundamental and probably insuperable.

First, two of his primary principles, glasnost and democratization, were incompatible with the third, perestroika, because perestroika was unpopular and glasnost and democratization facilitated opposition to it.

Second, Gorbachev violated every historical canon of Russian tradition. As head of that ancient hypertrophic leviathan and Stalin's legatee, he was a populist, a democrat, a civil libertarian, a quasi capitalist. And he demanded of the people *at once* spontaneous, self-assertive, public initiatives. This was a recipe for real revolution under the rubric of reform, a revolution of the most pervasive kind, a revolution of mentality. Or it was a recipe for disaster. Tradition does not tolerate such insults submissively. To paraphrase Pascal, tradition has its reasons which reason does not know.

Third, all three of his fundamental principles, glasnost, perestroika, and democratization, were incompatible with two Soviet traditions, the exclusive power of the party and the maintenance of the multiethnic empire. It was precisely the implementation of glasnost, perestroika, and democratization that eventually ruined the party and the empire, and it was Gorbachev's unwillingness to relinquish them that cost him his own power. The most graphic evidence of this error occurred upon his return from house arrest in the Crimea after the August 1991 coup. Before all the TV sets in the world, he had the folly to reaffirm his faith in Leninist socialism. At this point, the triumph of Boris Yeltsin, who was willing to jettison both party and empire, was assured.

Yeltsin had long exhibited a more impatient and radical attitude toward reform than Gorbachev. Having begun as allies in the cause of reform, they parted company over the pace of it. Perhaps Yeltsin realized at some point that the natural thrust of Gorbachev's program automatically doomed party and empire. In any event, he was temperamentally equipped to dispense with them. As one ethnic constitutent of empire after another began to fall away, Gorbachev, civil libertarian that he basically was, refused to use the traditional Russian weapon of massive force to hold things together. In the meantime, Yeltsin emerged from Soviet disgrace to become a Russian national hero in the elections of March 1989, the only major player on the national scene who could then lay claim to the mandate of genuine popular prerogative. In retrospect, the bungled coup of 19–21 August 1991 seems to have been a blessing in disguise for the new democrats. The hard-liners overplayed their hand; and in botching the affair so frightfully, they forfeited the political authority that competent conspiracy might have conferred. Gorbachev might have returned a near-martyred hero had he had the insight to assess the political landscape clearly. He did not, and Yeltsin had perhaps inadvertently upstaged him, in any case, standing on an army tank while dramatically defying the putschists before, again, all the TV sets in the world. Within a matter of months, in December 1991, what had become inevitable was recognized, and the Soviet state was dissolved.

Gorbachev had embarked on a quest as if to expunge from national life a kind of curse, an un-Holy Grail, Stalinism. He is one of history's heroes, like Parsifal, a brave man slowly wise. Like the heroes of classical mythology, engaged as he was in a kind of Sisyphean striving, he was endowed by the gods with faults and frailties without which his trials would not have been epic.

Much to the sorrow of humanitarians and civil libertarians everywhere, his legacy is not at present a happy one.

Conclusion:
A Cautious Prognosis

The market cannot create a political community by itself. It has never done so in the past, and it would be a mistake to think that it can do so now. Even at its best, the market aims only at efficiency. For justice, one has to appeal to the polity.

Dusan Pokorny, *Failure of the Soviet Experiment*

The Russian public is not imperialist.

Charles Fairbanks, "A Tired Anarchy"

In the ever so volatile present, there are three compelling questions on the Russian agenda: the nature of the government, the nature of the economy, and the fate of the former Russian/Soviet empire.

The Struggle to Govern

If the Gorbachev phenomenon was principally a characteristically Russian revolution from above, still there was initially more than the usual support for it at the grass roots. Much the most careful study of public opinion yet to appear on the attitudes of the Soviet public toward the Gorbachev reform yields several informative findings.[1]

The public initially welcomed the program as a genuine and honest effort to tell the truth about present and past, to bridle the corrupt bureaucracy, and to improve economic opportunity without surrendering the guarantees of the welfare state. Only when the reform palpably failed and exacted a high price in living standards, ideological comfort, and national pride did the tide of public opinion turn against it. From that time, we have witnessed a deterioration of the Russian situation that has yet to be clearly arrested.

At the present time, Russia has merely the shadow of a government at best. The contemporary political chaos is from two sources. On the one hand, the executive institutions of government have atrophied. As they lack their former force, they do not get the respect that they formerly got. There is a huge and spontaneous revolt of the provinces against the capital. Moscow no longer counts for much in the hinterland. Except through the application of military force, it lacks the power to do either good or evil. It can be ignored. In many respects, this is a constructive phenomenon. It erodes that concentration of power formerly capable of international catastrophe and domestic tragedy.

On the other hand, the new parliamentary institutions have not developed the capacity to articulate policy in a coherent fashion. They cannot do so because they reflect the frightfully fragmented opinion of the land. The proliferation of parties and programs leads to deadlock and paralysis. This fact, too, encourages the migration of initiative from capital to provinces and compels the population to learn the dynamisms of self-reliance.

For a time the most troubling phenomenon, inextricably associated with the name Vladimir Zhirinovskii, was that motley coalition known as the "red–brown bloc." As a headline in *Izvestiia* put it, "Communists, Nationalists, and Monarchists Have Concluded an Alliance to Overturn the President of Russia."[2] For many of these people, the Gorbachev reform was the root of all evil. They have coined the term *katastroika—katastrofa* plus *perestroika*—to describe it. The democrats, *demokraty*, they call *dermokraty*, shit-ocrats. The communists, of course, want to restore the Soviet Union, and some of them are conventional Stalinists. The monarchists are of various kinds, some of them mere sentimentalists, not all of them dangerously obnoxious. One camp in this bloc not familiar in the West is that of the National Bolsheviks.[3] They embody the idea that Bolshevism alone saved Russia from destruction in the wake of the disaster of World War I and the mortal threat of Nazism. By 1945, Bolshevism had reconstituted the old Russian Empire and, including the new Soviet bloc in Eastern Europe, in many respects exceeded it; therefore, Russian nationalists must be grateful to the Bolsheviks. Of course, a lot of them are not, pointing to the huge sacrifices of population in Stalin's purges, to the destruction of both life and a characteristically Russian way of life among the collectivized peasantry, and to a long list of gifted artists annihilated in the purges.

As elsewhere in the world, however, there are in Russia many varieties of nationalism, and fortunately several of them are more benign than the more or less undisguised racist fascism of Zhirinovskii's "Liberal-Democratic Party of Russia." Moreover, Zhirinovskii's problems are developing more quickly than his movement is. Documents in his place of birth, Alma-Ata, appear to show that his father's name was Eidelshtein, that his grandfather's name was Isaak Eidelshtein.[4] Evidently born Jewish, he makes an implausible anti-Semite. According to a recent poll, support for his party among the Russian electorate has already fallen significantly.[5]

In our frustration at the fact that the perpetual peace and good order promised by the Soviet collapse has only yielded disappointment, we sometimes overlook the fact that the worst has not happened there. In retrospect, it is clear that our expectations of the Soviet disintegration were grossly inflated and never realistic. The history of Eastern Europe ought to have suggested to us a skeptical reaction, at least a reserved reaction. It was not a question whether it was desirable to maintain Soviet civilization and the Soviet bloc. It was rather a question how benevolent or malevolent a form their transformation would take. Though the transformation has been troubling, and its outcome is by no means yet clear, many knowledgeable people would have predicted much more vicious consequences of the Soviet breakup than we have yet seen. In spite of the regrettable affair of Chechnya, there is as yet no large Russian civil war, and there is not yet a war between Russia and Ukraine. Both, of course, remain possible, though the former seems increasingly unlikely.

If we consider our decidedly uncertain and self-serving penchant for thinking that liberal democracy is the natural goal toward which the progress of nations tends—we will know more about this proposition several thousand years hence—still the time and the travails through which they have passed in order to arrive at this imagined state of bliss are impressive. The great progenitor of constitutional democracy was England. If we do not put too fine a point on it, the process lasted in England from the early seventeenth century—the struggles of James I and his successors—through the coming of equal women's suffrage in 1928. The process of evolution in England was slow in part because the English were inventing the idea before they accepted it as an institution. Success appeared to attend the enterprise of constitutionalism—Voltaire was its press agent—especially in the age of imperialism, and imitation abroad naturally followed. Imitation being less grueling than invention, the process ran its course in other nations somewhat more quickly. Still, in France it required more than a century and a half, 1792 to the 1960s, to stabilize itself. Similarly in Spain: from 1808, Napoleon's destruction of the old monarchy, to 1975, Franco's posthumous establishment of Juan Carlos's new constitutional monarchy. In the United States, a country favored by geography, economics, and natural strategic defensibility—a country perfectly remarkable, with one brief exception in 1861, for political stability—the Senate was subjected to popular vote in 1913, and women were enfranchised in 1920. In some modern nations, Germany and Japan, liberal democracy did not evolve; it was dispensed.

In other words, the Russian road to a stable popular sovereignty, if that is the course that Russia chooses, will likely be a long and awkward one yet. As the Russians grope their way (forward?) to a more satisfactory future, they must seek to find it in the context of some of their own traditions, the less vicious and grim ones, we hope.

The Evolution of the Economy

Though it may be found surprising here, the bulk of the Russian public maintained throughout the Soviet period a basic attachment to the socialist ideals of the Soviet system. Fewer people approved of the Communist Party and Soviet administration. The particular Soviet model most approved was not Stalinism but rather the New Economic Policy of the 1920s, liberal communism, a mixed economy in which the state was significantly involved in heavy industry, less involved in the consumer economy. The welfare state was distinctly popular, but younger people and better-educated people preferred less comprehensive versions of it. Collectivization of farming was generally condemned. The blue-collar proletariat was less dissatisfied with the old order than the more privileged sectors of society were, but even it grew slowly more critical of both government and party.[6]

When the new economic regime began to produce its now notoriously painful consequences, however, it generated massive confusion and disapproval. Myriads of Soviet and post-Soviet opinion polls have demonstrated a steady retreat from the heady rejoicing of the early phase of reform. All known forms of populist politics have been discredited as the population finds in them no effective remedies of its affliction. The people are scrambling hectically to find sustenance, and they lack the luxury of leisure to concern themselves with the question of desirable forms of new political and economic institutions. The election results of December 1993—the success of parties taking the mantle of communism and of their counterparts on the nationalist fringe of the right wing—demonstrated just how far public opinion had swung against the new dispensation. Given the suffering that the new regime has inflicted, it is not surprising.

At the same time, it is undeniable that commerce unleashed and enterprise emancipated have made giant strides in Russia. This, too, is unsurprising, as it was unavoidable. The government veritably legislated its own destruction as well as that of its economy. In the midst of the collapse of the whole of the Soviet institutional infrastructure, the new style of Russian economy is the only one that at present fairly functions. Hustling for oneself is the only way to survive, and the imperatives of survival are compelling teachers. In the chaos and confusion, the shock and pain of post-Soviet Russia, an inchoate, rapacious, and somewhat primitive protocapitalism is the decidedly uncivil economy of a kind of Hobbesian state of nature.

Will capitalism succeed in Russia? Undoubtedly, in spite of all contrary precedent and tradition. Why? Because at present it is the only reliable system of distribution and acquisition. And the bureaucratic mandarins of the Bolshevik old order have used their levers of power to position themselves advantageously in the free-wheeling new order; therefore their own material interest commits them to the new present as it formerly did to the old past. One of our best-informed authorities, Anders Aslund—he was part of the Jeffrey Sachs team imported to advise the government on the transition—says flatly, "However messy and imperfect, Russia is a market economy, and has been at least since the end of 1993."[7] Anders is accounted an optimist, however, and his opinion is open to objection.

What do the Russians think of the matter? A distinguished Russian writer, Daniil Granin, has recently summed it up properly ambiguously. On the one hand: "The Russian has never had a normal attitude toward private property. . . . The government is offering land to collective farm workers and the people are saying they do not want it! . . .

The businessman was never a positive figure in Russian literature. . . . Trading has been considered the occupation of swindlers." On the other hand:

> A new third estate is taking shape. . . . Factory engineers are becoming managers of companies or directors of large firms. This is a time for transformation and unheard-of careers. The visible changes are breaking through all cracks. In the St. Petersburg district where I live almost all the ground-floors in the buildings have been remodeled and furnished. . . . The buildings are now being repaired for use by private firms. You enter another neighborhood and do not recognize the new signs and new store windows.
>
> The stores are filled with goods. . . . The people of St. Petersburg can buy pineapples, bananas, and kiwis in the wintertime.[8]

Only someone who has wintered in the old Soviet Union can appreciate the novelty of finding fruit of any kind, not to speak of tropical fruit, in Russia in that season.

An extensive public-opinion poll recently produced conclusions like Granin's. "It has taken most Russians just a few years to cast aside values that traditionally have been regarded as inalienable features of their national mind-set: an omnipotent state possessing quasi-religious authority, disdain for wealth, egalitarian beliefs about property, conformity of opinion, collectivism, anti-Western attitudes, and the rejection of democracy and liberalism."[9]

This judgment requires some qualification. Russian society is by no means so uniformly transformed. It is divided in complex ways but most conspicuously by a generation gap. Russian youth had long been disaffected from the dreariness of Soviet life.[10] As plain among Russian émigrés in the United States as among Russians at home is the radically different rate of adjustment of different age groups to a new way of life. In addition, support for socialist principles remains strong both among the poorly educated and among the politically inactive.[11] And 88 percent of Russians still favor the establishment of a minimum standard of living; 96 percent favor a guaranteed right to work.[12]

One element of this problem is the rampant criminality, the notorious Russian mafia so conspicuous in our headlines. The mafiosi were the original Soviet entrepreneurs. While the Soviet government still functioned with some degree of effectiveness, the criminal element bought protection by cutting civil servants, especially the police, in on its profits. The phenomenon is universal, of course, but in Russia at present it is unusually massive. When the government began to disintegrate and then collapsed, the mafia was in a position to establish itself as little less than the economic administration of the country. No one goes far in business before being forced to purchase protection, a "roof" (*krysha*) in street parlance. The multiple murders, daily fare in contemporary Russian news, are chiefly a form of economic warfare. They target turf rivals, nosy journalists, and politicians who do not play the game. Given the weakness of the government and the strength of the mafia, this disturbing element of the new civil society will not soon be brought to heel.[13]

Reconquest of Empire?

The war in Chechnya has filled our headlines with humanitarian dread and foreign-policy alarm. Fortunately, the conflict is as small as it is grisly, and even it bears distinctly hopeful signs (for those not savaged by it). The Russian populace and the Russian press alike have taken a ferociously hostile attitude toward it. The Russian army in many respects proved as reluctant, even mutinous, as it was inept. More and more the Russian intervention appears to have been prompted by a conspiracy of the security forces to enhance their claim on the state budget. The media have emphasized the sorrow that the war has brought to victims on *both* sides. The government in Moscow continues to take a hard line in the question. Its negotiating position does not appear to have been altered in the least by the Chechen seizure of the hospitals in Budennovsk and Kizliar. The Russian Federal Security Service has voiced suspicion of support of the Chechens by Turkey, Jordan, and Afghanistan (15 August 1995).[14] A conflict with these ramifications can benefit no one, least of all the Russians.

One of our most experienced Russian observers, former ambassador Jack Matlock, dismisses the prospect of a rebirth of the Soviet Empire. "Russia can't afford an empire again and the regions will not go along with it." Further military operations against its neighbors are likely to catalyze rather than contain fragmentation. More serious than the threat of empire is that of further disintegration.[15]

Perhaps it is natural for us to scan the horizon for traditional Russian imperialism in an alarmist fashion. In fact, one of the most agreeable surprises of the breakup of the Soviet Union is a manifestation of public opinion downright hostile to imperial adventure. As Charles Fairbanks has put it, "the Russians of today do not like fighting, killing and dying. . . . *the Russian public is not imperialist.*"[16]

We must recognize, however, even if grudgingly, that the collapse of the Soviet Union is not an unmixed blessing. This evil empire, a prisonhouse of nations—as Lenin called the Russian Empire and he and Stalin made the Soviet Empire—also kept a modicum of peace and order in a notoriously disorderly part of the world, the "crescent of crisis" that joined the southern Soviet frontier with the Near East and the borderlands of Eastern Europe that ignited two world wars. The Caucasus and the Balkans presently exhibit some of the evils that the Soviet Union—and the cold war—formerly preempted.

Solzhenitsyn has made a similar point in an interview in *Forbes.* He suggests, most realistically, that in the twenty-first century, the United States and NATO will need a Russian alliance for the sake of keeping a tolerable international order.[17] (And what to do with China?)

What may we expect the legacy of Russia to show us next? Prognosis in contemporary Russia is bedeviled by a series of unusually vexing circumstances. The experience of transition from communism to capitalism is unique. We have no analogies for comparison. The old Soviet infrastructure has collapsed, and a new one has not yet evolved. The former culture has been rejected, too. Finally, all of the analytical tools that we applied to Soviet Russia have now grown useless. Thus social science is impotent to deal with the question.

Neither is the historian properly a prophet. Historical development is subject to the intrusion of ever so many things that cannot be foreseen—barbarian invasions, the Black Plague, the personality of Martin Luther, earthquakes, droughts, implausible wars that no one can afford, stock-market crashes, Holocausts, Gulags, Lenin, Stalin, Gorbachev. Still, the historian ought to be able, within flexible and forgiving limits, to define the present and near future as the product of the past such as to place it in a somewhat better-than-average perspective of intelligence.

George Urban, a student of Stalinism, recently made a remarkably sound suggestion. He imagined a future Russian leader reasoning as follows:

> Marketization, a laissez-faire economy, and liberal democracy have failed in the Third World and are unlikely to succeed in [Russia]. They

presuppose Western traditions, Western education, and the spirit of Western enterprise. Whether we approve of these or not is unimportant. What is important is that we have not got them and, therefore, cannot build on them. But we can build on what we do have and need not be ashamed of—a tested tradition of centralization, a robust respect for authority, a spirit of social justice and even egalitarianism, a strong sense of national identity, a fine contempt for utilitarianism, and a love of spiritual values. These are great assets. . . . Will their cultivation slow down our development to Western levels of technological efficiency? Yes, they probably will. Will they retard our growth to Western levels of prosperity? Yes, they will. . . . But we are ready to accept these disadvantages provided we can make some progress towards a better life while remaining true to ourselves.[18]

Here is an authentic appreciation of Russian prospects, but it may still be somewhat amplified. A review of the history of Russia suggests the fateful influence of four forces.

First is, as Urban suggests, the power of the state, discredited for a time during the halcyon days of Gorbachev, the object of increasing nostalgia now that its disintegration has itself occasioned such widespread suffering. The Russians would gladly put together again some kind of coherent statecraft, but they cannot at present agree on what kind it is.

Second is a deeply ambivalent attitude toward the West—love, hate, respect, envy, admiration, suspicion, disgust. Their present experience of it and its commercial invasion are not enhancing affection for it. Russia today seems to absorb by preference the more philistine features of Western culture, and the result is far from pretty.

Third is Orthodox Christianity, which has enjoyed a lively, but not unambiguous, renaissance since 1985. It has a distinctly anti-Western bias. We have seen its "spiritual radicalism" manifest in "indifference to the world," the basis of its "hostility to the bourgeois world." (Of course, there is a long and venerable Western Christian tradition, chiefly Catholic, of antagonism to the ethos and values of capitalism as well—most conspicuously, Leo XIII's *Rerum Novarum* [1891].)[19]

Last is a primordial social and economic democracy, a pre-Marxist protosocialist egalitarianism, a devil-may-care attitude to getting ahead, an attitude complementing or deriving from the outlook of Russian Christianity and supplemented by a resentment of privilege.

None of these four facets of Russian culture is accepting of Western capitalism, and the present massive invasion of Russia by the cheapest and tawdriest forms of Western culture makes it doubly offensive.

It is tempting, if foolhardy, to think that the most natural, perhaps fortunate, development to imagine in the Russian future is Christian socialism. There is nothing so explicit as a doctrinal variant of it to be found in the history of the Russian church, but the spirit of the religion is remarkably close to it—St. Sergius of Radonezh, the Trans-Volga Hermits, the holy fools, St. Serafim Sarovskii, Leo Tolstoy, Father Georgii Gapon. It has been prominent in the religious and intellectual life of the twentieth-century Russian church in emigration, especially around Father George Fedotov and the journal *Novyi grad*.[20] The Orthodox religion and social egalitarianism are at the heart of the spirit of Russia. They represent a conservative return to the most humane traditions of the people's heritage.

In a broader perspective, it is increasingly apparent by now that socialism is not yet dead. Virtually every report from Eastern Europe brings us news of disillusionment with the new order there. Every election in Eastern Europe bears evidence of socialist revival. It is unlikely ever to die. Envy is its inextinguishable inspiration, as greed is that of capitalism.

Of course, Russian national politics in the Christian socialist form would preclude that effective technological race with the West, the quest for power and modernization, that has been one of the principal themes of the Russian past. Yet in the new world order—and disorder—nothing is plainer than the fatigue of the ambitions of the great powers, and a less demonically developmental society would be acceptable. In fact, it might well be welcome—and not only in Russia.

In any event, a stable and comfortable future for the Russians—and therefore, for all of us—depends upon their finding a way simultaneously to a rejection of the violent absolutism of their past and yet to something more nearly their own than a perfunctory replication of liberal capitalism and its attendant values. Perhaps in the process they will learn something of use for the ills of our society as well.

Notes

Chapter 1. Origins

1. Omeljan Pritsak, "The Origin of Rus'," *Russian Review* 36 (1977): 249–50. There is a fuller account in J.L. Black, *G.-F. Müller and the Imperial Russian Academy* (Kingston/Montreal: McGill-Queen's University Press, 1986).

2. Edmund Burke, *Reflections on the Revolution in France*, ed. J.G.A. Pocock (Indianapolis: Hackett, 1986), 54.

3. Richard Pipes, *Russia under the Old Regime* (New York: Scribner's, 1974), 223.

4. George Vernadsky, *The Mongols and Russia* (New Haven, CT: Yale University Press, 1953), 127, 219; John K. Fairbank, Edwin O. Reischauer, and Albert M. Craig, *A History of East Asian Civilization*, 2 vols. (Boston: Houghton Mifflin, 1958–65), 1: 212.

5. This is not to deny the presence of a belt of Asian peoples running from Central Asia through the southern Urals to Finland.

6. William McNeill, *The Rise of the West: A History of the Human Community* (Chicago: University of Chicago Press, 1963).

7. Ivan III was not utterly without Renaissance contacts. In 1472, he married Zoë Paleologue, the niece of the last Byzantine emperor, whose family had found asylum in Rome after the fall of Constantinople to the Turks in 1453. Zoë was educated entirely in Italy. Ivan invited to Moscow a variety of Italian technicians. Among those who came were Aristotle Fioravanti, Marco Ruffo, Pietro Solario, and Alevisio Novi. Fioravanti built the Cathedral of the Assumption (*Uspenskii sobor*) in the Kremlin. Alevisio rebuilt the Cathedral of the Archangel Michael (*Arkhangelskii sobor*). The Cathedral of the Annunciation (*Blagoveshchenskii sobor*) was built about the same time by architects from Pskov. The one structure that reflects a distinctly non-Muscovite style is the Palace of Facets (*Granovitaia palata*), done by Ruffo and Solario. The Italian visitors also built a gunpowder factory and cannon foundries.

According to Dmitrii Likhachev, Russia did not experience a Renaissance for the following reasons: inadequate economic development in the fifteenth–sixteenth centuries; construction of a centralized state and the destruction of cultural contacts; destruction of the free communities of Novgorod and Pskov, where the Renaissance was most likely to take root and grow; the force and influence of the church, which was hostile to the Renaissance. This latter was the most important factor, as the church supported the centralizing state. D.S. Likhachev, *Kul'tura Rusi vremeni Andreia Rubleva i Epifaniia Premudrogo (konets XIV–nachalo XV v.)* (Moscow: AN SSSR, 1962), 170.

8. Apparently in deference to popular demand, Ivan formed new institutions of elective local self-government, though they were in fact controlled by his own appointees who were found unfit for military service. A.A. Kizevetter, *Mestnoe samoupravlenie v Rossii, IX–XIX st.: Istoricheskii ocherk* (Moscow: Tip. Moskovskogo universiteta, 1910), 46–64.

9. Maureen Perrie, *The Image of Ivan the Terrible in Russian Folklore* (New York: Cambridge University Press, 1987).

10. George Vernadsky et al., eds., *A Source Book for Russian History*, 3 vols. (New Haven, CT: Yale University Press, 1972), 1: 132–33.

11. Ibid., 149.

12. R.G. Skrynnikov, in *Ivan Groznyi* (Moscow: Nauka, 1975), gives a devastating impression of the reign.

13. This is the argument of Richard Hellie, *Enserfment and Military Change in Muscovy* (Chicago: University of Chicago Press, 1971).

14. Adam Olearius, *The Travels of Olearius in Seventeenth-Century Russia*, ed. and trans. Samuel H. Baron (Stanford, CA: Stanford University Press, 1967), 62–63.

15. Henceforth, there were three religions in Ukraine: Russian Orthodoxy, Roman Catholicism, and an awkward combination of them, the Uniate Church (1595).

16. Fedor II was the very transient successor of Boris Godunov.

Chapter 2. Politics and Religion

1. Igor Shafarevich, *Sotsializm kak iavlenie mirovoi istorii* (Paris: YMCA, 1977), 349. A general and somewhat skimpy introduction to the school of thought can be found in Anatole G. Mazour, *Modern Russian Historiography* (New York: Van Nostrand, 1956). Much better, surprisingly good given the scope of the book and the brevity of coverage of individuals, not to mention the date of its publication and the atmosphere of Soviet historical scholarship at the time, is N.L. Rubinshtein, *Russkaia istoriografiia* (Moscow: Gospolitizdat, 1941). A convenient short and articulate statement of the idea is in P.N. Miliukov, *Ocherki po istorii russkoi kul'tury*, 6th ed., 4 vols. in 3 (St. Petersburg: Aleksandrov, 1909–13), 1: 137–61.

2. My recollection is that I took this articulate characterization from Perry Anderson, *Lineages of the Absolutist State* (London: NLB, 1974), but I cannot now find it there. If I have quoted incorrectly, my apologies to the real author.

3. Quoted in J. Russell Major, *Representative Government in Early Modern France* (New Haven, CT: Yale University Press, 1980), 191.

4. Nicholas Henshall, *The Myth of Absolutism* (London: Longman, 1992).

5. Ibid., 168. Also useful is William Beik, *Absolutism and Society in Seventeenth-Century France: State Power and Provincial Aristocracy in Languedoc* (London: Cambridge University Press, 1985).

6. A.A. Kizevetter, *Mestnoe samoupravlenie v Rossii, IX–XIX st.: Istoricheskii ocherk* (Moscow: Tip. Moskovskogo universiteta, 1910), 64–90.

7. Roland Mousnier, *The Institutions of France under the Absolute Monarchy 1598–1789*, vol. 2: *The Organs of State and Society*, trans. Arthur Goldhammer (Chicago: University of Chicago Press, 1984).

8. *Six livres de la République*, quoted in Roland Mousnier, *The Institutions of France under the Absolute Monarchy 1598–1789*, vol. 1: *Society and the State*, trans. Brian Pearce (Chicago: University of Chicago Press, 1979), 664.

9. Major, *Representative Government in Early Modern France*, 181.

10. Quoted in ibid., 182.

11. Quoted in Mousnier, *Institutions of France under the Absolute Monarchy*, 1: 664. Loyseau was right: Trajan Stoianovich, "Land Tenure and Related Sectors of the Balkan Economy 1600–1800," *Journal of Economic History* 13 (1953): 398–411.

12. Sigmund von Herberstein, *Description of Moscow and Muscovy*, ed. Bertold Picard, trans. J.B.C. Grundy (New York: Barnes and Noble, 1969), 43–44. Herberstein was there on diplomatic missions for the German Empire in 1517–18 and 1526–27.

13. Giles Fletcher, *Of the Rus Commonwealth*, ed. Albert J. Schmidt (Ithaca, NY: Cornell University Press for the Folger Shakespeare Library), 1966), 30–32.

14. Adam Olearius, *The Travels of Olearius in Seventeenth-Century Russia*, ed. and trans. Samuel H. Baron (Stanford, CA: Stanford University Press, 1967), 173.

15. Mousnier, *Institutions of France under the Absolute Monarchy*, 2: 485–501.

16. Daniel Rancour-Laferriere, *The Slave Soul of Russia: Moral Masochism and the Cult of Suffering* (New York: New York University Press, 1995).

17. George P. Fedotov, *The Russian Religious Mind*, 2 vols. (Cambridge, MA: Harvard University Press, 1946–66), 2: 341.

18. Miliukov, *Ocherki po istorii russkoi kul'tury*, vol. 3, pt. 1: 51.

19. *The Way of a Pilgrim, and the Pilgrim Continues His Way*, trans. R.M. French (New York: Harper, 1954), 1, 14.

20. D.S. Likhachev, *Zametki o russkom*, 2nd ed. (Moscow: Sovetskaia Rossiia, 1984), 14.

21. Fletcher, *Of the Rus Commonwealth*, 122.

22. Leo Tolstoy, *Childhood, Boyhood, Youth* (New York: Scribner's, 1929), 17–21.

23. Konstantin Paustovsky, *Story of a Life*, trans. Joseph Barnes (New York: Pantheon, 1964), 173.

24. Likhachev, *Zametki o russkom*, 13, 15.

25. Ieromonakh Ioann Kologrivov, Society of Jesus, *Ocherki po istorii russkoi sviatosti* (Brussels: Izdatel'stvo "Zhizn's Bogom," 1961), 8–9.

26. James Billington, *The Icon and the Axe: An Interpretive History of Russian Culture* (New York: Knopf, 1967), 69.

27. George Vernadsky et al., eds., *A Source Book for Russian History*, 3 vols. (New Haven, CT: Yale University Press, 1972), 1: 256.

28. Fletcher, *Of the Rus Commonwealth*, 121.

29. Saint Thomas Aquinas, *Summa theologica*, 3 vols. (New York: Benziger Bros., 1947–48), 1: 74.

30. John Calvin, *Institutes of the Christian Religion*, trans. John Allen, 2 vols. (Philadelphia: Presbyterian Board of Christian Education, n.d.), 2: 176.

31. Fedotov, *The Russian Religious Mind*, 2: 344. Georges Florovsky, *Ways*

of Russian Theology, ed. Richard S. Haugh, trans. Robert L. Nichols, 2 vols. (Belmont, MA: Nordland, 1979–87), 1: 1. There is an interesting account of the lives and intellectual orientations of Fedotov and Florovsky in Marc Raeff, *Russia Abroad: A Cultural History of the Russian Emigration, 1919–1939* (New York: Oxford University Press, 1990), 150–55, 176–86.

32. Max Weber, *The Sociology of Religion*, trans. Ephraim Fischoff (Boston: Beacon Press, 1963), chap. 10: "Different Roads to Salvation."

Chapter 3. Reason and Progress

1. Carl Becker, *The Heavenly City of the Eighteenth-Century Philosophers* (New Haven, CT: Yale University Press, 1932).

2. François Quesnay, *Oeuvres économiques et philosophiques*, ed. August Oncken (Paris: Jules Peelman, 1888), 329–31.

3. Pierre LeMercier de la Rivière, *L'Ordre naturel et essentiel des sociétés* (Paris: Geutiner, 1910; 1st ed., 1764), 50, passim.

4. Frederick II, *Die politische Testamente*, ed. Gustav Berthold Volz (Berlin: Reimar Hobbing, 1920), 37, 39, 77.

5. Quoted in Albion W. Small, *The Cameralists* (Chicago: University of Chicago Press, 1909), 320, 325.

6. Reinhold August Dorwart, *The Prussian Welfare State before 1740* (Cambridge, MA: Harvard University Press, 1971), 3, 18.

7. Nicholas de La Mare, *Traité de la police*, 2nd ed., 4 vols. (Amsterdam: "Aux depens de la Compagnie," 1729–38), 1: Preface, not paginated.

8. Frederick II, *Die politische Testamente*, 182–83.

9. Jean-Baptiste-Charles Le Maire, "La Police de Paris en 1770," *Mémoires de la Société de l'histoire de Paris et de l'Ile-de-France*, 51 vols. (Paris: Champion, 1875–1930), 5: 1, passim.

10. Quoted in J. Michael Hittle, *The Service City: State and Townsmen in Russia, 1600–1800* (Cambridge, MA: Harvard University Press, 1979), 88.

11. A.V. Anisimov, *Vremia petrovskikh reform* (Leningrad: Lenizdat, 1989), 238.

12. Reinhard Wittram, *Peter I, Czar und Kaiser: Zur Geschichte Peters des Grossen in seiner Zeit*, 2 vols. (Göttingen: Vandenhoeck und Ruprecht, 1964), 2: 114–15.

13. Natan Iakovlevich Eidel'man, *"Revolutsiia sverkhu" v Rossii* (Moscow: Kniga, 1989).

14. Quoted in Tibor Szamuely, *The Russian Tradition* (London: Fontana, 1988), 139.

15. Nicholas V. Riasanovsky, *A Parting of Ways: Government and the Educated Public in Russia, 1801–1855* (Oxford: Clarendon, 1985).

16. Arnold J. Toynbee, *A Study of History*, 12 vols. (London: Oxford University Press, 1934–61); idem, *A Study of History*, ed. and abridged D.C. Summervell, 2 vols. (London: Oxford University Press, 1946–57); idem, *Civilization on Trial* (New York: Oxford University Press, 1948); and idem, *The World and the West* (New York: Oxford University Press, 1953). These last two volumes present a provocative summary of Toynbee's ideas.

17. Quoted in Hans Rogger, *National Consciousness in Eighteenth-Century Russia* (Cambridge, MA: Harvard University Press, 1960), 50–51.

18. Isabel de Madariaga, *Russia in the Age of Catherine the Great* (New Haven, CT: Yale University Press, 1981), 38–43; David Ransel, *The Politics of Catherinian Russia: The Panin Party* (New Haven, CT: Yale University Press, 1981); John T. Alexander, *Catherine the Great: Life and Legend* (New York: Oxford University Press, 1989); David Griffiths, "Introduction: Of Estates, Charters and Constitutions," in *Catherine II's Charters of 1785 to the Nobility and the Towns*, trans. and ed. David Griffiths and George E. Munro (Bakersfield, CA: Charles Schlacks, Jr., Publisher, 1991), xvii–lxix.

19. My account of the Legislative Assembly follows A.A. Kizevetter, "La commission de 1767," in Paul Miliukov, Charles Seignobos, and Louis Eisenmann, *Histoire de Russie*, 2nd ed., 3 vols., (Paris: Ernest Leroux, 1935), 2: 552–70.

20. De Madariaga, *Russia in the Age of Catherine the Great*, 62, 63, 74, 127, 133–34, 161–62, 182; Alexander, *Catherine the Great*, 116, 119.

21. Quoted in Robert E. Jones, *The Emancipation of the Russian Nobility, 1762–1785* (Princeton, NJ: Princeton University Press, 1973), 136–37.

22. Daniel Field, *Rebels in the Name of the Tsar* (Boston: Unwin Hyman, 1989).

23. Jones, *Emancipation of the Russian Nobility*, 293–95.

24. My account of Catherine's interest in encouraging the development of a middle class relies entirely on David M. Griffiths, "Eighteenth-Century Perceptions of Backwardness: Projects for the Creation of a Third Estate in Catherinean Russia," *Canadian-American Slavic Studies* 13 (1979): 452–72.

25. Roland Mousnier, *The Institutions of France under the Absolute Monarchy, 1598–1789*, vol. 2: *The Organs of State and Society*, trans. Arthur Goldhammer (Chicago: University of Chicago Press, 1984), 159.

Chapter 4. Reaction and Revolt

1. Such was his caution and his attachment to secret proceedings that Alexander did the business of state largely without committing anything to writing. He issued his instructions chiefly in conversation. This circumstance has made the course of his policy unusually difficult to document and define. In the account that follows, frightfully condensed and simplified, I am especially indebted to the assiduous archival research of two recently published Russian authors: M.M. Safonov, *Problema reform v pravitel'stvennoi politike Rossii na rubezhe XVIII i XIX vv.* (Leningrad: Nauka, 1988); and S.V. Mironenko, *Samoderzhavie i reformy: Politicheskaia bor'ba v Rossii v nachale XIX v.* (Moscow: Nauka, 1989). I am indebted to my colleague Valerii Nikolaevich Ponomarev for bringing Mironenko's work to my attention. Also useful is A.V. Predtechenskii, *Ocherki obshchestvenno-politicheskoi istorii Rossii v pervoi chetverti XIX veka* (Moscow: AN SSSR, 1957).

2. Several of them are published in *Plans for Political Reform in Imperial Russia, 1730–1905*, ed. Marc Raeff (Englewood Cliffs, NJ: Prentice-Hall, 1966).

3. Alexander's "young friends" were Adam Czartoryski, Pavel Stroganov, Viktor Kochubei, and Nik'olai Novosiltsev.

4. F.V. Rostopchin, Aleksandr Kurakin, A.S. Shishkov, and others.

5. Allen McConnell, "Alexander I's Hundred Days: The Politics of a Paternalist Reformer," *Slavic Review* 28 (1969): 376; Mironenko, *Samoderzhavie i reformy*, 116.

6. Safonov, *Problema reform v pravitel'stvennoi politike Rossii*, 229.

7. Mironenko, *Samoderzhavie i reformy*, 69–73; Safonov, *Problema reform v pravitel'stvennoi politike Rossii*, 97–106, 141–46, 166, 180–81.

8. Raeff, *Plans for Political Reform in Imperial Russia*, 92–109; idem, *Michael Speransky: Statesman of Imperial Russia* (The Hague: Nijhoff, 1957).

9. Raeff, *Plans for Political Reform in Imperial Russia*, 110–20.

10. Mironenko, *Samoderzhavie i reformy*, 63–64, 79–80, 114, 157–60, 198, 217.

11. Hugh Ragsdale, *Détente in the Napoleonic Era: Bonaparte and the Russians* (Lawrence: Regents Press of Kansas, 1980).

12. Hugh Ragsdale, "Evaluating the Traditions of Russian Aggression: Catherine II and the Greek Project," *Slavonic and East European Review* 66 (1988): 91–117.

13. Alfred J. Rieber, ed., *The Politics of Autocracy: Letters of Alexander II to Prince A.I. Bariatinskii, 1857–1864* (The Hague: Mouton, 1966).

14. P.A. Zaionchkovskii, *Otmena krepostnogo prava v Rossii*, 3rd ed. (Moscow: Prosveshchenie, 1968); Terence Emmons, *The Russian Landed Gentry and the Peasant Emancipation of 1861* (Cambridge: Cambridge University Press, 1968); Daniel Field, *The End of Serfdom: Nobility and Bureaucracy in Russia, 1855–1861* (Cambridge, MA: Harvard University Press, 1976); W. Bruce Lincoln, *The Great Reforms* (DeKalb: Northern Illinois University Press, 1990).

15. The peasant view of this question is authoritatively documented, among other places, in Letter XI of Aleksandr Nikolaevich Engelgardt, *Letters from the Country, 1872–1887*, trans. and ed. Cathy A. Frierson (New York: Oxford University Press, 1993), 228–38.

16. S.M. Dubrovskii, *Stolypinskaia zemel'naia reforma* (Moscow: AN SSSR, 1963), 29.

17. Franco Venturi, *Roots of Revolution: A History of the Populist and Socialist Movements in Nineteenth Century Russia*, trans. Francis Haskell (New York: Knopf, 1960), 347.

18. Lincoln Hutchinson, ed., *Hidden Springs of the Russian Revolution: Personal Memoirs of Katerina Breshkovskaia* (Stanford, CA: Stanford University Press, 1931), 35.

19. Avrahm Yarmolinsky, *Road to Revolution: A Century of Russian Radicalism* (New York: Collier, 1962), chap. 10.

20. Ibid., 195–97; Venturi, *Roots of Revolution*, 581–84.

21. I have drawn here on Yarmolinsky, *Road to Revolution*; Venturi, *Roots of Revolution*; and David Footman, *Red Prelude: The Life of the Russian Terrorist Zheliabov* (New Haven, CT: Yale University Press, 1945).

22. P.A. Zaionchkovskii, *Krizis samoderzhaviia na rubezhe 1870–1880 godov* (Moscow: Izd. Moskovskogo universiteta, 1964).

23. Reginald Zelnik, *Labor and Society in Tsarist Russia: The Factory Workers of St. Petersburg, 1855–1870* (Stanford, CA: Stanford University Press, 1971), 24; Walter M. Pintner, *Russian Economic Policy under Nicholas I* (Ithaca, NY: Cornell University Press, 1967), 98.

24. Walter M. Pintner and Don K. Rowney, eds., *Russian Officialdom: The Bureaucratization of Russian Society from the Seventeenth to the Twentieth Century* (Chapel Hill: University of North Carolina Press, 1980), esp. chaps. 8–11.

25. W. Bruce Lincoln, *In the Vanguard of Reform: Russia's Enlightened Bureaucrats, 1825–1861* (DeKalb: Northern Illinois University Press, 1982), 12.

26. Dominic Lieven, *Russia's Rulers under the Old Regime* (New Haven, CT: Yale University Press, 1989), 120.

27. Richard Wortman, *The Development of a Russian Legal Consciousness* (Chicago: University of Chicago Press, 1976), esp. 221–22, 264.

28. Daniel T. Orlovsky, *The Limits of Reform: The Ministry of Internal Affairs in Imperial Russia, 1802–1881* (Cambridge, MA: Harvard University Press, 1981), 4.

29. Wortman, *Development of a Russian Legal Consciousness*, 288–89.

30. Lincoln, *In the Vanguard of Reform*, 165.

31. Ibid., 141–52.

32. Raeff, *Plans for Political Reform in Imperial Russia*, 121–31.

33. Ibid., 132–40.

34. Robert Brenner, "Economic Backwardness in Eastern Europe in Light of Development in the West," in *The Origins of Backwardness in Eastern Europe: Economics and Politics from the Middle Ages until the Early Twentieth Century*, ed. Daniel Chirot (Berkeley: University of California Press, 1989), 15.

35. E.L. Jones, *The European Miracle: Environments, Economics, and Geopolitics in the History of Europe and Asia* (Cambridge: Cambridge University Press, 1981).

36. Walter H. Mallory, *China: Land of Famine* (New York: American Geographical Society, 1926).

37. Samuel H. Baron, "The Weber Thesis and the Failure of Capitalist Development in 'Early Modern' Russia," *Jahrbücher für Geschichte Osteuropas* 18 (1970): 336.

38. Samuel H. Baron, "Who Were the *Gosti*?" *California Slavic Studies* 7 (1973): 1–40.

39. Samuel H. Baron, "The Fate of the *Gosti* in the Reign of Peter the Great," *Cahiers du monde russe et soviétique* 14 (1973): 492.

40. Alexander Gerschenkron, *Europe in the Russian Mirror: Four Lectures in Economic History* (Cambridge: Cambridge University Press, 1970), 90.

41. Alec Nove, *Economic History of the USSR* (London: Penguin, 1969), 12, 15.

42. Paul R. Gregory, *Russian National Income, 1885–1913* (Cambridge: Cambridge University Press, 1982), 192.

43. J. Pallot, "Agrarian Modernization on Peasant Farms in the Era of Capitalism," in *Studies in Russian Historical Geography*, ed. R.A. French and James H. Bater, 2 vols. (London: Academic Press, 1983), 2: 430. Robert Bideleux makes the contrary argument: "Agricultural Advances under the Russian Village Commune System," in *Land Commune and Peasant Community in Russia: Communal Forms in Imperial and Early Soviet Society*, ed. Roger Bartlett (London: Macmillan, 1990), 198, 201.

44. Heinz-Dietrich Löwe, *Die Lage der Bauern in Russland 1880–1905: Wirtschaftliche und soziale Veränderung in der ländlichen Gesellschaft des*

Zarenreiches (St. Katharinen: Scripta Mercaturae Verlag, 1987), 370–77, passim; Peter Gatrell, *The Tsarist Economy, 1850–1917* (London: Batsford, 1986), 232.

45. Gregory, *Russian National Income*, 155–57.

46. Richard G. Robbins, Jr., *Famine in Russia, 1891–1892: The Imperial Government Responds to a Crisis* (New York: Columbia University Press, 1975), 3.

47. Gatrell, *The Tsarist Economy*, 33, 34, 36, 37, 101.

48. Paul R. Gregory, *Before Command: An Economic History of Russia from Emancipation to the First Five-Year Plan* (Princeton, NJ: Princeton University Press, 1994), 44, 54.

Chapter 5. Culture, Character, Psyche

1. D.S. Likhachev, *Zametki o russkom*, 2nd ed. (Moscow: Sovetskaia Rossiia, 1984), 13, 15.

2. I have used here *Russian Fairy Tales*, trans. Norbert Guterman, collected by Aleksandr Afanas′ev, commentary by Roman Jakobson (New York: Pantheon Books, 1973); and a Soviet children's book, *Russkie skazki* (Moscow: Russkii iazyk, 1987). From the former: "Shemiaka the Judge," "Emelya the Simpleton," "Ivanushka the Little Fool," "Ivan the Simpleton," "Right and Wrong," "Know Not the Simpleton"; from the latter: "Sestritsa Alenushka i bratets Ivanushka," "Po shchuch′emu veleniiu," "Sivka burka," "Finist—iasnyi sokol," "L′etuchii korabl′," "Mar′ia Morevna," and "Ivan-tsarevich i Seryi volk."

3. Ivan Turgenev, "Khor and Kalinich," in *A Sportsman's Notebook*, trans. Charles and Natasha Hepburn (New York: Viking Press, 1957).

4. Leo Tolstoy, "The Power of Darkness," in *Redemption and Two Other Plays* (New York: Boni and Liveright, 1919), 55–143.

5. Ronald Hingley, *Chekhov: A Biographical and Critical Study* (London: Allen and Unwin, 1966), 233.

6. Chekhov to Aleksei Suvorin, 30 May 1888, in *Anton Chekhov's Life and Thought: Selected Letters and Commentary*, trans. Michael Henry Heim, ed. Simon Karlinsky (Berkeley: University of California Press, 1973), 104.

7. Avrahm Yarmolinsky, "Introduction," in *The Portable Chekhov*, ed. Avrahm Yarmolinsky (New York: Viking, 1968), 5.

8. Chekhov to Suvorin, 27 March 1894, in *Anton Chekhov's Life and Thought*, 261–62.

9. *The Portable Chekhov*, 312–53.

10. "Russian Camera Obscura: Ten Sketches of Russian Peasant Life (1916–1918)," in Geoffrey Gorer and John Rickman, *The People of Great Russia: A Psychological Study* (New York: Norton, 1962), 21–89.

11. Gleb Uspenskii, "From a Village Diary," in *Readings in Russian Civilization*, ed. Thomas Riha, 2nd ed., 3 vols. (Chicago: University of Chicago Press, 1969), 2: 358–67.

12. Obituary, *The Times*, 11 January 1919, p. 6; quoted by Cyril E. Black, "Introduction," in Donald Mackenzie Wallace, *Russia on the Eve of War and Revolution*, ed. Cyril E. Black (New York: Vintage Books, 1961), v.

13. Ibid., 345–47.

14. Ibid., 349–50.

15. Ibid., 352.

16. Aleksandr V. Chayanov, *The Theory of Peasant Economy*, ed. Daniel Thorner, Basile Kerblay, and R.E.F. Smith (Homewood, IL: Irwin, 1966), 4–6.

17. Wallace, *Russia on the Eve of War and Revolution*, 142–43.

18. Eric Wolf, *Peasants* (Englewood Cliffs, NJ: Prentice-Hall, 1966), esp. 35ff., 73–77, 93.

19. Ibid., 69.

20. Robert Redfield, *Peasant Society and Culture* (Chicago: University of Chicago Press, 1956), 27, 46, 59.

21. Oscar Handlin, *The Uprooted: The Epic Story of the Great Migrations that Made the American People* (Boston: Little, Brown, 1951), chap. 1, "Peasant Origins," 23–24. I am endebted to Redfield, *Peasant Society and Culture*, chap. 4, "The Peasant View of the Good Life," for reference to Handlin.

22. Redfield, *Peasant Society and Culture*, 105ff.

23. Ibid., 75, 77.

24. Barrington Moore, Jr., *Social Origins of Dictatorship and Democracy: Lord and Peasant in the Making of the Modern World* (Boston: Beacon Press, 1966).

25. Ivan Goncharov, *Oblomov*, trans. C.J. Hogarth (New York: Macmillan, 1915).

26. Nikolai Dobroliubov, "What is Oblomovism?" in Riha, *Readings in Russian Civilization*, 2: 339.

27. Milton Ehre, "Turgenev, Ivan Sergeevich," in *Handbook of Russian Literature*, ed. Victor Terras (New Haven, CT: Yale University Press, 1985), 489.

28. "The Cherry Orchard," in *The Portable Chekhov*, 531–94.

29. Chekhov to his sister, 14 January 1891, in *Anton Chekhov's Life and Thought*, 183.

30. Anton Chekhov, "An Anonymous Story," in *The Oxford Chekhov*, trans. and ed. Ronald Hingley, 9 vols. (London: Oxford University Press, 1965–75), 6: 250.

31. Wallace, *Russia on the Eve of War and Revolution*, chaps. 7 and 8.

32. Roberta Thompson Manning, *The Crisis of the Old Order in Russia: Gentry and Government* (Princeton, NJ: Princeton University Press, 1982), 8–9, 20, 37; Seymour Becker, *Nobility and Privilege in Late Imperial Russia* (DeKalb: Northern Illinois University Press, 1985), 29, 32, 45, 53, 172.

33. Ivan S. Turgenev, *Fathers and Sons*, trans. Constance Garnett (New York: Modern Library, 1950).

34. Fyodor Dostoyevsky, *The Possessed*, trans. Andrew R. MacAndrew (New York: New American Library, 1962).

35. The characterization that follows here is based on the excellent chapter, "The Intelligentsia," in Tibor Szamuely, *The Russian Tradition*, ed. Robert Conquest (London: Fontana, 1988).

36. *Vekhi; intelligentsiia v Rossii: Sbornik statei* (Moscow: 1909), 24–25; quoted in ibid., 202.

37. Szamuely, *The Russian Tradition*, chap. 10.

38. Alexis de Tocqueville, *The Old Regime and the French Revolution* (Garden City, NY: Doubleday Anchor, 1955), 138–47.

39. James H. Billington, *The Icon and the Axe: An Interpretive History of*

Russian Culture (New York: Vintage Books, 1970), 592 and 786, n. 5. I am indebted to Orest Pelech of Duke University Library for this reference.

40. Martin Malia, *Alexander Herzen and the Birth of Russian Socialism* (New York: Grosset and Dunlap, 1965), 12–13, 54–55, 110–19, 253–54.

41. This account of Kennan's introduction to Russia and the conception of his great classic is based on the Introduction by George Frost Kennan in George Kennan, *Siberia and the Exile System*, abridged ed. (Chicago: University of Chicago Press, 1958), ix–xix, and George Kennan's own Preface, *Siberia and the Exile System*, 2 vols. (London: Osgood, McIlvaine, 1891), 1: iii–x. A fuller account is available in Frederick Travis, *George Kennan and the American–Russian Relationship, 1865–1924* (Athens: Ohio University Press, 1990).

42. These examples are taken from Kennan, *Siberia and the Exile System*, 1: chap. 11, "Exile by Administrative Process."

43. Quoted in Franco Venturi, *Roots of Revolution: A History of the Populist and Socialist Movements in Nineteenth Century Russia* (New York: Knopf, 1960), 563.

44. Ibid., 642.

45. Ibid., 635.

46. Henri Pirenne, *Medieval Cities: Their Origins and the Revival of Trade*, trans. Frank D. Halsey (Garden City, NY: Doubleday Anchor, 1956), 82ff.

47. Alfred J. Rieber, *Merchants and Entrepreneurs in Imperial Russia* (Chapel Hill: University of North Carolina Press, 1982), 23, 29. Quotation is from Prov. 22:3.

48. Mikhail Saltykov-Shchedrin, *The Golovyov Family*, trans. Ronald Wilks (London: Penguin, 1988).

49. D.S. Mirsky, *A History of Russian Literature*, ed. Francis J. Whitfield (New York: Knopf, 1958), 281.

50. *Five Plays of Aleksandr Ostrovsky*, trans. and ed. Eugene K. Bristow (New York: Pegasus, 1969).

51. Jeffrey Brooks, *When Russia Learned to Read* (Princeton, NJ: Princeton University Press, 1985); Edith W. Clowes, Samuel D. Kassow, and James L. West, eds., *Between Tsar and People: Educated Society and the Quest for Public Identity in Late Imperial Russia* (Princeton, NJ: Princeton University Press, 1991), esp. chaps. 4, 5, 6, 7, 19.

52. Ruth Amende Roosa, "Russian Industrialists Look to the Future: Thoughts on Economic Development, 1906–1917," in *Essays in Russian and Soviet History in Honor of Geroid Tanquary Robinson*, ed. John Shelton Curtiss (New York: Columbia University Press, 1965), 198–218.

53. Quoted in Thomas C. Owen, *The Corporation under Russian Law, 1800–1917: A Study in Tsarist Economic Policy* (New York: Cambridge University Press, 1991), xii.

54. Brooks, *When Russia Learned to Read*, 355.

Chapter 6. Reform or Revolution

1. Nicholas V. Riasanovsky, *Russia and the West in the Teachings of the Slavophiles* (Cambridge, MA: Harvard University Press, 1952), 135 passim.

2. The standard study is Theodore H. von Laue, *Sergei Witte and the Industrialization of Russia* (New York: Columbia University Press, 1963). Witte's own memoirs are now available in a new English translation: Sidney Harcave, ed. and trans., *The Memoirs of Count Witte* (Armonk, NY: M.E. Sharpe, 1990).

3. Arthur P. Mendel, *Dilemmas of Progress in Tsarist Russia: Legal Marxism and Legal Populism* (Cambridge, MA: Harvard University Press, 1961).

4. My account of the events and background of "Bloody Sunday" relies on Walter Sablinsky, *The Road to Bloody Sunday* (Princeton, NJ: Princeton University Press, 1976).

5. Whether this phrase, attributed to Minister of the Interior V.K. von Plehve, was authentic or not, it typified much of the government's attitude.

6. Sablinsky, *Road to Bloody Sunday*, 344–49. I have ignored italics that indicate variations among different texts.

7. The most authoritative study is Geoffrey Hosking, *The Russian Constitutional Experiment: Government and Duma, 1907–1914* (Cambridge: Cambridge University Press, 1973).

8. Theodore H. von Laue, *Why Lenin? Why Stalin? Why Gorbachev?* 3rd ed. (New York: HarperCollins, 1993).

9. S.M. Dubrovskii, *Stolypinskaia zemel'naia reforma* (Moscow: AN SSSR, 1963), 200.

10. Dorothy Atkinson, "The Statistics on the Russian Land Commune, 1905–1917," *Slavic Review* 32 (1973): 773–87.

11. Dubrovskii, *Stolypinskaia zemel'naia reforma*, 222–30.

12. Orlando Figes, *Peasant Russia, Civil War: The Volga Countryside in Revolution (1917–1921)* (Oxford: Clarendon Press, 1989), 57.

13. Leopold Haimson, "Social Stability in Urban Russia, 1905–1917," *Slavic Review* 23 (1964): 627.

14. B.N. Ponomarev, ed., *Istoriia SSSR s drevneishikh vremen do nashikh dnei v dvukh seriiakh i dvenadtsati tomakh*, 11 vols. to date (Moscow: Nauka, 1966–), 6: 452.

15. Whether Marx and his disciples were democratic is quite another question. Democracy requires patience and tolerance, or indifference, and these are naturally not the qualities of revolutionaries.

16. Oliver H. Radkey, *The Agrarian Foes of Bolshevism: Promise and Default of the Russian Socialist Revolutionaries, February to October, 1917* (New York: Columbia University Press, 1958).

Chapter 7. The Awkward World of Leninism

1. For the somewhat obscure nuances, see T.H. Rigby, *Lenin's Government: Sovnarkom, 1917–1922* (Cambridge: Cambridge University Press, 1979), 26–28.

2. Hereafter, dates are given according to the Gregorian calendar, which the Bolsheviks began using 14 February 1918.

3. Richard Pipes, *The Russian Revolution* (New York: Knopf, 1990), 807, 811.

4. Oliver H. Radkey, *The Unknown Civil War in Soviet Russia: A Study of*

the Green Movement in the Tambov Region, 1920–1921 (Stanford, CA: Hoover Institution Press, 1976).

5. Evgenii Zamiatin, "The Cave," trans. Avrahm Yarmolinsky, in *The Portable Twentieth-Century Russian Reader*, ed. Clarence Brown (New York: Penguin, 1985), 91–102.

6. Paul Avrich, *Kronstadt 1921* (Princeton, NJ: Princeton University Press, 1970), 73–74.

7. B.N. Ponomarev, ed., *Istoriia SSSR s drevneishikh vremen*, 11 vols. to date (Moscow: Nauka, 1966–), 7: 33.

8. E.H. Carr, *The Interregnum* (New York: Macmillan, 1954), 139.

9. Alec Nove, *An Economic History of the USSR* (London: Penguin, 1969), 114–15; Carr, *The Interregnum*, 55, 59ff., 84–85 (quotation).

10. Quoted in Roy Medvedev, *The October Revolution*, trans. George Saunders (New York: Columbia University Press, 1979), 59–60. The first quote is from Engels's letter to Weydemeyer, 1853. The second is from his *Peasant War in Germany*, 1850.

11. Ilya Ehrenburg, *Memoirs: 1921–1941*, trans. Tatania Shebunina (New York: World, 1964), 66–72.

12. Robert V. Daniels, ed., *A Documentary History of Communism*, 2 vols. (New York: Vintage Books, 1962), 1: 223–25.

13. Adam Ulam, *The Bolsheviks* (New York: Collier, 1965), 567–68.

14. Lenin's own lineage was long contrived to remain obscure. See Louis Fischer, *The Life of Lenin* (New York: Harper Colophon, 1964), 1–4. His paternal grandmother was a Kalmyk, and both his maternal grandparents were of German background. His maternal grandfather, Dr. Aleksandr Dmitrievich Blank, was long believed to have been Jewish, an issue of considerable significance only in the context of traditional Russian anti-Semitism. The facts have recently been revealed. In 1932, Lenin's sister Anna prepared to confirm these allegations in print, but Stalin absolutely forbade it. The documents, originally housed in police archives, were at that time transferred to the party archive, where a Russian historian has at last consulted them. Dmitri Volkogonov, *Lenin: A New Biography*, trans. Harold Shukman (New York: Free Press, 1994), 8–9 and 486, nn. 15–18.

15. Donald W. Treadgold, *Twentieth Century Russia*, 3rd ed. (Chicago: Rand McNally, 1972), 167.

16. Isaac Deutscher, *Stalin: A Political Biography* (New York: Oxford University Press, 1967), 167.

17. Isaac Deutscher, *The Prophet Armed: Trotsky, 1879–1921* (New York: Oxford University Press, 1954), 176–77.

18. Leon Trotsky, *The Revolution Betrayed*, trans. Max Eastman (New York: Pioneer, 1945), 257.

19. Robert C. Tucker, *Stalin as Revolutionary, 1897–1929* (New York: Norton, 1973), 131–32.

Chapter 8. The Brave New World of Stalinism

1. Isaac Deutscher, *Stalin: A Political Biography* (New York: Oxford University Press, 1967), 328.

2. William J. Chase, *Workers, Society, and the Soviet State: Labor and Life in Moscow, 1918–1929* (Urbana: University of Illinois Press, 1987). There is also a purely political explanation. Perhaps Stalin, having used conservative allies who feared the provocation of a civil war with the peasantry—Nikolai Bukharin and company—in order to rid himself of the Left Opposition, now wished to turn left in order to rid himself of dependence on his previous allies, who thereby became the Right Opposition. This suggestion is logical, but it is mere speculation.

3. E.H. Carr, *Socialism in One Country*, 3 vols. (New York: Macmillan, 1958–64), 1: 268ff.

4. Moshe Lewin, *Russian Peasants and Soviet Power: A Study of Collectivization*, trans. Irene Nove (New York: Norton, 1975), 175–78, 216.

5. Eric R. Wolf, *Peasants* (Englewood Cliffs, NJ: Prentice-Hall, 1966), 45.

6. Robert C. Tucker, *Stalin in Power: The Revolution from Above, 1928–1941* (New York: Norton, 1990), 50–55.

7. Ibid., 57.

8. Lynne Viola, *The Best Sons of the Fatherland: Workers in the Vanguard of Soviet Collectivization* (New York: Oxford University Press, 1987).

9. As told to Markoosha Fischer, *My Lives in Russia* (New York: Harper, 1944), 49–51.

10. Fedor Belov, *History of a Soviet Collective Farm* (New York: Praeger, 1955), 9–10.

11. R.W. Davies, *The Industrialisation of Soviet Russia*, 1: *The Socialist Offensive: The Collectivisation of Soviet Agriculture, 1929–1930* (Cambridge: Cambridge University Press, 1980), 271.

12. Ibid., 257, 260. The police reports in the Smolensk Archive confirm the first of these reasons. Merle Fainsod, *Smolensk under Soviet Rule* (New York: Vintage, 1963), 250. The new evidence available in formerly closed Soviet archives is in substantial agreement with that of the Smolensk Archive and the occasional memoir literature that we have long possessed. Much the most systematic exploitation of it is in the new work of Sheila Fitzpatrick, *Stalin's Peasants: Resistance and Survival in the Russian Village after Collectivization* (New York/Oxford: Oxford University Press, 1994).

13. Fainsod, *Smolensk under Soviet Rule*, 252–53.

14. Robert Conquest, *Harvest of Sorrow: Soviet Collectivization and the Terror-Famine* (New York: Oxford University Press, 1986).

15. Lazar Volin, *A Survey of Soviet Russian Agriculture* (Washington, DC: U.S. Government Printing Office, 1968), 24.

16. Robert Conquest, *The Great Terror: Stalin's Purge of the Thirties* (New York: Macmillan, 1968), 24.

17. Maurice Hindus, *Red Bread* (New York: Jonathan Cape and Harrison Smith, 1931), 51–52.

18. Vasily Grossman, *Forever Flowing*, trans. Thomas P. Whitney (New York: Harper, 1972), 141–43.

19. Lev Kopelev, *The Education of a True Believer*, trans. Gary Kern (New York: Harper, 1980), 235.

20. Much of the factual matter of collectivization in the Soviet histories of the preglasnost era is in agreement with that of the Western accounts on which I have relied here, though the interpretation of the material is entirely different. For

example, the Soviet Academy of Sciences's official history, B.N. Ponomarev, ed., *Istoriia SSSR s drevneishikh vremen*, 11 vols. to date (Moscow: AN SSSR, 1966–), 8, passim.

21. Vasilii Belov, "God velikogo pereloma: Khronika deviati mesiatsev," *Novyi mir*, 1989, no. 3.

22. Conquest, *The Harvest of Sorrow*, 10.

23. John Scott, *Behind the Urals: An American Worker in Russia's City of Steel* (Bloomington: Indiana University Press, 1973), 97.

24. Naum Jasny, *Soviet Industrialization, 1928–1952* (Chicago: University of Chicago Press, 1961), 167.

25. Ibid., 6.

26. Ibid., 1, 10–11.

27. Holland Hunter and Janusz M. Szyrmer, *Faulty Foundations: Soviet Economic Policies, 1928–1940* (Princeton, NJ: Princeton University Press, 1992), chap. 3: 26–50.

28. Scott, *Behind the Urals*.

29. Stephen Kotkin, *Steeltown, USSR* (Berkeley: University of California Press, 1991).

30. Belov, *History of a Soviet Collective Farm*, 113–14, 122–23; John Littlepage, *In Search of Soviet Gold* (New York: Harcourt, Brace, 1938), 199; Scott, *Behind the Urals*, 166–70.

31. Conquest, *The Great Terror*, 27–31.

32. Theses of the Sixth Comintern Congress, 29 August 1928; Jane Degras, ed., *The Communist International, 1919–1943: Documents*, 3 vols. (London: Oxford University Press, 1956–65), 2: 459.

33. Theses on Tactics and Theses on Methods, Third Comintern Congress; ibid., 1: 241–71, esp. 263.

34. Programme of the Congress, 1 September 1928; ibid., 2: 485.

35. Tucker, *Stalin in Power*, 258, 379.

36. Ibid., 275.

37. Ibid., 251.

38. Conquest, *The Great Terror*. The recent opening of many of the Soviet records has both informed and confused us on the question of the number of victims. The statistics are in great flux and are likely to remain so until time has allowed the sober and comprehensive weighing of the archival material. For an interim report, see the various contributions in *Stalinist Terror: New Perspectives*, ed. J. Arch Getty and Roberta T. Manning (Cambridge: Cambridge University Press, 1993) and the somewhat more systematic recent article by J. Arch Getty, Gábor T. Rittersporn, and Viktor N. Zemskov, "Victims of the Soviet Penal System in the Pre-War Years: A First Approach on the Basis of Archival Evidence," *American Historical Review* 98 (1993): 1017–49.

39. An interesting dual biography is Alan Bullock's recent *Hitler and Stalin: Parallel Lives* (London: HarperCollins, 1991).

40. Review of the Russian translation of Robert Conquest's *The Great Terror* in *New York Review of Books*, 11 April 1991, 6.

41. Feliks Chuev, *Sto sorok besed s Molotovym* (Moscow: Terra, 1991).

42. Evgeniia Ginzburg, *Journey into the Whirlwind*, trans. Paul Stevenson and Max Hayward (New York: Harcourt, Brace, and World, 1967). A variety of these

attitudes are documented in Robert W. Thurston, "Fear and Belief in the USSR's 'Great Terror': Response to Arrest, 1935–1939," *Slavic Review* 45 (1986): 213–44. Some corroboration is to be found in the memoirs of the literary critic Lidia Ginzburg, in Vera Tolz, "How People Reacted to Stalin's Terror: The Notebooks of Lidia Ginzburg," Radio Liberty, *Report on the USSR*, RL 421/90 (10 September 1990), 10–12.

43. Grossman, *Forever Flowing*, 69–77.

44. The smaller figure is the one so often cited by Eduard Shevardnadze and the Foreign Ministry spokesman, Gennadii Gerasimov. It is supported by V.V. Gurkin, "O liudskikh poteriakh na sovetsko-germanskom fronte v 1941–1945 gg.," *Novaia i noveishaia istoriia*, 1992, no. 3: 219–24. It is based on the statistical reports from the battlefield. The larger figure is the product of a careful demographic study by V.I. Kozlov, "O liudskikh poteriakh Sovetskogo Soiuza v Velikoi otechestvennoi voine 1941–1945 godov," *Istoriia SSSR*, 1989, no. 2: 132–39.

45. Hans-Heinrich Herwarth von Bittenfeld, *Against Two Evils: Memoirs of a Diplomat-Soldier during the Third Reich* (New York: Rawson, Wade, 1981); Alexander Dallin, *German Rule in Russia, 1941–1945: A Study of Occupation Policies*, 2nd rev. ed. (Boulder, CO: Westview Press, 1981); P.A. Pal'chikov, "Istoriia generala Vlasova," *Novaia i noveishaia istoriia*, 1993, no. 2: 123–44.

46. We now have an excellent memoir of one of the accused, Iakov L'vovich Rapoport, *The Doctors' Plot of 1953*, trans. Nataliia Perova and Raisa Bobrova (Cambridge, MA: Harvard University Press, 1991).

Chapter 9. Reform or Revolution—Again

1. Martin Malia, *The Soviet Tragedy: A History of Socialism in Russia* (New York: Free Press, 1994), 319–20, 328.

2. Priscilla Johnson, *Khrushchev and the Arts* (Cambridge, MA: MIT Press, 1965).

3. Alec Nove, *An Economic History of the USSR* (London: Penguin, 1969), 346.

4. Lazar Volin, *A Century of Russian Agriculture* (Cambridge, MA: Harvard University Press, 1970), 510.

5. Ibid., 378–85, 406–15.

6. Eugen Wädekin, *The Private Sector in Soviet Agriculture* (Berkeley: University of California Press, 1973), xiv, 44–45, 247–315; Arthur E. Adams and Jan S. Adams, *Men versus Systems: Agriculture in the USSR, Poland, and Czechoslovakia* (New York: Free Press, 1971), 24–25.

7. Volin, *A Century of Russian Agriculture*, 458–78; Roy A. Medvedev and Zhores A. Medvedev, *Khrushchev: The Years in Power* (New York: Columbia University Press, 1976), 85–93.

8. Martin McCauley, *Khrushchev and the Development of Soviet Agriculture: The Virgin Land Programme, 1953–1964* (New York: Holmes and Meier, 1976), 82–83, passim.

9. Ibid., 88, 211, passim.

10. Harry Schwartz, *The Soviet Economy since Stalin* (New York: Lippincott, 1965), 42, 46, 51.

11. Michel Tatu, *Power in the Kremlin: From Khrushchev to Kosygin*, trans. Helen Katel (New York: Viking, 1968), 59.

12. Schwartz, *The Soviet Economy since Stalin*, 42, 46.

13. Newly published documents from Russian archives; *The New York Times*, 8 February 1993, 6. The events in Novocherkassk are more fully documented in *Soviet Law and Government* 30 (1992).

14. Chinese polemics, never denied in Moscow, assert that the Russians in 1957 promised to assist the Chinese in developing a nuclear weapon but that in 1959 they reneged on the promise. My interpretation of the Cuban missile crisis, especially the relationship among the Berlin crises, the Sino–Soviet polemics, and the placing of missiles in Cuba, relies on William E. Griffith, *The Sino–Soviet Rift* (Cambridge, MA: MIT Press, 1964), though I have made adaptations.

15. Andrei Amalrik, *Will the Soviet Union Survive until 1984?* (New York: Harper and Row, 1970).

16. George R. Urban, *End of Empire: The Demise of the Soviet Union* (Washington, DC: American University Press, 1993), 135.

17. Robert F. Byrnes, ed., *After Brezhnev: Sources of Soviet Conduct in the 1980s* (Bloomington: Indiana University Press, 1983), xvi–xvii.

18. Seweryn Bialer, *Stalin's Successors: Leadership, Stability, and Change in the Soviet Union* (New York: Cambridge University Press, 1980), 305.

19. The term Ottomanization was coined by Timothy Garton Ash.

20. Personal letter.

21. Paul M. Kennedy, *The Rise and Fall of the Great Powers* (New York: Random House, 1987).

22. Vladimir G. Treml, *Alcohol in the USSR: A Statistical Study* (Durham, NC: Duke University Press, 1982), xi–xii; Walter D. Connor, *Deviance in Soviet Society: Crime, Delinquency, and Alcoholism* (New York: Columbia University Press, 1972); Anthony Jones, Walter D. Connor, and David E. Powell, *Soviet Social Problems* (Boulder, CO: Westview Press, 1991).

23. Ben Eklof, *Soviet Briefing* (Boulder, CO: Westview Press, 1989), 93. A story that Russians repeated everywhere in the summer of 1986 blamed the Chernobyl disaster on the antialcohol campaign. The technicians at the nuclear facility were perfectly competent, according to the story, to operate it in a drunken stupor, as years of experience had convincingly shown. It was only the unfamiliar condition of sobriety that confused them.

24. Adolphe, Marquis de Custine, *A Journey for Our Time*, trans. Phyllis Penn Kohler (Chicago: Regnery, 1951), 105.

25. Hedrick Smith, *The New Russians* (New York: Avon Books, 1990), 122–23.

26. *Izvestiia*, 15 October 1992, 1, 5.

27. Theodore H. von Laue, *Why Lenin? Why Stalin? Why Gorbachev?* 3rd ed. (New York: HarperCollins, 1993), 158.

28. Natan Iakovlevich Eidel'man, *"Revoliutsiia sverkhu" v Rossii* (Moscow: Kniga, 1989).

29. Vladimir Voinovich, *Ivan'kiada* (Ann Arbor, MI: Ardis, 1976).

30. Smith, *The New Russians*, 77.

31. For a sophisticated documentation of this process—and in my opinion, an affirmation of my argument—see Linda J. Cook, *The Soviet Social Contract and*

Why It Failed: Welfare Policy and Workers' Politics from Brezhnev to Yeltsin (Cambridge, MA: Harvard University Press, 1993).

32. These quotes are from von Laue, *Why Lenin? Why Stalin? Why Gorbachev?* 106, 155, 92.

33. George Vernadsky et al., eds., *A Source Book of Russian History*, 3 vols. (New Haven, CT: Yale University Press, 1972), 3: 801.

34. Smith, *The New Russians*, title of chap. 10.

35. Philip Hanson, "Alexander Zinoviev: Totalitarianism from Below," *Survey* 26 (1982): 28–48.

36. *Izvestiia*, 4 June 1992, 1–2.

37. *The New York Times*, 17 November 1991, 1, 6.

38. *Izvestiia*, 14 January 1993, 1.

39. B. Khorev, Moscow State University, and O. Khoreva, Central Economic Research Institute, RSFSR, "Russia's Demographic Anomaly," *Sovetskaia Rossiia*, 26 December 1990, translated in *Current Digest of the Soviet Press*, vol. 43, no. 1 (1991): 22–23.

40. Address in Norfolk, VA, evening of 18 March 1994 (Southern Conference on Slavic Studies).

41. Edmund Burke, *Selected Works*, ed. W. J. Bate (New York: Modern Library, 1960), 209.

42. Raymond Aron, *Democracy and Totalitarianism* (New York: Praeger, 1969), 242–43.

43. *Izvestiia*, 24 August 1992, 2.

44. *Literaturnaia gazeta*, 1991, no. 42, 7.

45. This opinion is based chiefly on personal observations, but it is interestingly explored in *Moscow Women: Thirteen Interviews*, ed. Carola Hansson and Karen Liden, trans. Gerry Bothmer, George Blecher, and Lone Blecher (New York: Pantheon, 1983), and Francine du Plessix Gray, *Soviet Women: Walking the Tightrope* (New York: Doubleday, 1989).

46. *Pravda*, 3 October 1990, 1.

47. *Izvestiia*, 8 September 1992, 3.

Conclusion: A Cautious Prognosis

1. Donna Bahry, "Society Transformed? Rethinking the Social Roots of Perestroika," *Slavic Review* 52 (1993): 512–24.

2. *Izvestiia*, 18 September 1992, 1.

3. Mikhail Agursky, *The Third Rome: National Bolshevism in the USSR* (Boulder, CO: Westview Press, 1987).

4. *Chicago Tribune*, 4 April 1994, 12.

5. *Izvestiia*, 28 April 1994, 2.

6. Bahry, "Society Transformed? Rethinking the Social Roots of Perestroika."

7. Anders Aslund, *How Russia Became a Market Economy* (Washington, DC: Brookings Institute, 1995), 5.

8. Daniil Granin, "New Dangers, New Hopes," in *Remaking Russia*, ed. Heyward Isham (Armonk, NY: M.E. Sharpe, 1995), 69–75.

9. Sergei Filatov and Liudmila Vorontsova, "New Russia in Search of an Identity," in ibid., 277.

10. Allen Kassof, *The Soviet Youth Program: Regimentation and Rebellion* (Cambridge, MA; Harvard University Press, 1965).

11. David Mason, "Attitudes toward the Market and Political Participation in the Postcommunist States," *Slavic Review* 54 (1995): 395, 400, 405.

12. Ibid., 391.

13. Arkadii Vaksberg, *The Soviet Mafia*, trans. John and Elizabeth Roberts (New York: St. Martin's Press, 1991); Stephen Handelman, *Comrade Criminal: Russia's New Mafiya* (New Haven, CT: Yale University Press, 1995).

14. Open Media Research Institute, *Daily Digest I*, 15 August 1995.

15. Remarks at the Kennan Institute for Advanced Russian Studies, 1 May 1995, "Meeting Report" (vol. 12, no. 15).

16. Charles H. Fairbanks, Jr., "A Tired Anarchy," *The National Interest,* Spring 1995: 51.

17. Reproduced in *Izvestiia*, 4 May 1994, 5, in the author's Russian original.

18. Radio Liberty, *Report on the USSR*, RL 262/91 (26 July 1991), 17.

19. For example, the teachings of the Gospels (blessed are the poor in spirit); the communitarian ideals of the early Christian society of the Book of Acts; the church fathers, SS. Augustine and Jerome; SS. Thomas Aquinas and Thomas More; the Anglican Christian Socialists around the Reverend Charles Kingsley, chaplain to Queen Victoria; the English Catholics G.K. Chesterton, Hilaire Belloc, and C.S. Lewis; *Rerum Novarum*; Paul Tillich in German Social Democracy; and the leading influence in Christian theology in the United States, Reinhold Niebuhr. See J.C. Cort, *Christian Socialism: An Informal History* (Maryknoll, NY: Orbis Books, 1988).

20. Marc Raeff, *Russia Abroad: A Cultural History of the Russian Emigration, 1919–1939* (New York: Oxford University Press, 1990), 150–55.

Index

About the Author

Hugh Ragsdale studied at the University of North Carolina (A.B.) and the University of Virginia (M.A., Ph.D.). A past recipient of awards from Fulbright, the International Research & Exchanges Board, and the American Council of Learned Societies, he has conducted research in the foreign affairs archives of London, Paris, Vienna, Copenhagen, and Stockholm, as well as Moscow. *The Russian Tragedy* is his fifth book on the history of Russia.